W9-BWC-777

The Theology of Schleiermacher

KARL BARTH

The Theology of Schleiermacher

Lectures at Göttingen,
Winter Semester of 1923/24

Edited by
DIETRICH RITSCHL

Translated by
GEOFFREY W. BROMILEY

WILLIAM B. EERDMANS PUBLISHING COMPANY
GRAND RAPIDS, MICHIGAN

Copyright © 1982 by Wm. B. Eerdmans Publishing Co.
255 Jefferson Ave. SE, Grand Rapids, Mich. 49503

Printed in the United States of America

Translated from the Swiss edition of Barth's collected works,
Karl Barth: Die Theologie Schleiermachers, V, Vol. 2, of the *Karl Barth Gesamtausgabe*.
Copyright © 1978 by the Theologischer Verlag Zürich.

"Concluding Unscientific Postscript on Schleiermacher" was translated from *"Nachwort"*
in Heinz Bolli (ed.), *Schleiermacher—Auswahl* (Munich and Hamburg, 1968) by George
Hunsinger, and reprinted from *Studies in Religion/Sciences Religieuses* 7/2 (1978), 117-135;
published at Wilfrid Laurier University Press by Canadian Corporation for Studies in Religion/Corporation Canadienne des sciences Religieuses. It is used here by permission of
the translator, Wilfrid Laurier University Press, and the Theologischer Verlag Zürich.

Library of Congress Cataloging in Publication Data

Barth, Karl, 1886-1968.
The Theology of Schleiermacher.

Translation of: Die Theologie Schleiermachers.
Includes bibliographical references and index.
1. Schleiermacher, Friedrich, 1768-1834. I. Ritschl, Dietrich. II. Title.
PX4827.S3B313   230'.044'0924   82-2330
ISBN 0-8028-3565-1   AACR2

CONTENTS

TRANSLATOR'S PREFACE

Karl Barth never revised for publication these lectures that he gave on Schleiermacher early in his teaching career. Yet they are important for several reasons. First, they show Barth at work as scholar, professor, and theologian. Second, they provide the materials from which he drew the brilliant essays that he later wrote on Schleiermacher. Third, they testify to his early recognition of Schleiermacher as both the father of Liberal Protestantism and its most gifted theologian. Fourth, they give evidence of Barth's predominant concern, not for background, influences, and historical development, but for subject-matter. Fifth, they pinpoint already the sharp differences between Schleiermacher's thought and what Barth was not coming to see as a truly scriptural and Reformed dogmatics. While, therefore, much of Barth's ongoing debate with Schleiermacher is already available at a maturer level in the various essays and the relevant sections of the *Church Dogmatics*, publication of this basic and comprehensive examination can still serve a useful purpose, particularly as many of the issues raised in it are still, if in altered form, the living issues in the theology of our own time.

Pasadena, Epiphany 1982   G. W. BROMILEY

EDITOR'S PREFACE

In a letter dated October 6, 1921,[1] Eduard Thurneysen reminded his friend of the night in Leutwil when for the first time they said out loud that they could no longer believe Schleiermacher. Already in May of the same year Karl Barth had told Thurneysen that he planned to declare war on this church father and religious virtuoso[2] and that the muzzle of the gun was trained on him.[3] According to Barth's own account the passionate criticism which now began had much earlier roots.[4] On the manifesto of ninety-three German intellectuals who at the outbreak of war in 1914 supported the policy of Wilhelm II and Bethmann-Hollweg, he had found to his horror the names of almost all his German teachers (with the honorable exception of Martin Rade), and he had seen behind the theology of the time the figure of Schleiermacher, although even as late as 1968 he did not believe that Schleiermacher himself would have signed such a manifesto. At this point at the very latest, then, his criticism of the pillars of the theology of the age had begun, and with it the criticism of Schleiermacher.

Nevertheless the great attack on Schleiermacher did not come until some years later. The passages in the letters to Thurneysen in 1921 are the first indications that the Göttingen lectures planned for the winter semester of 1923/24 would open an assault that would continue unhindered for many years. In 1928 Thurneysen could speak confidently of an elimination of Schleiermacher,[5] and he wanted something of the same for Albrecht Ritschl, which would perhaps be even more crushing.[6] The target of the attack was not just Schleiermacher but all 19th-century theology.

It is worth noting that a shift in Barth's attitude to Schleiermacher has sometimes been seen in his epilogue to the Schleiermacher selection of 1968. One may admit that here—forty-five years later—the aggressive and not infrequently scornful tone of the Göttingen lectures has yielded to one that is

---

[1]K. Barth/E. Thurneysen, *Briefwechsel I, 1913–1921* (Zurich, 1973), p. 525.
[2]*Ibid.*, p. 489.
[3]*Ibid.*, p. 492.
[4]In his epilogue to the *Schleiermacher-Auswahl*, Siebenstern Taschenbuch 113/14 (Munich and Hamburg, 1968); see pp. 261–279.
[5]*Briefwechsel II, 1921–1930*, p. 595.
[6]*Loc. cit.*

more balanced and even critically resigned. But the content of the argument is the same. Man has been made the subject of theology and Christ his predicate. And what Barth's earlier interpretation of Schleiermacher clearly leads us to conjecture is now fully confirmed, namely, that Schleiermacher is understood in terms of his influence. The constantly emphasized line from Schleiermacher to Ritschl and Troeltsch (for which—if it were a valid interpretation of the Reformation—Barth would even have left the supposed evangelical church and "would in fact rather have become a Roman Catholic")[7] is now extended to much of the contemporary German-speaking theology which, starting systematically from Bultmann, constitutes a group or school and can undoubtedly be reduced to a single common denominator.[8] Asking what the denominator is, Barth concludes that "it was and is Schleiermacher." A long list of similarities may be drawn up which shows that modern theology is "a new and vigorous Schleiermacher renaissance."

For the Göttingen lectures of 1923/24 which are published here, and which were attended by some thirty to thirty-five students,[9] Barth makes use of earlier Schleiermacher studies, but he really set to work seriously only in September of 1923, "not without some feeling of antipathy as when getting a first scent."[10] In October he told Thurneysen that he was busy with Schleiermacher but took little pleasure in it,[11] and two weeks later he wrote that he was making only slow progress.[12] He then read Emil Brunner's book on Schleiermacher and praised it.[13] His plan of treatment was fixed only late. On October 31 he was thinking of religious philosophy as the third part, though he regarded this basically only as twaddle and not a serious matter.[14] This arrangement recurs in the Foreword to the lectures (see pp. xiiif.). On November 12 Schleiermacher is going well[15] and only now does he share with his friend an outline of the series, in which he is still planning sections on Christian morals and religious philosophy, though he had to drop these at the end of the semester for lack of time. In the circular letter of December 20, which offers a temperamental general criticism of Schleiermacher, he looks ahead to dealing with this material which he later had to omit, but is already asking whether he can squeeze everything in.[16]

In the lectures Schleiermacher is interpreted in terms of his impact on the 19th century, though this is not an explicit theme. Hardly a sentence—apart from occasional references to the Herrnhut tradition of Schleiermacher's family—is devoted to the theological and philosophical alternatives at the end of the 18th century. There is no real analysis of romanticism and the factors that conditioned Schleiermacher's thinking and vocabulary. Nor is there any

---

[7]K. Barth, "Der römische Katholizismus als Frage an die protestantische Kirche," in *Die Theologie und die Kirche* (Munich, 1928), pp. 338f., n. 3.
[8]*Schleiermacher-Auswahl*, p. 300.
[9]*Briefwechsel II*, p. 198.
[10]*Ibid.*, p. 189.
[11]*Ibid.*, p. 191.
[12]*Ibid.*, p. 193.
[13]Cf. his review in *Zwischen den Zeiten*, 8 (1924), 49–64.
[14]*Briefwechsel II*, p. 196.
[15]*Ibid.*, p. 198.
[16]*Ibid.*, pp. 207f.

express debate with other interpreters. Critical accounts and biographical materials stand in the forefront, but even these only in a limited way, since Barth in his interpretation deliberately places earlier and later texts alongside one another. Thus the lectures end with a chapter on the *Speeches* of 1799 in which Barth summarizes his questions and charges against the whole of Schleiermacher's theology. They do not close with critical comments on some later work.

Apart from being astonished that such firmly preplanned criticism could produce such a comprehensive interpretation, critics might ask whether one does not perhaps learn more about Barth from these lectures than one does about Schleiermacher. This view—even if exaggerated—receives indirect support from Barth's original intention to lecture on Dogmatics I in this winter semester, a project which he postponed. At the end of February 1923 he had suggested that next winter he might lecture on Schleiermacher instead of Dogmatics I.[17] It is as if there had to be a great settling of accounts with the cardinal theology of the 19th and early 20th century before Barth could lecture on dogmatics, as he did in the summer semester of 1924. We obviously have this settling of accounts in the Schleiermacher lectures.

This edition of the lectures follows the principles of the series of which it is a part. Editorial additions are in brackets [ ]. New materials to facilitate reading are marked by |. Minor corrections are not noted, but other alterations are indicated in the footnotes. Scripture references that Barth himself did not supply are given in brackets [ ]. Allusions are introduced by "cf." No special marks are used for Scripture references within quotations from Schleiermacher. Underlinings in the manuscript are represented by italics.

In regard to quotations from Schleiermacher the following procedure has been adopted. Unless otherwise noted, material in parentheses is Barth's. Where there are serious deviations the original form chosen by Barth has been retained and the original given in a footnote. If, however, the difference is simply for the purpose of incorporation into Barth's context, it has been ignored.

Barth's orthography has been modernized with a few exceptions. The same applies to the quotations from Schleiermacher. Titles added by the editor in the footnotes are given in their original form, but the Schleiermacher texts have been modernized in view of the lack of any standardization in 19th-century editions.

It might be mentioned in closing that while the indexes of Scripture references and names are complete, the index of subjects is not. The terms typical of Schleiermacher are often hard to differentiate and are even interchangeable. A full list of such words and their full documentation would have made the index unmanageable. Instead two aims have been adopted: first, to give terms that are important for Schleiermacher's theology (and in Barth's opinion) and, second, to enable readers to find again the catchwords that they recall.

Work on the text has proceeded in various stages with many different helpers. Hannelotte Reiffen typed the manuscript and made some helpful notes. Ursel Spies and Konrad Knolle checked the quotations and worked with my wife and me on the final text. Bernhard Neuschäfer gave assistance at

[17]*Ibid.*, p. 153.

some knotty points, worked on the proofs, and prepared the indexes. I wish to express my warmest thanks to all of these, and also to Dr. Hinrich Stoevesandt, who was unwearying in his counsel and who also worked with us on the text.

Reigoldswil, Baselland, June 1978   DIETRICH RITSCHL

FOREWORD [11/1/23]

These lectures need a short foreword.

1. Little need be said about the importance of the subject and the legitimacy of devoting a whole semester to it. Schleiermacher merits detailed historical consideration and study even if only because he was the one in whom the great struggle of Christianity with the strivings and achievements of the German spirit in 1750–1830, in whose light or shadow we still stand today, took place in a way which would still be memorable even if he were dead and his theological work had been transcended. None of his contemporaries with the possible exception of Hegel took up that struggle so comprehensively or with such concern, and none of the theologians of his age has anything like the same representative significance for what took place at that time. But Schleiermacher is not dead for us and his theological work has not been transcended. If anyone still speaks today in Protestant theology as though he were still among us, it is Schleiermacher. We *study* Paul and the reformers, but we *see* with the eyes of Schleiermacher and think along the same lines as he did. This is true even when we criticize or reject the most important of his theologoumena or even all of them. Wittingly and willingly or not, Schleiermacher's method and presuppositions are the typical ferment in almost all theological work; I need only mention the basic principle, which is so much taken for granted that it is seldom stated, that the primary theme of this work, both historically and systematically, is *religion*, piety, Christian self-consciousness. Who is not at one with Schleiermacher in this regard? In 1859 the Bremen preacher F. L. Mallet wrote concerning Schleiermacher: "It once seemed (even then!)[1] as though his day was over, as though he had done his work. . . . But it is not the same with Schleiermacher as with the discovering of thinking faith (Paulus in Heidelberg): he has a tenacious life, and to the surprise of his detractors and despisers he is suddenly remembered in a way and from an angle which cannot be overlooked or missed" ("Biographie," 16).[2]

The basic work of W. Dilthey (Mulert edition of 1922)[3] first appeared in

---

[1]Here and later, unless there is a note to the contrary, material in parentheses within quotations comes from Barth.

[2]W. M. Meurer, *Zur Erinnerung an Friedrich Ludwig Mallet* . . . (Bremen, 1866).

[3]W. Dilthey, *Leben Schleiermachers* (Berlin, 1870); Mulert ed. (Berlin, 1922); M. Redeker ed. (Göttingen, 1970f.).

1870; since then there have constantly been Schleiermacher renaissances. Historically the most remarkable is that the theological movement that originated with A. Ritschl, reversing the aversion of its master, after brief hesitation turned with new warmth at almost every point, not just to Schleiermacher, but to the Schleiermacher of the *Speeches*, whom Ritschl had made his target in 1874.[4] The two most striking representatives of this group, W. Herrmann on the one wing and E. Troeltsch on the other, would in fact be more easily conceivable without Ritschl than without Schleiermacher. That the school of religious psychology, which is in the forefront of interest today, seeks to go back to Schleiermacher and to advance from him (Wobbermin),[5] I may take to be well known in Göttingen.[6]

But Schleiermacher does not need such renaissances because he has been forgotten or overlooked. I find it hard to grasp how F. Naumann could write in 1910: "The collapse of Protestantism would not have been so great had it eaten more of the bread of Schleiermacher" (*Schleiermacher der Philosoph des Glaubens*, p. 8).[7] On what has it fed if not on the bread of Schleiermacher, and this not only on the liberal wing but on the pietist and orthodox wing as well, as Ritschl very rightly said in 1874? It has to be admitted that his impact is not by a long way exhausted or worked out, that there have been and are innumerable theologians who have never truly realized the real influence of the ideas of Schleiermacher even though they live in and by them. But of what factors in history would this not be true? That it is, therefore, a task for *our* generation in *our* age to understand Schleiermacher afresh and for the first time properly does not alter the fact that the two or three generations before us heard and understood him very effectively in *their* age. Seldom has a prophecy been so radically fulfilled as that which Gass the elder made in 1822 when under the impact of the first edition of *The Christian Faith* he wrote to Schleiermacher from Breslau: "But no one can argue me out of the view that with your dogmatics a new epoch will begin not only in this discipline but in all theological studies" (*Briefwechsel*, p. 195),[8] or the even more far-reaching one which A. Neander made to his students on the day of Schleiermacher's death: "A new period in church history will one day begin with him."[9] A new period did indeed begin with him just as an earlier one was summed up and closed with him. Note how little even accounts of modern theological history like that of Frank[10] or the latest one by Elert,[11] which would like things to be

---

[4] A. Ritschl, *Schleiermachers Reden über die Religion und ihre Nachwirkungen auf die evangelische Kirche Deutschlands* (Bonn, 1874).

[5] G. Wobbermin, *Systematische Theologie nach religionspsychologischer Methode*, Vol. II: *Das Wesen der Religion* (Leipzig, 1921), p. VI; cf. p. 133.

[6] Georg Wobbermin (1869–1943) was one of Barth's colleagues at Göttingen, being Professor of Systematic Theology from 1922 to 1935.

[7] F. Naumann, "Zur Einführung," *Schleiermacher der Philosoph des Glaubens. Sechs Aufsätze* (by E. Troeltsch, A. Titius, P. Natorp, P. Hensel, S. Eck, and M. Rade) (Berlin-Schöneberg, 1910).

[8] *Friedrich Schleiermachers Briefwechsel mit J. C. Gass*, ed. W. Gass (Berlin, 1852).

[9] A. Neander, *Theologische Studien und Kritiken* (1834), p. 750.

[10] F. H. R. von Frank, *Geschichte und Kritik der neueren Theologie* . . . , ed. P. Schaarschmidt (Erlangen/Leipzig, 1895²), pp. 54–131.

[11] W. Elert, *Der Kampf um das Christentum* . . . (Munich, 1921), pp. 36–74.

different, can avoid the ranking which Lülmann gave to Schleiermacher in his work "Schleiermacher der Kirchenvater des 19. Jahrhunderts" (Tübingen, 1907), in which he called him "the *genius* of the 19th century in the religious, ecclesiastical and theological field,"[12] a factual judgment which in my view cannot be refuted. It is to learn to know and to depict this theological genius of the 19th century that I want to study Schleiermacher with you. When we learn to know Schleiermacher we learn to know ourselves and the main characteristics of the theological situation today. There was, of course, an opposing theology in the 19th century which definitely did not originate with Schleiermacher and is not to be traced back to him. In relation to it we should have to talk about Gottfried Menken and J. T. Beck, Kierkegaard and the elder Blumhardt, the Lutheran Vilmar and the Reformed Kohlbrügge, Lagarde, and Overbeck, the younger Blumhardt and Hermann Kutter, and it would be well worth giving a series of lectures on these seven thousand who did not bow the knee to Baal [cf. 1 Kings 19:18]. But thus far they have had little or no determinative influence on the course of theological development or the form of the modern situation, and in the main, to use the phrase of Harnack, they belong more to the objects than to the subjects of scientific theological research.[13] Theologically the "genius" of the major part of the church is that of Schleiermacher. All the so-to-speak official impulses and movements of the centuries since the Reformation find a center of unity in him: orthodoxy, pietism, the Enlightenment. All the official tendencies of the Christian present emanate from him like rays: church life, experiential piety, historicism, psychologism, and ethicism. We need not ask how far he constituted this center personally and directly or simply as a proponent of the romantic and idealistic movement of his age—how far, then, the threads that link the past and the future also run back beyond him. Suffice it to say that almost all of them run by way of him, so that with a good conscience we can call him a type of what was determinative for a whole century, and are indeed forced to see in him the most brilliant representative not only of a theological past but also of the theological present.

2. A second introductory note is needed with reference to my personal attitude to this subject. Some of you will perhaps remember certain passages in my writings in which I have incidentally but fairly clearly expressed my suspicions regarding Schleiermacher and his genius.[14] I have indeed no reason to conceal the fact that I view with mistrust both Schleiermacher and all that Protestant theology essentially became under his influence, that in Christian

---

[12]C. Lülmann, "Schleiermacher der Kirchenvater des 19. Jahrhunderts," in *Sammlung gemeinverständlicher Vorträge und Schriften aus dem Gebiet der Theologie und Religionsgeschichte*, 48 (Tübingen, 1907), 1.

[13]Barth is alluding to a verbal remark of Harnack in which the latter told him that he, Barth, would one day be more of an object than a subject of theological research.

[14]C. K. Barth, *Der Römerbrief*[2] (Munich, 1922), pp. 209, 242 (ET *The Epistle to the Romans* [1933]); "Das Wort Gottes als Aufgabe der Theologie," *Die christliche Welt*, 36 (1922), 863f., reprinted in *Das Wort Gottes und die Theologie* (Munich, 1924), pp. 164f. and J. Moltmann (ed.) *Anfänge der dialektischen Theologie* (Munich, 1966[2]), pp. 205f.; "Reformierte Lehre, ihr Wesen und ihre Aufgabe," *Zwischen den Zeiten*, 5 (Munich, 1924), 25, reprinted in *Das Wort Gottes und die Theologie*, p, 197.

matters I do *not* regard the decision that was made in that intellectually and culturally significant age as a happy one, that the result of my study of Schleiermacher thus far may be summed up in that saying of Goethe: "Lo, his spirit calls to thee from the cave: Be a man and do *not* follow me."[15] Nor can I promise that things will be different in the course of these lectures. But I say this only for the sake of honesty, and I hope you will immediately forget it, for the aim of my lectures is not to make you hard on the universally venerated Schleiermacher but to see and know and learn to understand him with you, not to induce the arrogant view that you can become a match for him but to handle him modestly, not to condemn him but to comprehend him as he was and obviously had to be. One cannot possibly study Schleiermacher without getting a strong impression not only of the great seriousness of his moral and academic personality, not only of the dialectical and systematic skill which is displayed in all his works almost down to the last Sunday sermon, but also of the greatness of the task which he set himself and of the manly steadfastness with which he bravely trod his path to the end once he had entered upon it. The almost incomparable influence that he has had in the history of theology since the Reformation is not surprising. We have in him a classical figure. Those who have not noticed the brilliance of this figure or the charm that he exerted and still exerts; those who have not, I might almost say, succumbed to it, should not in this instance kick against the pricks [cf. Acts 9:5]. To be sure, they should not expect me to share the exaggeration of Lülmann and call Schleiermacher a "gigantic personality," "at one and the same time a priest and a prophet, and a king in the kingdom of spirits" ("Schleiermacher der Kirchenvater . . . ," p. 12). It would probably be better to restrict the doctrine of the threefold office to Christology. Nevertheless, you should not expect any iconoclasm either, but some simple and placid observations and statements which you should then amplify for yourselves. The works by and about Schleiermacher are a vast ocean where there is much to see that I, perhaps, have not seen and which can serve to expand and correct my presentation. Use this opportunity to check whether I am correct in the *immanent* debate with our subject which is naturally unavoidable in the predominantly descriptive and statistical procedure that I have adopted.

During this winter we may expect a comprehensive, consistently critical, and systematically polemical account of Schleiermacher from the pen of Emil Brunner (*Die Mystik und das Wort*; Tübingen: Siebeck).[16] I have come to know this work at least in part from the manuscript. Brunner's aim is not to learn to know Schleiermacher but to show those who already know him what is to be held against him, just as Schleiermacher himself in his *Grundlinien einer Kritik der bisherigen Sittenlehre*[17] did not seek to make known the history of ethics from Plato to Kant but dialectically to criticize what was known al-

---

[15]Literally, the concluding lines from Goethe's poem *Zu den Leiden des jungen Werthers* run as follows: Sieh, dir winkt sein Geist aus seiner Höhle:
Sei ein Mann, und folge mir nicht nach.

[16]E. Brunner, *Die Mystik und das Wort* . . . (Tübingen, 1924). Cf. Barth's review, "Brunners Schleiermacherbuch," in *Zwischen den Zeiten*, 8 (1924), 49–64.

[17]F. Schleiermacher, *Grundlinien einer Kritik der bisherigen Sittenlehre* (*Sämmtliche Werke*, 3, Vol. I) (Berlin, 1846).

ready. *My* aim in these lectures, although I agree, so far as I can see, with Brunner's criticism, is to know and to make known, and thus, if you will, to provide material for an understanding of Brunner's book, which will evoke serious discussion even beyond the circles of specialized Schleiermacher studies.

3. A third and final observation must be made concerning the nature of the procedure to be followed. The usual and apparently obvious way to get to know the historical phenomenon of Schleiermacher is naturally the *genetic* one of showing how his theology was born from the mother's womb of the community to which he alludes in the first *Speech on Religion* (p. 14),[18] how it was then embedded and achieved individuality in the intellectual life of the decaying enlightenment, upsurging romanticism, and Kantian-Fichtian idealism, and how it finally developed on all sides. I appreciate the validity and utility of this method, which I myself followed in my earlier lectures on Calvin and Zwingli,[19] but I have to say that in the case of Schleiermacher, and in view of the particular position in which I find myself regarding him, this path cannot be mine. Use of the genetic method presupposes the open or secret integration of the phenomenon concerned into a total view. This integration for its part presupposes a specific judgment, a historical value judgment about the phenomenon, an initial sign (predominantly positive or negative) that one has given to it (again openly or secretly) from one's own systematic standpoint. In such circumstances, especially if the indication is predominantly negative, there is cause for *mistrust* of the historical integration and also of the genetic depiction attached to it. A historian who, for example, is essentially hostile to Zwingli on the basis of a specific view of Reformation Christianity will probably assign to him, in his total picture of the Reformation, a position somewhere in the middle of the fatal triangle of medieval reforming Catholicism, Humanism, and Radicalism, and it will be easy for him to offer appropriate illustrations in his genetic depiction, though whether he really does justice to Zwingli in so doing, whether he sees him correctly, will finally depend on the thin thread of his own systematic position. Fundamentally the same applies, of course, when the initial sign that is given to a phenomenon is predominantly positive. But I would regard the *probability* of a just or accurate evaluation as much higher in this case, because love, when one *can* love, is *a priori*, in history too, a relatively surer way to knowledge than alienation or aversion. Since in the case of Schleiermacher I am unfortunately not in this happy situation as I was in the case of Calvin, but since I also want to do him justice and see him properly, I will not adopt the genetic method, which in these circumstances will inevitably and correctly be open to mistrust, and I will at best venture on a presentation of his development and the historical context only at the end. The allotted path, then, will not be that of integrating Schleiermacher into some openly or secretly imported schema, and interpreting him in the light of it, but rather that of letting him speak for himself and listening to him, and this as he presented himself, or wanted

---

[18]F. Schleiermacher, *Über die Religion. Reden an die Gebildeten unter ihren Verächtern* (Berlin, 1799). Barth used Otto's edition (Göttingen, 1906) but gives the page numbers of the original edition, which Otto supplied. The Otto reference is p. 10.

[19]Barth lectured on Calvin in the summer semester of 1922 and on Zwingli in the winter semester of 1922/23.

himself to be presented, not beginning with works which, interesting though they are for a genetic depiction, he transcended and set aside as provisional or incidental, but with those that are the most mature and decisive. In our case, then, he will especially have the chance to show his best and most important side, to speak in his own words and not in some combination of ours, to be what he finally was and wanted to be unequivocally, and not in the ambivalence of development. Only when it is necessary to explain what would otherwise be, perhaps, an unintelligible picture will I speak about the course of his development and the influences upon him. In the main, however, I will try to engage in a kind of stocktaking and let the man display himself as though I were under his pulpit or his podium, my interest focused not on his external or internal biography but on the things he has to tell us, and within the sphere of our present study on the *one* question of what he means by what he has to tell us, desiring *only* to hear *more* from him for a better explanation of what he means.

I have thus arranged things as follows. Schleiermacher was first (1) a pastor, then (2) a professor of theology, and last (3) a philosopher. (1) First of all, then, we shall have to speak about his sermons. We cannot do better in terms of Schleiermacher's own purpose and concern than begin here. Already in Halle in 1805 he described preaching as his "proper office" (*Briefen*, II, 16).[20] All his letters in this period bear witness to an urge to preach, an "enthusiasm for the pulpit," as the elder Spalding wrote to him in 1804 (*Briefen*, III, 376).[21] This filled him at the time, and the tenor of his later utterances shows that it is here that we must seek, on his own view, the center of his work. This impression is confirmed by the judgment of those who knew him best. Thus his oldest student K. Thiel says that preaching to the congregation to awaken faith was by far the sweetest desire of his life and what gave to it, much beyond his own age, "truly apostolic significance for the future" (*Friedrich Schleiermacher*; Berlin, 1835, p. 64). Gass the younger says that his primary office was that of preaching; he was faithful to the pulpit until death.... Academic teaching came second, a course of life which he had not sought and which he had to pursue to the end almost against his will.... One might describe his life as an entry into Christian piety by means of the preaching office, or even, if one thinks of his upbringing, ascribe to it the sense of a return (*Briefwechsel*, Vol. XI).[22] Dilthey, too, thinks the supreme impact of his spirit was by way of the pulpit (p. 76).[23] This first chapter will also, we hope, give a fairly complete if not a systematic account of Schleiermacher's theology, that is, of what he presented as Christian teaching. For the academic context which understanding demands we shall then again let Schleiermacher speak for himself by turning (2) to his theological works in the narrower sense, his *Kurze Darstellung des theologischen Studiums* and especially the big works *Der christliche Glaube* and *Die christliche Sitte*. If in the sermons we have the almost extemporaneous and hastily prepared expression of Schleiermacher's

[20]*Aus Schleiermachers Leben in Briefen*, 4 vols. (Berlin, 1858–1863).
[21]This letter (1/16/1804) was from G. L. Spalding of Cologne, son of J. J. Spalding (the elder, 1714–1804) and a friend of Schleiermacher.
[22]See n. 8.
[23]See n. 3.

Christian life—and for our purpose that is important as such—in this second, academic stratum of his work we have the considered, connected, and definitive formulations of his knowledge with special reference to the great interaction between Christianity and modern culture which one might describe as the true theme of his life. In this second chapter, however, I have in view and will discuss only his system as such, the academic nexus of his Christian ideas. I shall then turn (3) to Schleiermacher's philosophy insofar as this is necessary to understand his theology, that is, the predominantly philosophical parts of his theological writings (the introduction to the *Glaubenslehre!*),[24] his dialectics, his philosophical ethics, psychology, and the like, but also his *Reden über die Religion*, which definitely belong to this context in both form and content. We shall be dealing here, if not with his grounding of theology or even religion, at least with his scientific demonstration of their *possibility*. Thus (1) what did he preach? (2) how does this content of his preaching look as an academic totality? and (3) what is the whence and whither of his preaching and its content? If we can get fairly clear answers to these questions, we shall be able to say that we have seen and understood Schleiermacher as we have sought. That I have not invented this threefold division may be seen from Schleiermacher's own *Kurze Darstellung*, in which he himself divided theology in just this threefold way under the headings of philosophical, historical, and practical theology. The deviation that I have permitted myself consists only of a reversal of the order, though even for this I can appeal, as shown, to Schleiermacher himself. If time allows, we shall conclude with a fourth chapter in which, after allowing Schleiermacher to speak for himself without interruption, we shall attempt a very cautious and restrained historical integration.

[24]F. Schleiermacher, *Der christliche Glaube nach den Grundsätzen der evangelischen Kirche im Zusammemhang dargestellt* (1821, 1830); 3rd ed. (Berlin, 1835/36) (*Sämmtliche Werke*, 1, Vols. III and IV).

CHAPTER I
THE PREACHER

§ 1

SUNDAY SERMONS FROM THE LAST YEARS

"By self-contemplation we reach a situation in which pusillanimity and weakness cannot come near us; for from the sense of inner freedom and its work there spring eternal youth and joy. I have grasped these and will not let them go, and so it is with laughter that I see the light of the eye fade and comb white hairs between the golden locks. Nothing that can happen can oppress my heart; the pulse of inner life stays fresh even to death" (Schiele, p. 94).[1] These were the concluding words of the *Monologen* with which Schleiermacher greeted the new year and the new century at the age of thirty-one. What he here wanted, or rather boldly maintained in relation to old age and death, he fulfilled, so far as this was possible, in the last years of his life. "It may be the last time in this earthly life," he wrote in August 1833, on the point of setting out on a journey to Sweden, to Brinckmann, the friend of his youth, whom he hoped to meet there. "May you just be found in tolerable health by your whitehaired but still vigorous and unchanging friend" (*Briefen*, IV, 408). In keeping with these words are the features of Schleiermacher on the various portraits that come from this period. These show little sign of age. Schleiermacher had not merely not retired when he died; he was not[2] tired or exhausted but still in harness. He preached his last main sermon on Sunday, January 26, 1834, and his last early sermon on February 2 of the same year. He gave his last lecture on Thursday, February 6, fell ill on Friday the 7th, and died the following Wednesday, February 22, 1834. "He taught and preached until his voice failed him," said the philosopher Steffens at the funeral.[3] All this seems to justify our taking the sermons of the last years as the maturest, if not perhaps the most vital products of his pulpit work and—since I shall be dealing separately with the festal sermons—starting with the ordinary (main and early) sermons of the years 1831–1834.

To find the characteristic lines of Schleiermacher's thinking and utterance [11/5/23] (in which task Schleiermacher himself must put us on the track), we do best

---

[1] F. Schleiermacher, *Monologen. Eine Neujahrsgabe* (1800) (critical edition, F. M. Schiele [Leipzig, 1902]; revised by H. Mulert [Leipzig, 1914]); ET Chicago, 1926.

[2] The MS has another "merely" here.

[3] F. Strauss, F. A. Pischon, and H. Steffens, *Drei Reden am Tage der Bestattung des weiland Professors der Theologie und Predigers Herrn Dr. Schleiermacher am 15ten Februar 1834* (Berlin, 1834), p. 35.

to take a short sequence of his sermons and engage in brief analyses of their most important contents exactly as they are. For this purpose I will select— it makes little difference but may add some interest—the sermons from New Year's Day to Sexagesima Sunday (February 2) 1834, that is, the last six sermons that Schleiermacher preached (three main sermons—*Predigten*, III, 752ff.,[4] two early sermons—*Predigten*, VI, 164ff.,[5] and the last early sermon, ed. J. Bauer—Marburg, 1905).[6]

The New Year's sermon[7] has as its text the saying: "Peace be with you" [Jn. 20:19]. The preacher seeks to develop the content of this greeting of the Savior by "considering the variegated *life* that unrolls before us today."[8] Peace to the *nations* first. A long period of war (the French Revolution and the Napoleonic wars) is now happily behind us. Sages no longer need to struggle "to find out in what way and in what sense bloody war can also be a blessing."[9] Intelligence and the desire for concord have gained the upper hand. We may be glad about this. Each nation may go its own way, independent in its own way of life, but without the ill will toward others that finally can be based only on error. May the remaining barriers between nations fall more and more through the powerful hand of good will and brotherly love, so that the forces of all may be united to serve the great and noble purposes of the human race on earth. But may the nations also find inner peace. This is not unthreatened (an echo of the July revolution). The noble striving for equality, which is grounded in nature as well as Christianity, should not be extinguished. But a mechanically uniform equality is neither possible nor desirable. Let us seek a higher equality by means of the inequality which, guided aright, can only work for good in our relationships. Peace, second, among the Christian *communions*, whatever their names may be. To a large extent their multiplicity does not have a material basis. Attempts at union should not, of course, be forced, nor pursued by establishing common confessions, which can only be letters—"nothing more than one of many explanations of this or that in the divine Word or in the inner consciousness of Christians"[10]—"why seek ye the living among the dead?" [Lk. 24:5] (allusions to the moves leading up to the Prussian Union)—but with loving joy at the distinctiveness of each particular communion, which is its special gift presented to the Head who is willingly revered by all. "Love for the Savior cannot fail to be the deepest basis of all of them; for why else should they confess His name?"[11] But even within the communions peace cannot be sought by like-minded people banding together. Separation does not bring peace but leads to new divisions (we are to see in this an attack on Berlin pietism, which Schleiermacher had seen developing after the wars of liberation). "Let us perceive the blessing residing in our

---

[4]F. Schleiermacher, *Sämmtliche Werke*, 2: *Predigten*, 10 vols., Vol. III (Berlin, 1834ff.).
[5]*Ibid.*, Vol. VI (Berlin, 1835).
[6]*Schleiermachers letzte Predigt*, ed. J. Bauer (Marburg, 1905).
[7]New Year's Day 1834 (*Predigten*, III, 752–764).
[8]*Ibid.*, p. 753 (the emphases here and in what follows are mostly Barth's).
[9]*Loc. cit.*
[10]III, 756.
[11]III, 757; Schleiermacher has "innermost basis."

belonging to a widespread communion such as that represented by the German Evangelical Church."[12]

Within this great communion may each do the best he can according to the form in which God has made him, and let each also view every other form of Christian life with love and joy, and not just view it but so far as possible appropriate it, so that each and all may belong to all. Peace, third, to the universities. Here it is a matter of passing on and preserving what is old and good and of giving to our children the freedom to be better than their parents. Yet no intruding of individual personalities, no unstable seeking of novelty, no partisanship for what is ancient or modern, but a loyal uniting of forces. Peace, fourth and finally, to Christian homes. Are there not too many law-suits? Ought not civil courts some day to become superfluous in a Christian land? About how many new marriages do we not have to be concerned that they will not be centers of peace! Where will peace come in "the great and complicated human bustle of a city like ours and among such a farflung people as ours . . . if the power of the fear of God, in the good and true sense of the term, does not rule in our homes?"[13] We have gathered here, the preacher concludes, in order that the Savior may come among us. He has not come to judge the world—for there is nothing more to judge where his peace reigns—but to save the world [Jn. 3:17]. "In the peace of the Lord are enclosed all the good things which attract us as objects of our striving both in the inner spiritual life and also in outer public life. Therefore may his peace be with us!"[14]

On the Sunday after New Year's Day Schleiermacher preached the early sermon[15] on Mk. 12:13–27 (the tribute and the question of the Sadducees). He gave these early sermons[16] the form of homilies closely related to the text. Hence historical-exegetical instruction plays a bigger part here, there is as a rule no single theme, and detailed ideas taken from the text are not so strictly or richly developed as in the normally synthetic main sermons. At the beginning of 1834 Schleiermacher was near the end of a series on Mark's Gospel. He aimed to deal with the story of the passion in Holy Week (*Letzte Predigt*, p. 1).[17] He was thus preaching on larger segments than he usually did. The teaching that he finds in the saying about the tribute ("Render to Caesar . . .") is the postulate of the separation of church and state. "What is God's" relates primarily to the temple tax which the Jews paid in addition to the Roman tax: "Be grateful that the unjust authority which lies upon you does at least leave the practise of your religion unhindered."[18] They must learn how to differentiate the civil and divine orders. "This separation was intentionally contained in the Savior's teaching. The kingdom that he sought to build was to be apart from the civil union of men, and he wanted to prepare the way for this."[19] Apart from some historical notes, Schleiermacher ignored

[12]III, 759.
[13]III, 763.
[14]III, 764.
[15]VI, 164–178.
[16]By mistake the manuscript has a "für" before "diese Frühpredigten."
[17]See n. 6.
[18]VI, 169.
[19]VI, 171.

the answer to the Sadducees' question (on the resurrection). His interest focused on something other than the dialogue itself. In his view the Sadducees' lack of belief in the resurrection was due to the fact that "they did not want to accept anything as truth and revelation except what stood in the sacred books."[20] They were biblicists.[21] The Pharisees, in contrast, accepted the human dicta of older expositors as well. The preacher thus discerns "a great similarity . . . to the present situation."[22] The Sadducees, who are biblicists but in many matters unbelievers, are obviously rationalists, while the scrupulous Pharisees, with their "zeal for expositions of scripture which were given in the past by individual men of God and have become part of the Christian faith," are naturally the pietistic orthodox (for the sake of brevity I am simply labeling them; Schleiermacher, of course, gives a description), "and as then, so now, the people as a whole are involved in the debate, specifically in the Evangelical Church, though the people do not understand the differences."[23] The Savior did not favor either school but stood above them both."[24] "He went his own way. Christians should do the same."[25] Yet note that "he warned the people against the hypocrisy of the Pharisees but did not warn them against the unbelief of the Sadducees."[26] He did not require anyone to separate from them, for example, to refuse to bring a sacrifice if a Sadducee was the priest. "Hence Christians do not act according to his intention when they say that they can find no edification from the teachings of biblical scholars who are not of their opinion."[27] He let everyone go his own way in the search for truth and did not have in view the divisions that we see today. "Let us follow him, then, by teaching everyone to do as the Savior did," and not to shun parties, but to have dealings with the Sadducees *and* with the Pharisees, whom he censured more sharply, so that "true Christian brotherhood" is not disrupted. "May this consideration increasingly stir us all up to this end and help us to see the one thing that is needful for all the differences. Amen."[28]

From this point on—Schleiermacher obviously wanted to finish the early series—texts from Mark come in an unbroken sequence in both the main and early sermons. Thus he preached on Mk. 12:28–34 (the question about the chief commandment) in the main sermon on the First Sunday after the Epiphany.[29] The problem that occupies the preacher here is that of the relation between the two commandments, love of God and love of neighbor. "Let us see what the situation is in our inner consciousness regarding this relation, whether we can find the Savior's meaning there."[30] How can we satisfy both commands at the same time—different, yet one, as the Savior presents them and thus sets us between them? Undoubtedly there is no love of God where

[20]VI, 172; Schleiermacher has "in these sacred books."
[21]VI, 174.
[22]VI, 175.
[23]VI, 175.
[24]*Loc. cit.*
[25]*Loc. cit.*
[26]*Loc. cit.*
[27]VI, 176.
[28]VI, 178.
[29]III, 765–778.
[30]III, 766.

there is hatred or indifference for men, where there is no combination with their welfare. But it is not so obvious that there is no love of neighbor without love of God. "As we know not only from stories from the past, but not infrequently perceive, there are loud [enough] complaints about people who are unfortunate enough not to have faith in God in their hearts."[31] Objects of pity! But perhaps their unbelief is not their fault. ("There is nothing capricious about belief and unbelief.")[32] And if their benevolence, love, and friendliness are extolled, can we deny them love of neighbor and say it is all a mere appearance, and if not, can we deny them love of God? "I at least think" that their unbelief "is simply that certain ideas of God and his nature and qualities which they most hear on the lips of men are not natural to them."[33] Does this mean that the final basis of all things is lacking to them even though they are organized just as we are? How can we who live as Christians judge otherwise than that "where love is, there God is also." Those who have love have the essence of the faith that we ourselves have, and they should cling to this and "dismiss all specific opinions (concerning it)."[34] "Where there is love of neighbor, there, inadequate though it may be, unaware though one may be of it, love of God is also present."[35] Nor is it merely that love of God and love of neighbor are always present together; the one is there only through and by means of the other. Love of God is something other than mere admiration bordering on astonishment and amazement, the type of wandering on the frontiers of consciousness such as the natural world can cause, in which destructive forces, too, can hardly go undetected. "When we speak about love for God, where are we to deduce it if we do not pay heed to the human world?"[36] "As we consider God's revelation in man," "as we live and work lovingly among men, love for God arises within us too."[37] Similarly the criterion of love for man is that we love God, that is, that for ourselves and our neighbors we do not seek what is empty and corruptible but what is "spiritual," that "we have and want our neighbors, not merely as servants, but as fellow participants in spiritual gifts," and that we increasingly make them such. This is what it means to love them as ourselves, "and that is the same as love for God, for it means being conscious of his work and nature in us."[38] This twofold love, which is one, is finally "the same as our love for Christ our Lord,"[39] in whom we love the Father, but also all men. "And after that no one dared to ask him any question," the text concludes. Why not? Because there is nothing more to ask when the secret has been told that love of God and love of neighbor are one and the same. "On this alone the spiritual world rests, by this alone the kingdom of God can be established, and there can never be any other blessedness than this."[40]

---

[31] III, 771.
[32] *Loc. cit.*
[33] III, 772; Schleiermacher has "wird wohl nichts weiter (not Anderes) sein."
[34] *Loc. cit.*
[35] *Loc. cit.*
[36] III, 774.
[37] III, 775; Barth has "Liebe Gottes" for Schleiermacher's "Liebe zu Gott."
[38] III, 776.
[39] *Loc. cit.*
[40] III, 778.

The early sermon on the Second Sunday after the Epiphany[41] was on Mk. 12:35–13:13 (Christ as David's son and lord, the warning against the scribes, the widow's mite, and half of the eschatological chapter 13). With his saying about David the Savior wished to draw the attention of the scribes to the contradiction and inconsistency in their way of thinking. Christ is David's lord as the one whose destiny it is to found a spiritual kingdom greater and mightier than an earthly one. "We, beloved, have moved beyond these considerations. The true kingdom which he has founded is not only before us but we live and move and have our being in it, its rule is firmly established [among us], and ought to reign over us everywhere."[42] In the saying about the widow's mite the preacher finds the teaching that it is commendable for the individual to give up his possessions for the sake of big universal concerns, to keep all things in order, but that in such matters "one must not judge outwardly but inwardly."[43] The saying about the destruction of the temple yields the same lesson "that in the fellowship of Christians external things neither are nor can nor should be anything but a husk, the clothing in which the spiritual comes and works, but without the slightest value accruing to it in and of itself."[44] If the story teaches us that only too often there has been a confusion of the outward and the inward in Christianity too, we may be tempted to infer that full divine power is not available in Christ to save and bless men, that they need something else "which cannot come to them from outside but only from deep within their [own] inner selves."[45] Hence the saying: "Take heed that no one leads you astray" [Mk. 13:5]. True faith in the Savior differentiates itself from the delusion which has fastened onto the simple truth of faith, and in relation to the divine word that is manifested in him it is certain that he and his kingdom stand. The power of the divine Spirit is a present thing which every moment takes the form that we need and leads us to what is right. Otherwise, of course, Christ would not be the One on whom we set our hope.

In the main sermon on Septuagesima Sunday[46] Schleiermacher discusses Mk. 13:14–37 (the second half of the eschatological address). Here he finds on the one side things that have already happened and that continually happen in this life. Thus he discerns "the abomination of desolation in the holy place" in the fact that in times of great affliction the human mind completely loses sight of eternal things, and people "turn aside hopelessly from God as though no noble gifts could be expected from above." If, however, they think they can see divine revelations in the storms of devastation, if they imagine "that a totally new age is dawning which will leave all the past behind, and the spirit of destruction is breathing out unheard-of blessings"[47] (Schleiermacher possibly had in view the fanatical hopes kindled by the French Revolution), we have enactments of the saying: "Look, here is the Christ! There he is" [Mk. 13:21]. On the other side this chapter unavoidably raises the question of the

[41]VI, 179–190.
[42]VI, 183.
[43]VI, 184.
[44]VI, 186f.
[45]VI, 188.
[46]III, 779–789.
[47]III, 780.

future: "Will earthly existence continue always as it has been, will all things constantly recur as from the times of the fathers, or will it literally come about that the worlds will be rolled up and perish and human affairs on earth will come to an end?"[48] The preacher is thus stimulated by the text to deliver "an admonition . . . on the orientation of the human spirit to the hidden future."[49] What are the "signs of the times" that our Lord would have us note? As is shown by the parable of the fig tree, by which the approach of summer may be discerned, these signs are obviously "the actual beginnings of things"[50] in their natural connection with their completion. It is to this that our attention must be directed if we are to enjoy the present gladly and to make a powerful impact on it. We should thus take note of new human aspirations, of the forces which are at work in the human spirit, of new tasks that are set, so that "we may rightly estimate whether, in the circle in which we live, it is in fact a time to expect great changes in human affairs, or whether we can enjoy peaceful and gentle progress on the path we have entered,"[51] and so that we can then give to our own action either the one direction or the other. But no foolish curiosity regarding the future! Attention to human affairs, not turning from them, and no pious exercise without remaining active on the path that God has assigned! Fulfilment of present duties unchanged by looking to the future! The signs of the times and taking note of them also belong to the present. Naturally everything will then be done to which the future, serious and significant though it may be, has a modified claim. Watch! is the Savior's cry, not just to some but to all. This Watch! obviously refers to the beginnings of human things which lie concealed in the dark, that is, in the hiddenness of human minds, the point being that we should be ready when the hour of action comes. We should watch with confidence in the One who directs and determines all things from eternity. We should watch in love and not in fear. We should watch to see that the right is done always and everywhere, that evil is overcome by good [cf. Rom. 12:21]. Undisturbed in the equanimity of love, in the activity of each for all we shall fully discharge the Savior's commission in relation to everything that may lie ahead of us.

We now come to Schleiermacher's last sermon, the early sermon on Sexagesima Sunday[52] on Mk. 14:1–26 (the anointing at Bethany, arrangements for the passover, its celebration, and the institution of the Lord's Supper). The sermon opens with a discussion of the relation between Jesus and Judas. Nothing in the Savior's mode of being is in any way troubled by Judas: "his joy in life, his sympathy for others, his view of his work and of what was ahead of him, none of these was disturbed."[53] We should "not lose sight of this, so that our own life may not be troubled or our powers weakened by what is dark in the mind of others."[54] Concerning the anointing in Bethany it is noted that "what shows itself to be an expression of pious reverence is approved and

---

[48]*Loc. cit.*
[49]III, 780f.; Schleiermacher has "natural orientation."
[50]III, 781.
[51]III, 782.
[52]See n. 6.
[53]J. Bauer, *Letzte Predigt*, p. 2.
[54]*Ibid.*, p. 3.

sanctified by the Savior's declaration,"[55] so that we may assume that if the expenditure, which was censured by the disciples as wasteful, had not stood in a right relationship to the resources of the one who made it, the Savior would not have vindicated it. To the consideration that we hear the Savior speak here of his approaching end in the solemn but lively fellowship of the Supper, there is added the admonition: "The thought of death, no matter how it comes up, deals with something so certain for us all that it should never disturb us; it can be present any moment without disrupting either the cheerful activity of life or the happiness of disposition."[56] The passover was not a feast of the Israelite church but of the Israelite people in remembrance of the establishment of its free existence. Just before his death, then, the Savior did not disdain to concern himself with the affairs of his people—a lesson for the many Christians who value only religious fellowship and look upon other human relationships only as a matter of necessity. The institution of the Supper, however, was not just a uniting of the disciples in the fellowship of his life and of brotherly love for one another but also the full establishment of the Christian church as the fraternal union in which spiritual life would be shared and each would treat and love others not only as himself but also as a society for the mediated circulation and distribution of his spiritual powers, the fulness of grace and truth which they have in him and which continually flows to us from him. "How single-hearted he was, how untroubled in soul! How little did all that had happened and all that he foresaw affect his love for his people, and how totally oriented he was, in the narrow circle of his disciples, to spiritual life with God!" We see him thus in all his earthly relationships, but "in them we also see him in whom everything is included and who, as he instituted the spiritual union of men which is grounded in him, displays the power that resides in him. This, then, is the source on which we must draw; it is this that we must appropriate in all life's relationships: then we shall express our veneration for him as Mary did and we shall also be worthy to live in the narrow circle of those who know him fully and who live in him and through him and for him."[57] These were the last words of Schleiermacher the preacher.

We shall now turn to the task of trying to understand more precisely the meaning and context of what we have just heard. We shall do so by examining more closely some of the main threads in the pattern of the sermons presented, by using them so far as possible to look at the rest of Schleiermacher's preaching in the years 1831–1834, and by trying to understand this in its inner coherence. The result even of this first section should thus be a brief account of all Schleiermacher's theology, though this will naturally need to be supplemented, sharpened, and corrected by our later researches. The sources for what follows are Volumes III, V, and VI of the sermons in the complete edition of Schleiermacher's writings.

1. One might well say that the text of the last New Year's Day sermon: "*Peace* be with you" [Jn. 20:19], characterizes all Schleiermacher's teaching

[55]*Ibid.*, p. 4.
[56]*Ibid.*, p. 5.
[57]*Ibid.*, p. 10.

in these years (and perhaps not in these alone). Not so much the disposition of the preacher, for in many places, especially in the early sermons, this is critical and polemical almost to the point of a certain irritability, but rather in the purpose and intellectual content of his proclamation. The uniting of what is divided, the reconciling of what is opposed, communion between those that differ—this seems to be (in a very general sense) the concern which ultimately motivates him. Apart from the New Year's Day sermon, think also of that on the twofold command of love, less in relation to love and more in relation to the unity of the two commands which is the nerve of what Schleiermacher has to say. Think of what he has to say about the single-heartedness of Jesus at the end of the last sermon. How does this come about? With reference to the antithesis of joy and pain Schleiermacher says (Sixth Sunday after Trinity 1831, III, 22): "The Supreme Being himself has a part neither in the one nor the other; he is high above all change, and joy and pain exist only in the alternation of a life that is conscious of itself. The greater, then, our participation in the divine being, the more inward our fellowship is with him who without any change is always and eternally the same: the more we should thus reach beyond both and constantly draw nearer to a quiet peace, a total rest of the soul in God, where neither joy nor pain can strike us with its customary force."[58] Again (Early Sermon 13, V, 165): "In fact there is also no essential difference between good and evil except that good is one and evil is manifold and self-contradictory." Again (Second Sunday after the Epiphany 1832, III, 167): The saying in Jn. 1:51: "You will see heaven opened, and the angels of God ascending and descending upon the Son of man," "points to the union of heaven and earth . . . , that neither is to be apart nor separate from the other, but a union commences between them which will never cease." Originally this was only in Christ and "at first it was only seen by others, but then it was increasingly spread abroad by them. . . . What is this, beloved, but the most perfect expression of the most perfect and blessed experience of a believing mind?" It is because, for Schleiermacher, this union is in Christ, in God himself, because it is identical with the good, that this doctrine obviously has the scope that it does.

On the basis of the text: "My peace I leave with you" [Jn. 14:27] Schleier- [11/6/23] macher says (Second Sunday after Trinity 1831, III, 2ff.) that the Savior's peace was the union of his will with God's will, but God's will was his love for the sinful world, so that Christ's peace is the sympathy of the sinless one for sinners. Of this peace it may be said: "There is no greater good for the human soul, and no more satisfying human state may be thought of, than when one can say that the Lord gives and leaves his peace."[59] Here too, then, synthesis is the will of God and Christ and the true blessing of salvation. Again, each individual believing mind ought to be "a revelation, a visible and unmistakable representation of the peace which comes into the human soul through fellowship with the Savior of the world" (Second Day of Pentecost 1833, III, 597). For this reason Schleiermacher's exposition of the saying: "Rejoice with those who rejoice, weep with those who weep" [Rom. 12:15] (Sixth Sunday

---

[58]Schleiermacher has here "treffen könnte" (Barth: "treffen können").
[59]III, 6.

after Trinity 1831, III, 27) culminates in the promise: "The more all our inner feelings not only reflect themselves but clarify themselves in pure sympathy, the more we can approach the state where the alternation of opposing feelings in our mind grows weaker and we are less exposed to the rise and fall of hope and fear, of cheerfulness and melancholy. For both the increase of strength *and* the moderation of its excitement are brought into our souls by a sense of sympathy. They achieve an *equalizing common note* in those who are originally affected in their inner selves *and* in those who in the power of love share this with them. Indeed, we might almost say that *real truth lies only in this common feeling.*" And this achievement of stillness in sympathy is expressly called a preparation for entry into "the sanctuary of peace."[60] Cf. how in relation to the story of Herod's death [Acts 12:19–23] (Nineteenth Sunday after Trinity 1832, III, 410), discussing the contrast between an arrogant and distant prince and a flattering and obsequious prince, Schleiermacher observes that "the truth that *God* wills, the form of relationship in which his will can be achieved, necessarily lies *between* the two." Peace always means the overcoming of antitheses in a higher *third thing*, the achieving of a balance between the two arms of the great scales of life. This is shown in many different areas. Thus he says (Sixth Sunday after Trinity 1831, III, 29) that in the great "struggles for the most important goods in life," even in those in which we have a part, and even in those of the kingdom of God, "our sympathy should be on both sides." Again (Sixteenth Sunday after Trinity 1831, III, 89), we all share the same weakness and the same strength, and what is all our outer or inner *inequality* compared to this twofold *equality*? Again (New Year's Day 1832, III, 143f.): With God there is no difference between big and small. "To the degree that we see human things as illumined by God's Spirit, this distinction vanishes for us too." Or in the same sermon (III, 148): The secret of the divine wisdom is that "in it the best for the individual and the welfare of the whole are inseparably united." There is no conflict here. Again (Twelfth Sunday after Trinity 1831, III, 67): The climax of prayer is that "petition and thanksgiving flow into one another and there is thus peace without alternation or disturbance." It is in this that Schleiermacher finds the inexpressible sighing of the divine Spirit who intercedes for us [cf. Rom. 8:26]. Again (Fourteenth Sunday after Trinity 1831, III, 68f., expounding the saying: "Godliness is of value in every way" [1 Tim. 4:8]): "Since in the Supreme Being everything is undividedly one and the same"—and therefore blessedness and power too—"why should not divine power be poured forth on man through this blessedness in God, so that through its power that will be possible which would not otherwise be possible?" Again (Twentieth Sunday after Trinity 1831, III, 99): "The antithesis between activity, or the doing of duty, and pleasure, which so confuses us in this earthly life, is done away in the kingdom of God; every work that we do is nourishment and enjoyment for the soul that is dedicated to God. But nothing gives it pleasure that is not at the same time activity." Along the same lines (Early Sermon 5, V, 66f.): Every day should be "in the same way a day of rest and sabbath, of awareness of our own relationship to the Savior . . . ," "and the more our life is not divided in this way and

[60]III, 30.

that, the more the likeness of the Savior presents itself in us." Or finally (Early Sermon 26, V, 339—on the feeding of the five thousand): "Seek first the kingdom of God, and everything else will be added to you—not accidentally, but because it develops naturally out of this seeking of the kingdom of God, because you do not need to cherish *two* wishes or follow *two* laws, but everything proceeds from *one and the same* thing, spiritual welfare and physical welfare being *one and the same* and able to develop only from *one* source." A very remarkable passage which also belongs to this context (Third Sunday after Trinity 1833, III, 624f.) is as follows: "What, then, is our natural life? Of what does it consist? We breathe the air and expel it again, only to breathe it afresh. Is this a relation to something specific outside us? Is it a specific knowledge of *ourselves*? . . . No, it is the general relation of living beings to the immeasurable space that belongs to our earth; we breathe in from this and breathe out into it. So it is with love. Spirit seeks spirit because it belongs to it, and wherever it finds it the human heart opens itself to all human life and being on all sides without distinction. It feels satisfied when it takes into itself the knowledge of all that is beautiful and pleasing to God; but it also gives out its life again to make itself known and to strengthen other life by its communication. . . . This is how our love should be; when it is, it is like God's love." The antithesis that is overcome here is, then, that of the inner world and the outer world. An even more remarkable passage (Seventh Sunday after Trinity 1832, III, 332) runs: "Is not this the beautiful and lofty goal to which we all are moving, that the Spirit of God may so dwell in us that we can no longer distinguish between the impulse of our own mind and the inspiration and work of the Holy[61] Spirit of God in our soul? So long as the two are so separate that we can clearly distinguish them, so long there must be something in us that resists the divine Spirit. . . . When this is not so, when nothing occurs in our slightest feeling that in opposition to the impulsion of the Spirit we must recognize as human and corruptible in a movement of the heart: . . . then we may believe that what impels us is in truth a movement and work of the Holy Spirit" (cf. Early Sermon 24, V, 305). I think that this is enough for the present. This is Schleiermacher's main principle in his "Peace be with you," and he was right (in his own context) when he rejected the view (Third Sunday after the Epiphany 1833, III, 467f.) that "peace with God" is anything less than the divine Spirit, than the living fellowship with God which is the basis of our life. "Is it possible to have peace with the living God,[62] we who are also alive when through this preaching of peace spiritual life has been awakened in us, without the formation of the same blessed fellowship with God (as in Christ)? . . . in the one word [of] peace everything is in fact contained, we cannot think of the one apart from the other."[63] "The *sermon* of our life is simply the maintaining and spreading of the *peace* that the Savior has established."[64] The next sentence takes a further step.

2. He who greets men with the greeting of peace is Christ the Savior (or

[61]Schleiermacher has "divine."
[62]Schleiermacher has "with God, the living God."
[63]III, 468.
[64]III, 469.

Redeemer, as Schleiermacher usually says). In the words of the sermon just quoted we may continue: "[But] *Christ* is our peace; he it is who unites all that was separated, men who were separated, the creature and the Creator who were separated; he establishes peace."[65] He is "the incarnate Word, and what is God's Word but one that commands and establishes and creates?"[66] In the new covenant proclamation and impartation, proclamation and fulfilment, are one and the same. In the next section—§2 (on the festal sermons)— we shall have the opportunity to examine Schleiermacher's christological thinking more closely. In the Sunday sermons on free texts and themes Christ is everywhere very naturally and self-evidently in the background as the historical source and *authority* by which the wisdom presented is attested, the *fountain* from which flow forth the life and spirit and power to which these sermons so often refer, the *initiator* of the kingdom of God, as Schleiermacher likes to call the expanding sphere of this peace. This authority and source, this initiator and Savior, is a historically given and active factor like any other, except that we Christians in our faith live specifically by it, except that our preaching refers specifically to it, because what is given in this factor is no more and no less than the perfect and sinless union of a human will with the divine will, the incarnation of what Schleiermacher calls peace. There was a time when this factor was not given or active. Then all that we now know and have and live was only surmising, yearning, and hope, and it can hardly be overlooked that Schleiermacher is inclined to judge the state of those who languish under mere law as even worse than the confusion of the heathen. But according to him this lower stage of religious development has been followed by a higher one. For him the coming of the Savior means above all the abolition of the law in the strictly historical sense that from the year 30 the normal relationship with God is one in which the law, that is, mutual exclusion, the confrontation of God and man, has no more place, in which spirit, life, love, peace, and fellowship with God are all in all. Christ stood in this new relationship with God, and in him we, too, should and can and may stand in it. This is the essential content of the gospel; this relatively simple thing is what Christian proclamation has to present, clarify, and offer in the categories of revelation, redemption, reconciliation, forgiveness, the imparting of the Spirit, and the like. The normal structure of Schleiermacher's sermons, which is clearer in the homilies than in topical sermons, is thus as follows: (1) *Christ*, his nature and will from some specific angle; (2) *we*, in whom this nature, will, and being are to be increasingly realized. The following statements (Sexagesima Sunday 1832, III, 205f.) are typical: "So, dear friends, he was always the same. This was on his last journey to the capital city of his people; his passion was just ahead . . .; but we find him unchangeably the same. . . . All that was ahead of him brought no alteration in his manner of life; the same love and friendliness shown in his whole life, the same trait of good will to those who could make use of it, the same equanimity, the same unshakable calm in all relationships as is always found! And in this way alone can *man*, too, fulfil all the tasks of life, always remain happy and brave, never grow

[65]III, 468.
[66]*Loc. cit.*

tired, never vacillate on his way, not let slip any opportunity where he can work with his talent to do what his resources are able to do for the great common calling of all." In view of this significance of the Savior as the great paradigm of the true relationship with God in which we already stand and into which we are increasingly to grow, as the principle of the great divine life-process which controls humanity and ourselves within it—in view of this we need not be surprised that this figure sometimes takes on some formal, abstract, and self-evident elements, so that the question suggests itself whether what the preacher wants to say could not finally be said without the help of this paradigm or archetypical figure; and we shall see that this was a question which the preacher had in fact to think and speak about more than once. Conversely, in view of the close correlation between what is in Christ and what should be and will be in us, it is not surprising if the picture of Christ, when it does take on contour and color (as it not infrequently does), should usually have the features of the ordinary Christian, living at peace with God, as the spiritual eye of the preacher perceives him. Already in the homily on Jesus' relations to the Pharisees and Sadducees we have noted the statement that "the Savior did not favor either school but stood above them both. . . . He went his own way,"[67] and one may comment that this is strikingly similar to Schleiermacher's own theological attitude. When Jesus went up to Jerusalem, he did so in the *discharge of his commission* (Early Sermon 36, V, 442): "He could not have been so pure and free, nor had such a good conscience as [a] member of his people" if he had not done so. He did not talk to the Samaritan woman [cf. Jn. 4:1–42] (Fourth Sunday after the Epiphany 1832, III, 172) because he expected anything from this woman—he did not—but "he would have missed a moment when he could have been at work in his calling if he had not done so." In the same sermon (p. 176) we are assured that "he dealt with *earthly things* in an *earthly* manner and did not intrude the concerns of his calling in a forced and violent way into ordinary social relationships." He is also praised (Sexagesima Sunday 1832, III, 200) because what he said and did expressly as a teacher of the people on the one side and in social life on the other, "both were *always in the same spirit* and with the same orientation to the kingdom of God and the same love for men." The saying: "Go and tell that fox Herod . . ." [Lk. 13:32] (Nineteenth Sunday after Trinity 1832, III, 406f.) evokes the statement that "he must have been greatly concerned about this prince, for how else would he have been able to call him by such a name. . . ." The Savior judged "even public persons who lived totally outside his sphere." It would be easy to put together a full picture of the virtues that Schleiermacher expected in man from the qualities that he finds in his Christ and then apply them afresh to the Christian in his sense, fortified by this view of his own innermost ideal.

The decisive answers to the question of Christ we must leave, as stated, until we survey the festal sermons. We shall turn here to some difficulties that are connected with the christocentric character of Schleiermacher's sermons and that he himself brings to our notice.

3. The first difficulty to be noted obviously arises for Schleiermacher from

[67]VI, 175.

the fact that linking proclamation to the figure of the Savior unavoidably means linking it to the Bible. It was clear that even Schleiermacher could not self-evidently find his Christ, the Christ of synthesis, in the Bible. He was happy to find John's Gospel in the Bible, which he found to be congenial to his message. He gave homilies on it for four years from 1823 to 1826,[68] and afterward as well as before he turned again and again to Johannine texts. But no matter how he might interpret John, he could not preach only on this gospel. The whole of the Old Testament lay before him like a rock. The solution that Schleiermacher found here is as radical as it possibly could be. In all the years that concern us he never preached on an Old Testament text, and a glance at his lectures on practical theology (pp. 238f.), the printed version of which is from the same period,[69] shows us that this was no accident but by principle and design: "If I take a text from the Old Testament, I place myself and my hearers in a historical situation and give them an alien consciousness and evoke a train of thought that is not related to what I ought to derive from the text if I am to speak as a Christian. ... We must treat our hearers as Christians and not as people who have still to become such and who have to be led through the torment of the law." I cannot recall ever having come across a passage in these sermons in which Schleiermacher speaks of Old Testament man and his relation to God except as something that for us now has been completely transcended or in which he views them except with sorrow and indignation, quickly hastening past as by something abhorrent. It is obvious, however, that even the New Testament does not fit smoothly into the schematism of his teaching. Much in the attitude of Jesus and the apostles and in the wording of the biblical text seems to point in other directions than he would like and to breathe a very different spirit from his. The total impression of the relation of the preacher to his texts is that of violent wrestling in which one hardly knows which to admire most: the incontestable seriousness with which he exerts himself really to let the text speak for itself (in this regard he does not just preach on mottoes but gives real expositions in which he does not like to leave any term in the text unexplained); the exegetical thoroughness with which he often tests the patience of his readers for many pages with perspicacious historical explications leading up to what he wishes to convey; or finally the dialectical skill with which he is able to exploit the situation happily created by exegesis in favor of his own lessons and admonitions.) |

I will give you a few examples of this wrestling with the Bible. We have already seen how Schleiermacher struggled with a chapter like Mk. 13 and how for him the Sadducees became biblicists as compared with the traditionalist Pharisees. In the story of the Ethiopian eunuch [Acts 8:26–40] (Seventh Sunday after Trinity 1832, III, 326ff.) the preacher is first affected a good deal by the thought that "this (what Philip does) is a way of spreading the gospel that no reasonable exposition sanctions."[70] He is reconciled to the strange fact

[68]*Sämmtliche Werke*, 2, Vols. VIII and IX.

[69]*Die praktische Theologie nach den Grundsätzen der evangelischen Kirche im Zusammenhange dargestellt (Sämmtliche Werke*, 1, Vol. XIII).

[70]III, 327; Schleiermacher wrote: "the gospel, this greatest act of God's grace in the world."

that this Christian finds himself on the road from Jerusalem to Gaza at the behest of an angel, instead of being content with the quiet activity of calm and regular teaching in the community, by the consideration that his move was finally prescribed by external human relationships (i.e., the persecution in Jerusalem), so that he was not disobedient to divine order when he followed the angel, that is, "the inner impulse of the mind."[71] Regarding the suspiciously quick baptism of the eunuch, the thought consoles him that Philip did not wait for a fulfilment of the letter, for full acceptance of his teaching by the candidate, but rightly took note of the stirring of his inner disposition.[72] Why does Acts contain the story of the death of Herod [Acts 12:19–23] (Nineteenth Sunday after Trinity 1832, III, 400ff.), which belongs to secular history? So that by its mere presence it may shame and refute those Christians who "wherever they can want to avoid participation in the greater relations of social life in the Christian world."[73] The saying: "Let the day's own trouble be sufficient for the day" [Mt. 6:34] (Fourth Sunday after Trinity 1831, III, 11ff.) is reinterpreted to teach that a Christian should not recognize as trouble what is usually called such. On the forbidding text: "Do not give dogs what is holy" [Mt. 7:6] (Tenth Sunday after Trinity 1831, III, 44ff.) Schleiermacher preaches a truly warmhearted and powerful sermon to the effect that the upper classes must become much more aware of their social guilt and responsibility. The conversion of Saul [cf. Acts 9:1–19] (Ninth Sunday after Trinity 1832, III, 338ff.) seems to him to be an eloquent example of a conversion that does not involve inner conflict or despair or contrition but a quiet working through by contemplation. We "let all the reasons work on us: and we are secure in what results and begin afresh from there. . . . The apostle was in this state, and it was thus that the light found him, and in this state the voice from heaven could work on him and give him the final push."[74] The command of Jesus: [11/8/23] "Love your enemies" [Mt. 5:44] (III, 320, 465, 617) is continually emended to the effect that the Christian should have no enemies. As regards the question: "And if you do good to those who do good to you, what credit is that to you?" [Lk. 6:33] (Third Sunday after Trinity 1833, III, 621), Schleiermacher notes that in modern society the rich do good to the poor and the poor to the rich, so that there is no place for love outside this reciprocity. Of the cured Gadarene [cf. Mk. 5:1–20] (Early Sermon 19, V, 241f.) he says that Jesus did not let him go with him "because so many unusual and extraordinary things took place around him which might easily have upset again the state of order in his mind," and when in spite of Jesus' prohibition he goes off and tells the people of the ten cities what Jesus has done, he is gravely censured by the preacher: the good intention of the Savior has hardly been fulfilled in him. "The more regular and the simpler the life he had begun would have been, the more quickly, certainly, and visibly the proper order would have returned to his mind." The point of the story of the transfiguration [Mk. 9:2–13] (Early Ser-

[71]III, 329.
[72]III, 336.
[73]III, 404; Schleiermacher: "as much as they can."
[74]III, 342.

mon 37, VI, 9) is to be found in the simultaneity of the divine voice with[75] the disappearance of Moses and Elijah. The hard saying from the story of the boy with the unclean spirit: "This kind cannot be driven out by anything but prayer and fasting" [Mk. 9:29] (Early Sermon 38, VI, 21), is taken to mean that "you could not do this because you were in an excited state; you could do it only if you were in a quiet state of mind." The violent act of cleansing the temple [cf. Mk. 11:15–17] (Early Sermon 48, VI, 144) is softened and justified by the following consideration: "We must suppose that those who were responsible for order in the temple were perhaps a little too slack, that the outer tumult was penetrating too far inside the temple; but the Savior took it more seriously." So much for the biblical difficulty in general and for the way in which Schleiermacher tried to overcome it by vigorous *interpretation* of texts he did not like, interpretation which we can often describe only as *reinter-pretation.*

— 4. The preacher has a harder time with a second difficulty which constantly arises the more he takes seriously the derivation of his message from Christ. We refer to the miracles with which he sees this historical figure surrounded at every point. The unparalleled voices, visions, and events about which the sources tell us seem to be designed to indicate that the deity of this figure has *also*, at least, to be understood in terms of a qualitative distinction from all other being and becoming. But Schleiermacher will *not* accept this pointer. We now understand him sufficiently to see *why* not. As we have seen and will see again, between Christ and man there is supposed to be continuity in their being and becoming in the world inasmuch as he is the incarnation of peace between heaven and earth. Between him and us and our world the relation is that of original to derivate, of beginning to continuation, of source to flow, of perfect to imperfect, not of superiority in principle such as seems to be expressed in the idea of miracle. The general impression left by Schleiermacher's attitude can only be that the fact of the miraculous character of the historical figure of the Redeemer is for him a very unfortunate one with which he wrestles as best he can but which he would obviously prefer to have eliminated. Miracles are there (First Sunday after the Epiphany 1833, III, 456), "but we realize that we do not need them to believe in him." He himself would have written the Gospels very differently, putting all the stress on the spiritual, inward, and personal aspects of Christ's appearance and therefore—this is the point—on the elements which manifest the continuity between him and us, the peace between God and the world, unbroken and undisturbed by the intervention of that alien factor. But the Gospels and Acts (on which he preached seriatim in 1832) were in fact written in this way. An eminent and tasteful man like Schleiermacher could not consider two possible ways of escape: first, the transformation of the miraculous into natural processes, a solution much favored in the age of rationalism, and second, the thesis that the miracle stories are myths, a view trumpeted to the world by D. F. Strauss a year after his death.[76] Instead, he chooses two other possibilities which he

---

[75]The MS has "und" here ("und dem" cannot be correct in German, which must read either "mit dem" or "und des").

[76]D. F. Strauss, *Das Leben Jesu*, 2 vols. (Tübingen, 1835/36).

either combines or selects individually in specific instances. Even when no explanation is possible, as in raisings of the dead and the like, which he calls "direct" miracles, he lets the miracle stories stand but emphasizes strongly that the revelation of Jesus was not effected in the miracle as such but in the disposition disclosed by it, and that it is upon this and not upon the miracle that our faith must rest. Or else, wherever possible, as in the healing of Peter's mother-in-law [Mk. 1:29–31], which is for him a "direct" miracle, he finds the miracle in the unheard-of operation of the spirit on nature as this is revealed in Jesus. Either way, he arrives at the desired link to his total view of the direct and continuous relation between revelation and world, between Christ and us. But let us allow him to speak for himself and put things even more plainly in detail. What do the miracles of Jesus signify? According to the passage just quoted (III, 456f.) they are "joyous signs of God's good pleasure in him." "God placed these forces in the earthly appearance of the Redeemer in order that . . . he might demonstrate thereby the Spirit that dwelt in him." For "the Redeemer, whose business on earth[77] was purely spiritual, who could not have any other external calling, had he not necessarily to relate in some way to the actual life of men, had he not to show himself as the one whom the Father had sent in the demands of everyday life as well?" Note the restriction at the beginning of this sentence. Miracles are connected only indirectly with the real calling of the Redeemer. "Every such act of the Redeemer brings afresh to our awareness the love with which he commended himself to all men in their spiritual need and fills our minds afresh with gratitude not so much for what he did physically but more for the Spirit of love dwelling within him" (Early Sermon 6, V, 77). "Never did he make this his main business but always kept the call before him that he had come to preach [the message] of the kingdom of God" (Early Sermon 7, V, 84). Jesus did not heal the paralytic [Mk. 2:1–12] "for his own sake but for the others who were present." For the sick man himself it would have been enough that the Redeemer had told him his sins were forgiven. "This would have been the basis for the development of a glad and cheerful faith in him whom God had sent and in the spiritual kingdom of God which he founded by his life and being" (Early Sermon 18, V, 225). "Peace! Be still!" says Jesus to the wind and sea [Mk. 4:39]. "Here, too, we have something totally human; he did not really speak to the wind and storm but, while addressing them, really spoke to those who were with him; he wanted to declare his will to them so that they might recognize what happened to be the result of his will." |

For Schleiermacher, as already mentioned, all the passages are very important in which the nature of the miracle is obviously the extraordinary working of *psyche* on *physis*, so that the natural and the miraculous elements flow into one another. The story of Peter's mother-in-law [Mk. 1:29–31] "is a beautiful and inspiring example of the power of the will and especially the power of love over man's physical conditions" (Early Sermon 5, V, 55). It was "the meeting of her spiritual receptivity and his superhuman spiritual power that brought about these results" (58). The basis of the healing of the Gadarene [cf. Mk. 5:1–20] was found in his mind; "independently of the miraculous

[77]Schleiermacher: "in the world."

working of the Redeemer, it took place through[78] the direct working of his proximity experienced in a specific way" (Early Sermon 19, V, 243). In the story of Jesus' walking on the sea [Mk. 6:45–52] we are to see a scarcely distinguishable mixture of the natural and the miraculous (Early Sermon 27, V, 344) and therefore an example of the way in which they are so close in the Redeemer's life. As a result "we never find in it anything contentious or fantastic in total antithesis to the natural course of things." In the healing of the blind man at Bethsaida [cf. Mk. 8:22–26], whom Jesus touches with his spittle and who regains his full sight only by stages, "what was elsewhere an immediate outflowing of the divine power of the Redeemer may be seen here as something imparted and coming to pass only gradually" (Early Sermon 35, V, 427). But whether the relationship is more evident or less, Schleiermacher insists: "The fact that indirect or direct miracles took place through him was in and of itself of no significance for the true purpose of his mission; it was a demonstration of his power over nature, but the true salvation of men had to be established by his power over the mind, had to be effected upon it spiritually by him" (Early Sermon 39, VI, 37). He also distinguishes sometimes (Twenty-First Sunday after Trinity 1832, III, 419) between the miracles of Christ and the "miracle of Christ himself," the "miracle that the Word became flesh . . . that the glory of the only-begotten Son shone in a human face and a human figure," and he then declares that only the latter is "the miracle on which we all build, the miracle which is inseparable from our faith as its true, [deepest], and innermost ground." He makes this point again and again. The faith of Nathanael in Jn. 1:47f. (Second Sunday after the Epiphany 1832, III, 165) was a "perfectly established faith," resting as it did on a demonstration of the omniscience of Jesus. The power that converted Saul of Tarsus [cf. Acts 9:3] was not the shining of the light from heaven but the content of the words that he heard and whose effect upon his mind had already been prepared in various ways (Ninth Sunday after Trinity 1832, III, 341). The power which convinced Peter of the universalism of Christianity was not the vision of the sheet with unclean animals but the demand which in this instance, as distinct from that of Saul, had *prepared* his mind for the vision [cf. Acts 10:9–23] (Thirteenth Sunday after Trinity 1832, III, 369). It was more correct (Early Sermon 4, V, 49) that the people should be astonished at Jesus' teaching, and obey him, than at the power with which he commanded unclean spirits [cf. Mk. 1:21–28].

If we were to ask Schleiermacher why he says this, he would answer that it is less sound to argue from the lesser to the greater, from the physical to the spiritual, from the kingdom of nature to the kingdom of grace; that seeing miracles is in itself no way to knowledge of the Redeemer, to the stilling and satisfying of the soul (First Sunday after the Epiphany 1833, III, 450f.). Or he would answer (in the same sermon, 453) by drawing our attention to the fact that we have no criterion by which to say what a miracle is, since we have not set the boundaries of nature (III, 188; V, 50). Or he would answer (Early Sermon 4, V, 50) significantly in connection with this same concept of the unknowability of miracle that miracle is "something alien," a condition that

---

[78]Schleiermacher: "as."

our faith cannot meet ("totally unintelligible," as Harnack would say).[79] Or else he finds it sufficient to say that the faith which rests on something that is connected with Christ but removed from the order of human affairs, and even opposed to it, is not a saving faith, and to assure us that the only witness that Christ desires is that of "inner truth," that is, the "effect that he has on the soul" (Early Sermon 11, V, 144f.). Can one say in any sense that biblical miracles have a positive significance for *us*? He finds such significance (First Sunday after the Epiphany 1833, III, 457f.; cf. V, 58, 273, 347f.) in their ability to be a "stimulating prophecy relative to our own action." We are told that "he who believes in me will also do the works that I do; and greater works than these will he do" [Jn. 14:12]. What does this mean? You shall "rule the earth through the divine Spirit of love. He will increasingly enlighten the eye of the spirit; he will teach you to penetrate deeper and deeper into all the mysteries of nature; you shall arouse through him new forces within you which have been asleep, and in the common life of the spirit and nature the power of the former will spread from one generation to another with no possible end in sight until the whole earth, as it is handed over to man, will become open to him and serve the divine Spirit in him . . . and lo! all that the human understanding will progressively achieve as it is led by the Spirit is a continuation of the Lord's miracles;[80] and we are summoned not merely to believe in them and not merely to proclaim them but to do them." Where this takes place in "inner faith in the one great work of God," "the most glorious human powers will increasingly unfold," and "we shall become increasingly strong to do and achieve all things in his name."[81] In other words, biblical miracles are a happy prophesying of an increasing knowledge and mastery of nature in the endless progress of civilization. And has not this been in progress of fulfilment for a long time already? "Whether mountains can be moved may be a matter of indifference to us, but we go ahead as though they were not there," we are generously assured (III, 420). "Where are more forces at work increasingly to achieve man's original destiny of having dominion over everything on earth, where are more such forces at work than in the Christian world?" is the preacher's triumphant question. "The work of the Redeemer still goes ahead as it did, except that the helpful powers which once stayed as close to nature as possible now remain increasingly within its bounds" (V, 348f.). But for Schleiermacher this positive significance of miracle, at least for us, radically excludes the possibility of any other. The comforting assurance that miracles are still taking place today, though in the form of civilization, conceals the barb that they take place, and *may* take place, *only* in this form. At any rate, God does nothing today in such a way as to "stand in relief"

---

[79]Harnack did not relate this formula primarily to miracles, though cf. *Das Wesen des Christentums* (Leipzig, 1900), pp. 16–19 (ET *What is Christianity?*) where he says that individual miracle stories might have an alien effect and contain unintelligible features. In his exchange of letters with Barth (*Die christliche Welt* [1923]; cf. also K. Barth, *Theologische Fragen und Antworten, Gesammelte Vorträge* [Zurich, 1957], III, 7–31) he calls Barth's answer to his first thesis "totally unintelligible" (p. 14). Barth takes up the phrase on pp. 21ff. and extends its range (for Harnack) to the resurrection on p. 24.

[80]Schleiermacher: "signs and wonders."

[81]III, 458.

(Fifth Sunday after Trinity 1833, III, 637). In this sense the kingdom of God is no longer the kingdom of the supernatural and miraculous. "On the contrary, we find that individual miracles cease when God's kingdom has been founded on earth, and not just external miracles, but internal ones as well." Schleiermacher believes that he can appeal to the Reformation doctrine of the sufficiency of the Word for the thesis: "What comes from God, can come from God only through men; what God must do to achieve this or that, he does only through the ministry of those that perceive his will." "The miraculous, the supernatural, has now vanished," we are told (Early Sermon 5, V, 58); with the departure of the Redeemer from the earth it had to "return by God's grace to the sphere of nature." This thesis is a decree for Schleiermacher. He appends to the story of the girl with a spirit of divination at Philippi in Acts 16 (Twenty-First Sunday after Trinity 1832, III, 425) the application: "We should order in Christ's name that none should presume to prophesy and work miracles. . . . There is no miracle now . . . except the great miracle of God, that we should lay hold of all else as ordered by the great law of nature and grounded in the guidance of God." The more we see this, "the more we shall smooth the way for glad enjoyment of God's benefits, and for progress, well pleasing to him, in the proper knowledge and use of the powers of nature over which he has set us to have dominion."[82] This, then, is how Schleiermacher deals with biblical miracles. The question arises whether one can harmonize his vigorous negation of direct miracles today with his acceptance of them in the past. Did he seriously think that he could accept them only for the past? The question also arises in relation to his positive statements: If the real miracle of God today is civilization, who or what is the Christ who is called God's real miracle in the past? Would it not be more to the point, perhaps, to drop the concept of miracle in both instances and to give another name to the beginning here, and the continuation there, in their constant interconnection? But we shall set aside these questions and listen further.

5. The third difficulty which besets Schleiermacher's Christology is obviously the main one, for it involves no less than the question which ineluctably confronts the preacher: *Why call Christ specifically* the incarnation of peace with God, the perfect bearer and bringer of this saving benefit? Is he really this? Could we not perhaps have it without him? Might not some other be to us what Christ is now? The problem is that of the *absoluteness* of Christianity which vitally occupied Schleiermacher the preacher as well as the scholar right up to his final years. Let us first hear how it arises for him. In the next to the last early sermon (Second Sunday after the Epiphany 1834, VI, 188) we have noted already[83] that "we might easily be tempted to say that the light was not the right one but they need another which cannot come to them from outside but only from deep within their own inner selves." Here we obviously have the *mystical* objection to the absolute significance of Christ's coming. On another occasion (Early Sermon 17, V, 211), in a discussion of the parable of the mustard seed [Mk. 4:30–32], it is the consideration of *other religions* and their numerous adherents that gives rise to the question "whether

[82]III, 426.
[83]See p. 8.

the fellowship founded by Christ will last to the end of the days, or whether a time will not come when men will need something else and Christ will no longer satisfy them." On yet another occasion (Early Sermon 18, V, 229) more general considerations from the *philosophy of history* raise the problem: "Is it true, as we believe, that this covenant with the Redeemer will last to the end of the days, is it not just a passing form for a special period in the development of the human spirit, will there not come another time . . . when faith in the Redeemer will be superfluous and men can rely on themselves, each for himself and all in fellowship with one another going their own ways without the Redeemer and achieving even more immediate fellowship with God in spiritual independence?" And it is obviously under the influence of a *belief in progress* that the statement can be made (Seventh Sunday after Trinity 1833, III, 652) that a person might "seek to hold men together under Christ because that is best *for now* (Troeltsch!), but for him it is only a transitory state. A brighter light will rise; others will come after this Jesus of Nazareth and lead humanity further; he should thus adopt the attitude of not being tied by any prejudice that would prevent him from preferring the later to the earlier." Schleiermacher did not, of course, advance this view as his own but only as that of "some" or "many" contemporaries from whom he kept his distance. He called it a "delusion" (III, 298) and a "fable" (III, 10). But how much it occupied him may be seen from his constant return to it. Even if hesitantly he places its champions under the protection of the saying: "He that is not against us is for us" [Mk. 9:40] (III, 653). And he entered into their reasoning with great understanding. Let us hear what he could say on their behalf. Those concerned point (VI, 188f.) to the imperfections of the Christian church from the very earliest times and they attribute these to its nature. They say (Early Sermon 24, V, 312) that among Christian nations the same crimes have been and are committed as earlier. They say (Fourth Sunday in Advent 1833, III, 735) that "the purpose of Jesus of Nazareth was, of course, pure and his efforts were divine, but naturally in his age, and with the limitations of the insights of his people, he necessarily lacked the completely clear consciousness which can be achieved only in a later age and which alone can give him his proper place." Or they say (Second Sunday after Trinity 1831, III, 10): If Christ seriously wanted "to make the world perfectly free, then it was necessarily his will to free it from himself, so that God might be all in all. Men would then not only recognize that they have in themselves enough strength to do the divine will but with this correct perception they could exceed it if only they would. Indeed, only when the Christian name is forgotten will a universal kingdom of truth and love arise in which there will no longer lie any seed of hostility (between Christians and non-Christians)." |

Schleiermacher rejected this view and its reasoning, though not with un- [11/12/23] restricted enthusiasm. He admits (Early Sermon 18, V, 230): "There are times when it seems as if those who incline to such belief are right, when it seems as though all the objections that are made from time to time against the adequate basis of faith in the Redeemer press in upon us, so that all that can be said to mitigate them is not enough." He also admitted (V, 229) that if with such questions one believes in the divine wisdom and love, one can think of a post-Christian era of this kind as being "even more glorious." But let us hear some of his counterarguments. Sometimes, of course, he was content to base his rejection simply on an assertion of his conviction to the contrary, as on the Second Sunday after Trinity 1831, III, 10, when he simply declared: "It is not true, this fable." The image of the Redeemer is too deeply impressed on the human race, and he closes with the lines of Novalis: "If all were unfaithful," though he corrects the fatal: "But I will be faithful to thee" to: "Keep me faithful to thee."[84] As a rule, however, he gave reasons for his rejection. The imperfection of the church should not be blamed on Christ (VI, 188). The evil that is still done in the Christian world is opposed by a different "inner feeling" on the part of men; it is no longer extolled or tolerated (V, 312). Opponents do not see that the whole development of the human spirit and human life is connected with the seed of the divine Word and conditioned by it (V, 212). They overlook the fact that the universal sense of freedom with which we live today and which they set over against Christ does in fact derive from Christ, and they miss the point that we enjoy "much greater happiness" "when we have awareness of God" through the mediation of Christ (V, 304). They should learn from "the experiences of world history" that "all that is glorious and godlike in man can develop only . . . as a mirroring and reflection of him" (V, 230). He challenges them: "The idea of a soul that is constantly united with God, whence does it come? The climax of our consciousness would have been missing if he had not come. . . . No, without this fulness of vital force and joy surrounding the existence of the Redeemer, I would not want to live" (III, 9).

On one occasion (Sixth Sunday after the Epiphany 1832, III, 193f.) Schleiermacher said that considerable differences in viewing Christ can and must be accepted so long as it is agreed that he alone, and no other with or beside or after him, is the light of the world. Otherwise the Christian community could not continue with full validity or authority, and if anyone takes a different view, that person belongs to it only halfheartedly and provisionally. There can be no doubt that Schleiermacher did not want to espouse any other view, that his choice had been made. But whether the reasons that he urged in this matter against his doubting age, and against himself too, may be described as convincing, whether among the counterarguments that he advanced there is one whose ultimate seriousness is a match for the ultimacy of the matter, whether his rejection of the questioning of the absoluteness of Christianity not only has weight, but has *specific* weight—this is a question that must at least be raised and noted for future investigation.[85] But for the moment let us press on.

6. We shall return to the "peace be with you" [Jn. 20:19] in which we have provisionally sought the secret of Schleiermacher's genius. The reference here seems to be a *gift* to men, and we do in fact see that endowment with this gift is one of the outstanding characteristics of man according to Schleier-

---

[84]Barth is mistaken in thinking that Schleiermacher himself changed the text from "So bleib ich dir doch treu" to "erhalte mich dir treu." This emendation may be found in No. 557 of the 1829 hymnbook. It is possible, of course, that Schleiermacher had a hand in the original change, since he was a member of the commission which from 1817 worked on the preparation of the hymnbook.

[85]The MS has the marginal note: "cf. also III, 741f.; III, 128f."

macher. We must now speak about this man and first about this endowment. The Christian according to Schleiermacher is in happy possession in this regard. He is never told about Christ except with the emphatic promise that what was in Christ can and should be in you too, not excluding the very highest that was in him, but this most of all. Not only will this be in you but it is in you already if only you rightly understand yourself according to the best that you are and do not refuse to grow in this. One of the most common and typical terms in Schleiermacher's sermons is "increasingly." The divine life is increasingly to glorify itself in us, we are increasingly to live in fellowship with him, increasingly clearer, higher, more glorious, and so on. The special message that Schleiermacher has for the Christian is that he is already in this upward movement that has neither beginning nor end, and that he is to stay in it. God's Word in Christ, as we have seen, is one that commands and creates and brings forth. Proclamation in the new covenant is communication and fulfilment (III, 468f.). Along these lines Schleiermacher can thus speak of the "Christ sleeping in the soul" at whom we have only to look, whom we have only "to awaken afresh in our hearts," and he will live in us and we shall see the picture of his peace and receive it into our own hearts (Second Sunday after Trinity 1831, III, 4f.). Our task in relation to others is to show them in ourselves the blessedness to which we are called (Twentieth Sunday after Trinity 1831, III, 97). How does Christ come to sleep in our souls? one might ask. Schleiermacher replies: As "the innermost and most sacred basis of our peace" Christ has left us the recollection of himself, not in the letter, but in the power of the Spirit. But the Spirit has called forth the Word (and would have done so even without the letter), and the Word has carried his portrait through the ages. Hence the Word is Spirit and the Spirit is recollection. "Peace is given to us in this recollection; the more his image fills our souls, so much the more we draw near to his peace, his life permeates ours, and we feel drawn into the same unity with God that was in him" (III, 4). We have only to hold fast, then, to what is given to us by the power of the divine Word, by contact with the voice of God, of divine revelation within us (i.e., in that filling of the soul with his image, in that permeation by his life). The *result* of the process, then, is the real presence of a quantity of Christlike nature which may be modest but which is also capable of growth. "Faith in (Jesus) Christ, the Son of the living God, . . . is the revelation of God himself in the human mind" (First Sunday after Trinity 1833, III, 601). The forgiveness of sins is this: that "resistance to the kingdom of God declines, . . . minds that have been at odds increasingly come together to seek salvation at the same source, . . . the eye of the spirit becomes increasingly clearer in distinguishing the true from the false and in turning to the heavenly light" (Fifth Sunday after Trinity 1832, III, 323).

If we are to see what Schleiermacher has in view, the concept of *gift* must not be pressed, that is, taken too literally. Strictly, as Schleiermacher expressly declares, the new life which arises in this way in man is the result of *cooperation* between something divine outside him and something divine within him. Christ presupposes in man a receptivity to the truth and a love for it; we must orient our ideas of the corruption of human nature accordingly (Second Sunday after the Epiphany 1832, III, 161). This is how they are in fact oriented.

To be sure, Schleiermacher often says that "we are totally sinners . . ." (Rom. 3:23; e.g., III, 330, 358, 624). But the emphasis in his anthropology is wholly upon a demonstration of the "longing of the human soul" for "the eternal" (Eleventh Sunday after Trinity 1832, III, 358). Prayer is important because God regards nothing as more valuable than that "the deepest and innermost disposition of man should lift itself above the vain and corruptible things that surround us on all sides and so focus itself that for the first time it finds itself complete by finding the highest within, around, and above itself," no matter whether this takes place in the form of a "quiet awareness" that has "the way to salvation" already behind it or in that of a "profound yearning" for it (355). The disciples of Jesus, to whom he says that "the secret of the kingdom of God" is theirs [Mk. 4:11], are what they are, "not simply by a choice of his whereby he excludes others, but because they felt a need in themselves to support him and consult him" (and therefore, in a kind of reversal: "I have not chosen you . . .") [cf. Jn. 15:16] (Early Sermon 16, V, 200f.). For "the divine Spirit, of course, is in and for himself an infinite power, . . . yet in the Christian church at large and in each individual soul he works only as a power that is subject to the law of nature" (Fourth Sunday after the Epiphany 1832, III, 179). "The Redeemer worked with a divine power, but only according to the natural law of human affairs, according to the measure that each was capable of receiving what he had to impart, according to the measure of the readiness that each brought to him, according to the measure of preparation and prior work that had already taken place on the soil of each human soul" (Sexagesima Sunday 1832, III, 198f.). For "certainly no one can say, however frivolously a person has lived and drowned the voice of conscience in order to pander to the desires of the flesh, that nevertheless in such a soul, as in any other, a true desire for the Redeemer can readily arise" (204). We appreciate Schleiermacher's meaning best if we compare it with Luther's concept of the justification of the wicked. For Schleiermacher there is neither a justification as a free, self-grounded act of God nor is there a wicked person, truly lost. Instead we find a process that operates according to "the law of nature" in which both God and man are at work. Again questions crowd in upon us: What kind of God is this? What kind of grace? What kind of Spirit? What kind of relationship in which man stands? What kind of salvation that is mediated to him in this relationship? But be silent and let the questions be![86]

7. Let us consider what becomes of the possession that is mediated to man through Christ in the way depicted. There can be no question of a completion of the process when salvation or peace finds its human recipient or when its significance is perceived by this recipient. The individual, according to Schleiermacher, should feel himself to be only a "part of the living whole to which we belong," only an "instrument of the divine Spirit" (Fourth Sunday after Trinity 1831, III, 18). He should be "opened up" (Sixth Sunday after Trinity 1831, III, 22), he should be aware of being in a "nexus," an "order," a "kingdom" (Early Sermon 13, V, 166). For Schleiermacher evil is identical (loc. cit.) with multiplicity, that is, with self-seeking. The opposite of this is not altruism (on one occasion he extols "the pure and single eye which thinks

---

[86]Barth seems to be quoting here from a source that could not be discovered.

neither of itself *nor [of] others"*; III, 18) but surrender to the movement of the Spirit that lives in me as in others, a movement that is best pictured as a kind of physical blood circulation which flows through all the organs and gives them life. Schleiermacher gives the following definition of the good: "We must always view the good in relation to the whole. What this brings, what it represents in our circle in a glorious form, well pleasing to God, which increasingly reflects the image of the Redeemer, what promotes this spiritual temple of God so that it builds itself up higher even to heaven itself, this, dear friends, is the good" (Second Sunday after Trinity 1831, III, 64). As he saw it, the insight that brought about Saul's conversion is, along with the universalism of grace, the connection that he had not hitherto recognized "between one's own possession of heavenly blessings and the irresistible urge to share them" (Ninth Sunday after Trinity 1832, III, 346). We should rejoice with those that rejoice and weep with those that weep [Rom. 12:15] with the aim of awakening in them "the innermost slumbering sense of their higher calling" (Sixth Sunday after Trinity 1831, III, 28). Not judging, but "in the power of love intervening, helping, and defending, drawing on the strength of others on the one side and sharing our own on the other, we should view all human activity in its relation to the kingdom of God and interweave it accordingly into our own lives" (Eighth Sunday after Trinity 1831, III, 41). That there are people who are against Christ Schleiermacher lays upon the conscience of those who are for him as their fault: "If we followed him aright, we should attract all those around us until they would be forced to decide" (Seventh Sunday after Trinity 1833, III, 653). In this sense one can say that for Schleiermacher individual possession of salvation is only a means to the greater end of circulating this possession in humanity at large. "Those to whom God has given a privilege he has not blessed for their own sakes as individuals but solely because his kingdom will be best advanced according to this order" (Eleventh Sunday after Trinity 1832, III, 362). This is the rule which is explicitly applied, for example, to Jesus' conversation with the Samaritan woman [Jn. 4:1–42] (III, 176), to his staying with Zacchaeus [Lk. 19:1–10] (III, 199), to the baptism of the Ethiopian eunuch [Acts 8:26–40] (III, 331), and to that of the centurion Cornelius [Acts 10:1–48] (III, 359), in this case with the argument that there could have been no lasting peace for the faith if the number of adherents among the Roman people, and especially in the Roman army, had not become so big that the thing could no longer be checked. And a beginning had to be made somewhere (III, 361). Schleiermacher speaks with surprising force about the unimportance and even valuelessness of the individual as such compared to the task that he is given to serve the Spirit of life that flows through the whole. In his sermon on Cornelius he says (III, 360): "Let us try not to fix our eyes on the individual, for we shall find nothing there, but on the whole." On another occasion (Fourteenth Sunday after Trinity 1831, III, 78) he says: "How can a person … ever arrive at the point of regarding himself as indispensable in this life? … Of what importance can an individual manifestation of the human spirit be? Human life is corruptible, but not in such a way that it can ever fail to supply the Lord with servants to do his work. The Spirit produces unceasingly and his workshop cannot be laid waste no matter how illnesses, wars, and all the calamities of life destroy men; for the gates of hell shall not be able to overcome the kingdom of Christ." On yet another occasion (Fourth Sunday after the Epiphany 1833, III, 481) he says: "How the individual perishes, how he has to perish, when the Lord's regard is for the whole of the human race. . . . The words of eternal life that we speak, that we share with one another, by which we serve one another, are always to be spirit and life. . . . And if they have become spirit and life, then each of us should depart gladly, leave what is temporal, and realize that his life has been for the purpose that the words of eternal life should accomplish spirit and life and increasingly glorify in human life him who has brought life back." |

A double question mark needs to be put here too. First, what is man if his humanity, in this most fundamental sense, namely, as *individuality*, supposedly has only this *functional* significance? And the second question is closely related to the first: What is this "life" and "spirit" which destroys and eliminates its servants and instruments after using them as means to achieve its own ends? When he speaks about man, Schleiermacher does have in view the man who is made by *God* after his own image, and he does have in view the life and Spirit and kingdom of *God*. But would it not fit his depiction better if he viewed man as a particle of the whole of nature and Spirit and the like as this whole, or as its eternal content or the like? Or is the obliteration of the distinctiveness of man meant to suggest, not an immediate but an ultimate obliteration of the distinctiveness of God? It may be an accident, but I should call it a nonaccidental accident, that Schleiermacher, who is not usually a casual exegete, passes over in complete silence vv. 36 and 37: "For what shall it profit a man . . . ?" in his sermon on Mk. 8:31–38 (Early Sermon 36, V, 444). We shall postpone our exposition of this until later. For the moment I would simply ask that Schleiermacher's obliteration of the distinctiveness of the individual in favor of the purposes of the so-called whole *not* be confused with the *Calvinistic* definition of the aim of life as the glorification of God. If the two seem to be saying the same thing, it is not really the same.

8. The Christian community is the qualified agent of the movement of life or Spirit that derives from the Redeemer. "What he (the Redeemer) has become for us, (he could) not become through his life alone, but there also belongs hereto the fellowship of believers which he founded, so that the one cannot be separated from the other" (Fourth Sunday after the Epiphany 1833, III, 470). Schleiermacher's church is a free society of like-minded people founded on common love for Christ with the aim of the common contemplation, fructification, and extension of the stimulus received from him. Schleiermacher is a decided champion of the idea of a *free* church, not merely free from the state (though sometimes he says this too), but also free from any inner tie apart from the common nature of the subjective experience in its immediacy which is not constituted by any verbal confession nor subject to the norm of any external authority. This is what is meant by statements like the following: "You know very well that I do not mean that in our gathering together I have come to edify you and you to be edified by me, but that I seek only that I myself should be edified with and in you through the divine Word of the Lord and Master which we lay together on our hearts" (Twentieth Sunday after

Trinity 1831, III, 102f.). The Spirit has his locus in the *community as such*. Schleiermacher calls the Spirit "a clear and accurate foresight" which the apostles had when they "placed the first big issue that arose in the hands of the community." "What they definitely expected to emerge with increasing force and universality, they tried in this way themselves to call to life" (Sunday before Pentecost 1833, III, 584). Ecclesiastical *offices* have their origin in the community alone. This always stands *above* those who are its ministers. Hence no individual who holds such an office is a seat of the Spirit in any special way (Sixth Sunday after Easter 1832, III, 288). The apostles do not seek to differentiate themselves by any particular dignity from other Christians of their day or from us (Thirteenth Sunday after Trinity 1832, III, 366). A distinction in principle between givers and receivers of spiritual blessings would obscure the nature of the gospel and lead us back from the immediate relationship to God, in which we should all stand, to confidence in man. Every particular ministry of the divine Word takes place only on the commission of the community (Seventeenth Sunday after Trinity 1832, III, 396; cf. also Early Sermon 12, V, 153). Here again I would ask that the ideas of Schleiermacher on church and office not be confused with those of the Reformed Church in spite of their similarity. As in the previous point we have here a modification of the Reformed tradition to which Schleiermacher belonged.

Two striking marks of Schleiermacher's thinking about the community may be provisionally noted. The first is that Schleiermacher's church, like his Christian, is in happy possession. In the church "we perceive the full revelation of the Supreme Being in this world" (Second Day of Pentecost 1833, III, 591). The individual churches, of course, are as such broken and imperfect beams of the eternal light. "But when we consider Christianity in its total being, if for a moment we can so illumine the eye of the spirit and warm the fire of divine love within to such a glow that these differences no longer have a repulsive effect, then in them all taken together we not only find the total Christ and the total undivided Spirit of God, but we also see the Father who has revealed himself in the Son and provided that all the different and broken beams of the divine light should radiate from a common center" (III, 590). I also recall the passage quoted earlier (Early Sermon 51, VI, 183) which says that the true kingdom founded by Christ is not merely an object of vision but we live and move and have our being in it. I recall, too, the place in Practical Theology which, in speaking about the abrogation of the Old Testament, says that "we must receive its adherents as Christians and not as those who are still to become such" (p. 239).[87] The sermon on the invitation to the great supper in Lk. 14:15–24 (Twentieth Sunday after Trinity 1831, III, 93f.) presupposes that "we who gather here to think together about him who has called us into the kingdom of God" are not among those who in the parable were only invited but among the servants who have to take the invitation, since we have ourselves already accepted it. Thus the apostolic admonition that we should all seek to please our neighbors [Rom. 15:2] becomes incomprehensible only if in our neighbors "we have to do with people who stand outside our fellowship with God on the basis of Christ . . .; but this is not so" (New Year's

---

[87]See p. 16, n. 69.

Sermon 1833, III, 445). A particularly strong passage may be found in the exposition of the saying: "I came not to call the righteous, but sinners to repentance," in Mk. 2:17b (Early Sermon 8, V, 105f.): "This is not to be taken to mean that all those who are born and brought up in the Christian church, and instructed from youth up in the truths of salvation, must be converted and come to a different mind in the same way as the contemporaries of the Redeemer—for this mind, which they had to make their own with a total renunciation of their former mind, is impressed upon us from our youth up. ..." In other words, the repentance that Jesus demands is not necessary for the individual today in view of the general repentance of the Christian community that becomes his through his Christian upbringing, of the Christian history as such which is in no more doubt than the presence of the Spirit, of life, of fellowship with God, and so on, but is presupposed as given with the existence of Christianity (not, of course, as an outflowing of baptismal grace, nor as the direct working of the death of Christ or the Holy Spirit, but with the historical existence of Christianity transmitted and continuing from gen- [11/13/23] eration to generation). The question of the appropriate purifying, propagating, and depicting action based on this presupposition has to be and will be dis- cussed in a Christian ethics.[88] The question of an original becoming of the community, of a receiving of its possession in the strict sense, is no question in and for the community. But it is all the more a question for us who have at least to seek more light on the presupposition.

The second issue is this: Who is for Schleiermacher a member of the Christian community? He can say quite definitely: "It is always essentially a matter of two things: clarity of awareness of the divine counsel in Christ, of the worth that God imparts, of the glory that God gives, and faithfulness in discipleship which cannot be discouraged or deflected by anything" (Sixth Sunday after Easter 1832, III, 282). But the criterion of this clarity and faith- fulness is subjective, as is shown by the triumphant way in which Schleier- macher affirms at the beginning of the same sermon (on the election of the apostle Matthias in Acts 1[21f.]) that this important decision was taken prior to the outpouring of the Holy Spirit, from which he deduces that this out- pouring is among mutable external things and consists only of the reception of a higher measure or stronger stimulation of divine power, the Spirit himself being always the same in the Lord's community, so that there is no reason to ask whether anyone is born again of the Spirit (III, 277f.). If, however, the Spirit who makes a Christian a Christian is identical with subjective stimu- lation and is not called in question by the possibility of blowing where he himself wills [cf. Jn. 3:8], then it is not surprising that in spite of Schleier- macher's express statement the boundary between the Christian and the non- Christian is a *fluid* one—not, of course, in virtue of the secret of God the Lord, who alone knows who are his [cf. 2 Tim. 2:19], but in virtue of the secret of the *human heart* which we cannot penetrate and judge (Eighth Sunday after Trinity 1831, III, 36). As we have seen in the sermon on the twofold com-

---

[88]An allusion to the headings of Schleiermacher's *Die christliche Sitte*, ed. from Schleiermacher's literary remains and lecture manuscripts by L. Jonas (Berlin, 1834) (*Sämmtliche Werke*, I, Vol. XII).

mandment of love [Mk. 12:28–34], Schleiermacher does not count upon a prevenient love of God which embraces unbelievers too but on a real if unconscious love of man for God (First Sunday after the Epiphany 1834, III, 773). He believes (Early Sermon 8, V, 104f.) that there are many things in many people today that lead them on to the right path of life and that do in fact come from Christ, though they regard them as their own. There is in fact "no one who does not experience the Redeemer's help from the very first and find himself within his purifying and strengthening activity." Such people simply lack any awareness of the origin of what they are and have, an awareness with which they would be better "because they would then have increasing cause to go back to the source and draw upon it directly." It is understandable, and is stated explicitly in this context, that according to this doctrine of the church individual repentance is not a demand that a member of the Christian community must permit to be made and that the question whether one has received the Holy Spirit is an illegitimate question in the Christian church. Almost unavoidably, then, the twofold requirement of a clear awareness of the glory of Jesus and faithfulness in his discipleship degenerates into the description of a purely quantitatively different and higher stage of the natural and self-evident adherence to Christ which in principle can just as well be unconscious as conscious. The primary thing that makes a Christian a Christian and establishes the church neither is nor has to be an original encounter of God with man but the mediacy of a supposedly Christian history, the continuum of the religious stimulation which runs through this history and in which man can have a bigger or smaller share with no danger in principle (and in this regard Schleiermacher is only too right!). Whether this latitudinarianism can be the last word in the question of the church if God is really God and the Spirit is really the Spirit and not the stream of life, is a very different question.

9. We have come to know (1) Schleiermacher's view of salvation, then (2–5) his view of Christ as its mediator, then (6–7) his doctrine of its outworking and propagation in humanity, then (8) his doctrine of the church as the agent of this movement; we must now investigate in detail the specific content of the latter, or what might be called Schleiermacher's doctrine of the Christian life. If I am not mistaken, we are dealing here with the true nerve of Schleiermacher's proclamation, with the thoughts which together with his view of peace, which we considered first, were perhaps the innermost concern that led him to the pulpit. I believe I shall understand him best and with the greatest justice at this point if I begin with what he says about prayer, "this relationship which is so indispensable, which represents the essence of piety, and yet which is so mysterious," as he once described it (Twenty-First Sunday after Trinity 1833, III, 677). Between 1831 and 1834, if I am right, Schleiermacher twice devoted whole sermons to this theme (Twenty-First Sunday after Trinity 1833, III, 677 and Twelfth Sunday after Trinity 1831, III, 56ff.). The inner, though not the outer, course of the two sermons is the same. In both cases the starting-point is the question of prayer as the individual act of asking God for specific things. The upshot of both is that when prayer has been critically sifted its true point cannot be an individual act nor the desire for specific things, but a general and ongoing situation of man before God which

according to the 1831 sermon consists of the undisturbed synthesis of petition and thanksgiving, and according to the 1833 sermon of the equally perfect identity of stormy perseverance and the inner and active thrust of the heart. But the distinction is only one of emphasis. The first sermon says, along the same lines as the second, that it is given only to those who give, that is, who will be active for the kingdom of God, and the second sermon says, along the same lines as the first, that true asking is silenced when it becomes asking that God's will may be done. The two sermons have exactly the same ring and they supplement one another excellently. What we have in them is Schleiermacher's ideal of the Christian life in a nutshell. This life is a circular movement which begins with man's concentration before God, or in himself, as this is demanded by the centripetal multiplicity of the active life, which then carries with it an increasing awareness that this concentration cannot be an act that is done for its own sake alone, but because it relates to God, or to the point of perfection that is given within man himself, can be meant only as a spiritualizing concentration of the whole of life, and which descends from this high point to clarified and increasingly to-be-clarified activity, then returning to a new concentration and interiorizing as a separate thing that takes place for itself. The impression that Schleiermacher's depiction leaves, however, is not that of the necessity of this return from activity to concentration but of the necessity of the movement from concentration to activity. Schleiermacher's basic orientation is *ethical*; there may be seen here his *Reformed* origin and schooling, though I would ask you here, too, to distinguish between school and scholar. Let us try to describe in more detail his typical way from narrowness to breadth, from quietness to the world, from prayer to work. "Prayer is an affair of our spiritual life, the maintaining of our fellowship with God, the living and sure feeling that no matter how far we may still have to go in relation to the gradual ascent of man to dominion over the earth through work, even now the great miracle of God may be done for all" (Twenty-First Sunday after Trinity 1832, III, 424).[89] The beginning and end of the path are classically stated in this definition of prayer: first "maintaining fellowship with God," but then anticipation of the miracle of God, that is, of cultural fulfilment in the living and sure feeling.

At the beginning stands "the natural expression . . . of men's desire for the eternal" (another of Schleiermacher's definitions of prayer; Eleventh Sunday after Trinity 1832, III, 357). This desire is in the first instance something special and isolated, separate from the other functions of human life. As always when speaking about prayer, Schleiermacher hastens to give greater precision by saying that what is at issue is "the need of the heart, which must be renewed each day, to sustain spiritual life" (Twelfth Sunday after Trinity 1831, III, 59). This must not be confused with the other and very different concerns of life that can be met by work. Hence in what Schleiermacher calls "spirit" or "the spiritual" we can really expect to find something which is

---

[89]In the wider context Schleiermacher explains that problems arise on earth in order to show us where help may be sought and in this way to develop our powers, so that we may gradually achieve dominion over the earth through work. While the achieving of dominion may be slow, help comes at once through prayer.

superior to nature or the nonspiritual. And indeed "news of the Redeemer and witness to him do not ring out from the midst of busy human life with its manifold activities" but "draws those . . . who want to receive the witness to the Lord . . . away for a time from direct participation in the active promotion of the affairs of this world and their agitation by them, so that nothing should interrupt or disturb this . . . Word that the Redeemer is present. . . . Hence the witness to the Lord seeks first in every mind the profound stillness of the inward[90] so as to establish itself there and become there first the seed of a new life" (Fourth Sunday in Advent 1833, III, 727). On the basis of Jesus' sermon by the lake [Mk. 3:9] Schleiermacher advises us to "hold ready the little ship in which we may . . . retreat," that is, to "make a place for the spiritual, . . . and not to give ourselves so totally to the things of this world that we completely deprive ourselves of spiritual contact with those who are like-minded" (Early Sermon 11, V, 140f.). For all the civilizing work that God desires, the inner needs of man should not be neglected: "Obvious though it may be how many benefits have come to human society through Christ, it is not from these but only from the need of each individual mind respecting its relation to God, and only when each sees Christ as the Redeemer in this regard, that there can grow true and saving faith in the human mind. Hence we must in every way promote this retreat to the stillness of the mind from the pressure of the world" (Early Sermon 21, V, 271f.). As is once illustrated by a parable,[91] we should not spend too much time contemplating the grateful gifts and offerings which are brought to the Christian community and displayed in its temple (e.g., the work of the state in matters of order and welfare) but should penetrate to the inner sanctuary (Second Day of Pentecost 1833, III, 594f.). This applies not merely to the relation of the church to the state but also in general principle, as we have seen already: "The kingdom that [he] (the Redeemer) seeks to build is to be completely different from civil society" (Early Sermon 50, VI, 171).

But we have to go beyond this beginning of the movement of life. "If only the Word has come into the depths of the human heart and is planted there, . . . O then our life is no longer a mere voice in the wilderness like the witness of John." The life of Christ that is in us must come out of the wilderness into the world, "and there must then be no difference between the wilderness and Jerusalem, no difference between the moments of self-renewing assembly in the stillness of retreat (though these will always be precious and valuable and will always be needed because of human weakness) and our active life itself" (Fourth Sunday in Advent 1833, III, 728; cf. also Early Sermon 25, V, 319f.).[92] The feeding of the five thousand [cf. Mk. 6:30–44] was designed to show that the Redeemer "did not wish that the union of men with him for the sake of the spiritual life that he was to establish among them . . . should in any way be to the detriment of their external life" (Early Sermon 26, V, 334). We are

[90]Barth has "Inwendigen" here for Schleiermacher's "Innern."
[91]III, 594f.: In the parable Schleiermacher says that when visiting a temple we should not spend all our time looking at the inscriptions, for this will prevent us from reaching the inner sanctuary and the time that ought to be devoted to the contemplation of divine things will be wasted on external and secondary things.
[92]III, 728; Barth has shortened and simplified the more complicated original.

expressly told not to separate the calling of people in society and their calling in the kingdom of God. We must carry every obligation of ours in society "into our obligation to the kingdom of God; indeed, we must regard this as the fixed place that is allotted to each of us at that great feast" (Twentieth Sunday after Trinity 1831, III, 100). How does Schleiermacher arrive at this? The two sermons on prayer answer this question clearly. As man seeks and finds God in prayer, he finds the point beyond the antithesis of rest and movement, receptivity and self-activity; according to the model of Jesus prayer can be only the end of all our own desires (III, 66), only our orientation to God's will, and therefore prayer is not to be differentiated as a special thing from fellowship with God, nor from activity in God's kingdom that is pleasing to him (cf. Twenty-First Sunday after Trinity 1833, III, 682–687). Once this dam is opened we relentlessly move on to a complete and irreversible amalgamation of Christian life and civilization. Schleiermacher's Christian is transformed (we need not be surprised at this after what we learned about miracles and about the general aim of the movement of life that emanates from Christ), for after a short stay in the inner sanctuary he emerges, newly strengthened, as the ideal civilized man who is distinguished from others only by knowing what is the goal of civilization, namely, the divinely willed mastery of nature by spirit, so that he can be called more joyful, unhampered, free, and direct than anyone else: "homo sum, nihil humani a me alienum puto."[93] Remember the conclusion to his last New Year's sermon in which he says that the peace of the Lord enfolds all the blessings that are the object of our striving whether in the inner spiritual life or the outer public life (III, 764). "All that we do in virtue of the spiritual power with which God has equipped the human race is a work of God . . . , from whom the gift comes" (Sixth Sunday after the Epiphany 1832, III, 184). "All that concerns the true welfare of man in all its aspects stands in the closest relation to the kingdom of God" (Fifth Sunday after Trinity 1832, III, 317). "We know that everything great and good comes from him, that it is his blessing, and that its value[94] rests on the fact that he uses it for his praise and glory" (First Sunday after the Epiphany 1833, III, 458). This can only mean—we shall already meet in Schleiermacher almost all the terms that modern Christianity uses when it follows this path—that godliness ennobles all things by relating "all things to the spiritual life" (Fourteenth Sunday after Trinity 1831, III, 74), that the "wise sayings" of the Lord in the New Testament are *applied* to life (Second Day of Pentecost 1833, III, 596), that we permeate all the relations of human life with the life that Christ has brought (Fourth Sunday in Advent 1833, III, 728). And these directions find their objective basis in a full and unrestricted equation of the providence which rules over the actual course of human affairs with the purposes of the kingdom of God, in the assurance that "all arrangements relate to the kingdom of God" (Early Sermon 27, V, 346), that "the divine orders in the whole sphere of human affairs are totally dependent on Christ, on the salvation which God

---

[93]Terence, *Heautontimorumenos* I, 1, 25: "Homo sum; humani nil a me alienum puto" ("I am a man; I do not regard anything human as alien to me").

[94]Barth has "sein Wert" for Schleiermacher's "der Wert desselben."

through him has given to men"[95] (New Year's Day 1832, III, 144). "Everything takes place as it does to further Christ's kingdom" (p. 147). The secularization of the Christian life is thus projected as it were into heaven. That this cannot happen without interesting reinterpretations of the biblical text is palpable. "To cast one's care on the Lord" [1 Peter 5:7] means primarily "to trust in the common strength of those who are committed to the good, to trust in the wisdom, supported by piety, of those who by divine order lead the whole," and then, of course, to trust in the Lord himself, though with what inner right is by no means apparent (Fourth Sunday after Trinity 1831, III, 19). "Not to kick against the pricks," as Paul did [Acts 9:5], means going along with "the hidden moving force," that is, seeking "to establish and validate right, light, and order" (Ninth Sunday after Trinity 1832, III, 348). The "faith that moves mountains" [cf. Mk. 11:23] means "briskly striding ahead on the way we are told to follow and doing briskly all that we find to do, and acquiring even greater skill in doing any work that can be demanded of the man of God." Hence "if you have faith," he tells his disciples, "you will be able to overcome all difficulties in your calling and set aside all obstacles" (Ninth Sunday after Trinity 1833, III, 663, 656).

Four terms are used especially to describe the cultural process which is presented as a manifestation of the Christian life in these sermons. All these terms occur frequently and need only brief exposition. The first is the concept of *progress*. Remember the typical "increasingly" and the temple of the good which is being built up even to heaven.[96] For Schleiermacher it is obvious that Christ does not bring his disciples immediately "out of darkness into the fullest light, into the brightest radiance of truth," but leads them forward progressively and conducts them gradually nearer to the goal (Thirteenth Sunday after Trinity 1832, III, 366). If the divine is equated with a historical continuum, as in Schleiermacher, all the hortatory and emotional power of proclamation will naturally fall on this concept, and even the belief in invisible things, to which full justice cannot be done, will have to seek and find expression in it. Yet it is remarkable that on New Year's Day 1833 words like the following should have been uttered, not from the podium of a Swiss shooting match, but from the pulpit of the leading theologian of the century: "Are we not a happy and greatly blessed people, no matter how we look at ourselves? Does not God's Word dwell richly among us; has not a sense of its blessings developed more strongly again from an almost moribund state and spread abroad more widely? ... Do we not have to admit that Christian faith, and the piety that is grounded in it and clings to it, is nobler among us than it was before and is freer from the yoke of the letter? Do we have to say the same when we look at our civil condition? ... Do we not have a livelier sense of belonging to one another? ... We are people who in both ecclesiastical and civil life need only that God should keep us on the path on which we walk so that we may enjoy undisrupted progress" (III, 437).

The second distinctive term in these sermons is *activity* or *calling*. Here is one of the points where Schleiermacher and Ritschl are at one. "To be able

---

[95]Schleiermacher has "given to men through him."
[96]Cf. pp. 25, 27.

to look around circumspectly each moment and not to neglect anything that belongs to the work of calling or the tasks of the moment" (Fourteenth Sunday after Trinity 1831, III, 76)—that is the very image of Schleiermacher. The antithesis of duty and pleasure is transcended in the kingdom of God. Everything is a pleasure for the consecrated soul but nothing is a pleasure for it that is not also action (Twentieth Sunday after Trinity 1831, III, 99; cf. New Year 1832, III, 132). The man born blind in Jn. 9[1–41] is praised because he did not want to live any longer on the generosity of others; he "was the kind of person who likes to fulfil man's calling on earth with his resources" (Sixth Sunday after the Epiphany 1832, III, 189). On the other hand, in the story of the calling of Levi Jesus has to be protected against the dreadful suspicion that with his "Follow me," he gave the tax-gatherer occasion "to neglect the task entrusted to him to his own loss and that of everyone. The Redeemer certainly did not want that" (Early Sermon 8, V, 98). The sermon of Philip, which is frequently cited, refers to the relation between the Holy Spirit and this view of culture: "Everything new and also (!) original can begin only with this vital stimulation of man within, with this often incomprehensible pull of the spirit; but this should always be only the beginning of a regular and connected activity, of a well-ordered work which fits into all activity that is pleasing to God" (III, 334).

[11/5/23]   The third dominant thought that strikes me here is that of *order*. The first words of the text to be expounded in the sermon on the feeding of the five thousand [Mk. 6:30–44] are the remarkable ones: "And they sat down in groups, by hundreds and by fifties." "(The Redeemer) made order the condition . . . on which alone he could intervene in this way in the external relations of earthly life," "on which alone the spiritual and the physical can coexist . . . on which the spiritual does not founder upon the physical" (Early Sermon 26, V, 329f.). "Godliness is of value in all things and holds promise for the present life and also for the life to come" [1 Tim. 4:8] is the text on another occasion. The first promise of godliness is that it makes man's entire earthly life an object of pleasure. But what is the essence and basis of this, its most indispensable aspect? "No other than soberness and purity, order and moderation. Where we . . . find these we feel pleasantly satisfied, for we note the rule of the Spirit" (Fourteenth Sunday after Trinity 1831, III, 70f.). And the fact that with God it is possible for the rich to enter the kingdom of God [cf. Mk. 10:27] is boldly taken to mean that in a time like our own which is so rich in invention and progress the necessary thing must take place in order to "put the rule of order, custom, and discipline in all human affairs in the place of whim, caprice, and arbitrariness" (Fifth Sunday after Trinity 1833, III, 639). To this context belong Schleiermacher's frequent references to the *state*, whose purpose he finds not merely in the maintaining of quiet and safety but also in the organization of forces for the efficient and complete prosecution of the work of civilization (Early Sermon 50, VI, 170). Although his ideal is a free church, he demands "that the spirit of Christian life should be reflected and recognized in civil life as well." Christian nations should differ from others in respect of the rule of law and public order (Early Sermon 30, V, 375). We have seen earlier that he found this already achieved to a large extent in the

Prussian state.[97] Thus in the early summer of 1831, when cholera threatened Berlin, he could promise his congregation that they could leave all concern about the future to those appointed to see to it. "All that belongs to some specific art of calculating human and natural affairs is everywhere among us a matter of special calling," in this case the preventive authority, that is, the Royal Health Department, which must be supported in its good work by "general consensus" and if necessary by "the judgment of the public" (Fourth Sunday after Trinity 1831, III, 14, 17f.). So, too, in the summer of the same year, when there was much talk of unrest in connection with the July revolution, he could urgently request that there be no neutrality but powerful support for the authorities in the maintaining of order (Tenth Sunday after Trinity 1831, III, 50f.).[98] I would regard this sermon of Schleiermacher on revolution, which deals with things in a calm and objective spirit, as one of his best at this period except that unfortunately its poor exegetical basis is so disappointing.

This sermon leads me to the fourth of the principles which Schleiermacher's sermons proclaim in practice. At this point we have to respect his insight and vision, for this principle is no other than that of *social equality*. Like the question of the absoluteness of Christianity, this is a theme that is constantly mentioned and discussed in these sermons, and to the best of my knowledge this side of his ethics has never been investigated or presented in context. Even in a specialized work like that of Uhlhorn on the history of Christian benevolence[99] it is oddly omitted. In view of the topical interest of the theme, it might be worthwhile to look into it briefly. In his sermon on revolution Schleiermacher is not content merely to ask for the maintaining of public order. Rather surprisingly he turns the tables and brings against the upper classes of society the accusation that the revolts indicate "great communal guilt." What have we done, he asks, to remedy the results of the great spiritual inequality among men which is caused by material relationships? Could this oppressed portion of the brethren sink so low if we did not so often isolate ourselves from it and regard it merely as an object of violent restraint? This has to be changed, not by philanthropy, but by the establishment of spiritual fellowship with this group, by the binding insight that we possess our spiritual advantages on the basis of their external inequality, and that we are thus required to practice all the more our equality with them before God. We should take a particular interest in the young people of this section of society, but all of us in our different circles should do what we can to reach the hearts of our brethren, not in order to protect ourselves against them, but in such a way as to make it irrefutably clear to them that what moves us in relation to them is true love (pp. 52–55). In the same summer Schleiermacher takes what is obviously a further step. If he had implied in that sermon that nothing should be done about external inequality in society, in the fall he declares expressly that the oppressive cares of external life leave many people with no strength for spiritual enjoyment, and it must be the aim of our common activity in God's kingdom "that this excessive difference in external conditions should

[97]See p. 35.
[98]Marginal note in pencil on the MS: "To *what* events is the reference here?"
[99]G. Uhlhorn, *Die christliche Liebesthätigkeit*, 3 vols. (Stuttgart, 1882², 1884, 1890).

be increasingly equalized" (Twentieth Sunday after Trinity 1831, III, 103). It is interesting to note that in the intervening period (Sixteenth Sunday after Trinity 1831, III, 84)—a gleam of light in his otherwise rather murky relation to the Bible—it had become clear to him that a saying of Jesus like "whatever you wish ..." [Mt. 7:12] does not fit into "the whole structure of a human existence like our own" but presupposes an equality "that is not present." In the following summer union with the "hidden saving force" (Ninth Sunday after Trinity 1832, III, 348) means "not serving the interests of this or that portion of society but seeking an ordering of human affairs whereby the power of evil will be most surely controlled and it will be made easier for men to do the will of God." In the very next sermon he then shows that if the civilization that God wills has become on the one hand the occasion of great external inequality among men, the insight is equally necessary on the other hand that God has not merely put the poor and the rich *alongside* one another but has made them *for* one another and that that external inequality should be vigorously opposed. Sooner or later the position must be reached where almsgiving is no longer necessary. Misery and want should not occur in a Christian and civilized nation (Eleventh Sunday after Trinity 1832, III, 352–355). We are also told (Seventeenth Sunday after Trinity 1832, 390f.) that social inequality is a false result of civilization and that social service is thus a matter of justice. Nor did Schleiermacher scorn to give his support to insurance ("the praiseworthy attempt so far as possible to provide mutual safeguards in advance against all the accidents that can happen to us in social life," p. 392). More sharply he can say incidentally in the early summer of 1833 (Third Sunday after Trinity, III, 620f.) that "the strong and wealthy live by the efforts of the lowly and needy, while the latter are content to remain in this order of things." It is they that do good to the rich rather than the reverse. Note, too, Early Sermon 10, V, 127f., which speaks about keeping Sunday holy: The fact that so many have to work on Sunday should not lead, as in England, to strict measures against this, which make no sense so long as inequality persists, but to shame at this "common imperfection" and action to improve things. Then Early Sermon 33, V, 407 demands a shortening of the hours of work for all manual workers, partly as the presupposition of nurture of the spiritual life, partly as its necessary consequence. And in the last New Year Sermon of 1834 (III, 754f.) Schleiermacher speaks about the "hostile jealousy" which has grown up among all "strata and divisions of society," of the new movements which have gradually fermented and suddenly developed, and "concerning which we cannot know what havoc they will cause or how far they may go." Recognizing that various experiences show that full equality can be attained only in small circles, he advocates a *higher* equality on the assumption of continuing inequality—a noble *social liberalism*, if I am not mistaken.

If we consider that all this was said at a time when the pioneers of the social movement and of socialism were only just emerging [the French Utopians St. Simon (1760–1825)—Bretschneider's work *Der St. Simonismus und das Christentum* came out in 1832[100]—and Charles Fourier (1772–1837), and

---

[100]K. G. Bretschneider, *Der Simonismus und das Christentum* (Leipzig, 1832).

the Englishman Robert Owen (1771–1858)],[101] and if we also consider that in contemporary pietist preaching such as that of L. Hofacker we listen in vain for rousing notes along these lines, we cannot avoid concluding that in spite of, or with, or because of his cultural theology Schleiermacher discharged with openness of vision and a powerful voice a watchman's office which elsewhere and afterward was fatefully neglected in the Evangelical Church until it was too late. Whether his social message of higher equality in a social inequality— which was necessary, though it could and should be mitigated—would really have been enough to calm the storm that threatened society and the church even if it had sunk in and been accepted by the rest of the church; whether what he said about the Christian permeation of relationships, which half a century later, not at the eleventh hour, but when the twelfth had already struck, was adopted by modern Protestantism,[102] though without remembering this church father—whether what he said was hopeless from the very first in face of the onrushing elemental powers of capitalism and the proletariat, these are separate questions; but that Schleiermacher saw the problem, and in spite of his triumphant optimism about progress saw it fairly clearly compared to what was seen by others, that he recognized its significance for Christianity and issued a loud warning to the Christian community concerning it, should never be forgotten.

10. I now want to look at Schleiermacher's Sunday sermons of the last years from a final aspect. Having so far considered the positive side, we must now ask: What does he not like? What does he reject? What does he warn against? I have indicated already that there is much of a polemical nature in these sermons. You will see that the attempt to fix the general direction of this polemical material will not merely confirm and supplement significantly our previous findings but even give on its own a well-rounded miniature of the whole man.

You will join me in accepting the paradox if I first make the general point that Schleiermacher strives against all strife, against all that comes from it or might lead to it; he allows himself the liberty of being cross with all who are cross and sharp against all who are sharp; he fights zealously for peace and harmony; he is filled with a passion for mediation, agreement, and the quenching of all passion. This is the kind of Christianity with which he found himself to be in opposition as he saw it in colleagues and books and among the laity, and against which, or the dangers of which, he wanted to warn and preserve his congregation. To give the matter a historical name, we must say that what he had in mind was the new pietist orthodoxy championed in Berlin especially by the militant Old Testament scholar and church newspaper editor Hengstenberg. The opposite of this movement, the rationalism which was now in irreversible decline, was not in view because in the party strife of the period it was the group under attack, and alien though it was to Schleiermacher's genius, it did not offer him any grounds of assault through rigidity, narrowness,

---

[101]The brackets are Barth's.

[102]The reference is to the Christian and Evangelical social movements associated with A. Stoecker, F. Naumann, and others (1890 saw the foundation of the Evangelical Social Congress).

combativeness, or the like. He thus leaves it alone, only occasionally recognizing and protecting it as a possibility that has a place in the general peace. His attack (i.e., the attack on all attacks) is mounted exclusively against the party on the right. Rationalistic listeners could hardly feel that their concerns were directly disturbed or negated by Schleiermacher, but if a member of the contemporary pietist circle in Berlin, or a visiting candidate from the South German revival movement like my namesake C. G. Barth,[103] were to wander into Trinity Church, he would see at once how matters stood and there would inevitably be a good deal of alienation and shaking of the head.

For the sake of clarity I will divide Schleiermacher's negations into three groups which naturally overlap and are in fact no more than different stages in the same movement of defense or attack. The first is the most striking, the second the most characteristic, and the third the most decisive.

1. The most striking is that Schleiermacher is a foe of all sharp antitheses and divisions in the Christian community. He hardly misses an opportunity to point out that all the lines and angles by which some Christians might mark themselves off from others appear only to disappear again at once, or to refer to "the large-hearted meekness of the Redeemer which Christians cannot sufficiently take to heart; it is much different from[104] the exclusiveness to which we easily fall victim when we perceive that others do not agree with us in every word and statement, that they do not judge everything exactly as we do. ... Let us, then, free ourselves totally from the manner which bears any trace of such exclusiveness and increasingly recognize, and impress it deeply upon our hearts, that the only salutary thing is to seek to promote his kingdom with his gentle, indulgent, and loving mind" (Early Sermon 39, VI, 39f.). You may recall how[105] (Early Sermon 50, VI, 177), with a rather unfortunate exegetical use of the difference between the Pharisees and the Sadducees, an attempt was made to show that "each should go his own way of investigation, but each should speak in the spirit of love and none should separate from others."[106] Similar thoughts are expressed regarding the conflict between the Greeks and the Hebrews in the Jerusalem community (Acts 6[1]) (Third Sunday after Trinity 1832, III, 309) and the relation between the strong and the weak at Rome (Rom. 14[1ff.]) (New Year 1833, III, 440).[107] The saying about rejoicing with those who rejoice [Rom. 12:15] is expounded as follows (Sixth Sunday after Trinity 1831, III, 29f.): Conflict in matters of the kingdom of God should not stop us from feeling sympathy for both sides, "sympathy ... also for the hurts that others experience at our hands because we help people in other ways than they think right." Nothing (Early Sermon 13, V, 162f.) is more perverse for those "who really have the salvation of others on their hearts" than blind zeal. "Even in what we regard as false and corrupt" we should "seek traces of truth, and only as we look for this and bring it to

---

[103]Cf. K. Werner, *Christian Gottlob Barth, Doktor der Theologie, nach seinem Leben und Wirken* (Calw/Stuttgart, 1865), I, 320–322.

[104]Schleiermacher: "opposed to."

[105]See pp. 6.

[106]Schleiermacher: "Each goes his own way of investigation but speaks in the spirit of love, and none separates from others."

[107]The text is Rom. 15:1–3.

light can we do true and authentic battle with the element of falsehood that is mixed with it." Or (Twentieth Sunday after Trinity 1831, III, 105): "One and the same power of the earth produces thousands of different plants; but look at the most beautiful glories of the garden, go to the most unassuming flowers of the field: the bee buzzes and bores in both, and from all of them it carries the same precious honey. May we show ourselves to our brethren to be like bees that have learned to draw honey from everything in which some portion of the one power of spiritual life may be found." To the text: "And if any place will not receive you and they refuse to hear you, when you leave . . ." [Mk. 6:11], the fervent exhortation is added that one should never be so unloving as not to listen. If others "choose to present to us what they regard as salutary, is this not already a mark of love? . . . But if we judge it adversely in advance . . . , we shall also be unable to commend and validate our truth to them. . . . No one has the right to believe that his own insight or conviction is totally the work of the Christian Spirit, that there is nothing human or erroneous in it." Conversely the Spirit of Christ is in everything that "concerns itself with the eternally living Word." Where this is not perceived, "there can be no improvement of insight or of life, and human affairs cannot make progress." The saying: "Who are my mother and my brothers?" (Mk. 3[33]), which hardly fits in with this view, is expounded along the line (Early Sermon 14, V, 175) that we are never really in a position to apply this rule of the Redeemer, since today there is hardly any conflict between "natural relationships" and faith. "When similar disturbances occur in our days, they rest more on imagination than any real cause." We must know only those with whom we *have* already reached agreement and those with whom we *must* reach agreement. "Is there here any occasion of conflict or reason for it? Can a well-ordered disposition feel any requirement to break a natural bone?"[108] The saying: "I have not come to bring peace . . ." [Mt. 10:34], which also seems to be in opposition, is dealt with in a similar incisive way: "If discord breaks out in the Christian church itself; if what ought to be a common seeking and searching for truth is perverted into a conflict which, even though it is no longer bloody, still bears all the marks of a passionate surging of spirit in which love and well-wishing may no longer be detected, this is . . . not the work of the preaching of peace, nor does it have its basis in this." For this reason (New Year 1834, III, 759) like-minded people must not separate themselves from the rest. For "the spirit of separation will constantly develop afresh and only too quickly bring disunity even among these people themselves, dividing on even more minor points those who thought they were together even down to the smallest details."

2. Less striking but more characteristic is a second feature of Schleiermacher's pulpit polemics. He is an open enemy of all excitement, of all that is crude and sudden and direct in the Christian life. He cannot issue too many warnings against all possibilities that might entail an either-or, a break, an irreversible turn. In such surprise invasions of *higher* forces, in such experiences of *unusual* things, he evidently sees the main reason for the divisions of Christians that he dislikes so much. We have already seen how quickly he

---

[108]V, 177.

recommends the channeling of all possible promptings of the Holy Spirit into the orderly activities of calling.[109] This serious concern finds amusing expression in Early Sermon 1, V, 6ff.[110] on John the Baptist, a figure for which, for various reasons, he does not care too much. After periods "of general and widespread slumber in relation to the great things of the kingdom of God," we are told, with express reference to Schleiermacher's own day, that there is often a "far-ranging awakening in relation to matters of salvation" and that this "is in sharp contrast to those who still live in a state of sleep, and seems to be something big and arouses great expectations." But "the more such movements have a violent and stormy aspect; the more people suddenly reach a point, suddenly want to change something, and suddenly think they can attain to something different, the less we find the work of peace, and the more movements appear which have to be stilled, and only when they are stilled, only when their passionate character has been lost, shall we find that the true life will develop of which that has been only a presupposition."[111] Schleiermacher views the Baptist and the movement that he started in this light. It was an external and legalistic awakening. "Where we find an external approach like that of John," it is unmistakably "in antithesis to the approach and manner of Christ; where we find preaching that deals only with repentance and the recognition of sin, we can be sure that to this extent nothing good will come of it, but that it can only be an occasion for God to establish the right relationship . . . in isolation and stillness."[112] We must "hold fast" to "the inner awakening of the mind" for activity according to God's individual leading, and then we can "calmly contemplate" such movements and not be "snatched away by any misleading appearances."[113] Along the same lines (Early Sermon 4, V, 52) a warning is issued against a "praise the Redeemer" which, like that of the man with an unclean spirit in the synagogue [Mk. 1:24], proceeds from "a sick and disturbed mind" such as appears precisely in times of true acknowledgment of the Redeemer. There is also a warning (Twenty-First Sunday after Trinity 1832, III, 415f.) against a superstitious or occultist credulity (a matter on which Schleiermacher had cause to be concerned, for his own wife and more or less his whole family after 1819 came under the dominant influence of a pious somnambulist, Mrs. Karoline Fischer née Lommatsch (cf. Ehrenfried von Willich, *Aus Schleiermachers Hause*; Berlin, 1909, pp. 42ff.); also against an exclusive preoccupation with religion which devotes all free time outside one's calling "to only one thing, to confidential discussion with like-minded spirits concerning the inner experiences and affairs of the individual soul." "Who can censure this in itself? . . . They must admit, however, that it is not everything" (Nineteenth Sunday after Trinity 1832, III, 405). The famous birds that according to Mk. 4[32] live under the shadow of the greatest of all shrubs show that "we should not set up scarecrows everywhere like those concerned and anxious Christians," as though "other parts of life"

---

[109]See p. 36.
[110]V, 6–15; the quotations are from V, 9.
[111]V, 8f.; Schleiermacher has: ". . . only a preparation for. . . ."
[112]V, 12.
[113]V, 14.

did not also have a place in relation to the kingdom of God (Early Sermon 17, V, 213).

You will remember from the last early sermons that when Schleiermacher [11/19/23] has to deal with eschatological texts, he hardly knows what to do but give urgent warnings against enthusiasm.[114] In particular, as we have already seen, he protests against too strict and severe and radical a view of repentance and conversion. He often seems to be rejecting as unchristian not merely a pietistic abuse but the very concept and thing itself. He can say not merely of pietistic repentance but even of the *metanoeite* of Jesus in Mt. 4[17]: "This repenting, how very far it is from the state of peace; and the demand for it, how totally different it is from the preaching of peace!" (Third Sunday after the Epiphany 1833, III, 460). Insofar as he allows it positively, repentance for him means "that men should turn away from external service and seek what is spiritual, striving after this and being filled[115] with the quiet, with the inner peace that the Redeemer proclaimed, with the living fellowship with God to which he sought to lead men, as the good thing to which they should aspire" (Early Sermon 3, V, 33). But in "repentance" they should not think first of "a death through which they must pass," nor should there be depicted "a torturing of the soul about their former state," nor demanded "a sense of destruction." For this is how man is, "and nothing can alter it": that if we show him the greatest and most glorious things in the distance, but close by only conflict, toil, pain, tears, sacrifice, and self-destruction, he will hold back and be unwilling to go through the latter to reach the former—which is obviously reason enough to spare both him and oneself this message of death (Twentieth Sunday after Trinity 1831, III, 96). Christ never made a general demand for sorrow to the point of self-destruction. For as "the love of truth is a general possession of the spirit . . . , so that all life in all its ramifications rests upon it, so it is with the sense of guilt and sin. . . . the Christian does not need more violent outbreaks of this to be aware of his salvation" (Second Sunday after the Epiphany 1832, III, 164). A mind pressed down to the point of despair is not the only way of God, we are told on another occasion (Ninth Sunday after Trinity 1832, III, 348f.). Nor is it the general path of Christianity as a force "which directs and moves human affairs at large."[116]

In this battle against all religious excitement, against every either-or, Schleiermacher finally attacks all real *tensions*, all *crisis*. Those who bear witness to Christ (Fourth Sunday in Advent 1833, III, 729) do not speak in the wilderness where no one listens to them. No, if the place where it happens, primarily the church, is not paradise regained, then what takes place is not witness to Christ; such witness can never fail to be heard and to bear fruit. We are told in Early Sermon 15, V, 194f. on the parable of the four types of soil [Mk. 4:1–9] that we must be "firmly convinced" that "there is no power which might bear within itself an aversion to the onward march of divine salvation, but all obstacles have their basis in the constitution of human nature. Thus there is nothing that we have to destroy or that necessarily remains

---

[114]See pp. 8f., though the reference is to the last *main* sermons.
[115]Schleiermacher added "inwardly" (*in ihrem Innern*).
[116]Barth has "leitet und bewegt" for Schleiermacher's "leitet und treibt."

a target of hostility; but everything is destined . . . to become an instrument for the divine Spirit who permeates his spiritual body." We have to believe that Christ's "divine power will increasingly subjugate all things and make all human nature serviceable for his work and fill it with the peace and the direct sense of God and his living presence in which he lived." Regarding the saying: "If any man would come after me . . ." [Mt. 16:24] he says (First Sunday after Trinity 1833, III, 603f.) that there might be an anxious spirit, concerned about salvation, which would still be "in that very desirable state of rest remote from violent strokes of fortune and therefore from profound sorrows," so that it has no reason "to deny itself, to renounce anything that belongs to the ordinary circle of life." If we assume, too, that a person has already won an orientation to what is higher, "already has some knowledge of the kingdom of God on earth, and has already been received into fellowship with the Redeemer" (and we know that in the last resort this is a general assumption for Schleiermacher)—then the "most favorable climate for the cultivation of the seed of heavenly love and all good in the soul"[117] is surely to be found in this golden mean between special difficulties and afflictions on the one side and a special plenitude of earthly goods on the other. Is not this the goal of all wisdom and progress? Relative to it, how confusing it is to make the time-bound demand of Christ that we should deny ourselves into a general requirement! How dangerous it is artificially to put ourselves in the embattled situation of the first Christians and erroneously to believe that we should bear the cross in this or that matter, that we should suffer for Christ's sake, failing to see the higher Christian wisdom in the conduct of others who without being exposed to this "blind zeal" and the corresponding entanglements tread the path of Christian piety peacefully and quietly. If it be asked whether the significant word "cross" and possibly the word "sin" as well do not provide some vindication for what is here abhorred as empty religious excitement, Schleiermacher replies on the one hand that the Redeemer never viewed the human spirit as being in any special hostility to the divine Word (Early Sermon 15, V, 194), and on the other hand that the reality of sin is negatively at least, as an object to be fought and vanquished, the indispensable condition of art and science and every good thing. How life would be without either charm or conflict were there no sin: "If sin has a place in our nature, it is so closely connected with everything else that our consciousness cannot be complete until it, too, has really emerged" (Second Sunday after Trinity 1831, III, 8; cf. Third Sunday after Trinity 1832, III, 304f.: "Do we have any awareness of ourselves regarding matters of our salvation which may not be traced back to these two things, to sin and to redemption?" Cf. *Christian Faith*, II!).[118] And in relation to this ultimately harmonious if dialectical union of sin and redemption in the Christian consciousness Schleiermacher can say (Second Sunday after the Epiphany 1832, III, 164): As "love of truth is a universal possession of the spirit . . . , so is the sense of guilt and sin. . . . But more violent eruptions of the latter are not necessary for a Christian to have a sense of his salvation and thus to enter into a sure and firm relation to the Redeemer."

[117]III, 604f.
[118]Cf. p. xix, n. 24 and pp. 195ff.

3. We turn finally to the third line of Schleiermacher's criticism, which I have called the truly decisive one to the degree that in it we see the reason for his aversion to controversy and also for his fight against all excitement, against all the tragic element in Christianity. Schleiermacher is opposed to what I might call the view that there are *true words in the relationship with God*. The belief that some words may be naively taken to be true as they stand is what gives rise to the religious wrangling of parties. Naively taking certain words seriously as though they could mean strictly and in practice what they seem to be saying, for example, such words as repentance and sin, is the source of religious excitement and tragedy. We have to realize that strife and agitation are not worthwhile because they are without point. There are for us no true words in relation to God. The truth is not in words but—where? We shall have to see this later. The negation is what Schleiermacher tirelessly impresses on his congregation. The negation, if appearances do not deceive, is his real theological charge against the Hengstenberg group. In what we have to say here we are dealing with thoughts which for us who have grown up in the modern Christian world that has been essentially shaped by Schleiermacher have so taken flesh and blood, have so become not merely the theological but the general Christian consensus, that the statements that I shall adduce will sound almost like *banalities*. But it is worth it sometimes to meet banalities at their source. When they were new, whether they were really banalities or not, they were balsam and gospel for educated people.[119] "In the great and all-inclusive gift of God we have to distinguish two things" (Early Sermon 7, V, 85f.): "the first has no quantity or mass but is always one and the same, the second is subject to the law of time, divides in time, becomes more beautiful in its unfolding and development, and then returns to itself. The first is the sense of the restored relationship in which we stand to God, of the peace with which awareness of the eternal being rests in our souls, and rules and moves there, so that a whole new life gradually grows out of this seed." Unfortunately the thought was not completed and Schleiermacher never gave a more precise definition of the second. But there can be no doubt that, in contrast to what has no quantity or measure but is always one and the same, to the sense of peace which rests and moves within the soul, this second or secondary thing is the specific external word in which the inner thing comes to expression and which comes forward with the claim of truth. And the charge which Schleiermacher brings against his opponents of the right is that they "clutch on," as it were, to this specificity of the word and its claim to truth, and in this way, by robbing it of its multiplicity and vitality and comparative irrelevance, by clinging to it and asserting it, they freeze it into externality, into "doctrine," into "letter." Schleiermacher had no time for the "letter." He was a resolute opponent of the old and possibly new confessional church. Naturally he took the same view of the words or letters of the Bible too. That the letter kills and the Spirit makes alive—this Pauline text (2 Cor. 3:6), which he wrested exegetically like the innumerable others who have

---

[119]In the MS Barth had a relative clause here which he struck out: "who listened to it only too willingly because they had long since heard it already from Goethe."

since shared his view, is appealed to constantly (e.g., *Christmas Eve*, Preface)[120] as the biblical basis of his theory of the secondary character of the word. He says expressly that we come closer to Christ and are better Christians (Early Sermon 5, V, 61) "the more we eliminate this power of the dead letter." Conversely, "those who contribute to the strengthening of the ideas in men's minds that God is connected with something external of this kind are in this way turning aside from the true worship of God in spirit and in truth" (Early Sermon 29, V, 365). Can we link such external precepts "with the idea of a spiritual omnipotence which orders all things in the world, of a being which is the source of the good, whose nature is love, before which there is no distinction between the inward and the outward, but to which all things everywhere are present and close at hand?" (p. 366). For this reason (First Sunday after Trinity 1832, III, 300, a sermon on Gamaliel [cf. Acts 5:34ff.], who in contrast to John the Baptist has Schleiermacher's fullest approval), "no one should presume to think, whether alone or in company with others, that he is in a position to distinguish definitely and for certain, when someone with his protestations or efforts is calling upon Christ and seeking his safety and defense in the order of God, in the Christian church, how much of this is God's work and how much is futile human work, apart from the person himself in his own experience. All church history offers us advance warning against trying to make such distinctions." "Let us look at the kingdom of God, at the relation of people to this kingdom, at the proper orientation of their whole life and being, at their fellowship with God, but not at individual words, not at individual precepts, not at individual facts in their explication and interpretation" (Early Sermon 3, V, 41). We no longer need "this or that admonition in this or that form, but the one admonition to show forth love in our lives and to proclaim thereby that the love of God is shed abroad in our hearts" (Sixteenth Sunday after Trinity 1831, III, 90). The apostles (according to Schleiermacher's view of them) were far from putting any "trust in a letter, or from worrying about the concepts in which the new teaching would take shape in the mind, but they had regard only to the impression which this teaching made on the mind" (Seventh Sunday after Trinity 1832, III, 336). Naturally the Spirit has to communicate through letters, he once concedes, "but in many periods there are movements of the Spirit during which the inner life takes a very different shape; wings unfold which cannot work under the previous cover but have to break out of it; then the letter must waver. This is why nothing of this kind should be regarded as lasting for ever" (Sunday before Pentecost 1833, III, 582). The power of divine truth needs "little or no external help." Those who think it does are basically lacking in confidence in it (Early Sermon 28, V, 357f.). Only love counts in the Christian church, not statutes, nor a confession, nor customs. "And if it is countered that in this way the Christian church would be something that one cannot grasp or get a handle on, that one cannot tell where it is or where it begins and ends, then reply that so is everyone who is born of the Spirit; you do not know whence the

---

[120]*Weihnachtsfeier, Philosophische Bibliothek*, 117 (Leipzig, 1908), 58; ET *Christmas Eve* (1826, 1890).

Spirit comes or whither he goes, but you hear his blowing" (Fourth Sunday after the Epiphany 1833, III, 481f.).

Let us pause here to conclude the section with a brief review. I have not drawn on all Schleiermacher's Sunday sermons from this period. There is thus the possibility that I have missed one or another distinctive trait. But I have utilized almost without a break the series which were my special concern and I do not think that in the sketch that I have given any important point in the man's preaching has been omitted. As you have seen, I have proceeded in an orderly but intentionally not a strictly systematic way, letting myself be led from point to point as the things presented came to my notice either individually or connectedly, but without considering either Schleiermacher's theological system or a system of questions that I might have posed. I hope that in spite of this we have come to know him a little as he really was and thus laid a foundation for what follows. I am surprised indeed that Schleiermacher's sermons have not been used more in this way in attempting to gain an understanding of his theology.

Let us now take a look at the main features of what we have found. In the center as the true blessing of salvation is the great synthesis of all antitheses, love, or, more typically for Schleiermacher, peace. This has come into history through Christ as life, spirit, and power. It is a new and the only real relationship to God through which all legal separation between God and man is refuted and overcome. Thus the Old Testament must retreat into the background and everything in the New Testament must be expounded along these lines. The miracle that surrounds Christ is not to be taken to mean that between God's world and ours there is still division; it is to be understood as the work of the power of peace which reconciles God and the world, spirit and nature. Whether Christ is the only or final effective embodiment of this power of peace is a question which may certainly be asked but does not come into consideration for believing Christians. In these the life of the Redeemer moves forward directly in history. As man is able voluntarily to receive the Spirit of Christ, so he is able to become its adequate vessel, agent, and proclaimer; he can realize the original type of Christ in himself for all his remaining imperfection. But he can fulfil his life's task only in the community. Moved by the life that flows through this he becomes its agent and bearer and messenger to ever new people. He has achieved his purpose in life when he has become and been a channel for this river. Not he, but the community as a whole, is the true embodiment of Christ in history. Only by its religious function, however, does the community distinguish itself as such from modern society in its civilized state as this is essentially shaped by Christ. As the dialectic of prayer constantly calls the individual to stillness but then directs him to the active life, so Christianity as a whole has to be something distinctive in the world but then at once it must seek out and permeate the world as the principle of progress, of regulated vocational work, of order, of social equality, and to be and do this it must guard against all party strife, all exaltation, all claim to truth, a claim which can indeed be justly made for the content of its mind and spirit, but not for the individual concepts in which this expresses itself.

This is Schleiermacher's theology according to his mature pulpit work. I will let it speak for and against itself, quoting only the words of his enthusiastic pupil, the preacher Sydow, in which he recorded his impressions of Schleiermacher the preacher two years after the latter's death: "Apart from the edifying way in which he expounded the convictions and experiences of a mind that was wholly under the control of the Redeemer and was able to make these fruitful for life, as an orator he granted to the receptive mind another intellectual pleasure which is so rare today, namely, the sight of a highly gifted and thoroughly educated individuality in moments of its noblest expression in life. His speech was a living act, in this act the whole man, and in the man everything came to consciousness and expression that can be a worthy object of human concern, love, and enthusiasm. His sermons were not an isolated work of oratorical art; they gushed forth from direct unity with the congregation in the largest sense of the word, they were prominent and more powerful pulse beats of its [own] innermost life."[121]

Much might be said about this, but we shall refrain.

---

[121]F. Schleiermacher, *Sämmtliche Werke*, 2, Vol. VII, ed. A. Sydow (Berlin, 1836), Introduction, p. VIII.

§ 2

CHRISTOLOGICAL FESTIVAL SERMONS

You will gather from this heading that I do not intend to discuss with you Schleiermacher's festival sermons as a whole. In these lectures we cannot give a full account of all the material of Schleiermacher's theology. We are trying to understand its meaning and content and are thus choosing certain approaches. I shall thus leave aside the New Year, Penitential, and All Saints' sermons, and also those for Pentecost. You may read these for yourselves, and a broad and rewarding field will open up for you in this regard. Here I shall deal with the specific christological festivals of Christmas, Good Friday, Easter (and the Ascension). The reason for the selection should be obvious from the preceding section. From what we have already seen, Christ, his person and work, is, if not the center (this would be too much to say in a cautious judgment), at least one of the two foci of Schleiermacher's theology if we think of it as an ellipse. In subjecting what we have found to a specialized investigation, we shall be preparing the way for the most important presupposition and at the same time the most critical problem in Schleiermacher's dogmatics as we shall learn to know it in the second chapter. The other focus is man as seen from the standpoint of the problem of ethics, and we shall devote our third section to man as a special preparation for our later treatment of Schleiermacher's teaching on Christian ethics. The line which connects the two foci is the concept of the community, but we shall not deal with this apart, since strictly speaking it simply denotes the relationship between the two foci, the possibility of Christ and man increasingly drawing closer together, the prospect of a full meeting and union of the two, so that the ellipse does in fact become a circle. So, then, we shall turn to the christological festival sermons. Here, having learned to know the uniform picture presented by the man in his older and maturer years, we shall draw on the whole of his activity as a preacher, less with any independent concern to trace a line of development and more with the aim of finding the unity of thought in the earlier and later years. What has been said thus far will, we hope, help us to proceed objectively and not capriciously in this search. Relative to the content of this section I recommend especially the following works: H. Bleek, *Die Grundlagen der Christologie Schleiermachers* ([Leipzig and Tübingen], 1898); P. Kölbing, "Schleiermachers Zeugnis vom Sohne Gottes nach seinen Festpredigten,"

Zeitschrift für Theologie und Kirche (hereafter *ZThK*), 3[1]; H. Scolz, "Schleiermachers Lehre von der Sündlosigkeit Jesu," *ZThK*, 17.[2]

1. Christmas. Cf. the sermons in the collected works (10 volumes), and also Johannes Bauer, *Ungedruckte Predigten Schleiermachers* (Leipzig, 1903),[3] where there is a survey of all the Christmas sermons of Schleiermacher and on pp. 82f. a number of outlines of Christmas sermons from 1794 to 1802.

[11/20/23] We shall be dealing primarily with nine sermons and outlines from 1790 to 1810, though the last is separated by a gap of eight years from the one that precedes (1802). In this intervening period Schleiermacher either did not preach at Christmas or the sermons have not been preserved. But the important little work *Christmas Eve* dates from this time (1806). It is rightly regarded as one of the most significant accounts of Schleiermacher's Christology, and I shall therefore quote and discuss it in the form of an excursus. From 1810 to 1820 we then have another great gap in the tradition. A group of ten sermons from 1820 to 1833 then follows. I shall put these at the end, the work on Christmas in the middle, and the early sermons at the beginning. Some of these were preached at Schlobitten Castle, where Schleiermacher was tutor for Graf Dohna from 1790 to 1794, some at Landsberg where he was an assistant preacher from 1794 to 1795, some at Stolp in Pomerania where he was court preacher in 1802, and the last at Holy Trinity in Berlin in 1810. We have no Christmas sermons from his years at the Charité in Berlin (1796–1802, the years when he wrote the *Reden*,[4] the *Monologen*,[5] and the *Lucinde-briefe*[6]), nor from the period when he was professor and university preacher at Halle. We are thus dealing with scattered and defective material.[7]

[1]*ZThK*, 3 (1893), 277–310.
[2]*ZThK*, 17 (1907), 391–422.
[3]*Ungedruckte Predigten Schleiermachers aus den Jahren 1820–1828. Mit Einleitungen und einem Anhang ungedruckter Briefe von Schleiermacher und Henriette Herz*, ed. J. Bauer (Leipzig, 1909). This is not to be confused with the appendix of unprinted sermon outlines of Schleiermacher in J. Bauer, *Schleiermacher als patriotischer Prediger. Ein Beitrag zur Geschichte der nationalen Erhebung vor hundert Jahren* (*Studien zur Geschichte des neueren Protestantismus*, 4) (Giessen, 1908), pp. 306–356.
[4]See p. xvii, n. 18.
[5]See p. 3, n. 1.
[6]See p. 119, n. 26.
[7]The MS had here a paragraph which was cut out and which ran as follows: "a) A common feature of these nine sermons and outlines strikes us at once. The Christmas event is for the preacher the expression of a general truth. It serves to illustrate an insight or law which certainly stands in supreme need of this illustration but which also exists apart from it. In the introduction to the outline of the second Christmas sermon of 1802 (Bauer, p. 87) we read: 'Christmas and the end of our gatherings for the year seem hard to link. But it is easy. The birth of Christ is the symbol of all divine blessings and disposings. The order that is considered here is everywhere the same. Let us then think of the past.' The text is Gal. 4:4: 'But when the time had fully come, God sent forth his Son, born of woman, born under the law.' It is concluded from this that all the past is an advancement of wisdom for the future. The theme is the order of divine blessing. God blesses us 1. when the time is fulfilled, 2. by means of a transitory circumstance, and 3. according to the rules of righteousness and order. Christ's birth is simply an example of this truth, or, as the preacher says, though perhaps only on his draft, a symbol. Seven years earlier in Landsberg Schleiermacher preached on the same

a.[8] When we survey these nine sermons and outlines we are struck first by the external fact that Schleiermacher preached no less than three times on the text Gal. 4:4: "But when the time had fully come, God sent forth his Son, born of woman, born under the law": in 1790 (Schlobitten) (VII,[9] 54ff.); the second sermon in 1795 (Landsberg) (Bauer, p. 85); and the second sermon in 1802 (Stolp) (Bauer, p. 87). One may well ask why Schleiermacher kept going to this verse during these twelve decisive years in his development. The earliest of the sermons gives the unambiguous answer that what primarily interests him is the historical necessity of the coming of Jesus. The greater and smaller circumstances of the birth of Jesus, the land, the people, the age, the situation of his parents, the shepherds, Simeon, Herod: "they are all important for us because directly or indirectly they all affect Jesus and his character, because they all had to come together to make him what he was to be. Out of this a great increase of love for Jesus arises in my soul and I believe that this will be so for all of us. . . . The more the extraordinary leading of providence . . . was necessary from his very first moment, the more precious he becomes to us . . . and the more fully and inwardly we rejoice that he is, and that he is precisely in this way."[10]

In the two later sermons on this text this idea is increasingly brought to the forefront in the treatment, so much so that the birth of Jesus seems strictly to be no more than an illustration or application of a general law that all good things take place for us according to a necessity, an order, the plan of divine providence. The time has to come, everything proceeds according to the course of nature, everything is subject to law, declared Schleiermacher in 1795, and in 1802, with only a slight variation, he stated that God's blessings come, when the time is ripe, as transitory circumstances (the emphasis now is on historical relativity instead of naturalness) according to the rule of righteousness and order. Why Christmas, or Christ, is needed to demonstrate this truth, or whether Christ and Christmas have more than demonstrative value, is not clear from these sermons except in the conclusion of the first one, though this conclusion is not in keeping with the theme. We shall have to come back to it later. How the thinking of the preacher goes may be seen from the introduction to outline 2 of 1802,[11] which runs as follows: "Christmas and the end of our gatherings for the year seem hard to link. But it is easy. The birth of Christ is the symbol of all divine blessings and disposings. The order that is considered here (i.e., in the Christmas story) is everywhere the same. Let us then think of the past." The conclusion is then that "all the past is an ad-

---

text, Gal. 4:4, and used the same divisions, though this time he stressed the natural rather than the transitory character of the circumstance, and discussed the way in which one may recognize the circumstance that God wills to use for particular purposes (Bauer, p. 85)."

[8]The section that begins here and ends on p. 72 was published in revised form as an essay entitled "Schleiermachers 'Weihnachtsfeier,' " Zwischen den Zeiten, 3 (1925), 38–61, and reproduced in Die Theologie und die Kirche, Gesammelte Vorträge, 2 (Munich, 1928), 106–135; ET Theology and Church (1962), pp. 136–158.

[9]Cf. p. 80, n. 121. The subject of this sermon is: "What Interest Have all the Circumstances of the Birth of Jesus for Us?"

[10]VII, 63.

[11]The reference is to the outline of the second Christmas sermon of 1802 (Bauer, p. 87).

vancement of wisdom for the future." In the conclusion of outline 2 of 1795[12] Schleiermacher reversed the logical relationship: "The agreement of this example with experience" (i.e., with that general wisdom) "is a new proof that the sending of Christ was a work of God" (i.e., a new proof of the truth of the Christmas message). But either way the Christmas message is understandably in this treatment almost completely under the shadow of the general truth which is illustrated and confirmed by it or by which it is illustrated and confirmed. At the end of the 1790 sermon Schleiermacher himself seems to have felt this, for after viewing the birth of Jesus as a historical necessity he says there that this way of looking at it yields us the twofold joy of seeing all the wishes corresponding to our needs so richly satisfied in him. Man longs for "one of his own kind in whom he may realize how far he can go on the way of perfection with the help of God."[13] Christ's example represents "the supreme triumph of human nature" and thus gives us "a strengthening glimpse of the mind of God."[14]

What Schleiermacher preached twenty years later in 1810 (VII, 566ff.)[15] is along the same lines but even more explicit. We feel drawn to the child in the crib "with a holy awe" which "no outward representation can satisfy." We always feel something deeper that we want to express. There is "something uncomprehended and incomprehensible" here. What? The divine figure and human form united in Christ (the text is Phil. 2:6, 7: "Though he was . . ."): Humanity in all its need, and on the other side a divine element standing under the law of the age and gradually developing by degrees, an element which is then depicted as the "reverent love, oriented to higher things,"[16] by which Mary brought him up differently and more purely and properly than we are brought up, as the untroubled nature, in contrast to our vacillation, of the "original relationship which lies at the inner basis of [human] personality,"[17] in the antithesis and conflict between reason and the senses which, in contrast to the surprises that the senses prepare for us, is transcended in him. Thus a perfect picture of humanity, in contrast to our imperfection, is, at least at the end of the period under review, the specific and positive content of the Christmas message that has been missing hitherto.

The second main standpoint from which Christmas is seen, along with that of the rule of special providence, is in the early period that of the proper reception of the Christmas message by men, that is, a psychological standpoint alongside the historico-philosophical. Twice (1794[2] and 1801[1])[18] Schleiermacher preached on Lk. 2:15f. ("When the angels went away from them into heaven, the shepherds said to one another . . ."—the text of my own first

[12]The reference is to the outline of the second Christmas sermon of 1795 (Bauer, p. 85).

[13]VII, 63.

[14]VII, 64.

[15]First Day of Christmas; text: Phil 2:6, 7; subject: "The Union of the Human and the Divine in the Redeemer, How It Brings His First Coming to Earth Most Clearly to View."

[16]VII, 572.

[17]*Loc. cit.*

[18]Here and in what follows the elevated figures with the dates denote the first or second Christmas sermon in the relevant year.

Christmas sermon in 1908).[19] The subject in 1794 is "A Consideration of the Different Ways of Receiving the News of the Presence of the Redeemer," and the drift of this may be seen more precisely in the subject seven years later: "The Thoughts of Those Who Received the First News of the Birth of Jesus Applied to Our Own" (Bauer, pp. 83, 86). The development is again the same not merely in the general divisions but even in detail. The poor shepherds in the field are for Schleiermacher a type of "theoretical faith," and he goes on to speak of "a mere investigation of the matter." They are interested in the revelation, they examine the miracle, they have a zeal to spread the faith, and they have devout feelings. "But we are not told that they became Christians."[20] This kind of faith does not make us real disciples of Jesus. It is merely a saying "Lord, Lord" [cf. Mt. 7:21]. It does not bring us the true fruits of religion. These are not active members of the kingdom of God, though they have their uses. "All who heard it wondered . . ." [Lk. 2:18]. These are the deniers or doubters or, in 1802, the indifferent. The first sermon contains the threat against them that "a time will come when they will be sorry."[21] It is said of doubters that they are this "because the miraculous is thrust upon them and the moral freedom of religion is neglected." "They would be better disposed to religion if they could learn to know it better and also become better acquainted with the nature of the human soul and the constitution of human nature on earth"[22] (an important passage for the genesis of the *Speeches on Religion*).[23] In the second sermon it is said of the indifferent that while the miraculous will not attract them, it should not repel them.[24] Ideal reception, third, is the "pondering in the heart" [Lk. 2:19] which is embodied in the person of Mary: "Mary kept all these things. . . ." "The miraculous leads to investigation, the moral evokes approval,"[25] as is said along rather Enlightenment lines in 1794, and "this class is the smallest but the best, and we should reckon ourselves to be in it; like Mary, we are related to Christ."[26] In 1802 this "approval" is defined more precisely. We must be thankful for our election "through the planting of Christianity in our country and our early reception into it,"[27] we must follow attentively the further development of the kingdom of Christ, and we must resolve with redoubled loyalty to play our part in this development. Schleiermacher adopted a similar standpoint when he preached on Lk. 2:14f. ("Glory be . . .") in 1794[1] (Bauer, pp. 82f.). The subject this time is: "The Feelings of the Christian When He Contemplates the Birth of Christ," and the divisions are: (1) Feelings about God relative to

---

[19]From November 1908 to August 1909 Barth helped to edit the *Christliche Welt* and he often preached in Marburg and its environs. He preached his first Christmas sermon (on Lk. 2:15) at Niedergrenzebach near Treysa in 1908.

[20]Bauer, p. 86.

[21]Bauer, p. 84.

[22]*Loc. cit.*

[23]See p.xvii, n. 18.

[24]Bauer, p. 86; Schleiermacher says: "The miraculous will not attract here, but should not alone bring about a negative judgment."

[25]Bauer, p. 84.

[26]Bauer, p. 85.

[27]Bauer, p. 86.

the universality and wisdom of the salvation that has come in Christ; 2. Regulative Feelings: peace with heaven, among Christians as Christians and as citizens, and pleasure in the wisdom that lies in Christ's coming, in his teaching, in his example, by striving to imitate him. Obviously with this psychological approach, as with the historico-philosophical, the Christmas message itself and as such can have only a marginal place. As in the former case the dominant center is the general truth of the divine government of the world, which determines individual things thus and not otherwise, so here it is the rich multiplicity of human feelings, thoughts, and possibilities, from whose dialectic an attitude like that of Mary emerges as normal and desirable. Or if one wants to call the Christmas message itself the center, one might put it this way: What may be seen in the one group or the other is a system of relationships which ought to point powerfully to the center; but it is so much centered upon itself, and the Christian philosophy of history or the Christian psychology is so expressly the theme, that alongside this secure and vital reality one can hardly miss the emptiness of the center to which all the relationships are supposed to relate. I have indicated that Schleiermacher himself seems to have been aware of this shadow and how he tried to remove it at the end of the period when "God was in Christ" [2 Cor. 5:19] (we shall not discuss how) became programmatically the subject of the Christmas sermon.[28]

But a third point must be made. Note the term "example" which is occasionally used here. Later it becomes the classical term for Christ in Schleiermacher's theology. In relation to this prototype we are obviously copies, as the Platonic ideas are copies of the supreme idea of the good. But the perfect here is not in principle superior to the imperfect, or different from it, or unattainable by it. There is continuity and only quantitative difference, however great, between them. A real if not unassisted approximation is counted on. "Like Mary, we are related to Christ."[29] The actualizing of this approximation, the manifestation of this relationship, is the true problem of Christianity. The Christmas message runs into the question on man's side: What is that to *us*? Here is Schleiermacher's answer: We must become as Christ was. There is no doubt that this systematic connection was intended by Schleiermacher from the very first, the only point being that at this time it was rather diffuse and incidental in accordance with the uncertain and secondary position of the Christmas message itself. In place of it we find in the historico-philosophical sermons a "general application," as in 1795[2]: God can "ensure the enjoyment of blessings to us in no other way"[30] (than according to the universal rules of his providence); or in 1802[2]: "So, too, can we. . . . This is how it always goes. . . . Everything by which human welfare is promoted necessarily stands under the same conditions."[31] Naturally on the psychological view it is we ourselves who are the shepherds, those who wonder, and finally and ideally Mary. From first to last the 1794[2] sermon follows the schema of type and antitype. But direct traces of the systematic connection are not absent. Thus the concluding

[28]Cf. pp. 52f.
[29]Bauer, p. 85.
[30]*Loc. cit.*
[31]Bauer, p. 87.

words of the earliest sermon are to this effect: "Let us not uselessly dissipate this beautiful feeling of joy which is the distinctive mark of this feast. ... Christ is present and we rejoice at this, but let us also see to it that as much as possible he is present for us" (VII, 64). It also occurs in the subject of the 1791 sermon (VII, 117ff.).[32] Christ's life was a life for others; he was inspired "by the lofty feeling of warmest universal love of men, in the most far-reaching benevolence. ... This feeling rested on his first disciples as his legacy." In this treatment we sense the wish "that there might in truth be many means to maintain and quicken this outlook." We thus apply the festival of his birth in what is certainly a useful way "if we encourage one another in the mind which always rules in him and by which he has become everything to us."[33] After this introduction no less a figure than the aged Simeon in the temple has to be held up as a paradigm of "the participation of the good man in the true well-being of humanity," a subject which is then developed in the main body of the sermon, with no further reference to the theme of the festival, in an enthusiastic extolling of the true philanthropist which surely must have moved the hearts of the ladies of Schlobitten Castle, until at last in the conclusion there is a return to Christmas, the feast of human love: What Christ brings to individual hearts, he also brings to humanity: "Glory thus comes to God on high, peace on earth, and good will to men." "Our soul rises up to follow the footsteps of him who loved men so much. On the day of his birth let us vow to act always, at least in our own circle, with his lofty thoughts."[34]|

The specific content of this "candidating" sermon is not important, nor is the fact that the preacher, four years before a pupil of Herrnhut, obviously treads the path of rationalism. What is important is the underlying systematization: Christ, a specific outlook as his legacy, the need to maintain and quicken this, it is his gift to humanity, and the final imperative, let us act with the same mind. This is Schleiermacher's complete doctrine of Christ's work in a nutshell. Along these lines the 1794[1] sermon, as we have seen, develops also in what it has to say about "regulative feelings" and in its conclusion that "the attempt at imitation must always be the keystone of all Christian feelings."[35] So does the 1810 sermon (VII, 573f.), in which the text ("Have this mind among yourselves . . ." [Phil. 2:5ff.]) readily enough suggests that the threefold depiction of human imperfection and the perfection of Christ should lead in conclusion to the threefold exhortation that the divine picture of Christ should purify and permeate our instruction of the future generation, that "it should always hover before us whenever we ourselves have to act," and that it should "impel us to set aside every besetting sin, so that we may keep the divine pure within us," and to hold fast to his sacred image, "so that it may grow and increase in us." We reach at this point a third standpoint which with the historico-philosophical and the psychological approaches controls Schleiermacher's Christmas preaching during this period. This is the ethical standpoint. It, too, is obviously related to the center in a specific way.

[32]The text was Lk 2:25–32 and the subject: "The Participation of the Good Man in the True Well-being of Humanity."
[33]VII, 119.
[34]VII, 133f.
[35]Bauer, pp. 82f.

If this center is an *event* on the historico-philosophical view and a *theme* on the psychological view, on the ethical view it is a *norm*. The ethical side of the system, too, can seek to become an independent theme, as happened very plainly in the 1791 sermon on philanthopy. The norm itself then becomes relatively empty and subsidiary. It is purely accidental that it has to be Christ who is the source of this ethical relation and that it has to be Christmas when we say this. But there seems to be some advance on this in 1810 to the extent that with the doctrine of the divine life in the humanity of Jesus a *primary* content of Christmas preaching has been relatively unambiguously attained with which the "Have this mind among yourselves, which was in Christ Jesus" [Phil. 2:5] may be naturally linked.

So, then, the comparatively few documents of these twenty years have enabled us to construct a fairly uniform picture of Schleiermacher's Christmas preaching on the basis of which we may look ahead to what follows with curious expectations and questions. Will the peripheral proclamation be more strongly and consciously replaced by a central message? Will there be more extensive recognition of the primary content of preaching, declarations concerning the real miracle of Christmas? Will the peripheral approach, what was at the beginning undoubtedly the secondary (historico-philosophical, psychological, and ethical) content of Schleiermacher's sermons, prove to be a false trend which is later victoriously overcome, or will this approach prove to be typical and dominant, remaining so even with a stronger development of a central and primary content, and even for this content itself?

A biographical and psychological note might be made in conclusion. It ·will set the stage for replies to these questions. I have already drawn attention to the parallelism between the two historico-philosophical and the two psychological sermons. That Schleiermacher in 1802, when thirty-four years old, could cold-bloodedly go back to seven-or eight-year-old outlines (1794[2], 1795[2]) and with only slight modifications say again what he had said when only twenty-six or twenty-seven years old, is an obvious indication, since there can be no question of indolence or poverty of thought, that for all the possibility of variation and for all the lack of clarity in detail his main view of the matter remains the same. A further sign of this is the persistent return to Gal. 4:4 (1790, 1795, and 1802), although one has also to take into account that thus far Schleiermacher had not done a great deal of study of the New Testament (this began only when he became a professor at Halle in 1804), so that he existed on a few large-type texts, like so many theologians and non-theologians before and after him. Much more important is the agreement that we have found between the sermons of 1790–1791 and that of 1810, between the twenty-two or twenty-three-year-old candidate at Schlobitten and the forty-two-year-old pastor at Trinity: agreement in the understanding of the true Christmas miracle as the supreme triumph of human nature, as he puts it in 1790, or of the perfect man, as he depicts him in 1810, and then agreement in the particularly important ethical reference in which the slogan "mind" clearly forms a bridge from the young rationalist to the mature religious philospher who already has the second edition of the *Speeches* behind him. These agreements cannot be accidental. We obviously have to do with a uniform if in many respects indefinite view which, if the man is not born anew, will become deeper and clearer, but which can hardly be expected to change in its basic features.

b. Since sources are sparse between 1802 and 1810 we shall now engage [11/21/23] in the promised excursus on the little book *Christmas Eve*, which came out in 1806 when Schleiermacher was at Halle. It would obviously be a pity to ignore in this context a work devoted explicitly to the subject. (The recommended edition is that of Mulert, *Philosophische Bibliothek*, 117.[36] Cf. W. Dilthey is *Westermanns Monatshefte*, Vol. 47 and *Schleiermachers Leben²*, p. 765.)[37] It is not my intention to give an account of the genesis of the book nor to offer a full analysis of its contents. To provide at least some indication of its origin I will simply adduce what Schleiermacher said about the immediate occasion of writing it to the publisher Reimer: "Most wonderfully the idea came to me suddenly one evening by the stove when we had just come from Dülon's flute concert, and less than three weeks after its [first] conception, and I became aware that it really was such only a few days later, the work was finished" (*Briefen, IV*, 122).[38] You will find more detailed intellectual and biographical information and analyses in Mulert's Introduction and in Dilthey. My own aim is to draw a firm diagonal through the little work, not losing sight of the problems in Schleiermacher's approach to Christmas which have already emerged. But a few technical elucidations cannot be avoided in view of the fact that the book is unknown to most of you. It is very well adapted to convey a first acquaintance with Schleiermacher and his nature and life's ideal. Dilthey (p. 775) rightly calls it "the best introduction to the study of his dogmatics." *Christmas Eve* is a dialogue whose form was undoubtedly inspired by Schleiermacher's study of Plato, which is "full of choice Platonic mannerisms" (Dilthey, p. 796), but which, going further than most of Plato's dialogues, perhaps along the lines of the *Phaedo* or the *Symposium*, tends to become a didactic short story. The dialogue takes place in the bosom of a middle-class German family that has gathered with some friends to celebrate Christmas Eve. Eduard and Ernestine are the parents, and especially prominent among their children is a charming, clever, religious, and musical little girl called Sofie. Along with them are the engaged couple Ernst and Friederike "at the gate of the pinnacle of life" (Dilthey, p. 779), another young wife named Agnes, an adult woman named Karoline, and in contrast to all of them the lawyer Leonhardt, who is the champion of a critical rationalism and who in some sense plays the role of the devil's advocate. On the last two pages there comes on the scene a certain Josef who is not characterized in detail but who speaks the last and concluding sentences of the whole work and says things which relate to some serious difficulties in Schleiermacher's own sit-

[36]Cf. p. 46, n. 120.

[37]W. Dilthey, "Die Weihnachtsfeier," *Westermanns Monatshefte*, 47 (1879/80), 343ff. and in W. Dilthey, *Leben Schleiermachers*, 2nd ed., ed. H. Mulert (Berlin/Leipzig, 1922), I, 765ff.

[38]Cf. p. xiii, n. 3. Friedrich Ludwig Dülon (or Dulon) (1769–1826) was a celebrated flutist who often came to Halle on his concert tours. The concert mentioned by Schleiermacher was given on December 2, 1805, in the Ratskellersaale in Halle. Cf. E. Börsch, "Zur Entstehung der 'Weihnachtsfeier' von Friedrich Schleiermacher," *Theologische Zeitschrift*, 13 (1957), 354–356.

uation at the time, so that we may see the author here as the self-portrait of the artist may be seen in the corner of medieval paintings. But one should not derive from this any conclusion regarding the content of the dialogue. The words of Josef form a dialectical summary. But among the others there is none who says things that are totally alien to Schleiermacher's own thinking—not even the often disturbing Leonhardt. In the fictional and not very convincing depiction of the relations between these persons one can study what Schleiermacher understood by "community": men and women, children and grown-ups, sober and poetic souls, each what it is, yet all with the same denominator, so that at any moment they can all be brought together under a common denominator. They may differ, and even contradict one another, in detail, in character, experience, and ideas, but in sum they are all the more surely and profoundly united in the joy of the feast in the noblest sense, so that everything individual finally seems to be such only to prepare and strengthen its contribution to the common whole and to bring to light the more clearly the one thing necessary. We remember what we said about this concept under §1.[39] The dialogue is very carefully constructed so that the outward events of the family festival come first: the sharing of gifts, singing, a small lighted model of the Christmas story, and indeed of the main dates in church history (there is no Christmas tree), all of which are designed irresistibly to set the Christmas mood. As is natural when the presents are given, the wonder child Sofie stands at this point in the foreground with her thoughtful sayings, her delight in the gifts, her piano playing and singing, and her mystical touches. She it is who continually provides occasion for the first free-ranging series of talks by the adults, for instance, on educating children, religious enthusiasm, the church and art, the relationship of the sexes, the victorious center beyond joy and pain, and the like. Then—a second section obviously begins here—Ernestine, Agnes, and Karoline, at the request of the men, begin to tell their own experiences of earlier Christmas eves, all without exception on the theme of mother and child, while Friederike with her piano playing, which either accompanies or concludes what is said, gives to the proceedings the character of a melodrama. The men—Leonhardt the rationalist, Ernst the man of quiet inward experience, and Eduard the speculative mystic—respond (and often, although wrongly in my view, the true heart of the work has been found in this third section) by giving their views of the meaning of Christmas and the Christmas celebration in more didactic theoretical and theological conversation. Finally the long-expected Josef appears on the scene with a mild rebuke for discussion of this kind and a demand for "inexpressible joy" at an "inexpressible subject." Thus the end brings us back to the beginning: "Come along, and especially the child if she is not asleep, and let me see your beautiful things, and let us be merry and sing something religious and joyful" (p. 56).

In exposition it should be noted especially that we should not confine ourselves one-sidedly or even primarily to the theological speeches of the third part, as, for example, in Mulert's Introduction. Schleiermacher himself, in what he had Josef say about these, warned us not to take too seriously what would seem from this discussion to be the common theme and content of

[39]Cf. pp. 28ff.

Christmas joy insofar as this can be formulated. The first two parts of the conversation, in fact, are not just initial exposition preparing the ground for this climax, and for the general mood that Schleiermacher is trying to evoke, the drift of the free-ranging preliminary talk, the chatter and behavior of little Sofie, and the stories of the women are to be taken no less seriously than the men's discussion.

What is the significance of Christmas and its celebration? I should like first to quote briefly what is said by Dilthey, who is so well disposed to Schleiermacher and, indeed, so full of sympathy with him. I read his words with very different accents and thoughts from those with which he wrote them, but objectively they correspond exactly to my own very general impression of the work. The piece begins "with the quiet and profound expression of Christian life as exalted and true human life depicted in the fellowship of noble men; reflection is raised and elevated to conscious investigation of [the origin of] this higher life of humanity in Christ, and is then extinguished again and overwhelmed in the profound experience of this exalted Christian life, . . . in the vision of human existence perfected by Christianity" with which the scene opened (p. 774). The opening standpoint is not that of a definite and palpable dogmatic position but "personal experience in the fellowship of Christians" (pp. 775–776), its trigger is the individual religious impulse which is presented "simply as the exalted and liberated life of the human mind and emotions in general," its core and goal is "exalted humanity, completely sanctified humanity" (p. 777). "In living emotion, in its extension, in feelings of fellowship, in the interplay of effects in which this becomes certain of the external world, and of counter-effects which it has on this, in its final depth and breadth, in which it knows that it is one with all else and grounded in the unconditioned, there lies for [him] (Schleiermacher) the central point of our existence." "The life of the emotions constitutes that exalted existence in which the Christian finds himself" (p. 779). Thus the festal joy of Christian companionship, in which a number of people who have found completion in Christianity express their exalted religious emotions (p. 779), "not only forms the starting-point of the work, but to this it constantly returns and it is in a sense no more than a depiction of this" (p. 781).

But—after this undoubtedly excellent exposition of Dilthey—what is the specifically Christmas modification of this general emotion that is elevated in Christianity? What does "exalted existence" mean from the standpoint of this feast? From the very first page Schleiermacher never leaves us in doubt about the obvious insight that answers this question. When the curtain rises, the first person we see is the "cheerful and intelligent Ernestine"[40] lovingly and attentively occupied as a woman in preparing the table for the presents. And when the company streams in, "in the middle of the room where everything could be seen, all eyes turned on her. So beautiful was the arrangement, and such a perfect expression of her disposition, that unconsciously and necessarily feeling and sight were drawn to her. . . . She it was first in whom the whole company delighted. As though all else had already b⸱ ⸱ enjoyed, and she were the giver of it all, they gathered around her. The child clung to her

[40]*Weihnachtsfeier*, p. 3.

knees and gazed at her with wide-open eyes, not smiling but infinitely loving; her friends embraced her; Eduard kissed her lovely downcast eyes, and all of them in suitable ways manifested their sincerest love and devotion" (pp. 4–5). And when, after a first look at the presents, they all gathered in front of the miniature depiction of the Christmas story, we are told that little Sofie "suddenly realized that her mother was standing just behind her; she turned to her, without changing her place, and said with deep feeling: 'O mother! You could just as well have been the mother of the divine child, and are you not sad that you are not? And is not this why mothers like boys better? But just think of the holy women who accompanied Jesus and of all that you tell me about them. Truly, I want to become one of them as you are.' Much moved, her mother lifted her up and kissed her" (pp. 9f.). "Mother love is the eternal in us, the basic harmony of our being," is the way the thoughtful Agnes formulates this insight in the name of the women themselves, and she goes on to make it more precise: "Do you think that love is oriented to what we can make of our children? But what can we make of them? No, it is oriented to the beautiful and the divine which we believe to be already in them, which every mother looks for in every movement so soon as the soul of the child expresses itself."[41] And Ernestine seconds her: "In this sense every mother is another Mary. Every mother has an eternal divine child and devoutly seeks the stirrings of the higher spirit within" (p. 24). |

But all this is really set going and fully developed only in the stories told by the women in the second section. The decisive moment in the first story is the meeting which the narrator had in a church with an unknown woman who had "a small child at her breast." "Her expression seemed to me to be now smiling and now sad; her breath came now with tremors of joy and now with barely suppressed sighing; but the constant feature was above all one of friendly peace and loving devotion, which streamed radiantly from her great, black downcast eyes. . . . The child, too, seemed to me to be unusually attractive; it moved with liveliness, yet quietly, and was apparently engaged in a half-conscious exchange of love and longing with its mother. I had before me living embodiments of the beautiful pictures of Mary and the Child. . . ."[42] Friederike accompanied the story softly on the piano. "When Ernestine had finished, after some extemporaneous passages, she broke into a beautiful church melody. Sofie, who recognized it, ran up to her to add her voice, and they sang together the lovely words of Novalis:

> I see thee in a thousand paintings,
> O Mary, charmingly expressed,
> Yet none of these can e'er depict thee,
> As thou art on my soul impressed.
> I only know that inward vision,
> Dreamlike, the strife of earth dispels,
> And a heaven so sweet I cannot tell it
> Eternal in my spirit dwells (pp. 32f.).

The climax of the second story is the moment when a baby is baptized

[41]*Ibid.*, pp. 23f.
[42]*Ibid.*, pp. 31f.

by its father, a pastor, on Christmas Eve in the midst of a deeply moved company of guests. "When we all laid hands on the child in accordance with the good old custom of the area, it was as though rays of heavenly love and joy met on the head and heart of the child as on a new focus, and it was certainly the common feeling that these rays would kindle a new life and then beam out again in every direction. 'The same again,' interrupted Leonhardt, 'just like a reversed or negative Christ child into whom, not from whom, the heavenly radiance streams.' 'You put it excellently, dear Leonhardt,' answered Agnes, 'I could not have put it so well. Only the mother, whose love sees the whole man in the child, and this is the love that evokes the angelic greeting, also sees the heavenly radiance already streaming from him' " (pp. 36f.). The third story, however, tells of a mother who with great sorrow has inwardly accepted the loss of her mortally sick child on Christmas Eve and reconciled herself to the renunciation. But then in her absence there comes the crisis of healing and she returns and finds the child on the way to recovery. " 'It moved me with sadness and sweetness,' she said, 'to send an angel to heaven at the time when we celebrate the sending of the greatest of all to earth. Now both of them come as direct gifts from God. On the feast of the world's new birth the darling of my heart has been born to a new life' "—" 'like a Mary in reverse, who begins with the deepest grief that a mother can suffer, with the Stabat Mater, and ends with joy in the divine child,' was the comment, and then someone else, heightening the dialectic, said: 'or not in reverse, for Mary's grief must have been submerged in her sense of the divine greatness and glory of her Son' " (pp. 40f.).

From all this there can be no doubt that the Christmas aspect of Christianity is understood as "exalted and true human life"[43] (or, in the phrase of the 1790 sermon, "the supreme triumph of human nature").[44] The specific Christmas aspect of humanity, however, is obviously the relation of mother and child in its various modifications: first the tender mother alone as seen from outside, then the child which recognizes its ideal and its own future in the mother, then love for the child as the inward and eternal element in the mother, then mother and child seen together as a group, then the child alone with what it receives from society and gives back to it, with its "holy radiance" both negative and positive, the latter prophetically perceived only by the mother. Finally there is the sorrowful mother whose grief is comforted, comforted already, by the life of the child which overcomes death. Always Mary and always Christ, and, whether as Mary or Christ, always we ourselves, the woman honoring the divine child in the man, the child honoring the pure mother in the woman, both united in the same concept of the noblest and most exalted humanity. "Therefore," says the third and last of the theological speakers at the close of his presentation, "every mother who feels it . . . and knows it . . . sees Christ, too, in her child, and this is that ineffable and all-compensating maternal feeling. And each of us sees in the birth of Christ his own higher birth through which nothing lives in him but devotion and love, and even in him the eternal Son of God appears. . . . And this is the glory of

---

[43]Dilthey, p. 774.
[44]VII, 64. See above, p. 52.

the feast which you wanted me to extol too" (p. 55). Thus the center of Schleiermacher's preaching of Christmas, to which we referred last time, is not in fact empty, although in the sermons it may often seem to be bare and abstract in comparison with the fulness of historico-philosophical, psychological, and ethical considerations. Schleiermacher does know a Christmas miracle; it is the true existence of man himself as this is most purely and beautifully depicted in the relation of mother and child; it is the feeling for life which is kindled by seeing this relation, which is elevated by the feast, and which lovingly seeks and finds fellowship.

But if this is Schleiermacher's center, is not Christmas as the feast of Christ's birth again pushed out on to the periphery by a fourth heterogeneous consideration? Does it really have to be Mary and Christ that we celebrate? Could not another divine mother and another divine son take their place, with no essential change, if the upshot of it all is that in Mary and Christ we recognize in the best sense ourselves? Are Mary and Jesus merely an accidental paradigm (the word "symbol" is still in our ears from the outline of the sermon at Stolp only four years before)[45] of the mother-child relationship, of exalted humanity? Or, and in what sense, are they more than this?

With these questions we now turn to the theological discussion of the men which constitutes the third section of *Christmas Eve*. I accept the interpretation of this best-known part of the work which has it that not one or the other but all three of the speakers represent the opinion of Schleiermacher,[46] and so too, of course, does the fourth speaker Josef, who, like Elihu in Job, comes on the scene at the end and transcends them all. It is the musical Friederike who, as the evening draws on and their wait for the last guest is prolonged, proposes that the men should take the meaning of the feast as a topic of discussion. "It has so many aspects that each can extol it as he likes best" (p. 42). The first speaker, Leonhardt, is a rather refined creation less of the literary than the theological imagination of Schleiermacher.[47] He declares at the outset that (1) he does not want to forestall the men, that is, the parsons, who will have to preach the next morning and will thus keep off "their line" so far as possible; and (2) that he does not intend to "extol" the feast but to honor it in its own way for its excellence and perfection. Schleiermacher is speaking here to the extent that, as most moderate theologians often like to do, he sometimes feels and acts like a non-theologian, like a cultured worldling, like a spectator of Christianity from outside. Hence Leonhardt (this

---

[45]Cf. p. 51.

[46]D. F. Strauss, *Charakteristiken und Kritiken* . . . (Leipzig, 1844²), p. 43; C. Schwarz in the Introduction to his edition of the *Monologen* and *Weihnachtsfeier* (Leipzig, 1869), pp. XIX–XXII; H. Bleek, *Die Grundlagen der Christologie Schleiermachers* (Freiburg/Leipzig/Tübingen, 1898), pp. 188ff. Cf. H. Mulert in the Introduction to his edition of the *Weihnachtsfeier*, pp. XV and XXVII.

[47]Note in the margin of the MS: "Br. II 49." Here and in what follows Br. is an abbreviation for *Aus Schleiermachers Leben. In Briefen*, 4 vols. (Berlin, 1858–1863). The reference is to a letter to Henriette Herz, dated 1/17/1806, in which Schleiermacher says of the speeches of the men in *Christmas Eve:* "I cannot concede that there is a Platonic spirit in the first speech, since strictly it is frivolous in nature; a Platonic form, yes, but equally so in the third speech." The same note may be found on p. 64 alongside the date 11/26/23.

Schleiermacher) honors Christmas as the epitome of a festival. "If the first beginning of Christianity is to be regarded as a great and important matter"[48] (note the caution in the premise), then the feast is an apter way to keep it alive in human memory than the Bible or religious instruction. In proof, the Roman Catholic Saints' Days give more cogency to the legends of the saints than purely oral or written narration can do. The power of such observances may be seen from the fact that not infrequently the feast becomes the occasion for making up the corresponding story. So, Leonhardt thinks, "the memory of Christ is more widely preserved by the feast than by scripture" (43). [Schleiermacher omitted these words in the 1826 edition, proof enough that he did not want to have the worldling Leonhardt say things that he himself could not later espouse.][49] Christianity is certainly to be accepted as a strong force today, but this has little relation to the real person of Christ. [1826: "The personal activity of Christ on earth seems to me to be less related to this ... than is commonly assumed."][50] One may except the doctrine of the atonement, which, being supratemporal by nature, is to be regarded as "more mythical"[51] [1826: "symbolical"].[52] As the historical founder of Christianity Christ has, on the contrary, "only a limited significance" [1826: "only a small part of the present structure of Christianity is to be ascribed to him"].[53] He is closer to John the Baptist than to Paul; it is doubtful whether "a separate church[54] [1826: "such a self-contained and cohesive church"][55] ought to have developed at all according to his will." Similarly the concern of the older evangelical narratives to link Jesus to the house of David does not fit too well the founder of a world religion [1826: "at first the supernatural birth of Jesus, although attested in the earliest tradition, was unknown to many"].[56] Conversely, the message of the resurrection and ascension, which marks the founding of the church, brings the historical life of Jesus under suspicion [1826: "in some degree"].[57] The controversy between the ancient Docetists and Ebionites, who denied either the true humanity or the true deity of Christ, and that between the Lutherans and the Reformed concerning the purely spiritual or also bodily presence of Christ on earth, point beyond themselves to the fact "that Christ was not formerly on earth and did not live among his followers in any different or more distinctive way than he does now" (p. 45). In short, the feast, the Christmas feast, because the historical facts are doubtful, deserves the honor of being the best basis for a consistent faith [so positively in 1826];[58] its force is close to what was said about Roman Catholic legends, namely, "that by such ob-

[48]Schleiermacher has "achten" for Barth's "halten."

[49]Cf. *Weihnachtsfeier*, p. 67, ll. 41ff. The brackets here and in what follows are Barth's.

[50]*Ibid.*, p. 68, ll. 10ff. Schleiermacher has: "than is more assumed than believed by most people."

[51]*Ibid.*, p. 44.

[52]*Ibid.*, p. 68, l. 19.

[53]*Ibid.*, p. 68, ll. 31ff.

[54]*Ibid.*, p. 44.

[55]*Ibid.*, p. 68, l. 39.

[56]*Ibid.*, p. 69, ll. 2ff.

[57]*Ibid*, p. 69, l. 21.

[58]*Ibid.*, p. 69, l. 30.

servances history itself can sometimes be made."[59] This wonderful power (to preserve history if not to create it) Christianity owes to its introduction into the home and especially into the world of children. For this reason its traditional form must not be in any way abandoned. As a child is its main theme, so children in particular must take up and carry the feast, and by means of the feast Christianity itself. It is celebrated at night because night is the historical cradle of Christianity. Candles are lit as a symbol of the star without which the stable, and the child in the dark stable, could not be found "in the otherwise starless night of history."[60] Among the stories of the women, therefore, Leonhardt liked best the one about the "negative Christ-child" with the holy light not streaming out from him but toward him from his Christian environment. To this view [1826: "to the eternal continuation of our feast"][61] the speaker finally asks those present to raise and empty their glasses. Stripped of its wrapping of cautious reserve, his view may be briefly formulated as follows: Christ is not the occasion of the beautiful feast that we celebrate but the feast is so beautiful and powerful that it is instead the occasion of the historical figure of Christ. In purely negative terms, this figure is not historical at all, but the product of a cult-legend which is justified as the cult itself is ("there have to be feasts," as Leonhardt guardedly says at the outset, p. 43). From Leonhardt's standpoint, then, pure humanity and its exaltation in the celebration, which we earlier saw put in the center of the Christmas message, could be not only central but primary, and in relation to it the historical aspect could be secondary, derived, and accidental. Stated thus, this was certainly not Schleiermacher's own view, nor did he allow Leonhardt to put it so definitely. But there can be no doubt that dialectically at least he did conceive of it as a thought of his own, as may be seen from the careful way in which he later corrected and softened Leonhardt's speech and to some extent rendered it innocuous. He would not have been concerned to do this for a figure who meant nothing to him. That Leonhardt is Schleiermacher is also shown by the fact that he is not refuted in the further course of the discussion. He is simply rebuked at the end by the gentle, harmonizing Josef: "Your evil principle ... this Leonhardt, the thinking, reflecting, dialectical, over-intellectual man."[62] But within Schleiermacher's view of things even the evil principle, even the advocate of the devil, can only be in his own way an advocate of God too, or at any rate an advocate of Schleiermacher, and in spite of these words of Josef, Schleiermacher would have been the very last to renounce such predicates as "thinking," or "reflecting."

[11/26/23]   The second speech in the men's discussion is made by Ernst, the happy bridegroom. The representative of the real opinion of Schleiermacher has been found especially in this figure, and a hint of this has been sought in his name "Ernst."[63] I believe that to hold this view is to spoil the rich dialectic of the work and the general wealth of Schleiermacher's spirit. Schleiermacher was suffering at the time from the break in his relations with Eleonore Grunow,

[59]*Ibid.*, p. 45.
[60]*Ibid.*, p. 46.
[61]*Ibid.*, p. 69, ll. 34ff.
[62]*Ibid.*, p. 55.
[63]D. Schenkel, *Friedrich Schleiermacher* ... (Elberfeld, 1868), p. 279.

and if he had really meant to portray himself in Ernst he would hardly have presented him as a bridegroom. It is correct, however, that Ernst, too, is Schleiermacher, and indeed, the outwardly most attractive Schleiermacher, the representative of the most easily understood form of his Christology. Leonhardt's speech had upset the company a little, especially the women, and Ernst is asked to refute the "unbelieving rascal,"[64] a task which he evades with a clever excuse. Yet in praising the feast as a good thing in its own way he is not hesitant as Leonhardt was; he does not say that we have to have feasts and that this is a good one after its fashion,[65] as did Leonhardt, whose whole argument leaves the question open, but starts from the unproved but positive hypothesis. He also says that on the assumption that the feast is a good thing he needs to explain its content more fully than Leonhardt had done. "For you merely considered the fact that every feast is a commemoration of something; my concern, however, is: of what?" (p. 48). And he defines this "what" as something "by the representation of which a certain mood and disposition can be kindled in men."[66] The mood of Christmas is that of joy. But, he asks himself, is it really the true and essential element in the feast that has this effect and not perhaps the incidental element, the presents that are given and received? But no: the joy of a birthday, for example, and the joy of Christmas are not the same. The former is that of inwardness, of inclusion in a specific relationship; the latter is "the fire, the swift movement of a widespread and universal emotion."[67] Although in much of Christendom, at least, "everybody is busy preparing gifts, this consciousness is the magic that masters us all"[68] [in 1826 it is only "a great part" of the magic].[69] Specific instances of friendship are recalled such as "efforts to be ready for the appointed hour of the feast,"[70] the Christmas market, and so on. What does all this imply? "What is so universal can never be invented arbitrarily. It must have something inward as its basis. . . . But this inward thing can be no other than the basis of all the joy that moves hither and thither among these men"[71] [in 1826 Ernst moves on directly to his goal in this sentence: "This inward thing can be no other than the fact that the coming of the Redeemer is the source of all other joy in the Christian world, so that nothing else can deserve to be celebrated in this way"].[72] Postponing the feast to New Year is a deplorable custom because New Year can denote only the change and antithesis in time. But for all those who do not merely live in the alternation of time nor rejoice only in the renewal of the transitory, there can be no other principle of joy than redemption, "and the starting-point of this for us must be the birth of a divine child"[73] [1826: "In the unfolding of this, the birth of *the* divine Child is the first bright point after which we can expect no other and can postpone our rejoicing no

[64]*Weihnachtsfeier*, p. 46.
[65]*Ibid.*, p. 43.
[66]*Ibid.*, p. 48.
[67]*Loc. cit.*
[68]*Ibid.*, p. 49.
[69]*Ibid.*, p. 70, ll. 2f. Here and in what follows the brackets are Barth's.
[70]*Ibid.*, p. 49.
[71]*Loc. cit.*
[72]*Ibid.*, p. 70, ll. 19ff.
[73]*Ibid.*, p. 49.

longer"].[74] What does "redemption" mean? The removal of the antitheses between appearance and being, between time and eternity, which is the life and joy of original nature but not in the first instance ours This can come only from one who does not himself need it. In the divine Child, that is, in the first seed of "the new, undisrupted life," we also see its finest blossom, its supreme fulfilment. The Christmas feeling, however unconscious it may be in many people, can be finally summed up only "in this concentrated view of a new world" which can be present in a thousand pictures: as the rising and returning sun, as the springtime of the spirit, as the king of a better kingdom, as the truest messenger of the gods, as the loveliest prince of peace. The feast depends—"and so I refute you, Leonhardt, even as I agree with you"—not on historical evidence which is weak when considered in a lower critical sense, "but on the necessary idea of a Redeemer"[75] [1826: "On the necessity of a Redeemer and so on the experience of an enhanced existence which can be traced back to no other beginning than this"].[76] Whoever concedes, as Leonhardt surely will, that Christianity has power in the present must also recognize the "thread," however slight it may be, to which this present is attached as if crystallized. "With this small emendation," for which he hopes to win Leonhardt's approval, Ernst concludes his challenge, and he hopes—indeed, he predicts—that the "beautiful feast" will always maintain its essential character, that of "true joy in the rediscovery of the higher life" (51). |

What is the "small emendation" which this second speech contributes to the discussion? It is obviously to be sought in the same direction in which we saw the earlier Christmas sermons of Schleiermacher moving. The Christmas message is to acquire a center, a content. It is first a certain "mood" or "disposition," then its universality is stressed, then it is shown that as such it must be related to redemption, then there is reference to the divine Child in whom we see redemption and in whom we rediscover the higher life which transcends division. In closer definition of what is to be understood by the "divine Child" there is a certain unresolved tension between the first and the second editions. If we had only the former we should have to assume that what is meant is only "the necessary idea of a Redeemer" and that the "birth" of this Child is plainly to be construed as the unpretentiously germ-like presence of the truth of redemption posited by this idea, that is, the overcoming of the antithesis in us, pointing to the present if concealed fulfilment of this truth to us and in us. But the corrections which Schleiermacher made in Ernst's speech in the 1826 edition (they are materially no less important than those he made in Leonhardt's speech), linking up with certain expressions that are found already in the first edition, place alongside the idea of an enhanced existence the *experience* of it—an experience which points back in some way to a historical beginning, to the appearing of the Redeemer in the world, to the first bright point after which we expect no other. If this is so—and there can be no doubt that Schleiermacher's thoughts run in this direction—then the divine Child, who is incontestably the historical Jesus, is thought of as

[74]*Ibid.*, p. 70, ll. 41ff.
[75]*Ibid.*, p. 50.
[76]*Ibid.*, p. 71; cf. pp. 10ff.

the unpretentious germ, the beginning, the crystallizing center, and the like, to which the present is linked as the last and outermost ring, again in such a way that the fulfilment may be seen already in the beginning, but with everything now presented as a historical process. In the first edition it was not wholly clear how far Leonhardt's view, on which the historical aspect of Christianity is in principle secondary, is refuted by that of Ernst. It is not wholly clear how far the question posed for us by the Christology of the women's stories is answered: whether Christ is more than a paradigm of our own elevated humanity. In the second edition, however, the historical element is undoubtedly put first, though in such a way, be it noted, that it forms part, albeit the first part, of a series, all that follows being in continuity with it. Thus Christ, the divine Child, has nothing that we do not already have fundamentally, the only difference being one of degree. He himself is the idea, and in the second edition the historical beginning, of our "enhanced existence" or "elevated life." Clearly this does not provide a satisfactory answer to the question whether the child of Bethlehem has more than paradigmatic significance.

Before closing let us listen to the third speech, that of Eduard, the head of the house and host. Here again Schleiermacher is the speaker—not Schelling, as has been suggested[77]—Schleiermacher debating, of course, with Schelling, yet still Schleiermacher, as is shown by the externally dominant position of the speaker. Eduard begins by saying that he will rely less on the "mythical recorders of Christ's life" [he means the synoptists; 1826: "the more external recorders"][78] than on the *mystical* writer John in whom "there is almost nothing historical [1826: "in whom few of the external events may be found"],[79] who has no Christmas story, but in whose spirit an eternal, childlike joy of Christmas reigns. He it is who gives us the spiritual and loftier view of our feast" (p. 52). Eduard quotes a few words from the prologue to John's Gospel and then launches at once into the following flight of speculative theology. The flesh is finite nature. The Word is thought, understanding. The incarnation of the Word is the coming of *this* original in *that* form. "What we celebrate, then, is no other than ourselves as we are collectively, or human nature, or whatever you want to call it, viewed and understood in the light of the divine principle."[80] But why must we "set up" (!) one person, and why precisely this one person, as already at his birth the union of the divine and the earthly? The answer is provided by the following consideration. Man in himself is earthly spirit, that is, understanding in its eternal being and also in its ever changing becoming. Individual man, however, is only becoming, that is, fallen and corrupt. The identity of being and becoming possessed by the earthly spirit must arise in him, that is, grow and become. He must reach the point where he can see and love all becoming, himself included, only in its eternal being. He must want to be no other than a thought of eternal being, but of the eternal being which is one with becoming. In humanity this identity is eternal,

[77]Cf. H. Mulert in the Introduction to his edition of the *Weihnachtsfeier*, pp. XXIVf.
[78]*Weihnachtsfeier*, p. 71, l. 24.
[79]*Ibid.*, p. 71, ll. 27f.
[80]*Ibid.*, p. 53.

but in the individual it has to come into being as his thought, as the thought of community life and action. The individual must see and build up humanity as a living community. He must lose and find again his separate existence in it. "Only then does he have within himself the higher life and the peace of God" (pp. 53f.). This community is the church. It relates to the rest of humanity as the self-consciousness of humanity does to the lack of consciousness in the individual. He in whom this self-consciousness "arises," he who "truly and vitally has knowledge in himself,"[81] comes therewith to the church and can at most only deny it outwardly. But women, who do not have knowledge in themselves, have that higher self-consciousness in emotion, and are thus the more attached to the church. Now although this community is in process of becoming, it has also become. As a community of individuals it has come into being through the communication of fellowship. "We thus seek a point where this communication began, knowing that it must actively proceed from each of us, and that man in himself must be born and fashioned in each individual." He "who is to be viewed as the starting-point of the church . . . must have already been born as man in himself (="earthly spirit"!), as the God-man." We "are born again through the spirit of the church. But the spirit" proceeds from the Son, who did not need to be born again but was "born originally of God" and is thus "the Son of man in the absolute." "In Christ, then, we see the earthly spirit originally taking shape as the self-consciousness of the individual."[82] In him we celebrate not only ourselves but all who will achieve this. "Therefore every mother perceives, . . . and knows by a heavenly message that the spirit of the church, the Holy Spirit, dwells in her, . . . she sees Christ in her child, . . . and . . . each of us sees in the birth of Christ his own higher birth. . . . Hence the feast streams out like a heavenly light in the night. Hence a universal pulse of joy throbs in the whole reborn world which only those members who are sick or maimed for a time do not feel. This is the glory of the feast that you wanted to hear me praise."[83] |

Now where do we stand? This is our question in face of this final vote. Obviously the mediating position of Ernst has been taken by storm and a sharp antithesis achieved against Leonhardt. Or is it not quite so sharp as it seems to be at a first glance? Certainly we are now at the other focus of the ellipse. The center of Christmas seems to have been definitively reached and asserted. Christ is the One, *this* One. He seems to be sharply differentiated from us others. We need to be born again; he, the God-man, was born originally of God. The order of rank seems also to be definitively secured. What was in him is primary, what is in us is secondary. In 1826 Schleiermacher had to correct a good deal in Leonhardt's speech, less in Ernst's, but hardly anything important or incisive in Eduard's. This is an indication that in positive content, though not in speculative form, we have here the "advance guard" of his thinking, of the early thinking which he could most freely reappropriate in his later years. Does this mean that the questions which we have had to raise in the discussion thus far are finally laid to rest here? We need to proceed

[81]*Ibid.*, p. 54.
[82]*Loc. cit.*
[83]*Ibid.*, p. 55.

carefully. The formalism of Leonhardt, with his feast that seems to have no content, has certainly been left behind. So, too, has Ernst's rather hazy "idea of a Redeemer" or the corresponding experience. In their place there now stands in rich fulness man in himself, the earthly spirit, the Son of Man in the absolute, the incarnate Word. Is that not central, primary, and material enough? We certainly have to say so, and we certainly cannot close our eyes to the considerable enrichment which the whole cycle (or, better, ellipse) of thought has achieved through the development of the problem of the individual and the church. What possibilities seem to open up here! But at this very point we are brought up short. How does Eduard move from his church to Christ? "We seek a point where the communication starts,"[84] we are told, but we are told even more plainly at the beginning that we must *posit* One in whom alone human nature may be depicted thus. We ask: How does this Christ that is *sought* and *posited* by the church differ in principle from Ernst's "idea of a Redeemer," from that historical core or beginning to which our enhanced existence points back? If the primary character of Eduard's Christ is genuinely primary, how can there be any question of seeking and positing? Again, Leonhardt's theory, which reminds us of Feuerbach, and which has it that the feast—Leonhardt could have agreed with Ernst and said the church—could have produced Christ, can certainly stand unrefuted and uncontradicted alongside Eduard's theory. Can one not think of the seeking and positing along these lines too? We also ask: How does it come about that on Eduard's view the relation between the individual Christ and the individual Christian can obviously be reversed, that the communication which founds the church must originate independently again with each individual, and that man in himself can be born and take shape in each individual? How does every mother come to see Christ in her child, and how does each of us know that the eternal Son of God appears in him too?[85] How does the Son of Man in himself, the incarnate Word, remain One, *this One*, as we are told at the outset, if all of us obviously can be and already are the same? Is the unique dignity which seems to be secured by revelation really amphibolic? Can it be changed (as it must be here) into its opposite, into the universal dignity of man in general in his participation in being as one who is becoming? If knowledge—what is meant is the awakening of the individual to the consciousness of humanity—means participation in the church for man, and if emotion plays the same role for rather more foolish woman, what remains of the central position of Christ which seemed for a moment to be presupposed in establishing the concept of the church? Finally, what about the content of this Christ? Let us accept the brilliant originality of the description of Christ as the earthly spirit—the predicates that Eduard confers on this are indeed absolute enough. But can this absoluteness be meant seriously when Eduard can say that "what we celebrate is nothing other than ourselves as we are collectively, or human nature," and when we also consider that he goes on to say: "viewed and understood in terms of the divine principle"?[86] How does Pilate come into the creed? Is there

[84]*Ibid.*, p. 54.
[85]*Ibid.*, p. 55.
[86]*Ibid.*, p. 53.

anything to celebrate in ourselves and human nature when we view and understand them in terms of the divine principle? What does the latter mean if the former is possible? Is the incarnation of the Word or the Son of Man in himself anything other than again that elevated humanity which in the women's speeches, to which Eduard expressly refers, is so vividly depicted in the mother-child relationship as the true heart of Christmas? And if this is Eduard's view, what option is there but to accept a symbolic or paradigmatic Christ in his sense. This certainly leaves Leonhardt's Feuerbachianism unrefuted, nor does it resolve Ernst's vacillation between idea and experience, so that in the long run it does not matter much whether we put it the one way or the other.

Josef can now appear on the scene and speak the final word about the ineffable theme and ineffable joy, along with the positive statement: "The poor women have had to put up with a good deal (i.e.., the men's theological discussion). Just consider what beautiful tunes they would have sung to you in which all that is religious in your speeches would have resided far more inwardly, or how sweetly they would have talked with you out of hearts full of love and joy; this would have delighted and refreshed you much more than these solemn speeches. . . . Let us be merry and sing something religious and joyful."[87] One should not in any way overlook the literary and, indeed, the highly theological significance of this final page with its gentle triumphing over all earthly heaviness. Music and the eternal feminine are in no sense mere adornment in Schleiermacher's *Christmas Eve*. Somewhat epigrammatically I might venture the thesis that they are the real theological substance of this little masterpiece—for this is what it is no matter what view we take of its contents. Music: Not for nothing was it Dülon's flute concert, as we have seen, that inspired Schleiermacher to write this work in 1805. Whenever there was singing during the conversation, there came at once "some silent moments when all knew that the heart of each was directed lovingly to the others and to something higher still" (p. 10). Not for nothing is it little Sofie with her very significant name who, although definitely inclined toward feminine pursuits, shows a decided talent for music, especially for music "in the grand church style" (p. 7). "Every feeling," says Eduard, "emerges most fully when we have found the right music for it; not the word, this can only be an indirect expression, . . . but the musical notes in the proper sense."[88] To help to give common expression to religious feeling, song must be set again in a truer relation to the word. "What the word makes clear, music must make alive, transmitting it directly as harmony into the whole inner nature, and fixing it there."[89] Again: "Christianity is a single theme presented in infinite variations. . . . It is undoubtedly true that church music could dispense, not with the singing, but with specific words. In a Miserere, Gloria, or Requiem, what do the individual words matter? The music may be understood from its own character, and no one can say that he has lost anything if he does not hear the set words. These two, Christianity and music, must stay close to-

[87]*Ibid.*, pp. 55f.
[88]*Ibid.*, pp. 21f.; Schleiermacher: "every beautiful feeling."
[89]*Ibid.*, p. 22.

gether"[90] [1826: "and a piece of music like Handel's *Messiah* is for me at the same time a compendious proclamation of the whole of Christianity"].[91] "Yes, indeed, said Friederike, it is the most religious music that pierces the heart most surely. And it is singing religion, added Karoline, which rises most gloriously and directly to heaven" (pp. 22f.). Why music? one may ask. From all that has been said, the answer is plain: Because the word cannot do justice to what Schleiermacher takes to be the real Christmas miracle, that is, elevated humanity; because the word, as we have seen, sets man before riddles, entangles him in self-contradictions, and forces him into dialectical arts in which he is not really credible to himself. Words always end with a reference to the ineffable object and ineffable joy. But this object and this joy are elevated humanity, ourselves, and how fortunate it is that, harassed and threatened by words, we can flee for refuge to the realm of music, to Christian music and a musical Christianity. Music with its very lack of concepts is the true bearer of the Christmas message, for it is capable of expressing a human capability.|

Then woman: It is much more than an act of gallantry when Josef at the end assumes that the women with their singing and talking could have done better than the men did with their solemn speeches. It is the women with their stories, with their variations on the mother-child relationship, not the men with their Christology, who in Schleiermacher's mind say what is really essential about Christmas. For if (p. 28) Christmas speaks about conversion, about a change of mind, about something new by which the old is done away, the speakers agree that this demand comes to expression in the restless, aspiring, struggling nature of men, but it is already met in the quiet and gracious nature of women which combines holy seriousness and charming playfulness. "Christ himself, replied Karoline, was not converted; for this reason he has always been the protector of women, and while you have been arguing about him, we have loved and revered him. . . . We always (remain) children, . . . but you must be converted so as to become children again."[92] Thus the women *are* and *have* what we celebrate insofar as this is "the direct union of the divine and the childlike in which there is thus no further need of conversion."[93] As music is beyond logical dialectic, woman is beyond ethical dialectic. Woman, too, is capable of expressing the human capability in which Schleiermacher finally thinks he sees the Christmas miracle. In both cases the comparison lies in the freedom from conceptuality and the transcending of antitheses. We may leave on one side the question whether Schleiermacher with this characterization does justice to the true nature of either music or women, whether they do not both have good cause to reject the role assigned to them with an "I am afraid of the Greeks even when they bring gifts."[94] In my view, however, the impressive reference to the direct communication of the divine which takes place in music and the eternal feminine is the decisive proof that for Schleiermacher what Christmas imparts is in fact a human capability, "the supreme triumph of human nature." The dialectical tension

[90]*Loc. cit.*
[91]*Ibid.*, p. 63, ll. 10ff. The brackets here are Barth's.
[92]*Ibid.*, pp. 28f.
[93]*Ibid.*, p. 29.
[94]Vergil, *Aeneid* ii.49: *timeo Danaos et dona ferentes.*

has increased in comparison with the older Christmas sermons, the church's doctrine is set forth forcefully in sonorous formulae, the range of treatment and concepts has been greatly enlarged, and there is no lack of spiritual power, but in his basic theme Schleiermacher has remained true to himself. With these findings we now turn to the Christmas sermons of the later period.

[11/27/23]   c. When we survey the Christmas sermons of Schleiermacher's later years— and not by a long way are they all extant, the series only beginning in 1819— we note at once the familiar antithesis of the early sermons between his true and central Christmas thinking on the one side and his inauthentic and peripheral Christmas thinking on the other. Schleiermacher himself once (1833, III, 738f.) put it this way: "Sometimes it is the real subject of the feast that we celebrate with singing and prayer and public addresses; sometimes it happens that the event that is really celebrated . . . serves more as an occasion to lay upon the hearts of Christians in one or other of their essential relationships, not the individual factor itself, but rather the one thing that is really necessary." And it is worth noting that on the whole in his very last years Schleiermacher reverted to the second procedure which had characterized his early preaching, whereas from the beginning of the twenties we have some definitely central sermons (in intention at least) which stick to the real theme of Christmas. In a few others it is hard to say which course he adopts, the last one in 1833 (III, 738ff.) being an interesting combination of the two approaches. If we have been correct in our evaluation of the early sermons and *Christmas Eve*, then we shall have to see the true climax and goal of Schleiermacher's Christmas preaching in the sermons from the twenties and in everything in the other sermons that agrees with them in content, although naturally the other elements which are also present, and which come to the forefront again at the end, must be taken into account too. Let us again try to work from the periphery, which catches our attention first, back to the center, and then try to understand what the relation between the two implies.

In my view the most powerful and impressive Christmas sermon that Schleiermacher preached, although in it Christmas is definitely more an occasion than the theme, is one that cannot be dated for certain (II, 314ff.; J. Bauer thinks it might have been delivered as early as 1811–1812,[95] but I would be inclined to put it in the period 1818–1821). Its text was Acts 17:30–31 ("God overlooked the times . . . but now he commands . . . to repent . . ."). Let us look beyond the narrow sphere of individual life, Schleiermacher asks in the introduction, to the large and universal sphere. It is the Savior of the *world* whose coming we celebrate. A new world has dawned since the Word became flesh. His appearing was the great turning-point in the whole history of the human race. What is the change whereby the old age and the new may be distinguished? The fact that ignorance of God is no longer overlooked and tolerated by God. Christ's life was from beginning to end an increasing *revelation*. The world's childhood ended with it. Sin is now known and the image of God is evident. Hence judgment passes on all human action, and we ought to *rejoice* at this. We are now told that he commands everyone everywhere to repent. "This now . . . is the glad and glorious now from the day whose splen-

---

[95]Bauer, *Ungedruckte Predigten Schleiermachers*, p. 82.

did anniversary we are now commemorating together."[96] The transition from that ignorance to a new age—a transition which God commands through the inviting and life-giving voice of his own Son—is repentance, described as man's purification through the vision of the Son of God, and its inseparable companion faith, described as confidence in the eternal truth and reliability of the divine life which is revealed in the Redeemer and in the sacred bond of fellowship which he establishes among his people. As the Redeemer glorifies himself in individual souls he brings about the transformation and re-creation of the whole world. The new world is the world of repentance, which leaves ignorance behind, and faith, which recognizes the Son and with sure steps strides on to the eternal and imperishable crowns which can be won only with the Redeemer through love for him in firm fellowship with his people. In this new world "he is the First and the Last: the First because it has started with his appearing, and the Last because he does not cease to work in it with power until he has brought the whole race to himself and dispelled the darkness of ignorance on the whole circle of the earth."[97] Undoubtedly more than one question needs to be addressed to this, but I believe that we have here the best side of Schleiermacher, and I would like to say this. The only point is that the sermon gives little answer to the christological question put by Christmas, says nothing new in addition to what Ernst and Eduard said in *Christmas Eve*, and also does nothing to change the problems by which what they said is surrounded, as we saw.

Materially less essential, and standing in an even looser relation to the theme of Christmas, is a sermon of uncertain date preached on St. Stephen's Day (in 1819 according to J. Bauer)[98] on the text: "I have not come to bring peace, but a sword" [Mt. 10:34]—a text which he would have done better to have left alone (II, 69ff.). He believes that the fact that Christ and Christians are entangled in affliction and conflict on earth is a proof of their true *humanity*, that the fact that Christ foresaw this suffering without being frightened by it is a proof of the fulness of deity that dwelt in him—this is how the preacher links up with the Christmas theme—and finally that the confidence with which he sent out his disciples in spite of the overhanging sword is a measure of the security of the relation between him and them. In spite of everything Christ took up residence in the innermost minds of believers and therefore in spite of the sword that he brought, peace and goodwill have in truth come among us. We can only say that all this is rather artificial and not much can be gleaned from it concerning the meaning of Christmas. Even less is to be found in the two Christmas sermons of 1831. On the first day Schleiermacher divided his sermon on "Behold, I bring you good news . . ." [Lk. 2:10f.] as follows (III, 132ff.): (1) joy at the coming of the Redeemer is the true model of our joy in the future; (2) the faith that grasps this future joy is our only security in relation to our anxieties about the future. This beautiful but heterogeneous theme is related more closely than in the early sermons to the true Christmas message. Nevertheless—and the sermon is like the earlier

[96]II, 323.
[97]II, 328.
[98]Bauer, *Ungedruckte Predigten*, p. 82.

ones in this regard—there is only a loose connection. The same thought could obviously have been combined with some other joy than that proclaimed to the shepherds in the field. On the second day Schleiermacher came back to the text Lk. 2:15ff.: "When the angels went away from them into heaven . . ." (II, 329ff.) on which he had preached in Schlobitten in 1794, and then preached almost the same sermon in Stolp in 1802. He again followed the same outline: the people who wondered, the shepherds who investigated, and Mary who pondered these words in her heart, and he discussed again "the different ways in which the message of the Redeemer is received"[99]—a proof that we are dealing with something constant here. But now—the preacher has obviously become older and gentler—those who wonder and the shepherds fare much better than they did before. Schleiermacher finds in the former a preparatory stage and he even sees in what the shepherds did "a fine and noble step"[100] (he still thinks they represent those whose interest in Christianity is predominantly historical but with a reference to the humanists of the Reformation period these are now praised for their faithful services, although it is still alleged against the shepherds that they are nowhere said later to have become Christians). On the other hand the evaluation of Mary is now somewhat muted. It is asked whether this was real justifying faith in view of her later vacillating attitude toward Jesus. Yet in people like Mary steadfastness of heart is a work of time. The conclusion reached by Schleiermacher is that in the Christian church there should not cease to be wonder at the inscrutable guidance of the human race, or investigation of these stories, or personal experience and knowledge of the matter. All this has become much more harmonious and profound and rich, as may be seen, but in his psychological approach and in the whole method of marginal consideration Schleiermacher has remained remarkably true to himself, or has become true again toward the end. |

Along the same lines, finally, is the Christmas sermon of 1832 on "There is neither Jew nor Greek . . ." (Gal. 3:27f.) (II, 343ff.). The theme is that the Redeemer's appearing in the world is the true basis of the restoration of true equality among the children of men. The heterogeneous theme is again related meaningfully and cleverly to the Christmas theme. How is inequality among men removed? "In Christ," says the apostle. Not then, states Schleiermacher, by anything unique or special that Christ has done but by what he was as the incarnate Son of God, natural inequalities being done away by the incomparable superiority of *his* sinless birth and acquired inequalities by the incomparable perfection of *his* development. Inequality lies only in us. In Christ we do not compare ourselves and therefore there is no inequality. In conclusion Schleiermacher looks forward to the removal of all religious divisions and also to that of political and social distinctions—something which, as we have seen, lay with particular urgency on the heart of the older Schleiermacher. One cannot fail to note the beauty and seriousness of all these ideas and yet be surprised at the remarkably formal role that Christ plays in these sermons.

[99]II, 329. This is the theme.
[100]II, 336.

All possible locks are opened with this key, but one longs to see the Christmas message stand for once on its own.

A powerful but unsuccessful thrust in this direction may be found in the 1832 sermon (X, 718ff.). Schleiermacher was preaching a series on Philippians. At Christmas he had reached 4:4: "Rejoice, . . ." and he rightly took as his theme "The Special Nature of the Holy Joy of These Days."[101] But instead of working this out in terms of "in the Lord," the question is reduced to that of how far we can specially rejoice in Christ at Christmas, and he replies: First, insofar as we do not look at this or that feature but keep before us the quiet, total picture of all being, which is, of course, too big (we again remember *Christmas Eve*) to be expressed in words. Second, we Christians rejoice together, everything divisive or impure being left behind as we turn to Christ. Finally, we rejoice to see the maturing of Christ in his whole history as he develops from a child to a man on the presupposition of sinlessness. In a way that is very fine but a little perfidious this is worked out at every stage in terms of what a birthday can mean for us too. We do not look at people in their qualities and defects, but in their totality. We unite in our joy in and for them. We think with joy of every stage in their life. I need hardly point out that with this treatment the special nature of Christmas that is formally Schleiermacher's theme has again become something purely formal, a special type of consideration which yields only an incidental insight into what is being considered.

As already noted, the last Christmas sermon of 1813 (III, 738ff.) stands on the border between formal and material preaching. The text selected was 1 Jn. 5:5: "Who is it that overcomes the world but he who believes that Jesus is the Son of God?" Apart from its context this was a tempting text, so much do the words seem to say what Schleiermacher himself wanted to say. If by accident we had only the second part of the sermon, we should undoubtedly have to regard it as a classical example of his Christmas preaching in which Christmas is simply the occasion that Schleiermacher takes to say something he would have said anyway; and it is again his imposing belief in culture and progress that comes to expression. The same world is to be overcome and yet saved, judged and yet made an object of God's good pleasure. Evil is to be overcome but human nature is to be saved, that is, earthly existence to the extent that it can be governed and inspired and permeated by divine existence. This overcoming and saving of the world, as a collective work of God in us, is "the content of our total activity"; when we think about it our eyes cannot but fall "on Jesus the Son of God, on the beginning of his earthly life. . . . At this place and with this moment the victory began."[102] Hence it is one and the same thing when he says: "I have overcome the world" [Jn. 16:33] and when John says: "He who believes in the Son of God overcomes the world" [cf. 1 Jn. 5:5]. His work is our work and *vice versa*. Without deeds, yet enclosing in himself all that is to be, he is the object of our confession and celebration. For it is not by what he did but by what he is that he overcomes the world in us and through us. As, then, we work at overcoming the world,

[101]X, 720.
[102]III, 747.

first within ourselves, then in all those close to us, in all our larger public life, as we reflect upon ourselves in this undisrupted development of our being and thus come to self-certainty—what do we celebrate but again and again this beautiful feast of Christmas? Yes, "it is a beautiful feast that returns [to us] each year; but it has its truth and significance only in this ongoing work, only in our celebration of it afresh each moment. . . ."[103] Only as a kind of exponent of cultural activity does Christ come in at the end of this sermon, and again one might well ask: Why Christ? Why Christmas? Could not the overcoming of the world be proclaimed in some other way? The aim of the sermon, of course, was to show how the joy of the Christmas feast is related to the fact that faith is the victory that overcomes the world [cf. 1 Jn. 5:4]. Directly before the cultural program for Christians, then, the first part of the sermon outlines with bold strokes the features of the Christmas message itself as Schleiermacher understood it. We rejoice, he says unequivocally at the outset, that in Jesus the Son of God is born for us. This is more than we celebrate on the birthdays of children or adults or great men. We are not to stress the expression "Son of God." The essential thing is that God could take pleasure in him, that is, his sinlessness. For his sake God said of the world that he had made that it was good [Gen. 1:31]. And he upholds the world so that it remains an object of God's good pleasure.

In essence these are the positive ideas in the sermons at the beginning of the twenties which I have called the really decisive ones. We must again begin with a sermon of uncertain date (according to J. Bauer 1820–1825,[104] II, 55ff.). Its theme is that even at his birth the Redeemer was God's Son. This seems to be a hard saying. We are to put our trust in something that we cannot know by experience: divine power in the state of the most childish incompleteness. Was not Christ's divine sonship something that simply developed? Nevertheless, Schleiermacher boldly replies, giving up the faith on which this feast rests would be equally hard. It may be affirmed as common experience that sin is part of the purely natural endowment of men. If redemption consists of the purging of sin from our consciousness, then sinlessness must be manifested to us, "and this living sinlessness is the Redeemer, and only as we appropriate this in the most inward friendship and fellowship with him . . . can we share the peace and salvation which are the fruits of redemption."[105] No sinlessness that came subsequently could assure us of the Redeemer through whom we can feel perfectly satisfied "and retain no desire that another might come after him."[106] If Christ spoke truly when he maintained his oneness with the Father, could he intercede for us with God if he were not the sinless one? Again, would we be capable of anything other than a very earthly and broken love "if we had converse merely with ourselves and did not have any other object of love than companions in the same corruption"?[107] No, we can love only through and in a Christ in whom the divine essence was originally united with human nature. The universality of Christian love is intelligible

[103]III, 750.
[104]Bauer, *Ungedruckte Predigten,* p. 82.
[105]II, 59.
[106]II, 60.
[107]II, 62.

only on this basis. "From the beginning of his life, then, it must have been true that the divine Word became flesh in him."[108] Only with this faith can we say of our children: Of such is the kingdom of God [cf. Mk. 10:14].

The rest of Schleiermacher's sermons are to be understood in the light of this one. It is strongly doctrinaire; one cannot be happy about the heaping up of arguments. But it says what Schleiermacher wanted to say and could say. The center of his Christology, the point of his statement that Christ is God's Son, is the postulate that in distinction from all of us he is the *sinless* man. Traces of these ideas may be found in the other sermons previously mentioned, and naturally not in the Christmas sermons alone. When he wanted to say precisely what Christmas is, and what is the special element not merely about our joy but also about the Lord, *this* is what he said. The two other sermons that are still to be discussed, and that deal with the Christmas theme, are weaker and less clear in comparison with those already referred to. In 1823 ("God so loved . . ." [Jn. 3:16–18], VIII,[109] 185ff.) Christ is depicted as the supreme sign of love, as the supreme symbol of the grace of God. At the end it is said that his self-witness, and therefore the feeling that we are not lost, is what we must experience at Christmas. In 1824 ("The day has dawned upon us, . . ." Lk. 1:78–79; Bauer, pp. 74ff.) it is more the thought of the Spirit that is attested to us as the reality of mediation between Christ and us.

We are far from being able to say anything definitive about Schleiermacher's Christology as a whole. It is clear, however, that the Christmas sermons and *Christmas Eve* form a closed circle which is not broken by the sermons of the final years. We note that Schleiermacher wanted to posit Christ as an absolute in some way. But we have not so far seen him succeed, not even in these genuinely warm and inspiring and always well-thought-out testimonies. We are told about a beginning which we are all following up. We are told about a revelation which seems to have all the marks of a historical event. We are told about a sinless man as though this might in some circumstances be the sharpest underlining of the human and nondivine, a further repetition, perhaps, of the theme of "the supreme triumph of human nature" which is sufficiently familiar to us from *Christmas Eve.* We are told about a supreme symbol of the grace of God by which we feel reminded that the old has not yet passed away. Let us take note of these dubious elements and pass on to the next grouping.

2. Good Friday. The material for an understanding of Schleiermacher's view [12/3/23] of Good Friday is relatively incomplete as in the case of the Christmas sermons. I have augmented it with some other sermons on the passion as the texts or subjects demand. Unfortunately Schleiermacher never offered a systematically and dialectically valuable supplement comparable to the *Christmas Eve* of 1806. He did plan to deal with the other Christian festivals in the same semiplatonic and semifictional fashion. But unfortunately—at least for scholarly investigation—he never carried out this plan.

We shall begin with the sermons of the young Schleiermacher, then con-

[108]II, 67f.
[109]Cf. p. 16, n. 68.

sider monographically his treatment of the seven last words insofar as the
sermons are available, and conclude with the sermons of the final years.[110]

a. The four extant Good Friday sermons of the young Schleiermacher (the
initial sermon at Landsberg an der Warthe in 1794,[111] that which he preached
on March 22, 1799, in the garrison church at Potsdam in the presence of the
king,[112] and those of 1810[113] and 1811[114] in the Berlin period) all show the
same characteristics as we have discerned already in the Christmas sermons
of these years. The preacher seems to stand intellectually and emotionally at
a distance from the theme of the day, the death and passion of Christ. He
undoubtedly reflects on this but his reflections do not escape a powerful contrary tendency which changes the contemplation of the cross of Christ into
man's ethical and psychological self-contemplation—obviously from the
standpoint of the cross of Christ, but still *man's*. Naturally this affects the
way in which the cross of Christ is considered. The titles of the first two
sermons are indicative of this tendency and its effects: "That We Must Proclaim Gratitude to Jesus for His Death,"[115] and: "Some Experiences of the
Dying Jesus Which We Should Desire for Our Last Moments."[116] We have here
the familiar ellipse of Schleiermacher with its two foci: As Christ, so we. The
original sharp emphasis on the second softens with time. In the older sermons
we shall see how the Good Friday preaching increasingly becomes preaching
of Christ in the sense that the first focus becomes more and more incisive and
independent, but this does not mean that the second loses its force or that the
ellipse that comprises both is broken—quite the contrary. It is simply that the
naive moralistic one-sidedness disappears. The ethical and psychological depiction of what takes place in us becomes richer and deeper, and one can also
see how far the preacher may validly link his proclamation of supreme humanity, which is now that of obedient suffering, with the figure of the suffering Christ, inasmuch as this is now thought through and worked out as a
prototype in a very different way. To this extent even at the end of the series
we shall expect no more than the triumph of the beginning. Obviously in
interpreting *these* Good Friday sermons all memory of the depiction of the
crucifixion at Grünewald must be obliterated if this is possible; otherwise we
shall be filled from the very outset with *indignation* and even *disgust* at the
innocuousness—or already no longer innocuousness—with which the cross
is made a symbol of peace for the German home and our relation to it is made
into one of inspired uplift after the idealistic manner of Biedermeier. It is
shattering to have to say that, so far as I at least can see, the eloquent dialectic
which is at work here never found occasion even in the presence of *this* subject

[110]Marginal note in the MS: "S.S.45b"; at this earlier point, obviously by mistake,
we find the marginal note: "Account of an 1807 Good Friday sermon in Bauer, *Schleiermacher als patriotischer Prediger*, p. 44." (The reference is to a sermon preached in
Halle on Good Friday, March 27, 1807 on Jn. 12:24).

[111]VII, 205ff.: Good Friday 1794 on 1 Cor. 11:26.

[112]I, 41ff.: Good Friday 1799 on Mk. 15:34–41.

[113]VII, 383ff.: Good Friday 1810 on Jn. 19:30: "How the Lord Can Rightly Say That
It is Finished."

[114]IV, 778ff.: Good Friday 1811 on Jn. 10:17f.

[115]VII, 205.

[116]I, 41.

to halt for once with fear and trembling and to abandon the everlasting Christ and We, and We and Christ, in an attitude of qualified reverence. Neither the younger nor the older Schleiermacher can achieve this. The familiar handling of the Savior, and especially the crucified Savior, which was so typical of the older Brethren, is something that Schleiermacher never lost in spite of his leaving that communion. In this and other matters he simply became "a Moravian of a higher order," as he himself once put it.[117] Hence we had better forget Grünewald and the Middle Ages and the Reformation if we are not to be *angered* here. And it is not our concern to be angry at Schleiermacher but to understand him, or at least to let him have his say. So we shall *let* him have his say.

The initial sermon at Landsberg (which was a Good Friday sermon except in the final section, VII, 205ff.) had as its text 1 Cor. 11:26: "You should proclaim the Lord's death until he comes." I have already mentioned the theme. What does it mean to proclaim the Lord's death? Answer: "Not what the death of Jesus should and can be for men, but what its fruits have been for the Christian, how beneficently it affects his soul, how he constantly seeks counsel and comfort in its fruits, how he counts on their beneficent power in the future."[118] This proclamation consists first of "not being ashamed of the religion of Jesus which he founded and sealed by his death,"[119] whether by expressing our innermost convictions or our supreme emotions. In particular, however, by gaining the attention of others by putting a Christian disposition into practice, or simply by fulfilling our duty and obligations. We must gratefully cherish the teaching of Jesus and expressly proclaim Christ as the *author of our better mind.* Second, we must confess especially the impact of his death, for there is much here that can illumine all of us, for example, by increasing and strengthening faith through contemplating the *force of conviction* demonstrated in it. Or again we can point to the significance which his death had as a *grain of wheat* from which a great harvest sprang. Or again we can show how striking is the *last teaching* which was received here from a dying friend and teacher. This causes us to make our confession to the whole world. We cannot bury Christ again. Attentiveness and obedience are better, but they can be only an expression of gratitude. This must lie within as a constant feeling of blessing, the recognition of Christ as the author of all good and all salvation. From this expressions of gratitude will then arise of themselves.

The Potsdam sermon of 1799 (I, 41ff.) is interesting not only because His Majesty the king was present, as Schleiermacher observes in a footnote, but also because it was preached in the same weeks as those in which the *Reden über die Religion* were composed. [If the two are compared, along with the brilliant correspondence with Henriette Herz which was now at its peak,[120] we get a strange impression of the relation between the esoteric and the exotic

---

[117]In a letter to G. Reimer, April 30, 1802 (Br., I, 309): "I can say that in all these things I have become a Moravian again, but of a higher order."
[118]VII, 207.
[119]VII, 207f.
[120]Cf. Br., I, 201–210, 218–231, 236–243, 313f., 335–338, 344f., 352, 354–356, 361–364, 375f., 378, 379–390, 394f., 397, 401–403.

in the younger Schleiermacher, but this is beside the point here.][121] Both formally and materially the sermon is extremely well thought out and is worth noting for this alone. The author of the speeches on religion undoubtedly gave of his best in it. It begins with an animated prayer which refers to the "commemoration of the Holy One" and the "cross of God's Beloved" and then, in preparation for the theme, to the tears of sympathy which should never run dry until everyone present is "gripped by an inner desire to die the death of this righteous one" by the experience of holy reverence and amazement which is bound to grip all of us when we think of the dying Christ, and so on. The sermon itself begins with the following words: "I am assuming, brethren, that all of us will have at this hour a sad and compassionate heart, and it is to this alone that I will speak. At least for now, I pray you, let us set aside all the separate ideas that each of us may have about some of the specific benefits and blessings of the death of Jesus. I honor all of them if they reside in a heart that I honor; and it would be a pity if this holiest of days were spent in raising questions, sifting opinions, and instigating inquiries which would not do our minds any good but often divide them by bringing to light inevitable differences when we want to be most inwardly united. No, we will unite in thoughts which will be of equal importance and blessing for all of us to the extent that we all honor in Christ the author of our faith, that his death is for us all a death of love and obedience, that we all take his life even up to death as an example that we want to follow . . . not excluding the final thing that took place in his holy soul."[122] "Therefore"—he now comes to his subject—"let us learn to die as we see Christ die."[123] "There may well be an easier end and gentler falling asleep than the Redeemer's but none more lofty, none more worthy of a devout and virtuous heart. If any desire such, let them look with me now at the consummation of the Holy One of God."[124] After these fine words the preacher reads the text Mk. 15:34ff., beginning with the statement: "And at the ninth hour Jesus cried with a loud voice, My God, my God, why hast thou forsaken me!" The sermon then proceeds as follows: (1) "May we all die with the same regret for uncompleted acts."[125] Schleiermacher thought at that time (he changed his mind later) that he found such regret in the second of the seven last words. It cannot have been physical pain or a love of life that wrung this cry from him. But he loved his calling with all his heart and would have liked to do more to promote his mighty cause. He was asking: "Why is the Eternal God bringing his life to an end so as to continue the great work without his help" when he can see "how much he might still have done." The wish is then expressed that state officials, the well-to-do, scholars and sages, artists and artisans, the young, the mature, and the aged "will never cease to love their calling and dedicate new thought and all their resources to it"[126] without ever having had enough and giving up, so that finally they can commend even an incomplete work to God and say: It is finished. (2) "May we all

[121]The brackets are Barth's.
[122]I, 41f.
[123]I, 42.
[124]*Loc. cit.*
[125]I, 43.
[126]I, 44f.

die also with undisturbed peace in spite of the *ungenerous and unreasonable judgments* and very unloving and hostile conduct of men,"[127] with the "*equanimity* of the Redeemer" toward such things, "for this is the fruit of the ripest wisdom and the most genuine piety."[128] (3) "May we all die surrounded by loving and suffering *friends* as the Redeemer was."[129] No one is without a friend. If only we know how to cultivate friendship, we will never be alone in the world even in old age. We should not hold aloof from others when it is time to die. "On our own responsibility we should not break off the finest of human activities a moment too soon. We do not know what beneficent results the last outpourings of love can have, and if only we show our friends how high the power of piety and true wisdom can exalt man even in death, it will have a blessed impact."[130] In conclusion the preacher commends "the bond of brotherly love and true discipleship of Jesus,"[131] whose participants certainly cannot fail to fulfil these three desires.—At this time, then, when Schleiermacher was writing the canonical book of the new theology,[132] these were for him the experiences of the dying Jesus and their significance for us.

The next fully extant Good Friday sermon is from the year 1810 (VII, 383ff.). This time "It is finished" [Jn. 19:30] is the text and the sermon runs as follows. Why does Jesus say that it is finished? Not with reference to the brief sufferings and sorrows of his death, the preacher maintained, and he refused to believe "that the great and sacred moment of his death was the beginning and end of the whole work of redemption"[133]—a negation which in his own way, as we shall see, he later retracted. Jesus says it is finished (1) because he had brought his *earthly life* to a necessary end. Chance did not rule here. No trace of human weakness could be seen in his death. Faith had led to it. But "there is nothing greater or more glorious than the death of the martyr who for the sake of what is present in his heart as the law of his life can leave life itself."[134] This is why his death had to be repeated so often in the story of his disciples and why we can and should hold fast to the same purpose in life and thereby have a share in his glorious death. (2) It is finished because Christ's "*personal work* in the world was now fully ended and completed,"[135] on the one side the *separation* of his own from the great mass (and this "great work of spiritual creation still goes on strongly"[136] and should be promoted by us), on the other side the assuring of the *continuation of his teaching*, from which it follows that none of us should think so little of himself as to imagine "that what he was there for will perish with himself."[137] As he finished his work, then, so let us finish ours. "This holy day is appointed in

[127]I, 46.
[128]I, 48.
[129]I, 49.
[130]I, 51.
[131]I, 52.
[132]*Über die Religion. Reden an die Gebildeten unter ihrer Verächtern* (Berlin, 1799) (ET *On Religion* [New York, 1958]).
[133]VII, 384.
[134]VII, 386.
[135]VII, 387.
[136]VII, 389.
[137]*Loc. cit.*

order that we may impress the example of the Redeemer more firmly on our hearts, pursue the goal of a similar completion, and in thinking of his death lead our lives as those who wish to die as he did, in obedience to his law being transformed into his image."[138]

We have only a brief outline of the sermon of the following year 1811 (IV, 778ff.), though this gives us a clear picture of it as follows. From the text Jn. 10:17f. the preacher takes the saying: "I have power to lay it [my life] down." The subject is the honor and advantage for us of having the power to lay down our lives (naturally for the sake of the good for which we live), for (1) nothing more than this lifts us above all the power of the earthly, and (2) nothing so much as this pacifies us concerning the insignificance of our works. To what could we cling but a readiness to exert all our force to fulfil obligations? What greater proof does even the Redeemer give us of his unrestricted obedience than by going to death to fulfil his Father's will? And finally (3) nothing can purify us so much from all suspicion as to the insincerity of our efforts. "Nothing cleanses the reproach of impurity more than martyrdom. Indeed, even the bitterest enemies of the Redeemer could no longer suspect him of impure motives when he really went to his death."[139] The Redeemer can lift us up to himself only insofar as we take up our cross and follow him [cf. Mk. 8:34], and he is at the same time our guarantee that our sense of the power to lay down our lives is not mistaken. "Beneath the cross of Christ our hearts will not deceive us in this regard. Here each of us finds ... either the conviction that he is one who can do this or that he has the power to become such a one."[140] This was the lesson of the cross with which Schleiermacher and his congregation approached the wars of liberation.

b. We shall now turn to a group of six sermons on the last words of Jesus.[141] In time only the four middle ones are connected; they seem to belong to the years 1820–1823. The first may be considerably older, being put by Bauer as early as 1812 (?),[142] while the last may be dated in the middle or toward the end of the twenties. In spite of some slight overlapping with the third group I am treating them together because in relation to their texts they are well adapted to show us what Schleiermacher really wanted to bring out regarding the passion and Good Friday.

"Father, forgive them ..." (II, 430ff.).[143] The introduction makes the point that the passion and glory of Christ belong together. "He could not be the Son of God without suffering, and his suffering could be redemptive only because he was the Son of God."[144] And he now prays for those who are guilty of putting him to death. In the light of his passion we thus see sin on the one side and forgiveness on the other. His suffering was caused by sin. He certainly

---

[138]VII, 390.

[139]IV, 781.

[140]Loc. cit.

[141]Marginal note in the MS: "II,123, II,399, IV,293, II,138, II,151 form a series (cf. Bauer, p. 80)." Cf. p. 50, n. 3 (b).

[142]Bauer, p. 80.

[143]A Good Friday sermon. The text was Lk. 23:33f. and the subject "The Mystery of Redemption in its Relation to Sin and Ignorance."

[144]II, 431.

had to suffer to be who he was, but this does not excuse those who were responsible. He did not suffer, then, from the loss of enjoyment of life or honor, nor from physical pain, nor from death as such, but from sin. We, too, must be ready to suffer similarly through and from sin, and we must be a match for every other pain. Then we may hope that our suffering, like Christ's, will contribute to redemption from sin. The redemption effected by Christ's death leaves sin without excuse. The times of ignorance have passed [cf. Acts 17:30]. None of those who have known Christ can say any longer that he knows not what he does. The Redeemer has taken this excuse with him to the cross. It avails now only for mistakes and frailties. Furthermore, we can count on forgiveness only as we judge ourselves and the power of sin is increasingly blunted in us by the resistance of the divine Spirit. We shall see our fellows caught in the same movement from excusable ignorance to the witting falsehood and deceitfulness of the heart and therefore when they do us wrong we should pray for them—conditionally, as with every prayer—"Father, forgive them *insofar* as they know not what they do."[145] For they *seldom* do know that what they are doing to us they are doing to the Redeemer. I may sum up the content of this sermon with some astonishment as follows: The death of Christ has for us Christians the significance that we should neither expect unconditional forgiveness ourselves nor have it granted to others. How limited Luther must have been not to have seen this!

"Truly, I say to you . . ." (II, 123ff.).[146] One should not use this saying to 12/?/23 find an example of salvation through belated repentance in the one to whom it was made. A sudden inward conversion of this kind is in conflict with the divine order. We are rather to infer that the thief on the right hand was not such a vile criminal as the other. His request: "Remember me, . . ." gives evidence of quiet reflection. The Redeemer's efforts and promises cannot have been alien to him even at an earlier time. Nor should we infer anything about life in the hereafter from the saying of Jesus. Why should Jesus withhold information about such things from his disciples and then at the last moment reveal it to this man? Neither "today" nor "paradise" is to be taken literally. The heart of the saying is rather that "you will be with *me*." This sets the man alongside the oldest and dearest and most worthy of the disciples, for the saying: "This man has done nothing wrong" [Lk. 23:41] bore witness to his real *faith*. In the feeling of eternal spiritual fellowship with Jesus and his Father the difference between joy and pain was transcended for the malefactor. Today can only denote eternity. The glory of God's presence in the soul is the immortality and life that Christ manifested and that the dying thief is to share with him today and always. Under the most unfavorable outward circumstances he comes to participate in the consciousness and emotions of the Redeemer himself from his childlike submission to the will of God to his holy joy in the salvation of the sinner so happily achieved. Schleiermacher stresses the fact that the thief would still live a few hours so that that consciousness—his whole theory depends on this—could attain to realization in *time*. At issue

---

[145]II, 440.

[146]A passion sermon. The text was Lk. 23:43 and the subject "The Comforting Promise of Christ to Those Crucified with Him."

in it is not a miraculous gift but a growing life. He thus reaches the practical conclusion: "Let us . . . as we are all graciously offered, be with him already today."[147] In short, the malefactor is not a real malefactor but a secret believer; paradise is not paradise but acceptance into Christ's self-consciousness; and the promise "You will be" is not a promise at all but denotes a state that begins at once to become the present, and indeed the temporal present.

"My God, my God, why . . ." (II, 399ff.).[148] We have seen that Schleiermacher expounded this saying in 1799[149] as the expression of noble sorrow, worth imitating by us, at unfinished work. The sermon twenty years later begins with an admission that it is hard to think of this saying on the lips of the Redeemer, representing as it does "such a change and such a decline in spirits from solid trust to a despondent sense of dereliction."[150] That the dereliction was part of what Christ had to suffer for us the preacher calls an artificial explanation. He himself finds the key to the riddle in the fact that Jesus did not frame these words himself but was quoting Psalm 22. Unlike Jesus, the psalmist was not confronting death but even if under great affliction still had hope of life. In adopting the words Jesus shows that this is not so for him but that even at this moment he could think just as clearly and cheerfully about his death as in his last addresses to his disciples. He could never be other than himself. "My dear friends, it is a great blessing for mortal man when he can maintain daily equanimity in regard to this universal human destiny and as he approaches his end learn to look forward with increasing calm and cheerfulness of soul to his departure from this world."[151] One may also infer that since Jesus must have had the most complete understanding of scripture and a very lively memory he would have before him not just this verse but the context of the whole psalm and therefore the way in which the psalmist himself was conscious not merely of dereliction, that is, the non-hearing of his prayer for help in this hour of great need, but even more so of the holiness of God and of joy in him. And in taking to himself the words of another sufferer he shows that he has not become selfishly absorbed in the physical sensation of suffering but even in the deepest need can still take to himself the suffering of others. Precisely in this saying, then, the kindness of the Redeemer triumphs in his passion. Finally the preacher derives from the acquaintance of Jesus with the holy scriptures of his people displayed by this saying both a kindly regard for the glorious and precious treasure of our Evangelical Church and a summons to the reading of the Bible, especially, of course, the New Testament, which is now translated into foreign languages and thus made known to foreign peoples, something to which we should make our contribution but from which we should also diligently profit. In sum, the word of dereliction loses all its offensiveness and changes into a statement of its opposite once (1) we put alongside it the rest of the psalm, which Jesus un-

[147]II, 136.

[148]A passion sermon; the text was Mt. 27:46 and the subject "The Redeemer's State of Mind during His Last Hours."

[149]See pp. 80f.

[150]II, 400.

[151]II, 404.

fortunately did not quote, and (2) we interpret it as peaceably as possible. In fact, nothing is simpler than that.

"I thirst" (IV, 29ff.).[152] What are we to gather from this "frank admission of his need,"[153] as Schleiermacher calls this saying of Jesus? It shows, first, that the merit of the redemption accomplished by him does not lie, as many think, in his suffering as such. Otherwise he would not have asked, as here, for its alleviation. The cup that he had to drain to the last drops was not physical, his death, but the spiritual victory that he won. He will not boast of any strength of spirit but that of obedience. He *avoids* whatever suffering he *can*. We infer from this that we do not gain worth in God's sight by despising any good gift from above. We should also consider that those to whom Jesus made his request, if they were not the same, were the companions of the soldiers who just before had had their wicked and mischievous way with him. Would not many people in his position have been too proud to make this request? With it, however, he expresses in model fashion his sense of universal belonging and relationship, not this time by extending help to his enemies, but in what is almost a higher and greater way by himself receiving it from them, which sometimes can be an equally sacred duty. And since he is undoubtedly serious in making his request and expects it to be granted, he shows his faith "that the malicious passion which had so wantonly manifested itself against him was now spent and the original goodness of human nature would reemerge with the mounting of his suffering even to death itself."[154] It was the Redeemer's principle that "everything good could never completely disappear from human nature because otherwise the ability to accept him as Redeemer would necessarily disappear as well."[155] We, too, must neither overestimate people nor, when we learn to know their other side, lose all faith in them. "We must be on guard against great vacillations in our view of people and make our own the Redeemer's equanimity of spirit."[156] The saying also shows us, then, the unruffled inner peace and purity of soul of Jesus "in which not even the slightest cloud of ill-will arose to disrupt his equally indestructible fellowship with the Father who is love and with the human race which is the subject of this love."[157] May we be increasingly shaped into his likeness, and so forth. In short, the saying "I thirst" displays the purely spiritual nature of his reconciling and unavoidable suffering, offers us an example of passive love for enemies that surpasses even the Sermon on the Mount, and manifests the faith of Jesus in the original goodness of human nature.

The saying, "It is finished" (II, 138ff.)[158] is described by Schleiermacher as incontestably the greatest of the Redeemer's sayings. We have seen[159] how he interpreted it in 1810. It denoted at that time the martyr's triumph and the model completion of Christ's work. But what was then expressly questioned,

[152]A passion sermon; the text was Jn. 19:28f.
[153]IV, 294.
[154]IV, 303.
[155]IV, 304.
[156]IV, 305.
[157]IV, 306.
[158]A passion sermon; the text was Jn. 19:30 and the subject "A Last Look at Life."
[159]See pp.81f.

namely, that Jesus' death is as such the beginning and end of redemption, is now affirmed: "The sharp eye of the Redeemer saw everything completed at the sacred moment of his death and for this reason it is for us, too, the center of our faith."[160] Schleiermacher now tries to expound the "finished" in relation to the disposition of all those who trusted in the Lord with what was still a weak and imperfect faith. They still looked to him with all kinds of false earthly expectations. But they now knew that his whole work had been purely spiritual. It should also be noted that Christ was speaking not only of what he had *done* but also of what had *taken place* to him and through him. We involuntarily prick up our ears. Does this mean: Of what *God* had caused to take place to and through him? No; Schleiermacher says: "His death was the great moment for which *all human affairs had had to work together* from the first beginnings of our race,"[161] certainly according to the counsel of divine providence but with *"human affairs"* as the real acting subject in the fore-ground. Schleiermacher does not set in opposition "what man does" and "what God does" but *"what man alone does"* and *"what all the forces do together* that the Most High sets in motion."[162] "The divine counsel is fulfilled"—and this is the meaning (one would say today, the *cosmic* meaning) of the death of Jesus—*"through the interaction, profoundly concealed from us, of all times and places."*[163] In similar fashion we, too, are taken up into the great context of divine leading. The present of every living generation is one of imperfection and longing and yet it carries fulfilment within it. Hence we are to look, not so much at what we have done, but rather at what has taken place to and through us, and in this way to take into account the counsel and providence of God. In this way we shall be like him in the sense that at the end of our lives we shall be able to join in a joyful: "It is finished."[164] In sum, Christ and we can say "It is finished" when a "last look at life" (the title of the sermon) can be taken with the sense that our allotted function has been fulfilled in the total context of God's plans and dispositions and that to this extent the meaning of this totality has been achieved in and to us.

We now turn to the last of the words: "Father, into thy hands . . ." (II, 151ff.).[165] Schleiermacher calls this the final communication of the human soul of Jesus with his Father. For it could not proceed from what was *God* in him. This saying, which is again taken from the Psalms, is spoken by one who expects to live on, not to die; it is thus a proof that Christ made *no decisive distinction* between life and death. The addition of the word *Father* expresses the unruffled *equanimity* of his mind. For him as the Son of the Father tran-sition from life to death was no more than the kind of change he had often gone through in life. The Redeemer commends us, too, to the same fellowship

---

[160]II, 139.

[161]II, 143.

[162]II, 143f. Schleiermacher said: "The divine counsel with man is never fulfilled merely by what man does, and this is true of him, the only man in grace, of him, the only righteous one. The divine counsel is fulfilled only by the interaction of all the forces that the Most High sets in motion."

[163]II, 144.

[164]II, 149.

[165]A Good Friday sermon. The text was Lk. 23:46 and the subject "Christ's Last Saying to His Father in Heaven."

with the Father as he enjoyed. For us, too, God is not merely to be an external being in whom we trust; he is to be in us and we in him, so that we can no longer separate our will from his or his from ours. For Christ leads his people after him to this firm inward confidence, indeed, to this total unity of will with the Father. But this *dying* of Christ in harmony with God was possible only because of the harmony of his *life* with God. Coming to the end of his series, then, the preacher looks back again at the preceding words and briefly recapitulates their content, always from the standpoint of antithesis or synthesis: As the Redeemer. . . , so must we. This does not merely apply, however, to the last moment of life. The *whole* life of the Redeemer is reflected in the glorious words with which he left it. In faith in him, then, it ought to be that the comforted soul of a believer flees *at every moment* "from the earthly and corruptible to the eternal; at every moment it separates itself from the world to sink into the sea of the divine love; at every moment it surrenders itself and the work in which it is engaged . . . into the hands to which alone we can commend everything, and thus the spirit returns constantly to its eternal source."[166] To sum up, the last saying of Jesus (like all the rest) expresses his absolute superiority to the antitheses of the world in virtue of his total union with God, and all this is a model of what *does in fact take place at every moment* in our case too (note the indicative—not merely what might or should or could take place in our case, but what does).

We will refrain from putting the question marks and exclamation marks that might be put behind almost every sentence. You will see that the one-sidedness and aggressiveness of the earlier sermons has now disappeared. We are dealing with a rounded and consistently-thought-out whole which moves over the toughest biblical sayings, as over all other possibilities of thought, like a roller, levelling and harmonizing everything, triumphantly removing all difficulties. To raise individual objections is useless. As was undoubtedly Schleiermacher's intention, one can only receive the impress of the whole and then from the heart either accept or reject it as such. We shall now try to get a clearer picture of what is meant by this whole.

c. The sermons of the last decade are distinguished in the main from the earlier sermons by a sharper concentration on the true dogmatic theme of the commemoration. The very texts and subjects of the sermons raise the expectation that we shall be led close to the heart of Schleiermacher's thinking about Good Friday. This is not yet true, however, of the earliest in the series, a Good Friday sermon on "The Circumstances Attending the Last Moments of the Redeemer" (II, 442ff.),[167] one of the rare instances when Schleiermacher obviously took the path of allegory. The darkness during the three last hours before the death of Jesus and the tearing of the temple curtain provide him with the occasion for reflection on "a great and mysterious connection between the realm of nature and that of the spirit and grace"[168] as this may be discerned in these important events. As regards the sign of darkness, its *cessation* when Jesus died is significantly more important for him than the *dark-*

---

[166]II, 159.
[167]The text is Lk. 23:44–49.
[168]II, 443.

ness itself, for he takes it to mean that heavenly light has now come permanently into human nature, and the great turning-point has come in human history and the development of the human spirit, while tearing of the curtain naturally points to the "unrestricted spiritual house of God."[169] Finally, there may be seen in the *centurion at the foot of the cross* a mind which the death of the Redeemer shakes out of most blatant indifference to recognition of the Redeemer's worth,[170] while "the relatives of Jesus and the women of Galilee who stood afar off"[171] give Schleiermacher the chance to put in a good word for those who do not crowd around the Redeemer's cross but have still savingly received in their innermost minds the impress of his sacrificial death.

[12/6/23]   Of central importance are four sermons on texts from Hebrews and Romans, the last two preached in 1832 and 1833 (II, 161ff.,[172] 666ff.;[173] III, 242ff.,[174] 524ff.[175]). I will try to present their thoughts systematically. The common concept under which he understood the work of Christ in his death, and in which his doctrine of the cross obviously found its definitive formulation, is in all of them that of obedience. According to Schleiermacher the obedience and death of the Redeemer are one and the same in Paul. Christ's death is sacrificial because it is a death in obedience. It is God's will to give up his Son to death because leaving life in fulfillment of the divine will is the supreme climax of obedience. And the Son obeys because it is the Father's will. Inseparable from this obedience to the Father, however, is Christ's love for men, which could not be demonstrated more plainly than by his obedience. His was the *greatest* love and the *most perfect* obedience because in distinction from what martyrs did, what he did was done by the sinless one in favor of all sinners. If Christ had hesitated but for a moment, if human weakness had stopped him even inwardly or in the very slightest, man would have remained isolated from God and would not have known God's presence. Everything depends on the *perfection* of his obedience. We note how the doctrine of the cross impinges here on the doctrine of sinlessness which was so important a part of the Christmas gospel for the later Schleiermacher. What does this obedience mean for us? "The end of all sacrifices," replies the first sermon,[176] explaining more precisely that the crucifixion of Christ has shown what the final depths of *sin* are. All individual sins are only accidental expressions of this inner corruption. It is thus unnecessary and wrong to think of any other sins than this one sin in which we all have a part. In one of these sermons, then, Schleiermacher launches an unusual general *attack* on the Roman Catholic doctrine of the repetition of Christ's sacrifice in the mass which is sup-

---

[169]II, 446.

[170]II, 448.

[171]II, 450. Schleiermacher: "And all his acquaintances stood afar off, and the women who had followed him from Galilee, and saw all these things" (Lk. 23:49).

[172]A Good Friday sermon; the text was Heb. 10:8–12 and the subject "The Death of the Redeemer the End of All Sacrifices."

[173]The text was Heb. 10:12 and the subject "The Perfect Sacrifice of Christ."

[174]Good Friday 1832; the text was Rom. 5:7f.

[175]Good Friday 1833; the text was Rom. 5:19.

[176]II, 161ff.

posedly necessary for the forgiveness of individual or actual sins.[177] On the positive side the obedience of Christ means *righteousness* for us. Righteousness, however, is something that is ahead of us. We have still to reach it. We are to strive after it. We do not yet have it. It is a standard by which each of us will be measured and which each of us must achieve. Prior to Christ there is only an imperfect and humanly limited righteousness. Christ had to be perfected by obedience unto death in order that the image of the divine nature in human form should not be limited by any finitude, particularity, time, or place, but should be established among us as the standard which we should all try to achieve. We are righteous through his obedience when we take him into ourselves as the standard and to that extent the source of our lives; as we never cease to keep his image before us; as we love one another with his love so that he is among us in all life in the most diverse ways. We have already come to the third and decisive question: How and *how far* does the sacrifice of Christ *avail* for us when it is defined as perfect and sinless obedience? In a decisive turn in his doctrine of the cross Schleiermacher says that it does so as we are buried with Christ in his death and rise with him to a new life (Rom. 6[4]). Naturally we must believe in Christ. But what does believing in Christ mean if not *acknowledging* him and therefore wanting nothing other than his life? "Believers could not have wanted to put the Redeemer to death; with faith then—or it is no real faith—we must renounce all that brought the Redeemer to his death."[178] We take his life into ourselves and acquire another consciousness, namely, that of our living fellowship with him in which there is no more sin but only blessedness. The will of God is written in our hearts so that all the weakness that still dwells in us as the result of sin is in us against our will, our will being wholly one with God's will. This happens as we link ourselves to Christ and build up God's kingdom with increasing strength. Hence the guilt of sin is taken from us; God looks at us, not as we are in ourselves, but in the Beloved, and as we have become through him. On another occasion Schleiermacher describes the same process as follows. As the pinnacle of obedience Christ's death is the fulfilment of God's will. "But we should set ourselves alongside him by our obedience to him and then, he himself being made perfect, he will be the cause of our blessedness too."[179] Of immediate *blessedness* and not first of sanctification; certainly of sanctification *too*, but where the Spirit effects this, there peace and joy are already present, that is, blessedness. At any rate, by what he did all else develops in and for those who are obedient to him. Or on another occasion, there is no better celebration of his death than when, as he proffers himself, so "we receive him by receiving the words of life as we have them from him, . . . as we never cease to keep his image before us; as we love one another with his love."[180] Or in his last Good Friday sermon: "We become righteous through the obedience of the One to the extent that *the same life is both his and ours*." "This receiving of the spiritual life that is imparted by Christ is living faith."

[177]II, 671–676.
[178]II, 168.
[179]II, 669.
[180]III, 251.

"In this union of life, then, we are *in fact righteous.* we have become so through his obedience, however imperfect our own may be."[181] As the mercy seat stood in the innermost sanctuary of the people of Israel, so the demonstration of God's mercy in Christ is linked to the fact that we are a people that has dedicated itself to his sanctuary. In sum, the cross is the sacred site where we constantly *renew* our vows when sin seeks to renew itself in us, where we *purify* ourselves from doubts about him in whom the fulness of deity has manifested itself and around whom we gather as the people that is consecrated his spiritual body.

In the four sermons just summarized we have become acquainted with the last and ripest documentation of Schleiermacher's doctrine of the cross. In this form, which is saturated with the fulness of Bible and church, it seems far removed from the aridity of the previous sermons on the experiences of the dying Jesus.[182] But here as in the Christmas sermons there can be no doubt that Schleiermacher remained true to himself, that the relation between then and now is only one of prophecy and fulfilment. As he sees it, the significance of Christ's death is simply that it is the summit of what man can do in relation to God when the human will is submerged in the divine will (just as the incarnation is simply the triumph of human nature, or enhanced humanity). The result of this view of the cross, as of the mystical idea of the union of God's will and man's in every age, is on the one side the *excluding* of every nonmystical, supposedly external, and in fact contingent relation between God and man, and on the other side the establishment of an *ideal*, of a very spiritual and vital law which we are to strive to keep and to which we are to approximate ourselves. Finally, as the imparting of this blessing of salvation to us, there is the infusion and reception in us of the same obedience as was in Christ—the false doctrine of Andreas Osiander concerning essential righteousness which the Lutherans and Reformed of the Reformation period thought they should banish from the Evangelical Church. The church fathers of the 19th century brought back this teaching in all its fulness.

3. *Easter.* The material relating to Easter is even more defective than that relating to Good Friday. Between two early sermons and one in 1812 yawns a gap of eighteen years. We then have a sermon that is thought to come from 1820, and finally one each from 1832 and 1833. The line to be traced here has thus to link six fairly widely separated points, and even if [we] can supplement the material here and there, it does not give us much to go on. Let us see if we can at least pick out the general direction of that line.

Schleiermacher's earliest Easter sermon, probably preached in 1791 at Schlobitten (VII, 77ff.),[183] surprises us by its extraordinarily positive statements about the subject of the feast. It begins by declaring that Paul was right to say: "If Christ has not been raised, then our preaching is in vain and your faith is in vain, you are still in your sins" [1 Cor. 15:14, 17]. "The whole

---

[181]III, 528; Schleiermacher: "In this union of life we, too, are in fact righteous. . . ."
[182]Cf. pp. 79ff.
[183]The text is 1 Cor. 15:26 and the Theme "The Victory Which Christ Won over Death by His Resurrection."

strength of our faith in religion (rests) on the resurrection of Christ."[184] If Christ had not risen, the apostles would either be deceivers or deceived, Christ himself, who foretold it, would have had an empty notion of the importance of his person, and we would have no express assurance from God to give us certainty that his death was a death for the salvation of humanity. But since Christ *is* risen—the young preacher does not raise the question how—the resurrection is the most radiant affirmation of Christ's mission and the surest proof that God viewed favorably his teaching, work, and passion. On the basis of the text: "The last enemy to be destroyed is death" [1 Cor. 15:26], he then speaks about the special consequence of this event—the complete vanquishing of "the sorrowful figure of death."[185] Both for the sensual *and* for the moral person, even though this person be fully convinced of the immortality of the soul, death is terrifying. None of us leaves the known sphere of life for the unknown without anxious and bitter feelings. The separation of the soul from the body, apart from which we know no life, is no small matter. There is nothing comforting about the obscure ideas of the hereafter held by many peoples, including the Jewish. What do we know of the inner conflicts of soul of even those whose apparently complete composure in death we admire? Only Christ's resurrection gives us real strength in face of death. It also gives us a glorious picture of the state that awaits us. As Christ's conflict was crowned in glory by the resurrection, as it snatched him away from every temptation, as he triumphed over all his foes by means of it, so it will be at every point with us. Through a consoling look at the resurrection "the calm of a good man is assured in relation to the main thing."[186] The fact that Christ after his resurrection had the same feelings as those that graced his beautiful soul in his earthly life grants us a glorious prospect of even nobler joys, an enhanced capacity to love, and a freer enjoyment and activity in the life to come, and his promise, which is not, of course, "fully" applicable to us: "Lo, I am with you . . ." [Mt. 28:20], allows us to entertain without fanaticism the sweet hope of future reunion. But above all, higher than all these hopes, there is the prospect of a higher and more excellent fellowship with God, and the exalted state that awaits us there is worth the pains of committing ourselves patiently to God's providence until the last enemy is overcome for us too. And as Christ appeared in his transfigured body to his disciples, so our soul will not be without an instrument that it can handle just as easily as the present composition of earth. Nor will this new body be capable of dissolution, for Paul tells us that death is not merely overcome but destroyed by Christ [1 Cor. 15:26]. We are perhaps reading the candidate of Schlobitten aright if we sum up these thoughts as follows. The resurrection of Christ is both the *presupposition* and the *prototype* of human immortality envisaged at the time in the fairly concrete and cheerful features of Enlightenment piety. The relation between the ideas of the preacher and the theme of the festival is unmistakably analogous to that found in the earliest Christmas sermons. To a good man the resurrection of Christ guarantees what *needs* to be guaranteed

[184]VII, 77.
[185]VII, 79.
[186]VII, 87.

to him in face of the sorrowful figure of death. The only point is that the dogmatic side of the theme seems obviously to be slighter here and more related to his own reflections, so that the presupposition is made with even greater definiteness, but it is less closely thought out and explained.

A very different picture is presented by the sermon preached at Landsberg an der Warthe (1794–1796) (VII, 218ff.).[187] Expectation is kindled by the title of this: "Unbelief Relating to Things of the Other World." Unfortunately, as in the previous sermon, we do not have the conclusion, which would perhaps have resolved its present unevenness. It, too, opens fairly strongly with the declaration that the doctrine of the resurrection does not deal with the continued life of the *soul* of Jesus but with the fact that his *body* did not see corruption and was thus summoned back to life. This makes somewhat surprising the elucidation that the receiving back of his body was necessary to refute errors that might be caused by the disappointment of material messianic hopes and that it is still today the clearest proof "for the weak for whom the inner worth of the religion of Jesus is not enough to convince them of its divine nature."[188] Although he still expressly describes the bodily resurrection as the theme of the feast, Schleiermacher does not now speak so emphatically of its *indispensability* as he had done in the first sermon, and it is only to be expected that the theme of the feast, being expressly described as important only for the weak, will now be less prominent than before as the subject of proclamation, as the object of special investigation. In fact something other than the Easter miracle interests both the candidate of Schlobitten and the vicar of Landsberg—and something very remarkable, namely, the saying from the inauthentic Marcan ending: "But when they heard that he was alive and had been seen by her, they would not believe it"[Mk. 16:11]. In the first part he deals with a *salutary and necessary unbelief.* All possible caution must be used in face of real or supposed revelations of God so that we not be deceived by shams and led into terrible and foolish things. It is a matter of reason and circumstance whether we can accept the demand for faith or not. "This is how the disciples of Jesus acted. They believed in the risen Jesus, yet they did so, not because of the appearance or the miraculous element, but because Jesus convinced their minds through reasons."[189] Unbelief may also be called prudent when it consists of the rational view that beings from another world, spirits, angels, or men in their future state, do not appear to our senses and hence cannot be perceived by us. How destructive is the credulity which is the opposite of this wise unbelief! "Therefore let us cling fast to what sound common sense teaches us. Our present senses are made for this world, and the things of this world again are made for our present senses."[190] We need other epistemological organs for another world. That which presents itself to us visibly is a thing of this world; it may be hard to explain, or even perhaps unexplainable, but it cannot teach us about another world. According to this canon, that is, strictly according to Kant's canon of pure reason, which the

[187]The text was Mk. 16:10–14.
[188]VII, 219.
[189]VII, 223.
[190]VII, 224.

preacher has obviously appropriated in the meantime, the disciples of Jesus also operated, for although they saw and touched the risen Jesus, they did not draw from this any conclusions about our future state, for example, about the transfigured body. They perceived the inconceivable fact with their senses but they did not cease to halt with sound common sense before the border that is drawn for human thought. Obviously, then, the argument of the first sermon proceeds less according to the general *method* ("as Christ, so we") and more according to the specific *content*. Schleiermacher, as we shall see, could preach freely on Easter, too, according to the formula "as Christ, so we," but in its special relation to continued life after death his knowledge of critical philosophy posed an irremovable obstacle.

The second part of the Landsberg sermon deals with injurious unbelief. This consists of being ready to accept only what is confirmed by our senses, of rejecting the invisible, "what we can properly know by reason or other divine instruction."[191] This is an excess of rigor which is not appropriate to our state on earth. In most affairs we live by faith and not by sight, and in particular we have to have faith in our reason. The foolish wilfulness which restricts itself to the eyes and ears, and which may be seen, for instance, in the case of Thomas [cf. Jn. 20:24–29] and some of the other disciples, is said to derive "from an unhappy disturbance of the powers of the mind by suffering and worry."[192] But we should not allow great misfortune to crush us so much that we timidly deny reason and the true dignity of humanity. What remains of God's creation, what advantage do we have over other creatures, what will be our hope of either eternal or terrestrial bliss, where is the cheerfulness and peace of the soul in face of death, the best of all life's spices, if we act in this way? The sermon breaks off here. But one may conjecture that Schleiermacher would have said in conclusion that the seeing of the invisible that may be known by reason or "other divine instruction" includes the true belief in the resurrection to which the disciples attained even though at first they rightly distrusted the miracle as such. Note that the Easter proclamation has become considerably more tenuous and muffled. The eloquence of the first sermon could not hold up against the assaults of criticism. Decidedly more emphasis is put on depicting prudent unbelief than on contesting injurious unbelief, let alone on commending true belief, which was not committed to paper and [which] I have freely supplemented. And the acknowledgment of the Easter miracle, which is no longer possible in the form of that self-evident presupposition, which for its part obviously rested on a particular metaphysics that had now been undermined, has only the fairly weak support of that "other divine instruction" which is somewhat imprecisely set alongside reason as a source of true knowledge of eternal things. The whole pressure is toward the replacement of the Easter miracle, which is necessary only for the weak, by an appropriate substitute, or, to put it more cautiously, toward seeking and finding an interpretation of the Easter miracle that sits better with the preacher.

Unfortunately the gap of eighteen years in the Easter sermons of Schleier- [12/10/23] macher prevents us from gaining any picture of the development of his view

[191]VII, 225.
[192]VII, 226.

of the resurrection. The only certain thing is that it must have become definitely much more consolidated and settled during this time. We have an account by Twesten (cf. Bauer, *Schleiermacher als patriotischer Prediger*, p. 75) of a sermon by Schleiermacher that he heard on Easter Sunday of that year[193] from which it seems that he had now successfully overcome both the poorly grounded positiveness with which he had once affirmed the bodily resurrection and the dangerous confronting of this center of the Easter miracle with critical philosophy. The preacher now seems to be clear that there is at this center a kind of transition from death to life which can be related in some way to our present existence. Hence Twesten can describe what he heard as a "fine sermon," which could hardly have been said of the Landsberg sermon with its untypically Easter attack on everything that is contrary to reason. "How we, too, should be witnesses to Christ's resurrection," was the subject. For us as for the disciples of Jesus there is a time of Christ's earthly life, that is, of knowing about him without understanding or grasping the true essence of his teaching; there is then a time of his death when we forget him in the joys and sorrows of our own lives; finally, there is a time of his resurrection in which we press on into the divine spirit of his religion. For all the apparent death of his religion and church we may hope for their glorious resurrection, not, of course, believing that their preservation and restoration depend on something sensory and external, but attempting inwardly and spiritually to propagate them and pass them on to future generations.

Along the same lines methodologically is the Easter sermon of the following year 1812, as the heading shows: "Christ's Resurrection a Picture of Our Own New Life" (II, 176ff.).[194] This new life is the *immediacy* which all who believe in Christ *already possess* as having passed through death to life and from which they should draw new force as they celebrate Easter Day. The sermon itself is figurative from first to last. The resurrection of Jesus is the sign and our new life is the thing signified. Our natural life corresponds to the Redeemer's mortal body insofar as it is not yet life from God. Parallel to his violent death is the pain of self-knowledge through which we must pass. Selfish hindrances caused by others correspond to the guarding of the tomb. The miraculous angel represents the contacting by God of the soul that rests in the grave of self-destruction. The identity of the buried and risen Christ stands for the identity of our old and new man: "We are wholly the same except that the fire of the higher life is lit in us."[195] As the Risen Lord is gradually strengthened and receives new powers(!), so it is with us. The marks of the nails which do not fear to be touched point to those sensitive places in our inner lives that will heal with time. As Christ's risen life is not a ghostly one but real, so we are referred to a real life which does not merely feed and grow strong on the Word of the Lord but also has an effect on others, speaking to them with increasing power about God's kingdom. The retirement and concealment in which he lived as the Risen Lord tells us that while we should be effective we should not force our inner history on others nor be overanxious, for the

[193]April 14, 1811.
[194]The text was Rom. 6:4–8.
[195]II, 180.

initially alien spirit that blows toward them from us cannot but reveal to them sooner or later that a life as yet unknown to them is present here. And as the appearances of the Risen Christ took place only[196] at isolated moments and hours but were based on a self-consistent being, so the hours when we feel the new life in us may come and go, and often give rise to doubt whether it may not all be an illusion, but we can seek and find the constant element in it until, "drawing upon it, we reach the point where his heavenly gift in us is a fountain of spiritual and eternal life that never runs dry but continually resounds and gushes forth."[197] This final turn of speech is to be noted. Schleiermacher's *prototype* is not just a *model*, a heavenly analogy of the human copy, as it may often seem to be. Schleiermacher himself often protested against such an idea. As we saw in the last two Good Friday sermons in relation to his doctrine of righteousness,[198] it also has generative force; it is a "gushing fountain" to which one can constantly return to gain new strength as the giant Antaeus did to mother earth. We have in Schleiermacher an idealism which at the last moment can take a naturalistic turn and become a philosophy of *life* annexed to the figure of Christ.

The other Easter sermons of Schleiermacher follow the same pattern. They offer in principle the same investigating and presenting of analogies of the resurrection in our own *new, inner, spiritual* life, usually in the *church*, sometimes in the *world at large*. As Christ, or, for a change, as the other characters, the apostles, the women at the tomb, and the like—so we. And the point of the analogy is that Christ, as we have seen, should be the fountain of continual renewal. There would be nothing to gain by working through these sermons in detail now that I have expressly set an example before you. Simply out of curiosity I may mention that Schleiermacher finds no difficulty in explaining the saying of the angel: "Remember how he told you, while he was still in Galilee" [Lk. 24:6]. Galilee is the theater of the Redeemer's greatest and most imposing works. "As the disciples of the Lord were told to go there, O let us, too, leave the spectacle of death and hasten in spirit to the place of the outstanding activity of our dear Brother who has gone before us; to the place where the relation of love and sympathy has forged a bond with them; let us hasten to this place, reviving all our beautiful recollections and recalling the picture of their life and work! then they will be among us with their spirit and with the power with which they have affected us" (II, 462f.). In distinction from the Christmas and Good Friday preaching, the Easter sermons never broke through this framework to give an independent treatment of the theme of the feast. The reason for this striking fact is openly stated in § 99 of *The Christian Faith*. Schleiermacher did not regard the doctrines of the resurrection, ascension, and return of Christ as essential parts of Christian teaching or as original elements in the faith. They were accepted only because they were in scripture.[199] This explains why he cannot overcome the parabolic method. It also explains the contrasting attitudes that we noted in the first

[196]MS: "only took place. . . ."
[197]II, 186.
[198]See above, pp. 89f.
[199]*Der christliche Glaube*, § 99 (ET *The Christian Faith* [Edinburgh, 1928]).

two sermons, the one so directly dogmatic, the other so directly critical. Even if it emerged only gradually and in spite of many obstacles, Schleiermacher had from the very first an interest in the Christmas message of the union of the divine nature with the human and an interest in the Good Friday message of the sacrificial death of Christ, although only, of course, as *he* understood them.[200] But from the very first he paid only peripheral attention to the "Christ is risen" and in regard to it was obviously "poking about in the mist" until he could find some workable relation to its theme, coming to rest finally in the analogical or parabolic method—a method in which the question that we raised regarding *Christmas Eve*: Why Christ as the subject of this observance? is left wide open, although it finds a tolerably if not completely satisfactory answer in the later Christmas and Good Friday sermons. But we still need to know more about the *reason for this reason*, more than can be gathered from that section of *The Christian Faith*. In closing, then, I will attempt a systematic survey of the last Easter sermons, to which I will add some of the sermons preached on the Sundays after Easter whose texts and subjects ask for inclusion. We have in mind the sermons in II, 452ff.,[201] III, 253ff.,[202] III, 265ff.,[203] II, 466ff.,[204] and III, 537ff.[205] The first is of uncertain date but belongs to the middle twenties. The second and third come from 1832 and the last two from 1833. We already know what Schleiermacher was *aiming* to say in these sermons and need not return to this. Instead we shall focus on what was said more incidentally. This will help us to answer the question: How does he finally view the *fact* that is *asserted* at the heart of the Easter message? What *significance* does he attach to it in principle? What *effect* does he see it having on *men*, on us?

So as not to relax the tension, we shall begin this time with the third question. Instructive material regarding it may be found in the sermon for the Second Sunday after Easter in 1833 on the meeting of the Risen Lord with the fishermen at Tiberias [Jn. 21:1ff.] (III, 543f.). This is compared to the story of Jesus' walking on the sea [Mk. 6:45ff.], which says of the same disciples that they were even more afraid when they saw the Lord, whereas this time we have the calm saying of John: It is the Lord!—and they *believed* him. "Here, my friends, they took a fine step forward."[206] Disquietude of soul vanished. The Spirit became the rule of life. The story is also compared with that of Peter's great catch of fish when he said: "Depart from me, for I am a sinful man, O Lord" [Lk. 5:8]. What weakness of faith, what confusion of mind! the preacher thinks. But now all this was far behind him and nothing like it occurred this time.[207] He still has a sense of sin but it is no longer

---

[200]There may be an ironical allusion here to a popular usage such as is found in, for example, the title of a book by J. Müller, *Jesus, wie ich ihn sehe* (Leipzig, 1925).

[201]An Easter sermon; the text was Lk. 24:5f. and the subject "How a Sense of the Incorruptible Overcomes Pain at the End of the Corruptible."

[202]The Second Sunday after Easter 1832 on Lk. 24:1–3.

[203]The Fourth Sunday after Easter 1832 on Jn. 14:9.

[204]An Easter sermon; the text was Acts 3:13–15 and the subject "Why the Apostles So Specifically Call Themselves Witnesses of Christ's Resurrection."

[205]The Second Sunday after Easter 1833 on Jn. 21:2–8.

[206]III, 544.

[207]III, 545.

disruptive even though his denial had taken place in between. "Here too, then, we see the *mature joy* of faith."[208] For, as Schleiermacher had said in his real Easter sermon of the same year (II, 468), the disciples' own inner experience could not have been damaged by Christ's death and passion. "No, we cannot believe that! How else could we maintain any confidence in our own faith? . . . As they were *believers* in him in the full sense, they would have *remained his disciples even if he had not risen.*" The result of the resurrection, then, is the strengthening rather than the awakening of their faith. It gives especially the courage to go out to others to witness to him where merely with witness to the crucified Jesus they could not hope to overcome the offense of the cross. It was in relation to the human life of Jesus renewed by the resurrection that they became what the New Testament calls "witnesses of the resurrection" [Acts 1:22], that is, of his life in general, of his activity as this was essentially liberated from any kinship with an earthly mind and from all the opposition of evil, and as it completed God's whole work upon the human spirit. It was in this sense that they could and should be witnesses of the resurrection. As Schleiermacher had said in the earliest sermon of the series (II, 464f.), "it simply depends on us, that is, on the power of faith and love in our souls, which we enjoy, of course, only by God's grace in Christ, whether already in the domain of death, which this earthly world is, we, too, enjoy *such moments as the disciples did,*" that is, "not just a glad expectation of incorruptibility . . . but a direct sense of it and solid confidence that we . . . rise already with the Redeemer to the new life of the spirit in virtue of which death is swallowed up in the victory of faith and the kingdom of God . . . and in virtue of which we receive him *directly into our souls* and enjoy fully this inner and spiritual activity of the Lord." Thus the sermon on the Second Day of Easter in 1832 (III, 264) can close with an expression of "firm confidence that the incarnate Word, though no longer here physically, will not cease to be present spiritually and to reign on earth; that the Spirit that illumines him will constantly take possession of the human world." We may thus sum up as follows Schleiermacher's view of the effect of the resurrection, of what Paul called its *dynamis* [Phil. 3:10]. In the disciples and in us, too, it denotes a transition, but only a transition between two qualitatively *equal* states of consciousness, a transition from an assaulted faith to a secure faith, from battle to triumph, from expectation to feeling, but in no sense, even within the consciousness, from death to life, which would involve a transcending of the consciousness. As one would expect from the uncritical character of his doctrine of the cross, Schleiermacher does *not* want any transcending of this kind. Hence the effect of the resurrection can never be for him more than a relative one.

If, secondly, we ask about the *primary significance* of the resurrection, we are first pointed to the fact that it is "the prototype of our new and spiritual life" (III, 254f.). How? Because we have before us here a mysterious and unsearchable beginning that is wrapped in impenetrable obscurity. But obviously the mystery of this beginning is not principial or absolute. How else could Schleiermacher say in another place that our situation in relation to Jesus is very different and better than that of the first disciples, that our faith can

[208]III, 547.

never be so feeble or even so near extinction as most of theirs was? Why not? "Our faith rests *on the long history* of [so] many centuries" in which it has been shown, in spite of all opposition, that there is salvation in no other name and that all good comes from Christ (II, 452f.). How could even so long a history represent an approximation to the principial mystery of an absolute beginning, of a life that is really life from death, we must ask, and we must thus assume that in spite of all that he said about obscurity and unsearchability Schleiermacher did not have any such mystery in view. Let us listen closely to what he did say about this beginning. It is, he stated in 1833, "the first link in a long and great series of similar demonstrations of the divine grace and kindness" (II, 470). What does the preacher have in mind? From what we have heard about the continuation of the miracles of Jesus in our time we shall not be too wide of the mark if we make the following inference. On the one side the long series includes the rapid spread of Christianity in spite of every reverse. On the other side the preacher tells us: "If, dear friends, we now consider the world as it has been shaped for many centuries, where else shall we find all the workings of spiritual development in such majesty and fulness, where else has the dominion of man over the forces of nature reached such a pinnacle on earth, that we find it hard to believe that anything greater can be achieved, and yet there is constant advance. And where has human life purified itself more from everything unworthy in outward custom, in the mutual relations of men both domestic and public, or in the expression of thought and emotion, than among Christian peoples?"[209] Hence church history on the one side and the history of civilization among Christian peoples on the other are demonstrations of God's grace alongside the resurrection. Can the mystery of this beginning be fundamentally any greater, then, than the mystery of all other beginnings? In the same sermon Schleiermacher makes the remarkable point that the resurrection is *only one expression* of the divine power that resided in Christ, of the divine activity that radiated from him (II, 467). An *expression*? *Only one* expression? How can a mystery that is worthy of the name be only one expression? If it is a mystery in principle, then it obviously cannot be *only one,* nor can it be an *expression,* for even if only one expression may be a mystery, it can be only a relative mystery. Obviously, then, the mystery that Schleiermacher mentions here is only a *relative* one. And this agrees with his statement in the same sermon (II, 472) that the Redeemer "did not just become a Lord and Christ through the resurrection," but was so from the very first—a statement which, though half right, hastily overlooks Rom. 1:4 (designated Son of God in power by his resurrection from the dead). But what does this mystery mean if, as we have seen, it becomes less of a mystery with time, if it is a mystery alongside a series of other mysteries, if it is only one expression and *not* the qualitative thing that makes Jesus the Christ? It denotes (in the same sermon, II, 473) "an extraordinary divine act . . . by which God in human fashion and *for human weakness,* yet . . . clearly and definitely . . . acknowledges afresh what men . . . had rejected." Decisive for our present question are the words "for human weakness." To this interpretation belongs a view of the operation of the resurrection whereby

---

[209]II, 471.

its result was essentially the confirmation of the weak but existent faith of the disciples. The disciples *needed* the resurrection "if only that they in turn might bear witness to him with confidence and courage."[210] "The magic of their lips, of course, had to be so great" that what they said would pierce the hearts of their hearers even if they had testified only to the crucified and not also to the risen Christ—for their hearers could not themselves see the risen Christ. If, then, they call themselves witnesses of the resurrection, this, too, is a confession of the weakness of their faith, which should not have needed this "deciding event"; yet the Father in heaven compassionately came to help their weakness through this event and gave them the confident hope that their witness, given credibility by the fact "that he lived again after death,"[211] would be able to overcome the offense of the cross in some people, if not in all. |

In this doctrine of the resurrection we are also dealing with a resurrection (or rather, in terms of this teaching, with an ongoing life uninterrupted by real death), namely, with that of the theory that we found presented forty years earlier by the young vicar of Landsberg an der Warthe—the theory of a demonstrable proof "for the weak for whom the inner worth of the religion of Jesus is not enough to convince them of its divine nature."[212] If *this* was both the first *and* the last word of Schleiermacher about the significance of the resurrection, we need not be surprised that he could not get beyond a parabolic treatment of the theme and in his *Christian Faith* could not ascribe to it any principial significance for his doctrine of the person of Christ. This resurrection is unimportant, incomparably more so than the birth of Christ, with which there may at least be linked the prototypical idea of the triumph of human nature, or than the death of Christ, with which may be linked the idea of man's mystical union with the will of God. The prototypical element that Schleiermacher sought to link with the resurrection, his doctrine of the mystery of beginnings, was rightly so little convincing or important even to himself that, rightly again, he could not find for it any more than an incidental place in his total picture of Christianity.

Having clarified this point, we can move on confidently, third, to the cardinal question of the *fact* that stands at the heart of the Easter message. What is Schleiermacher's attitude to the *historical* issue that is so acute here? Understandably the parabolic method that he consistently follows enables him to avoid this question for long stretches, to set it on one side, and we might do the same and leave him in peace regarding it. I myself am not of the opinion that what glimpses we get of Schleiermacher's answer to this question will add any decisive feature to the picture that we have already sketched. Yet it will contribute a noteworthy feature that we should not ignore in illustration of what is truly significant. Our first step involves a general inference [12/11/23] from what has been said about the significance and effect of the resurrection. As we have seen, this has the *significance* of an extraordinary act of God undertaken with a view to human weakness. Its corresponding *effect* is the strengthening of an existing but weak faith. If we may take Schleiermacher at all seriously in his use of the parabolic method, then by inference something

[210] II, 469.
[211] *Loc. cit.*
[212] VII, 219; see p. 92.

general must also result in relation to what the resurrection *is* as a *"picture of the new life"* (1812),[213] in relation to the picture that Schleiermacher actually saw quite apart from its significance and the influence that it exerted. In the second *Speech on Religion* (p. 119) Schleiermacher described as *prophecy* what I have here called the parabolic method. Prophecy is "anticipation of the other half of a religious event, one half being given."[214] Here we shall have to reverse the process, deducing the first half from the second, the prototype from the copy. If the significance and what it effects are subjectively *strengthening* and objectively *help* in weakness, there must obviously be something similar in the signifying factor, in the original, in the Easter miracle itself. But what can this be? Resurrection as a strengthening or as help—what ideas can Schleiermacher have had in mind in this regard? Could he have viewed the resurrection of a dead man to new life as a strengthening or as help in the sense of giving support in weakness? Is a dead man a weak one whom one can help and who can let himself be helped? This dead man must have been precisely that if the analogy is to hold, if he is to be a model of faith that was once strong, then unfortunately became weak, and was then happily strengthened again. If the analogy is to hold—and there can be no doubt that it does—then on Schleiermacher's view did this dead man not really die at all? Did he simply become weak as the faith of his disciples did? There are only a few places where Schleiermacher in the pulpit gives any hint of what he really thought—or that *this* is what he really thought. I must go back once again to the 1812 sermon. There at the beginning he draws a parallel between the nature of the rise of the new life of the Redeemer and what takes place in us (II, 177): "It was not an easy transformation," we read, "but he too, if he did not have to see *corruption,* had to let *the shadows of death* pass over him." "The mortal body of the Redeemer was an expression of the power of death and a witness to it."[215] "But . . . at the summons of the Almighty life returned afresh to the deceased husk."[216] These expressions obviously attract attention by reason of their restraint. One cannot say more. But what are we to think when, continuing the great analogy, he says: "If the old man of sin died and we now live in Christ and with God, we are still the same as we were before. As *the resurrection of the Lord was not a new creation* but the same man Jesus came forth again from the tomb into which he had gone down, so there must have been in the soul, before it died the death that leads to life from God, the *capacity* to receive life from God when the body of sin would cease and die away," and so on (II, 180). The resurrection of the Lord not a new creation in spite of 2 Cor. 5:17? A direct and continuous identity between him who died and him who was raised again? And how does the new life of the risen Lord become an analogue of ours even in the fact that *"he is gradually strengthened*

---

[213]II, 177.

[214]See p. xvii, n. 18. The reference in Otto's edition (Göttingen, 1926) is p. 75 (ET New York, 1958, p. 89).

[215]II, 178; Schleiermacher: ". . . this life, which scripture calls being dead in sins . . . is no other than what the mortal body of the Redeemer also was, an expression of the power of death and a witness to it. . . ."

[216]II, 177.

and has won new powers"?[217] What are we to say about the following medical considerations: "When the Redeemer first appeared to Mary, *as though his new body were still nervous and sensitive,* he said: Do not touch me. . . . But after a few days he presented himself to Thomas and told him boldly to feel him, to thrust his hand into the Master's side and his fingers into the marks that the nails had left, so that *he was not afraid of contact in even the most sensitive places.* And on the first day, *as though to gain strength thereby,* we find him walking from Jerusalem to Emmaus and back again from Emmaus to Jerusalem . . ." (II, 181)—which obviously implies that he was taking a convalescent walk! |

Once in the sermon for the Second Day of Easter 1832 (III, 257) Schleiermacher stated plainly what he was obviously thinking. He warns against even raising the question whether the resurrection was a natural or a supernatural process: "What a futile debate, dear friends, and how much greater indeed is the wisdom of those who do not initiate it." But he can hardly deny that he himself was involved in the controversy and that he took up a definite position in it. He says: "When we read that Christ was raised up *by the glory of the Father,*" this leaves the impression at least that "this was an extraordinary, unique, unrelated, and incomparable revelation of the Father's glory." On the other hand one has to admit that "*glory in the strict sense*" is identical with all the essential orders of the world and specifically with "all the regular directions and demonstrations of his omnipotent love." And again in this connection: "When . . . the apostle in his sermon at Pentecost relates the saying from the old covenant to the resurrection of the Lord: 'Thy Holy One shall not see corruption. . . ,' and we ask what is corruption but the subjection of the living body, which was ruled by the law of life, to the law of dead nature when the spirit has departed from it, *corruption begins with the end of life, and death and corruption are simply one and the same. Does not this have to mean, then, that if the words of the apostle are taken strictly and properly his thought was that the life of the Redeemer had not completely ebbed away?* for otherwise would he not have seen corruption even if only in its first stages?"

Whether the apostle had to have been thinking this may be left on one side; there is no doubt, however, that Schleiermacher thought it. As may be seen from his extant lectures on the "Life of Jesus,"[218] he espoused the theory that in historical research goes by the name of the swoon theory. I repeat that we should not overestimate the importance of this fact. If we want to regard Christ as "a link in the universal chain in the development of all human affairs" (III, 258), as Schleiermacher did, we may, of course, speak very seriously of mysteries in his life, but it is clear that as rational people we can find a plausible *explanation,* analogous to other human processes, for each of the mysteries, and we will more or less frequently and plainly make much of such explanations. We will then have to *decide* for one or other of the familiar theories of the resurrection. Schleiermacher was in this situation. The *denial*

---

[217]II, 181.

[218]F. Schleiermacher, *Das Leben Jesu* (Lectures at the University of Berlin in the Year 1832 from Schleiermacher's Written Remains and Students' Notes), ed. K. A. Rütenik (Berlin, 1864) (*Sämmtliche Werke,* 1, *Zur Theologie,* vol. VI), pp. 442ff.

of the resurrection which we undoubtedly have to ascribe to him in the New Testament sense does not consist of his snatching after such a theory but may be found already in the total thrust of his Christology, which, as we have constantly had to state, knows *nothing* of any either/or, of any antithesis of heaven and earth or God and man, of any crisis of movement from real death to real life, of any overcoming of these antitheses that is not nature but miracle. This is in keeping with the further points that we have already learned in relation to Schleiermacher, namely, that there was for him no bondage of the will in the sense of the reformers, no sin that meant real and effective lostness, no word of truth that was more than one of many possible expressions of subjective experience, no justification that was not viewed as an infusion of righteousness after the manner of Roman Catholics or Osiander, no repentance that meant a conversion in principle, no church that was not secretly identical with civilized society in general, no eschaton that was not already in the soul, that we have literally to *wait for.* Just as Christmas finally offers us nothing but contemplation of perfect man in his *being,* and Good Friday finally offers us nothing but contemplation of perfect man in the *action* that culminates in mystical union with God, it is no surprise that Christ's resurrection, and resurrection in general, is "no new creation" but only resurrection from apparent death. There is nothing particularly wicked about this. Schleiermacher's whole view is mistaken, at least from the standpoint of 1 Cor. 15,[219] and this specific teaching, of which he made only a very restrained use (and not at all, so far as I know, in *The Christian Faith*), is simply one expression of the whole. Yet one may also say that it was no accident, and certainly that it was not for some *historical* or scientific reason, that he decided for this theory and not for an objective or subjective vision theory or for the theory of a theft of the body, which was occasionally championed in the criticism of his age. One needs to have penetrated a little into the law of his whole thinking to be able to say that he could not arrive at any other model of what he calls "new life" than that of *apparent* death and awakening from this *apparent* death.

An examination in depth of Schleiermacher's sermons on the ascension would round out the picture but not change it in any way. The ascension too, according to § 99 of *The Christian Faith,* is not one of the essential elements of faith. The point on which Schleiermacher fixes is that the temporal and visible presence and work of Christ end here and we see in this event the beginning of his invisible and spiritual presence and work. His thinking about the feast, then, takes both a negative and a positive turn. Negatively it was *necessary* that Christ should not remain on earth (the young Schleiermacher in particular can find many palpable reasons for this; Bauer, *Ungedruckte Predigten,* pp. 31f.);[220] "the eye of faith must look away from all sensory phenomena and

[219]Barth is alluding to his 1923 course on 1 Cor., which many of his listeners probably knew and which had been published as *Die Auferstehung der Toten* (Munich, 1924) (ET *The Resurrection of the Dead* [New York, 1977]).

[220]See p. 50, n. 3 (a). Outline of an Ascension Sermon 1795; the text was Jn. 16:5–7 and the subject "The Need for Jesus' Ascent to the Father: I. For the Propagation of the Religion of Jesus, II. For the Preservation of the Spirit of Religion."

—102—

... ideas to something higher" (VII, 403);[221] specifically in time we have nothing more to expect from him (II, 513).[222] Positively he is still among us as Friend and Teacher (Bauer, pp. 32f.),[223] or in a loftier speculative flight (1810): "There is nothing greater or more glorious, nor can all heaven point to such, than human nature that is permeated by the divine, and transformed into an instrument of the divine Spirit, fully presenting an image of the divine Father. ... This is how it is with the race of earth, its feet in storms and entangled in conflict and difficulties, but its eternal head in the rays of the sun, the Son of God at the right hand of the Father (i.e., in the spiritual and eternal), and from him streams that beatifying feeling, the fulness of power and love, and this fulness also dwells in us" (VII, 406f.). If temporal blessings are over, if the temporal house is broken down, even that of the humanity of Christ—and this has to happen so that the eternal should not become temporal again—all the more do we have the life and work of Christ in us, "that by fellowship with him we might also share in bearing the divinity within us" (II, 510f.).

Allow me yet another observation to close the section. I have not concealed from you the disquiet with which this Christology fills me, not just at one point but at all the points that we have touched upon, all along the line, and not in a secondary question but in the *central* one. Is this Christ really *Christ*, the revelation of *God*? This member of a series even though his significance for the whole series is strongly emphasized? This revelation in which we have a share all the time if only in a reduced form and at a much lower stage? This sinless one if sinlessness is no more than human nature completely permeated by the divine? This *symbol*, no matter how attentively we listen when we are told that this symbol is also power? This fulfiller of a *supreme achievement* which is then said to be half the law and half the means of our own achievement? This *prototype* of the new life which in the light of day signifies only the reawakening of the old life that is apparently dead? Or finally this *eternal head*, bathed in the rays of the sun, of the human race whose feet—ourselves— are in storm and conflict? Certainly, if God is one with the infinitude of spirit, as idealism teaches, or if he is more broadly one with the infinitude of life whose all-permeating soul is everything spiritual, as modern evolutionism demands, or, even better, if we can think of the two together, and if a great admirer of Schleiermacher like Heinrich Scholz defines what we have in Schleiermacher as "evolutionism under an idealistic sign,"[224] and if with the changing times Christianity can be one thing in our age as it can be another

[221]VII, 402ff.: Ascension 1810; the text was Mk. 16:19; Acts 1:10f. and the subject "The Glory Allotted to the Redeemer after His Disappearance from the Earth."

[222]II, 504ff.: Ascension Day; the text was Heb. 8:1f. and the subject "What Christ is for Us after His Exaltation."

[223]Outline for Ascension Day 1796; the text was Mt. 28:18–20 and the subject "The Last Promise of Christ as a Consolation at His Departing: I. He is Still among Us as a Friend; II. He is Still among Us as a Teacher."

[224]H. Scholz, *Christentum und Wissenschaft in Schleiermachers Glaubenslehre* ... (Leipzig, 1911[2]), p. 118: "The basis of his picture of Christ is, as we have shown, the evolutionary view of history given an idealistic sign, and therefore the best scholarship of his age."

in other centuries and people, then Schleiermacher's Christ may really be Christ. But if God is not at all that spiritual life or living spirit, or, more cautiously, it is not worthwhile calling that double being God, if on the other hand concepts like Creator, Redeemer, Spirit, faith, death, and resurrection, taken in their precise connotation, point to a synthesis in which entities like spirit and nature, which Schleiermacher joins in symbiosis, form only *one* *side* of a very different antithesis whose overcoming is really a last, an *ultimate* word, and if the Bible and classical Christian dogma are right to see in Christ this final word, then it must be said at least that in Schleiermacher's Christology with its great quid pro quo, executed with so much intelligence and piety, we have a heresy of gigantic proportions. But then the 19th century, which adopted this Christology wholesale and—which is almost worse— without noting the consequences, must have displayed an almost incredible theological dilettantism. |

I will not pursue this aspect. What I wanted to say was something different. Positively, no matter whether Schleiermacher's Christology was the work of a heretic or, as the official version reads, of a true church father of the 19th century, or of a combination of the two whereby the true church father of *this* century could not possibly be anything other than a heretic, one thing cannot be forgotten or contested. If it could be imagined that Christ did not figure in this theology at all, or that Christ were deliberately and expressly depicted as one of the many religious geniuses that could exist alongside one another or in succession as proponents of the great vital process of divine and human fellowship, how much better this would really fit in with the total thrust of Schleiermacher's thinking, how much more acceptable would his theology have been to the century of Goethe, how much more convincingly would it have spoken to those whom it was seeking to convince, to the idealists and the evolutionists on the right hand and the left who offered such shabby thanks to him and his successors for their demonstrable attempt to meet them halfway! Why did they do this? Because the stone of stumbling in Christianity, the problem of contingent revelation, was still present and caused difficulties in spite of this very sincere and brilliant attempt at modernization. It was still with the *biblical Christ* that the great game of analogy was played here and this unavoidably means that the "ugly ditch" between faith and history to which Lessing had referred[225] had not been filled in. The *prototype*, even though it be rendered innocuous and sucked into the dialectic of the whole process, is still the *proto*type and is very energetically presented as such: This and no other! This means, however, that the provocative isolation of Christ has not faded from view. To be sure, one cannot seriously speak of an absoluteness of Christ in Schleiermacher, but one can certainly speak of a supreme relativity which was most incisively maintained and which was tirelessly established lifelong with both brilliance and warmth. And even if a supreme relativity can never be more than that, it can still be a very disturbing recollection of the absoluteness that is no longer maintained. To be sure, in the end

---

[225]G. E. Lessing, *Über den Beweis des Geistes und der Kraft* (1777) in *Lessings theologische Schriften*, ed. C. Gross (Berlin, n.d.), III, 13 (ET *Theological Writings*, ed. H. Chadwick [Stanford, 1956]).

result this Christ bears a striking resemblance to a cultivated modern Christian who knows how to deal liberally with educated people in any position, who repels nobody, who has a clever word for everybody. In short, he bears a striking resemblance to Schleiermacher himself. But the way this result is reached is always one of a long and serious juggling with ancient biblical truths, preferably from John's Gospel or Hebrews, with which Schleiermacher undoubtedly drove dozens and hundreds of the educated people he had in view out of his church; for along this path he had sometimes to express serious and authentic Christian thoughts which could not be merged into the harmony of the whole. And what rocks he, the great leader of theology, has left in the path of his successors simply because nothing could wash away the fact that his was a real Christology, not the unfolding of some universal doctrine of religion and revelation and God in terms of the unconditioned, but in spite of all the concessions to those who thought otherwise, in spite of swoon hypotheses and the like that reduce the contrasts, a definite doctrine of faith that differs from others by reason of the fact that "everything in it is related to the redemption accomplished by Jesus of Nazareth," as the well-known thesis § 11 of *The Christian Faith* puts it.[226]

Why did Schleiermacher put this rock in his own path and that of others? Why did he not freely and frankly liberate himself theologically by starting at only one point, namely, the present religious consciousness, instead of working with the two focal points that we have continually mentioned, whose duality necessarily forced so many wrestings and artificialities upon him and finally meant that he had to suffer (or perhaps no longer to suffer) from such radical opponents on the left as D. F. Strauss the slander that through the little back door of the religious consciousness he had smuggled the whole of the older dogmatics back into theology,[227] as a superficial glance might suggest? It is not very perspicacious to suggest that regard for the *church's tradition* was what prevented him from taking the final radical step.[228] What does this mean? Schleiermacher's thinking is bold and free even in the pulpit. His scholarship and churchmanship are so united that I do not doubt for a moment that *if* he had found that last step inwardly necessary he would have taken it. Naturally he takes the church's tradition into account when he does not take that step, but *with* conviction and not without it, with *growing* conviction, although even the *young* Schleiermacher, the Schleiermacher of the *Speeches*, never thinks of cutting the rope that binds him to Christ or venturing a balloon ride into the absolute. One may accuse him of approaching his contemporaries too gently and musically and pleasantly with the true conviction which he maintained intact from his Herrnhut unbringing, but his intentions are pal-

---

[226]*Der christliche Glaube*, § 11, Thesis (3rd ed. p. 67).

[227]Cf. D. F. Strauss, *Das Leben Jesu*, 2 vols. (Tübingen, 1835/36), II, 715–719; *Die christliche Glaubenslehre*, 2 vols. (Tübingen/Stuttgart, 1840/41), II, 175–193.

[228]Cf. F. C. Baur, *Geschichte der christlichen Kirche*, ed. E. Zeller (Tübingen, 1862), V, 205: "Often enough one cannot suppress the idea of an intentional deception when one considers the too great caution with which Schleiermacher's *Christian Faith* tries to avoid and soften as much as possible any conflict with church teaching and the far-fetched artificiality with which it explains ecclesiastical doctrines and formulae in a sense which Schleiermacher could not possibly regard as the true and proper one."

pable from his candidate years. Nor can I agree with those who speak of Schleiermacher's *piety*, his heart's relation to Jesus, and the like, to explain the problem of the christocentric element in his theology.[229] That, too, was undoubtedly a factor. If it is still necessary, I will take this occasion to say expressly that for all the serious objections that I have against his theology, I regard Schleiermacher as not just an outstandingly clever person but also as a sincerely devout Christian. Perhaps he never broke free from a certain gentle yearning for the savior-cult of the Brethren. But to this relation, to his particular piety with its background of a gentle waft of Zinzendorf, I would rather ascribe the erroneous *content* of Schleiermacher's Christology. I cannot go into that here, but I believe that the intolerable humanizing of Christ that triumphed under the aegis of Schleiermacher in the 19th century was very closely related to pietism, especially in the form that it had been given by Zinzendorf. In itself Schleiermacher's piety might not have stopped him from taking that radical step. One should not forget that from his grandfather, a preacher of the Eller sect of Ronsdorf, and then from his father,[230] he had Anabaptist blood in his veins. If in spite of this he himself was not an Anabaptist when he did *not* take that apparently obvious step but preferred to create that enormous difficulty to plague himself and others and become and remain a christocentric theologian with an intensity paralleled by few famous theologians, in the last resort I would pass over the historical background and simply focus on the *force of the problem* which is posed in the Christian church and to which one of the strong has become a prey here even though he might have wished it otherwise [cf. Isa. 53:12]. The general thrust of his thought does *not* lead us to expect that he will develop a Christology at the important point. This Christology itself is suspect. It breaks in our hands when we touch it. Yet it is a real Christology. It exists. It is *there* at a central point. It is tirelessly presented in constantly new turns. Why? Again, not out of ecclesiastical conservatism nor out of piety. These play a part but they are not decisive. The only reason I can think of is that this is how it has to be in the Christian church. This is how it has always had to be, and always will have to be, in spite of all the extravagancies and caprices and open errors which clever people have committed in every age and always will. Even though the greatest folly has sometimes occurred at the point that we call Christology, it seems to be *unavoidable* that this cannot be surrendered, that the problem that it poses *has* to assert itself in a way which will either be illuminating or, if not, disruptive, possibly upsetting the calculations of whole centuries. Schleiermacher, too, was subject to this compulsion of the matter itself, which a thinker and teacher who wrestles seriously with the New Testament ob-

[229]Cf. H. Bleek, *Die Grundlagen der Christologie Schleiermachers*, pp. 23, 232; J. Wendland, *Die religiöse Entwicklung Schleiermachers* (Tübingen, 1915), pp. 153f., 170f.

[230]His grandfather, Daniel Schleyermacher (*c.* 1695–1765) was from 1741 to 1749 a preacher connected with the chiliastic Philadelphian Society founded by Elias Eller at Elberfeld in 1726 and transferred to Ronsdorf in 1737. His father, Gottlieb Adolph Schleyermacher (1727–1794) was brought up in this sect but later became a Reformed chaplain and then a Moravian.

viously cannot avoid. His Christology is the incurable wound in his system. It is so by its very presence. It is the point where the system involuntarily breaks up. When we see it from this standpoint, thanks to its own fragility we cannot part from Schleiermacher implacably even at this point.

§ 3

THE HOUSEHOLD SERMONS OF 1818

We shall be dealing with a series of nine sermons which have rightly become famous. They were published in 1820 in a first edition and in 1825 in a second edition. Two are on marriage, three on the upbringing of children, two on servants, one on hospitality, and one on philanthropy: I, 567–692.[1] I bring them in as a *counterpart* to the previous section, in which we have considered the central outlook of Schleiermacher's *dogmatics*, in order that we may have what I believe to be an equally central example of his *ethics*, and in this way, having come to know his view of *Christ*, arrive at a closer acquaintance with his view of *man*. As Schleiermacher said in the introduction to the first of these sermons (I, 571f.), life in the world cannot detach us from fellowship with God and the Redeemer because it simply consists of relationships that are grounded in the Lord himself, life being *"his sacred body which ought to be permeated by his living power."* This is perhaps enough for the moment to indicate the connection between the two standpoints regarding the many things that we have already seen. If we had more time, I would have dealt with this theme, which is undoubtedly the strongest side of Schleiermacher, from two angles, devoting a further section to the political sermons in addition to the domestic ones. I must let you study these on your own and would also advise you to read J. Bauer's book, *Schleiermacher als patriotischer Prediger* (Giessen, 1908), which deals exhaustively with this side of Schleiermacher's preaching, at least in relation to the wars of liberation, though less in relation to the notable decades that followed, and which, although it is a special study, is still the most incisive and comprehensive account that we have of Schleiermacher as a preacher. We also find in it several valuable references and notes relative to the other sermons. I need hardly say that my own theological and political understanding will be rather different from that of Bauer and that not altogether unwillingly I will for various reasons steer clear of the political side. If the political sermons are materially more interesting, these family sermons—and this is what counts here—are more *distinctive* or *typical*. We

---

[1]Marginal note in the MS: "In the 3rd vol. of the Braun edition (1910, ed. Joh. Bauer, pp. 181–398)." The reference is to F. D. E. Schleiermacher, *Werke. Auswahl in vier Bänden*. With a portrait and an introduction by Prof. A. Dorner, ed. O. Braun and J. Bauer (Leipzig, 1910–1913). In Vol. III (1910), pp. 181–398: *Der christliche Hausstand. Predigten von Schleiermacher*, newly ed. by Johannes Bauer. Barth quotes from *Friedrich Schleiermachers sämmtliche Werke*, 2: *Predigten* (Berlin, 1834), I, 567–692.

get to know Schleiermacher best as a man when we understand him as a virtuoso of family life in the broadest sense in the society of relatives either of blood or of his own choosing. We see this—to take just a single example or two—from his correspondence with his sister Charlotte, the loyal Moravian,[2] and also with his bride,[3] and perhaps most of all from the masterly way in which he dealt with the rather unhappy relations in his own household during his later years.[4] In this connection he was undoubtedly skilled in the art of life in a way that is hard to imitate. The *family* was for him the narrowest, most intimate, and most important circle within the concept of *community* that dominated his ideas of Christian ethics, and it is here that we can see most concretely how he regarded the great correlation of spirit and nature, or, theologically, of Christ and community, from the standpoint of the active life. His heart certainly beats no less strongly when he speaks about Christ or, in the field of ethics, when his concerns and enthusiasm are directed to the affairs of people and country. Yet in this area he is unmistakably in his own most proper and certain field, so that in it we can get to know him at what is perhaps his best and most brilliant.

Let us, then, consider this ideal of the family as a demonstration of Schleiermacher's understanding of the art of living. We shall study it in the five variations that he himself presents. For specialized reading I would commend Martin Rade, *Die Stellung des Christentums zum Geschlechtsleben* (Tübingen, 1910), where in addition to the views of Jesus, Paul, Augustine, and Luther (perhaps not too successful a combination), we also find a fairly acute presentation of those of Schleiermacher in this area.

1. Marriage.[5] This is the first divine institution. All other human relations develop out of it. The Christian household rests upon it, and Christian communities are then based on the Christian household. The propagation of the human race rests on marriage and with this (listen!) the propagation of the divine word from one generation to another. *Nothing* in it should draw us away from Christ the Lord; *everything* in it should be connected with the great relationship of our hearts to the Redeemer. It is on the famous passage Eph. 5:22–31 that Schleiermacher thinks he can find a biblical basis for these decisive equations of the orders of nature and grace and what he combines

---

[2]*Briefen*, I, *passim*.

[3]*Briefen*, II, *passim*.

[4]The reference is to the strong influence exerted by Frau Karoline Fischer (cf. p. 42) on Schleiermacher's wife and children. Looking back, his stepson E. von Willich commented as follows: "Inevitably a relation like that of Fischer to my mother had the profoundest effects on our life as a family, on her relations to her children, her friends, and my father himself. . . . But did it disrupt their innermost personal relationship? This was the most difficult problem for my father, and as I look back I am full of astonishment and admiration at the way he overcame it. . . . In short, my father had to share my mother's confidence with Fischer, and the greater share of it went to the latter. But love did not suffer on this account, and the most tender self-giving of my father (and of my mother to him) continued to the end of his life" (*Aus Schleiermachers Hause* . . . [Berlin, 1909], pp. 59f.).

[5]Cf. *Predigten*, I, 571ff.: "On Marriage. First Sermon" (Second Sunday after Trinity 1818; text: Eph. 5:22–31).

with them. There is in marriage, he says, an earthly element and a heavenly element. The two are one and are not to be separated. The *earthly* element ("two become one flesh" [Mt. 19:5]) consists for him of a love in which individual wishes and aspirations on the one side or the other not only stop asserting themselves but cease to exist altogether. Three forms of marriage are depicted which future husbands and wives may profitably consider, since they run more or less severely contrary to this ideal. Marriage in its *ghastly* form is when there is such hostility that conflict is not only not avoided but intentionally sought. Marriage in its *insecure* form is when the husband and wife have no joyous conviction of belonging to one another but avoid conflict by politeness, flexibility, and renunciation, trying to replace love by a carefully observed compact. Marriage in its *adverse* form arises when the two live together harmoniously and peaceably, making as few claims as possible on one another, and seeking and finding satisfaction in other relationships. Nevertheless, *wherever* the two still have their own desires and sufferings, even though they may look on the things of the other as their own; *wherever* it is necessary that they must admonish one another, the wife to stillness and the husband to regard, no matter how scrupulously these admonitions may be observed; *wherever* adjustments have to be made, excellently though this may be done—there the two are not yet one flesh, and the love that truly brings this unity is not enthroned and has never yet been enthroned. One can see at a first glance that according to Schleiermacher's ideal of a perfect marriage there has to be an application of his doctrine of peace, of neutrality, even indifference, the overcoming of all antitheses, in which we have learned to meet the climax of his view of life and the world. |

But let us hear more. Where this earthly perfection of marriage is present, it is necessarily one with a higher, *heavenly* perfection. That close relationship cannot develop out of external life alone but only as the one sanctifies the other and is ready to be sanctified by the other. Marriage cannot be simply a harmonious play of natural forces. It is Christian marriage insofar as both parties are mutually stimulated in the Spirit, what is contrary to the Spirit in the nature of the one being restrained by the other, "each reflecting himself the more purely in the eye of the other in order to see how it is with him in regard to fellowship with God,"[6] so that with united strength both may move closer and with redoubled steps to the common goal of sanctification. Such marriages are made in heaven. Where this is not so, true fidelity and constancy, the true content of married life, is missing. |

Now a third point: this heavenly element cannot be present without the earthly, without the most intimate *fellowship* in the joys and sorrows, the cares and activities of this *world*. No more than the individual Christian can a married couple withdraw from the world and be sufficient to itself. Love can bless only those who fulfil a calling and do not try to evade their destiny. Two people can be self-sufficient only to the extent[7] that they have to stand together in active life, dealing with temptations and trials and mutually helping one another; we can find joy in even the most beloved soul only when we see

[6] I, 576.
[7] The MS has "dann" here but Schleiermacher has "insofern" (I, 577).

it in its natural activity. It is in relation to this common standing in the active world, to the necessary involvement of each Christian household in a greater order of human affairs, that the imperative applies: "Wives, be subject to your husbands" [Col. 3:18], for it is the husband who must represent the household on the outside, the wife participating only indirectly in civil society. The commandment is explained by recollection that the husband must eat bread by the sweat of his brow while the wife is destined to bear children with pain. We are not to see in all this a work of necessity but a divine order by which alone we arrive at a proper awareness of the gifts that the divine Spirit puts to work specifically in each sex. Hence this does not establish a disruptive inequality, but everything that has the appearance of such leads to the most perfect equality. We read that a man will leave his father and mother and cleave to his wife [Gen. 2:24; Eph. 5:31]. This points to a *power* that emanates from the *female* disposition and *seizes the male*. Only when the man detects this separating and attracting power will he be sure of his choice. And "if the woman pronounces the Yes by which the man becomes her head, a Yes that is spoken freely ... she feels that he has become her head by the universal order and particular counsel of God through an unconscious and instinctive operation of this power residing in her," on whose continued operation it depends whether the marriage will be, and will continue to be, what it ought to be, *"a work of eternal love that is itself eternal* . . . , worthy to be compared to the holiest and mightiest work of the same."[8] When the husband returns from the great affairs of life in which, without his wife's cooperation, he secures joy and honor and also pain and anxiety for his household, and is thus the head to which she is subject, he continually turns back again to the wife whom God has given him, and she for her part "senses *her own* strength and blessing in all that he does and orders and achieves," so that the two of them stand "equal before God in a single consciousness as at the moment when by an equally free Yes the husband first became the head of the wife and she became subject to him."[9] Hence Paul does not compare the relation of the wife to the husband to that of the community to Christ in the sense of Christ being everything and we nothing, or as though the wife could be only passive and dependent in relation to her husband, but in the sense that Christ gave himself for the community and sanctified it. The husband should take this self-giving and liberating love as an example by increasingly freeing his wife both inwardly and outwardly from the servility to which her sex so easily inclines, "putting away every restriction from her so that the power of their common life may rule in her unhindered."[10] With *increasing rapidity* there should be achieved in the wife what is promised in the far distance of eternity to the community in its relationship with Christ, namely, that when what we are to be has fully come, we shall be like him [cf. 1 Jn. 3:2]. In other words, while staying in her quiet and modest circle, the wife will become like her husband because she understands and penetrates him in all that he is and does, *daily experience happily teaching* that "our wives really enjoy a fair

---

[8]I, 581.
[9]*Loc. cit.*
[10]I, 583.

share—and are glad of this—in all that their husbands accomplish or attempt in the various spheres of public life or in human art and scholarship."[11]

We are thus confronted here by the truly happy fact that according to the parabolic method the copy is not merely engaged in rapid approximation to the original but even gets far ahead of it and leaves it behind in the everyday experience of Berlin life in 1818. It should be clear by now that materially at least there is something exegetically amiss at this point. For favorable though the Pauline passage may at a first glance seem to be to this method, it is surely evident that Paul can hardly have been thinking of *this* interpretation of the relationship between Christ and his community. However that may be, according to Schleiermacher any appearance of inequality vanishes in the higher and more beautiful sense of a perfect community of life, just as, Schleiermacher adds—and we must again put a little question mark after this—even the heavenly and glorious images vanish for the apostle in the one thought that two become one—for we have to ask whether (and this puts a different complexion on the matter) Paul really uses the heavenly as a mere illustration of the earthly—for it is not at all the same thing if one says conversely that the earthly serves as an illustration of the heavenly. The perfection of marriage, which is the foundation stone of the community of the Redeemer, is thus achieved when in a purely spiritual *unity*, in which one may see a glorious picture of the love that brings every blessing and lifts us up to fellowship with God, and with enhanced *force*, the husband and wife give themselves with *purified hearts* to an active life in which they do the work of God. The innermost unity not merely of the two spouses but of the earthly and heavenly elements in marriage is what is meant by holding marriage in honor in Hebrews [13:4]. "This can happen only when both parties have received our Lord and Master into their hearts and he is the third party in the covenant that is sanctified by love for him."[12]

Let us pause for a moment. All this is so beautiful that there can be no objection to it, and perhaps the only objection that one can raise is that it is beautiful, *much too* beautiful. I will leave on one side all that we must admire and extol in the ideas that we have just considered. I hope that they will have spoken for themselves in my presentation. But I must say a few words, or put a few questions, concerning the "too beautiful" side of these ideas. Particularly in relation to the first part of the sermon we certainly cannot say that Schleiermacher was lacking in psychological perspicacity. But he is a good example of the truth that one may be a great psychologist and still have little conception of the real dialectic of life or marriage as we find it in the Bible and precisely in this section Eph. 5:22ff. How could this clever man miss the fact that directly before his text, though not included by him, we have the verse: "Be subject to one another in the *fear* of Christ" [Eph. 5:21]; that Paul was not speaking about the husband and wife becoming one *spirit* and one *flesh*; that the distinction at whose direct transcending his whole admonition is aiming is maintained right up to the last line: "Let the wife see that she respects her husband" [Eph. 5:33]; and that Paul does not speak about a heav-

[11]*Loc. cit.*
[12]I, 584.

enly marriage with Christ as the third party in the covenant(!), about an "eternal work of eternal love," but about an earthly reality which is seriously and soberly called by its earthly name, about a *mystery* which certainly has to be interpreted but does not for that reason lose its character as such. Where are the eyes of this clever man that he does not seem to have seen that in marriage, even in Christian marriage, the one is for the other above all a question, if not a test or purgatory or cross, and that only in this indirect way and not directly can the husband be compared to Christ and the wife to the community, and the union of the heavenly and earthly be maintained in marriage, in this incomparable place of testing and conflict? What kind of ethics can that be whose demands are obviously directed, not to fallen man, but to the man who already stands in at least some corelike being of the good in virtue of his natural fellowship with Christ? Are its demands the expression of an imperative? If not, can they be called demands? If not, is not ethics the description of a higher process of nature? If so, with what right may it be called ethics?

But let us hear on. The second sermon[13] is devoted to a special theme, the question of divorce. I will be briefer here. Authentic Christian marriage as the source of true joy in life, the preacher begins, ought to rob of their strength all the difficulties and sufferings that afflict us. Instead marriage itself is largely a source of dissatisfaction. The increasing number of divorces bears witness to this. What are we to think about this possibility? To anticipate, Schleiermacher arrives at an almost unrestricted *rejection*. This is biographically interesting because thirteen years earlier in 1805 it had come about that the wife of a Berlin preacher, Eleonore Grunow, had been ready to leave her irksome husband for Schleiermacher and to become his wife. The affair fell through, not because of Schleiermacher, but because of Frau Grunow, who at the last moment was arrested by "her old scruples of conscience" (Letter to Gass,[14] p. 38) and returned to her husband. Rade is probably right when he comments: "So far as Schleiermacher was concerned, the act was inwardly complete and done."[15] When he met Frau Grunow some years later in some society he is supposed to have said to her: Dear Eleonore, "God has been good to us."[16] When we put this alongside his 1818 sermon on divorce we can only conclude that we have here one of the few points in an otherwise almost completely harmonious life where a certain break is detectable, an earlier stage and a later one. Schleiermacher could not have preached the 1818 sermon in 1805 and he could no longer have done in 1818 what he did in 1805. Whether, with Rade, "in the interests of a more thorough handling of the problem in the Evangelical Church and theology,"[17] we should regret that the matter did not go through, is another question. Schleiermacher touched on his own not so old scar when in 1818 he took up the theme on the basis of Mt. 19:8: "For your hardness of heart Moses allowed you to divorce your wives, but from the beginning it was not so." He begins by saying that those [12/17/23]

[13]I, 585ff.: "On Marriage. Second Sermon" (text: Mt. 19:8).
[14]Cf. p. xiv, n. 8.
[15]M. Rade, *Die Stellung des Christentums zum Geschlechtsleben* (Tübingen, 1910), p. 64.
[16]Quoted in Rade, p. 63.
[17]Rade, p. 64.

who wilfully leave their people or parents or spouses can do so only in *hardness of heart*. The purpose of Christ's mission, however, was to soften this hardness. Man should find his *full satisfaction* in marriage and calling. If he does not, if his calling becomes a burden and his married life too narrow, hardness of heart is present. Marriages must be distorted, and wrongly contracted, in which things reach the point where the spouses think they should separate. But even a wrongly contracted marriage will break up only when a *new* hardness of heart is added—that of the intention to seek divorce. The common participation of the spouses in the life of the church ought unconditionally to shatter this intention and bring the spouses back together again. One ought not to say that there are cases where not lack of love but love itself, love for the suffering party, justifies the desire to end a marriage that has become intolerable. This is an unpardonable deception or hypocritical pretext. Only with a hardened heart can one overlook the fact that higher *Christian* love, not false love but the love that seeks the happiness of the other, can and should support and heal the other instead of pushing him or her to one side. To want to end a loveless marriage for love of *Christ* is a sophism. How can we honor by loveless separation the one who will *not* break the bruised reed or quench the smoking flax? Christ, then, does *not* authorize divorce. If it is still desired and achieved by the pronouncement of the state, we are doing what is *contrary* to the Lord's *will*, we can have little confidence in a successful outcome, and we can hardly expect that the suffering party will recover when freed from the link with the other. Whenever divorce does take place contrary to the Lord's will, we should be *ashamed* of the imperfect state of our common Christian life and we should undertake to build for the future, especially among our young people. It is not the *church* but the *secular* authority that to the church's *sorrow* breaks up marriages. The Evangelical Church, unlike the Roman Catholic, does, of course, bless the remarriage of divorced persons, and in so doing it simply obeys the state, sanctioning it by obeying it. There are reasons for this obedience. (1) It does not want to punish too severely individuals who perhaps deserve it less than others. (2) It does not want to encourage concubinage by refusing second marriages. (3) It wants to protect genuine Christian marriage against [the threat of] the unworthy environment that might be produced under (2). In his lectures entitled *Christliche Sitte*[18] Schleiermacher added a fourth reason: "Marriage is not an exclusively ecclesiastical matter but a civil[19] matter too," and the Evangelical Church cannot "try to achieve the kind of superiority over the state that the Roman Catholic church has arrogated to itself" (p. 351). But no one should boast of this as a "noble freedom" of our church. Its ministers can have no great joy in second marriages nor confidence as they "hear Yes from lips that have once already changed this Yes into a No."[20] The time when public opinion seemed to express itself with tepidity and indifference on this issue was a time of general tepidity. Now, when this stagnation in church life has been

---

[18]Cf. p. 30, n. 88.
[19]Schleiermacher: "political."
[20]I, 595.

overcome, our sense of piety will inevitably be scandalized by such events "in *most* cases,"[21] and view them only as a matter of necessity.

I want to add the following. In his philosophical *Sittenlehre*[22] Schleiermacher formulated the more general principle: "*Moral marriage is indissoluble,* for it is problemtatical whether a second marriage is possible after its dissolution" (§ 259). Note that he is speaking here about dissolution and indissolubility *in general*. And in the *Christliche Sitte* he said expressly that strictly speaking the remarriage of widows and widowers ("deuterogamy") as well as divorced persons ought to be ruled out. Church life might be structured in such a way that the remaining spouse could find assistance without having to remarry. Deuterogamy would cease of itself if universally and individually all things were so structured morally that it would be impossible to seek *and* to find a substitute after the death of the first spouse.[23]

One can hardly miss the moral enthusiasm and seriousness of these ideas. Indeed, one might be inclined to see for once an old-fashioned Christian rigorism in Schleiermacher at this point. In relation to the sermon in particular it may be asked whether he said anything other than what *Jesus* himself said according to Mt. 19[8f.]: "For your hardness of heart Moses allowed you to divorce your wives, but from the beginning it was not so. And I say to you, whoever divorces his wife . . . and marries another, commits adultery." Nevertheless, one should note some distinctions in evaluating the content. In rejecting divorce Schleiermacher undoubtedly defends the sanctity of marriage as one of the chief blessings of human life, as a special point of union between the heavenly and the earthly, as "an eternal work of eternal love."[24] His rigorism in relation to divorce is understandable against this background. He himself shows what positive factor he was defending by his strict prohibition, if an express name has to be given to it, when in his philosophical *Sittenlehre* (§ 260) he calls "*absolute union*" the "*ideal of romantic love.*" When he is speaking about marriage, he is speaking consistently and unrestrictedly about the marriage, the fellowship of husband and wife, which finds fulfilment in the *unconditional* fellowship of *one* man with *one* woman. If he speaks about the *Lord's* will in this regard, for him this amounts to no more than a definitive and eternal affirmation and confirmation of this ideal of marriage and its truth and dignity. As he sees it, the ideal of romantic love is the will of God. Hardness of heart for him is being closed to this ideal, and the softening effected by Christ is a new opening up to it, the Christian church being the place where this sanctuary, among others, is maintained and guarded and proclaimed. All this undoubtedly has a slightly different aspect in Mt. 19[3ff.], although the negation in which the words of Jesus culminate: No divorce, coincides exactly with that of Schleiermacher. The dignity that Jesus seeks to protect by this negation, the positive thing that stands behind his prohibition, is obviously not marriage, least of all in the form of the ideal of romantic love,

[21]I, 596.
[22]F. Schleiermacher, *Entwurf eines Systems der Sittenlehre*. From Schleiermacher's MS remains, ed. J. H. von Kirchmann (Berlin, 1870) (*Sämmtliche Werke*, 3, *Zur Philosophie*, Vol. V).
[23]*Die christliche Sitte* . . . , p. 352.
[24]I, 581; cf. p. 111.

but God's command relative to marriage, as *God's* command. About marriage as such, as a human value or as a place where heaven and earth unite, the whole passage from which Schleiermacher takes his text has nothing positive to say at all, although in relation to it, at least in Matthew's account, a three-fold question of some weight is posed at the end in the sayings about eunuchs (v. 12). According to this saying there are necessities, including the supreme necessity of the kingdom of heaven, which make it impossible that the normal ideal of love and marriage should be universal. Even when Jesus speaks about marriage, there is for him something higher than marriage, and if we look at the matter closely we can only say that even when he is speaking expressly about marriage he is not really speaking about marriage and its sanctity but about a very different thing, namely, the sanctity of the divine *order* that is present from the very first. This and not marriage is challenged by the casuistical question of the Pharisees which initiates the whole dialogue. Lack of respect for this, not lack of mature sexual morality, is what he calls hardness of heart. It is to restore this, not to proclaim a positive ideal of love and marriage, that Jesus rejects divorce. Here, as throughout the New Testament, monogamy is a sign of repentance and obedience set up against human licentiousness and caprice. It is a likeness of the uniqueness of God over against the plurality of the world's biotic forces. As a human ideal monogamy can hardly be called a *Christian* preference in comparison with polygamy. It is a *Christian* preference because in it the shadow of the cross falls on the area of sex. This is why its proclamation causes fear and trembling: "The disciples said to him, 'If such is the case of a man with his wife, *it is not expedient to marry*' " [Mt. 19:10]. These disciples understood what it was all about: not a further deepening, enriching, refining, or spiritualizing of marriage, but in opposition to the human impulses which are at best ordered and restricted in marriage, and hampered from their most flagrant outbreaks, the assertion of *God's* right to the *whole* man. And if we ask whether the primary distinction that is suggested here is merely a verbal distinction we should consider what results from it on the two sides.

1. The prohibition of divorce in Mt. 19[3ff.] is, in the form of a material demand, a *categorical imperative* precisely because its content is the command of God and for no other reason. When the Pharisees ask whether divorce is right they are referred to God, and the answer that it is *not* right carries with it an appeal to God and nothing else. In virtue of its content, for which the whole problem of marriage is merely an occasion, the prohibition of Jesus—who dare contest this!—is grounded in the autonomy of God and it is for this reason of universal validity for all times and circumstances. It is a first and last word in this matter. In contrast, Schleiermacher's prohibition is unequivocally based on a *material* principle and it is *not*, therefore, a categorical imperative. It presupposes something other than God himself, namely, the supreme good or value of marriage. Hence Schleiermacher obviously cannot succeed even in asserting its universality, although he obviously wants to do so. How can an *ideal*, no matter how lofty, ever be universal if it is not grounded in God but in a good? It holds good in the fellowship of the Christian church. Here, and according to Schleiermacher *more* after the wars of liberation than in the sad period of church lukewarmness that preceded them, the power that emanates from Christ is at work to counteract that hardness of

heart and to promote mature sexual morality among the peoples of western and central Europe. But obviously the establishment, if not the validity, of the Christian prohibition of divorce depends on the fluctuating state of the church's barometer. It plainly did not affect the Schleiermacher of 1805 in the same way as it did the more mature Schleiermacher of 1818. Only today can the prohibition of divorce be established, and later, with the further progress of the Christian communion, deuterogamy will be forbidden, and who knows what further refinements may come in the future as Christians are increasingly transformed into moral supermen. The question arises what relation there really is between the validity of Christian truth, or truth of any kind, and these processes of development. Should this validity be dependent on whether Schleiermacher as an individual, or the Prussian church as such, made progress between 1805 and 1818 and will, it is hoped, continue to do so? With what authority is one demand made today, another tomorrow, and another, perhaps, the day after tomorrow? Is this the authority of the Spirit or of nature? Can *real* pneumatic authority be delegated to such a relative and fluctuating construct as the fellowship of the Christian church? In other words, is this fellowship of the Christian church which moves with time, and develops and improves itself, really the Christian church, the place where true pneumatic authority is validly established?

2. In Mt. 19[3ff.] the prohibition of divorce is undoubtedly established as a rule with no exceptions. Those who transgress it have to consider how they will answer for it to God. The Mosaic exception proves the rule: Where hardness of heart and rebellion against God have to be presupposed, there a bill of divorce is a possibility, but only there, that is, only where what is ruled out from a Christian standpoint is presupposed. In contrast, Schleiermacher's prohibition, although it is vigorously upheld against all kinds of excuses, can conclude only by saying that in *most cases* we Christians should be ashamed of the incidence of divorces among us. Why only in *most* cases? The preacher seems to be sure of his point, but not *completely* sure as he would be if a "good" and God were one and the same. How are we to agree whether in a given instance we have one of the "most cases" or one of the other possibilities? In his *Christliche Sitte*[25] Schleiermacher is even more reticent about the compass of the prohibition than in the sermon: "The church must achieve a greater influence over the *contracting* of marriages before it can think that the time is ripe to declare all existing marriages to be indissoluble." Until that time comes we must have serious objections to negating all divorce in puristic fashion (p. 351). "The time is ripe." Until then? What needs to be said about this has been said already. The point is obvious that there are exceptions and that there will be for some time. But is a demand that allows exceptions a *real* demand, that is, a wish, a command, of authority? If not, with what right dare the church pester the public with demands when it is sure, but not completely sure, that they are true and valid? Are not such demands merely principles derived from the natural history of the human race?

3. What was said in Mt. 19[3ff.] *was* said. The Christian church is the fellowship in which people let what Christ said according to the witness of

the apostles *be said to them*. Naturally we can always ignore the authority of the apostles and that of Christ. We can appeal from these authorities to that of God himself. But what can this mean when the apostles' demand for faith refers us to Christ and that of Christ refers us to God and his command, when the point of all revelation is referral to this final court? In what can the Christian church find its real meaning if not in accepting and promoting this referral as it is given by Christ according to the witness of the apostles, and naturally in doing so with all the means at its disposal? Any exception to this rule in the form of not letting this be said to us, and not saying it, can obviously again be only a proving of the rule, which consists of the fact that when the church thinks it can evade the referral to God, no matter on what grounds, it is *not* the Christian church. But clearly Schleiermacher cannot champion the view that a prohibition with the kind of validity and authority described under 1. and 2. must be accepted and promoted as one that is fully, unconditionally, and unrestrictedly spoken by Christ. This explains his fatal defense of Evangelical practice regarding divorce as compared with Roman Catholic practice, the upshot of which, in my view, is simply that at this point the Roman Catholic Church *is* the Christian church and the Evangelical Church, as things now are, is *not*, since at the decisive point it *evades* the task of accepting and promoting that referral to God. Has it not struck you how brilliantly Schleiermacher argues so long as he can engage in an abstract discussion, against the background of the ideal of romantic love, of divorce and its sophistical justification, but how tenuous are the four reasons he gives in opposition to the demand that the church should refuse to remarry divorced persons? If the church is sure of its cause that there ought to be no divorce—and in the sermon it looks at first as though this is true of Schleiermacher—then obviously it should not simply preach this on Sunday and impress it upon hopeful young people at the confirmation class on Monday, working toward the possible honoring of the truth one day in the future, but then on Thursday bless a marriage of divorced persons with exactly the same rite as is used on other occasions. What sentimentality it is to say that the Evangelical Church deplores all this, that its ministers find no joy in hearing Yes from lips that once already have changed the Yes into a No, that it does not approve, but that it still obeys, that it obeys the state, being then able to make out that it is the wicked state that wants this, though even on its own ground it does not object but assents in the name of God. What has the regard for possibly fatal consequences; what has the pitiable fear that will not claim superiority over the state, as though this superiority were not self-evident; what has the scrupulosity that will not punish the innocent, as though there were any question of punishment here: what has all this to do with the truth that is proclaimed on Sunday if this is resolutely believed to be the truth, if it is realized that the prohibition of divorce carries a reference to God and not a mere reference to a "good"? The church should not lament, nor should its ministers make solemn and disapproving faces, but they should do their duty and proclaim the prohibition of divorce as an inalienable part of revelation, and proclaim it *totally*, that is, not merely in words but in deeds that unequivocally pronounce the needed No, that is, in a *refusal* to remarry divorced persons, as is rightly the rule in the Roman Catholic Church. All the worse if even there they can sometimes evade this rule with casuistical wiles and tricks, yet it is the rule there, whereas with us the opposite is the rule. Or should the Evangelical Church, or, let us say, the church of Schleiermacher, accept the fact that with the contradiction of word and deed it does not really take its *word* seriously, its prohibition that is not promoted unconditionally or without loopholes? That it really knows—and this alone really explains its inconsistency—that its prohibition of divorce along the lines of Schleiermacher and on the basis of the ideal of romantic love is not Christian truth, nor even truth at all?

Our only remaining task is to gain acquaintance with the positive factor which is to be found in Schleiermacher's doctrine of marriage at the point where the concept of divine order occurs in his texts in Eph. 5[22–31] and Mt. 19[8]. I refer to what we have thus far described in his own phrase as the *ideal of romantic love*. We shall do this best in the announced excursus on his famous *Vertraute Briefe über Friedrich Schlegels Lucinde* of 1800 and some passages from his *Monologen* that appeared in the same year [*Lucindebrief* (*Philosophische Werke*, I, 421–506, ed. Gutzkow [1835], ed. Fränkel [1907] [Diederichs], Reclam).[26] *Monologen* (*Philosophische Werke*, I, 345–420, Reclam; *Philosophische Bibliothek* [1902], ed. Schiele [Vol. 84]).[27] Schlegel's *Lucinde* (Reclam; Diederichs)[28]].[29] The *Briefe über die Lucinde* were written by Schleiermacher to defend his best friend's novel when it ran into a storm of almost universal protest from the public. The intellectual, literary, biographical, and psychological questions that are posed by Schlegel's book, Schleiermacher's apology, and especially the relationship between the two, need not affect us here. [For details see Dilthey, *Leben Schleiermachers*[2], pp. 530ff.;[30] R. Haym, *Die romantische Schule*[2], pp. 493ff.][31] I will summarize the essential points. Friedrich Schlegel, a highly talented but in every respect undisciplined writer of the first order, thought it to be appropriate to present to his contemporaries his confession of a chaos of spirit and nature, or nature and spirit, which he regarded as a new morality. He did this very suitably in the form of a glorification of Eros Pantocrator, if not Venus multivaga, which only displays his own lack of any stability or critical ability and leads at every point only into sand, if not something less clean than sand. The material triviality of this enterprise is not redeemed by any *esthetic* qualities, for from this standpoint, too, it has in it nothing worthy of note. All the same Schleiermacher, who was then preacher at the Charité, took it upon himself, at first anonymously

---

[26]F. Schleiermacher, *Vertraute Briefe über Friedrich Schlegels Lucinde (Sämmtliche Werke, 2, Zur Philosophie)* (Berlin, 1846), I, 421–506; ed. K. F. Gutzkow (1835); ed. J. Fränkel (Jena/Leipzig, 1907).
[27]F. Schleiermacher, *Monologen (Sämmtliche Werke, 3, Zur Philosophie)* (Berlin, 1846), I, 345–420; Schiele ed. [Mulert], see p. 3, n. 1.
[28]F. Schlegel, *Lucinde. Ein Roman*, ed. J. Fränkel (Jena, 1907); joint ed. of *Lucinde* and the *Briefe* (Stuttgart, 1835; Leipzig, 1907; Frankfurt, 1964 Insel-Bücherei, 759).
[29]The brackets are Barth's, both here and in what follows.
[30]See p. xiii, n. 3.
[31]R. Haym, *Die romantische Schule* (Berlin, 1906[2]); unrevised photocopy of the first edition (Berlin, 1870) (Darmstadt, 1961).

and then openly, to defend the book. In spite of some freely expressed formal and material criticisms, he refers to his constant enjoyment of the "lofty beauty and poetry of this unique and excellent work" (*Philosophische Werke*, I, 506), of the "infinity" of *Lucinde* (p. 496), of the thousand expressions of regard and affection (p. 424) that he has for this "divine book" (p. 491), of this "work which is like a phenomenon of a future and God alone knows how distant world" (p. 423, cf. p. 466), of the "gigantic and colossal morality" on which it rests as on an "eternal foundation" (p. 491). He declares as strongly as possible his *solidarity* with Schlegel. That the classical exponent of Christianity in the age of Goethe did at least display a gaping lack of *esthetic* tact and taste in this matter is something on which even the most enthusiastic of the more recent followers of Schleiermacher are regretfully agreed. Apart from all else, he was *taken in* here by something which competent children of the world like Friedrich Schiller at once stated candidly to be trash, or empty chatter, that could only do harm (Haym, p. 518). The unselfish *chivalry* with which he would not leave his compromised friend in the lurch explains a little but not everything and not the main thing; the letters are written with much too much personal involvement for that. The same applies to the problem of his own very difficult relationship to Eleonore Grunow at this time, for while this motivated him to speak out on the subject, it does not explain why he could not equally well, or better, have done this independently. Nor can one appeal to his happy knack of finding and acknowledging something *great* and beautiful and noble and true in *everything*, even under a contrary form: "I deal bashfully and prudently and respectfully with everything that shows itself to be cultivated, whether a person, a thought, or a civilized work" (p. 423). For he did not deal this way with Kant, whose theological agent and executor he is now lauded as being,[32] but the very opposite. Why then with someone like Friedrich Schlegel? And if it is rightly pointed out[33] that he simply imports *his own esthetic view* of love into Schlegel's novel, and then reads it out of the novel in the approved manner, this is simply to draw attention to the obvious puzzle how it was possible for so acute a critic of all existing moral teachings not to notice the heavenwide difference between his own ethics and Schlegel's but guilelessly to offer his own variation of the latter. If we can be satisfied on the esthetic side that we simply have a blind spot on the part of the great man here, we are forced to say of Schleiermacher the *ethicist, philosopher, and theologian* that he *must* unconditionally have noted the irreconcilable difference between himself and Schlegel—provided it was really there. It would seem from the extant correspondence, however, that in spite of reservations on both sides Schleiermacher's *Reden* and Schlegel's novel were regarded and reviewed by both authors as twin productions, and that each enthusiastically recognized his own genius in the work of the other, Schleiermacher more so than Schlegel,[34] the only difference being that the one book proclaimed the mysteries of religion and the other the mysteries of love.

[32]Cf. A. Titius, "Schleiermacher und Kant" in *Schleiermacher der Philosoph des Glaubens* (cf. p. xiv, n. 7), pp. 36–56; G. Wobbermin, *Systematische Theologie nach religionspsychologischer Methode* (cf. p. xiv, n. 5), pp. 4f.

[33]Haym, pp. 523f. and 530.

[34]Cf. Br., I, 237ff., 286f., 289f.; Br., III, 105.

But Schleiermacher could also offer a religious commentary on Schlegel's message of love, while Schlegel only toyed with the idea—which as a dilettante he happily never carried out—of composing a new "Bible" which would be in harmony with the message of *Lucinde* (Haym, p. 495). As was not the case in later Schleiermacher research the two participants, whom we must allow to speak first, did *not* view the difference as irreconcilable. As the later break between the two friends shows, it was in fact irreconcilable given their characters, personalities, attitudes, and modes of life. But this does not prove that their messages as they themselves felt and taught and stated them were not products of the same kitchen or apples from the same tree. This does not in any way affect Schleiermacher personally—quite the contrary—but it does throw *light* on his view of *religion* and his view of *love*, which we can now discuss without further reference to Schlegel.

In the household sermons of 1818 as well as in the writings of 1800 this was a doctrine of *romantic* love even though some things were said in 1800 that were no longer said in 1818, other things, especially the emphasis on monogamy, were stated later with greater *definiteness*, and everything was given a more Christian or *churchly* emphasis. Freethinking critics of Schleiermacher as well as theological apologists are mistaken when they suppose that he retreated or changed in the intervening years. Those who do not understand that the old *and* the young Schleiermacher wanted to be a romantic as a Christian and a Christian as a romantic do not understand him at all. *"Love shall rise again"* (*Philosophische Werke*, I, 428), declares Schleiermacher, and the expression reminds us immediately how the sermons of 1818 culminate in a kind of sexual eschatology, in the prospect of a type of marriage that far surpasses the present state of things in intensity and duration. What does he mean when he says that love shall rise again? He continues: "Its divided members will be *united* and ensouled by a new life so that it will rule merrily and freely in the *minds* of men *and* in their *works*" (p. 428). How will this union and this free and merry ruling take place? What is there to unite? The sensual and the spiritual aspects of love, replies Schleiermacher. (We remember from the sermons that marriage is a union of earthly and heavenly elements.)[35] It must not be that "sensual desire takes the form of (an) instinct that does not know what it wants or an appetite that aims at direct sensation" (p. 447), "that we do not know how to make anything but a necessary evil out of sensuality" (p. 430). "Love as the fulness of living power" should not be opposed to its "intellectual, mystical counterpart" (p. 481), "as the separate work of a powerful deity on its own" (p. 482). Joy in the sensual element in love can never be too loudly expressed, but it must always "be related to fusion with the spiritual element; once it loses this reference[36] and stands alone it sounds a hostile note"[37] (p. 446). There should be no pleasure in love "without inspiration," without enthusiasm (= being in God), without the mystical element that consists of God being in lovers, "their encirclement," and therefore "properly speaking his enclosing which they feel together at the

---

[35]Cf. p. 112.
[36]Schleiermacher has "accompaniment."
[37]Schleiermacher has "too loud a note."

same moment and then desire" (p. 447). Nor should the *"spiritual constituent"* in love be isolated and cultivated separately, for we do not know what to do with this either and in face of it we can only ask why people "finally take refuge in a normal and fruitful marriage and do not in love embark on the heroic feat of living together in a sublime spiritual fellowship without thinking of anything for which according to their assurances they have no cause in their feelings" (p. 430). It is "English practice" (pp. 435, 439, 441) even for a wife, and especially for a wife, not to confess any "love in reality" (p. 437). True *modesty* is not avoiding a consciousness of certain ideas in oneself and others but having regard to the disposition of another, not violently cutting it short (pp. 450f., 456), but respecting the other's freedom where it is vulnerable and insecure (p. 457). It can also be shameless violently to cut short (p. 458) the state of enjoyment and dominant sensuality, which is also holy, by a dry objectification of the animal or physiological element in love (p. 460). A modesty that rests on this interruption (i.e., modesty in the usual sense) "has its basis only in the sense of a great and universal distortion and a profound corruption" (p. 462). The aim is to get back to innocence by the completing of culture, and this will mean the end of true as well as false modesty to the extent that it merges here into the general disposition in which it is involved (p. 463). The task of *women* in particular, "in whom the union of the inner and the outer is much more delicate and tender" (p. 463), is to open the way to this innocent freedom for "the most beautiful and tender of all things . . . in the art of living" (pp. 463f.). Over against every one-sidedness we have the longing—fulfilled in Schlegel's *Lucinde*—"to see love for once fashioned in all its fulness and not in torn off buds and leaves" (pp. 430f.). "Here you have love all of a piece, its *most spiritual* and *most sensual* elements not only together in the same work and the same persons, but *united as inwardly as possible* in every expression and feature" (p. 431). In face of this composition Schleiermacher calls it a crime even to *mention* the two parts of love separately, and he asks its genius for pardon that he has done so even if only for a moment (p. 431). "Nothing divine can be split up without desecration into its elements of spirit and flesh, of choice and nature" (p. 447). In love we cannot stop at the antithesis; "the ideas produced by the new development of man" (Schleiermacher is obviously thinking of contemporary philosophy) must be applied and progress must take place. "Should one not demand that men should be able to realize them here, too, in this simple matter? They know about *body and spirit and the identity of the two*, and this is the whole secret" (pp. 481f.). The extraordinary thing about Schlegel's *Lucinde* is that it brings into "chemical union" the two elements in love which elsewhere are wrongly set in antithesis.

In the *Monologen*, which we will use only by way of supplement (III "Weltansicht," IV "Aussicht"), Schleiermacher does not stress so much the union of spirit and nature as that of husband and wife, of *one* husband and *one* wife. It is the second of the two sermons on marriage in 1818[38] that becomes understandable in this light. Husband and wife—"from the harmony of their natures" a *new and common will* should develop as they themselves

[38]Cf. pp. 113ff.

come forth from the womb of their love (p. 57).[39] Every home should contain "the beautiful body, the beautiful work of an individual soul, and have its own form and features. . . . Does she make him happy and live wholly for him? Does he make her happy and is he all kindness? Does nothing make both of them so happy as sacrificing the self for the other?" (p. 58). "I yearn for a new world," soliloquizes the author, and among the first and most important things that he has in mind he mentions this: "But the most sacred union must lift me to a new level of life; I must fuse into one being with a beloved soul, so that *in the most beautiful way my humanity may work on humanity*; so that I may know that after the resurrection of freedom the transfigured higher life may be formed in me as the old man begins the new world" (pp. 74f.). Now of course fate, the freedom of others, the course of the world, and the mysteries of nature seem to oppose the fulfilment of this longing. "Where might she dwell with whom it is fitting that I should join my life? Who can say where I must go to seek her? . . . And if I find her under an alien law that keeps her from me, can I release her?" (p. 75). (To his friends this was obviously a reference to Eleonore Grunow.) Yet even if everything is impossible, the author will not think of himself as vanquished by fate. "The impossibility of the outward act does not prevent inner action; and more than for myself and her I will lament for the world . . . which is losing a rare and beautiful example, which is forfeiting a manifestation from the better future by which it might have received new warmth and life for its dead concepts. As for us, as surely as we belong to one another, imagination will carry us even unknown into our beautiful paradise. Not for nothing have I seen many forms of the feminine mind and come to know the beautiful modes of their quiet life. The further I stand from its boundaries, the more carefully I have investigated the sacred territory of marriage; I know what is right there and what is not; I have fashioned every possible form of what is appropriate as only a later and free age will reveal it, and I know very well what is fitting for me. Hence I know incognito the one with whom I might find the most inward life-union and I am at home in the most beautiful life that we might live together. As I now sadly plan and begin many things in arid solitude, I must be silent and hold back and withdraw into myself in little things and small; but there always hovers vividly before me how it would all be different and better in that life. *And so it undoubtedly is with her too, wherever she might be*, who is so made that she might love me and that I might satisfy her; the same longing, which is more than (an) empty desire, raises her up, as it does me, out of the bleak reality for which she was not made, and if a magic stroke should suddenly lead us together, nothing would be strange to us; as though we were bound to sweet and ancient habit, we should walk so sweetly and easily in the new way of life. Hence even without that magic stroke the higher existence is still present in us; we are formed for [and through] this life, and only its outward representation is missing to the world. Oh if only people knew how to use the divine power of imagination . . . !" (pp. 76f.).

I have given you this famous passage in full because it shows that what seems to be the ecclesiastically rigorous prohibition of divorce that Schleier-

---

[39]The page references are to the F. M. Schiele edition.

macher pronounced, not in 1800 but in 1818, is grounded in the contemporary ideal of love by which he was sustained as a young man, and obviously grounded in this *alone*. The author of the *Monologen* in 1800 believes, as we have seen, in an *invisible* marriage which is actually *contracted* (later he will say in heaven) apart from its actualization or nonactualization. Two people *belong to one another*, no matter what may lie between them, and when they *find one another*—or even if they do *not*, then, in defiance of fate, by the divine power of imagination—their predestination is fulfilled. No wonder that a bond of this kind is declared to be indissoluble. One might well say that Schleiermacher would have had to make this declaration even if he had not found Mt. 19[3ff.] in his New Testament. The asserted break in his development whereby he wanted to release a separated woman in 1805 and then in 1818 maintained that this is against the Lord's will cannot, then, have been a break in principle. Incidentally, note in the extracts from the *Monologen* the quasi-*eschatological* significance that Schleiermacher accords to his ideal of love even though this is already a present reality. As one who was "alien to the thinking and life of the present generation," as "a prophetic citizen of a later world," he felt in this connection "that he was strongly drawn to it by living imagination and strong faith, that every act and thought belonged to it" (p. 61). From these very individualistic-sounding references to a better future develops later his doctrine of the evolving fellowship of the church as the bearer of a purer sexual morality.

Let us turn back again to the Lucinde letters. We have not yet mentioned the most distinctive feature of Schleiermacher's doctrine of love. This is the religious transfiguration which according to him comes upon the union of man and woman, or nature and spirit, in marriage. As we have seen, God has to be in those who love and their embracing is really his (*Philosophische Werke*, I, 447). This point is made in Schlegel's book too. "Everything in it is both human and divine, a magical breath of holiness comes out of its innermost depths and spreads through the whole temple and consecrates all whose organ has not become ossified" (p. 483). "I cannot describe to you how I feel," says one of the fictional letter-writers after reading *Lucinde*, "I feel within myself the omnipotence of love, the *divinity of man*, and the beauty of life. . . .' 'To follow the rhythm of companionship and friendship and not to disrupt the harmony of love,' is there any higher wisdom or *deeper religion*?" (p. 495). There is supposedly a return of the ancient idea of the "sanctity of nature and sensuality": "the ancient delight and joy and the mingling of bodies and life" is supposedly one "with the most profound and sacred feeling, with the fusing and uniting of the two halves of humanity in a mystic whole. Those who cannot contemplate the inwardness of divinity and humanity in this way and grasp the mysteries of this religion are not worthy to be citizens of a new world"[40] [p. 482]. Is it saying too much to speak of the bedazzlement with which the one Friedrich expressly attributes to the other the dignity of a "priest and liturgist of this new religion" (p. 482)? It is certainly not surprising to hear the admirer speak of the "most holy worship of humanity and the universe in the beloved" (p. 431) and to read from the pen of his female coun-

[40]Schleiermacher has "the new world."

terpart, who addresses him as "Thou infinite one" (p. 487), the following rhapsody: "When, leaning on my breast, in the direct proximity of my heart, you whisper all your joy in me, and all your longing for the beautiful life that we contemplate together, then we both have the most profound feeling that we are wholly one, and like a divine lightning which almost consumes me, there flashes through me an infinite nexus of similar thoughts and feelings that stretches from highest heaven to the center of the earth and illumines and transfigures for me past and future and you and me and all things" (p. 489). Immediately before, the same lady offers an *even* clearer paraphrase of the doctrine of identity which I will spare both you and myself. I think I have said enough. This is "the ideal of romantic love." |

For the sake of completeness I will at least mention certain subsidiary points which arise out of this basic thought and which have claimed some attention. Here as in the sermons Schleiermacher, in a slight criticism of Schlegel, demands that *civil calling* should be a correlate of love. "The light-hearted person should still have something of the knight about him and should be like Hercules in his deeds." "Those who cannot play their part in the world ought not to love," and a depiction of love apart from this relationship is just as alien to Schleiermacher "as it was to our blessed father when there was talk of faith without works" (p. 444, cf. p. 503). This was a plain hint to the other Friedrich, the eulogist of sophisticated indolence, and it was over this difference that their friendship later foundered. |

Another secondary doctrine in the work is that of the lack of any ulterior motive in true love. Even the thought of future parenthood is not an original feature but signalizes the need to take note again of the outside *world* which has at first faded from the view of the lovers, the resurgence of the *care* which is alien to the first joy of love in which it sees itself rather "in its divine invulnerability and immortality" (p. 494). |

Schleiermacher evoked much opposition and criticism (even from Dilthey)[41] with a third subsidiary teaching of the same kind in a passage in which he describes love as an *art* that must be learned like eating and drinking. "In love too" there have to be *"preliminary attempts"* which have no lasting results. Mistakes may arise about the *object* of our feelings, but these can only help to make our feelings "more definite and to make the prospect of love greater and more glorious." "To demand love here and to try to establish a lasting relationship" would be "an illusion no less damaging than empty." Instead we should distinguish with holy awe between relationships that are futile attempts and those that can become "the beginning of a beautiful and authentic love" (pp. 473–475). I cannot agree with the condemnation of this passage but find it reasonable and full of insight from a pastoral standpoint. From it we can figure out how the *younger* Schleiermacher could have arrived at a theoretical justification of divorce as the ending of an unsuccessful attempt of this kind. But from the same passage we can also understand how the *older* Schleiermacher could come to reject divorce, for with the entry into marriage as a definitive recognition of predestination for one another such

[41]Cf. Dilthey, *Leben Schleiermachers*, pp. 544–546.

attempts are in principle left behind and unconditional fidelity is the only possibility.

In my view there is only one serious objection that one can raise against the *Lucinde-Briefe*. All the individual objections that can be and have been leveled against it make sense only if it is perceived that they boil down to this one objection. But because for understandable reasons this is usually not perceived it is dangerous to consult the critics of this little book. It can happen only too easily that we appear to be, and are, no more than scolding philistines and moralists who do not understand the man, who do not do him justice, and who reject his logic even before he has opened his mouth, and all this precisely because we adopt the same basic position, that of an affirmation of life which for all its perspicacity is disturbingly uncritical, that of the secret quid pro quo that we men are gods, that the good is a power of nature at work in us, and that the highest conceivable thing in this world is the commencement within it of the world to come. Those who share this basic conception with Schleiermacher, those who do not with *total* clarity know something different, cannot really contradict his doctrine of love and marriage, whether in the sermons or in the *Lucinde-Briefe*—for the doctrine is *the same* in both.

2. *Bringing Up Children*. This is not merely the most important business of Christian parents. All members of the Christian church should lay it upon their hearts. The younger generation as a whole is brought up by the elder generation as a whole. There are those who think they can achieve everything by educating children and there are others who expect nothing from it. Both must be told that in relation to children we must pay heed to the will of God and do it. In the three sermons that Schleiermacher preached on the theme in 1818 he based his thoughts on the familiar passages from Paul's household tables in Col. 3[20f.] and Eph. 6[1–4].

He is first interested by the statement: "Fathers, do not provoke your children," μὴ ἐρεθίζετε (I, 598ff.).[42] It is bad enough already that the fatal inclinations of the parents that slumber in the children are aroused by living with the parents and by their example, that older sin gives rise to younger, and that often new and individual sins will arise in children through opposition and antithesis to those of parents. All this is regrettable and humiliating. It is also *unnatural* if children are set in a movement of *hostility* to their parents when they are more closely related to them than the parents are to each other, and when by God and nature they ought to find themselves together with them in the innermost and most undisturbed sanctuary of love. But the same applies to the aversion of children to the teachers whom their parents provide for them and who are brought into the same holy circle of nature whose disruption by the extinguishing of love is against nature. Such provocation, however, is *pernicious* as well as unnatural. Combatting the faults of children demands that they come to us for healing, and that in their respectful trust we should find an ally in place of the enemy. What contact can we make with them if they are only bitter and hostile? *This* enemy, mistrust, must be starved out by the withholding of nourishment, by inexhaustible

---

[42]The subject was "The Christian Upbringing of Children," and the text Col. 3:21.

patience, by full self-control, by the purest self-denial. In contrast, the crude way of force is a dangerous one. Entering upon it shows that we either lack or do not know how to use the reason and love by which we should be guided. We certainly do not get through to our children by force and we usually emerge resigned and defeated, leaving the children to their own devices and to God's instruction. Yet if only we see to it that they do not become withdrawn, the situation may easily be remedied. If that disaster befalls, all is ruined and lost. It should also be considered that we adults need the young no less than they need us. To what can the pious retreat from the eternally shifting theater of confused secular relations, from the maze of business, from the multiplicity of provisions and projects, from disturbing intercourse with all the vain and selfish ideas of the earthly minded mob, to what can they retreat if not primarily to the narrow circle of their own homes? And where can we find the needed forgetfulness of the world, where can we meet the original placid form of life, if not in the carefree and eager youngsters who, when we return home, see in us only our joy at being there and feel only that they have missed us. Happy are we if this is our daily experience! But woe to us if through our egotistic indifference or capriciousness, through the coldness or unevenness that we bring with us from outside, our children come to share our worldly cares and concerns, meeting us anxiously, hiding all kinds of things from us out of regard for our moods, so that we are responsible for continuing the unworthy features of the wider spheres of life in our own homes! How can we believe in something perfect beyond the imperfections of society unless we can already see something of it, and where and how can we see it except in our children? We can see in them not only our own failings but also something of a hopeful future: "that the sons will be better, and because better, better off, than their fathers."[43] There is nothing more uplifting in face of vicissitudes of life than the way in which Jacob, when he blesses his sons [cf. Gen. 49:1–28], "allots to each his special place . . . in the affairs of the kingdom of God and the enjoyment of its blessings." "This prophetic vision in Jacob was not just the fruit of his faith in the impregnable divine word" but also the result of his accurate knowledge of the qualities of his children. So we, too, should be open to what is in our children. We should be able to see into the depths of their minds and perceive all the folds of their hearts. If through bitterness they become withdrawn in relation to us, then they will be closed to us and we shall be deprived of this joy. For the children's sake, therefore, and for our own too, sacrificial love above all. If sometimes our conduct might cause temporary bitterness in our children, there is divine forgiveness. God has equipped the human soul with the gift of *forgetfulness* on the one side and *discernment* on the other. Young people easily rise above details and learn to distinguish between transitory movements and the fixed direction or dominant orientation of our lives. If only the totality of our lives and the innermost core of our hearts might be pure before God and our children!

In the second sermon (I, 612ff.)[44] Schleiermacher turns to the positive goal of education. It concerns the *development of their spiritual gifts* in a way that

---

[43]This and the quotations that follow are from *Predigten*, I, 609.
[44]"The Christian Upbringing of Children. Second Sermon"; text: Eph. 6:4.

is right and pleasing to God. It should be and is a matter for the work of the divine Spirit. We declare confidence that this is so through the sacrament of *baptism*. Hence we adults are simply tools of this divine Spirit who, believing in progress in all that constitutes human dignity, seek to be educators to God's glory. The essence of all Christian upbringing is to make children capable of accepting the image of the Redeemer. The emphasis now falls on the text: "Bring them up in the discipline and instruction of the Lord" [Eph. 6:4]. In this verse Paul is not speaking about some of the many individual features of training and instruction but about the *totality*. He mentions *discipline* first, that is, moral upbringing. Discipline is not the same as *punishment*. It presupposes obedience. It promotes action, not suffering. It asks from the child the effort from which inner joy will flow. It is the love that drives out all fear and inclines the heart to the good. It gives a wholesome knowledge of the power of the will and a sense of freedom and inner order. True discipline makes punishment superfluous. Yet it is also the opposite of the *inactivity* that would simply watch the free development of the children "as though a work of the divine Spirit could begin in (them) without God using the parents and others as his instruments for this purpose . . . as though the good could be awakened and could develop by nature without the Spirit that dwells in the community of Christians."[45] We offend against the admonition to use discipline if we unthinkingly follow common custom and order in bringing up our children no less than if we try to force them into our own particular way of life and make them as much like ourselves as possible, or if we view as the goal of education the reaching of certain external earthly goals, or if out of vanity we overtax their powers. From the standpoint of discipline the *dealings* of the children with one another must also be considered and directed, "so that they may learn how to maintain fellowship with those of very different temperaments and by being helpful and obliging produce a happy life, learning to subdue disruptive and hostile moods."[46] The same with their games: "In these they should learn to use and control all the powers that will least be claimed by their work,"[47] so that for them enjoyment is not just the opposite of effort and the seeking of it will no longer be a danger. Nevertheless— and here the preacher turns to *religious* instruction—it is not enough to tame the flesh; we must also awaken the *joy of the spirit* in our children. The powers that are stimulated and exercised must find their true Lord. Beyond discipline, then, there is needed the "instruction of the Lord." It is true that the Spirit blows where he wills, but when he comes he opens our lips to extol the mighty acts of God. "Especially those that he does in the human soul, for there are none more mighty."[48] One should never say that it is too soon to speak to young people about the things of God. Ungodly things are all around us and threaten us on every side, flattering the minds of the young. It is appropriate, then, "to give the wandering soul a sense of the need for higher assistance, to bring God near to it."[49] It is said that young people *cannot as*

[45]I, 616.
[46]I, 619.
[47]*Loc. cit.*
[48]I, 621.
[49]I, 622.

yet understand what we can tell them about God and the Redeemer. "But let us simply ask, do *we* comprehend God? are we able to encompass and measure the Redeemer?"[50] And do we refuse to concern ourselves with him because we cannot put his influence on us in precise and universally valid and understandable expressions? Are the things of this world more comprehensible to our children than the Eternal? Understood in their childlike terms, is not the kernel of truth already present which will develop with increasing strength and put off its childlike husk? It is for us to see to it that the early teaching about God and divine things will not become a *dead letter* for our children; let us take care to link it to the realities of their own lives. They can understand the difference between what is godly and ungodly, and the meaning of dependence on God and blessedness in the doing of his will, only when they know something about the obligations and complications of life. But they are well able to know about *Christ* and to see God in the image to which he has directed us too. "As soon as they can take note of us and our whole life and begin to see its inner and spiritual side," the question necessarily arises: Where does this come from? and this is identical with the question: Who is this? How could we then withhold from them the one whose life in us all this is that they honor and love in us? Would it not be trying to snatch for ourselves the glory that belongs to him if we were not to refer them to him who has given it so that they might become the same themselves . . . ?"[51] (cf. Good Friday sermon at Landsberg, 1794).[52] Nor can this instruction be restricted to purely religious teaching; *all* instruction must be in the Lord, and beyond words our whole lives must become instruction, so that our love should be for them a weak but not too opaque or unrecognizable reflection of the eternal love. Here again we finally have to be pure in heart.

In the third sermon Schleiermacher spoke finally about the *result* of upbringing (I, 628ff.[53]). "Children, obey your parents" now stands at the center [Eph. 6:1]. He is still speaking to parents, not children, trying to show them what the effect of the Spirit that glorifies himself in the Christian community can and should be. Whether children obey is the test whether our discipline and instruction are right or not. Here, too, we must avoid as false extremes the harshness that simply awakens servile fear and the softness that seems not to require obedience but to incite to disobedience. The apostle appeals to "the ancient divine commandment,"[54] that is, to the natural relation between children and parents or the young and the old more generally. This obedience should not be evoked by the prospect of reward or punishment. Nor in true obedience should there be any reasoning or disputing as though the conviction and understanding of the children were its true source instead of respect, as though there could be argument and counterargument between parents and children. The first foundation of the obedience that rests on respect is laid in all children with the sense of the dependence of their being in all external matters. This sense is perfected in the *discipline* that sets before them the

[50]I, 623.
[51]I, 625.
[52]Pr., VII, 205ff.; cf. pp. 79f.
[53]"The Christian Upbringing of Children. Third Sermon"; text: Eph. 6:1–3.
[54]I, 631.

higher element in humanity that should rule the lower and by the *instruction* of the Lord that stirs up in them the highest and holiest that human beings possess. Why is obedience demanded? Paul refers to the promise in the Mosaic command: "that it may be well with you and that you may live long on the earth" [Eph. 6:3]. Schleiermacher takes this to mean that we can satisfy our great calling on earth, to build up and control our common patrimony for God's kingdom, only by a variegated alternation of command and obedience. Caprice is the enemy of everything that is good. For the sake of future respect for the common life we must learn to obey so that perhaps in part we may one day be able to command with authority. The second foundation for Paul is simply: "for this is right" [Eph. 6:1]. Schleiermacher defines the right, in contrast to the righteous, as the decision that proceeds without the letter from an inner sense and right evaluation of relationships (though the basic text is τοῦτο γάρ ἐστιν δίκαιον!). There comes a time when children, taking their own place in society, become responsible for their actions, when parental oversight changes into paternal and maternal friendship. But this change takes place only by degrees and perhaps with many a conflict. The required rightness consists of the children's respect for the decision of the parents beyond the measure of the obedience demanded in this transition. They will later need the same rightness when, commanding themselves, they must loyally and unselfishly promote the common good. In conclusion, the point is reiterated that the children should become *better* than their parents were, so that each upcoming generation will in its day *surpass* that by which it was instructed. For only thus can the kingdom of God be built up. And "if something great cannot always be developed from one generation to the next, nevertheless something in humanity can become better in each generation."[55]

3. Servants (I, 640ff.).[56] Schleiermacher is well aware how difficult is his subject here. Slavery has been set aside by the mollifying force of Christianity but not the justifiable complaints of dissatisfaction on the part of employers and servants, palpably so where servants are finally no more than that and have no hope of becoming independent as on the land. A new and more perfect arrangement must be made between employers and servants, but this can be done only on the basis of God's Word. In particular it must be admitted that this whole relationship, except when it is transitory, is to be regarded as a *necessary evil*, and this on both sides: It is no pleasure for employers to have to have others in their homes with their different habits, exerting an influence on the upbringing of the children, learning to know the weaknesses of the family, being under the embarrassment of having to perform all kinds of external services for reward. We should be glad that the number of real domestic servants has been generally reduced by the rise of all kinds of independent trades, so that by the general march of world events many are free today who once would have been servants. One can well understand the desire of many employers and servants to part company and the attempts by frequent moving about to find a substitute for the unhappy element in the relationship, though

---

[55]I, 639.
[56]"On Christian Servants. First Sermon"; text: 1 Cor. 7:20–23.

this, of course, only makes the evil worse. We need to see the relationship as one of an *inequality* that needs to be *corrected*. This will be done (Schleiermacher is using the text 1 Cor. 7:20ff.) when masters sense that they are the servants of *Christ* and view their relationship to servants as a part of their Christian calling. Torn from their own families, these are assigned to them in order that they might provide a replacement. In their homes servants should be affected by the gentle spirit of a moral and cultured life; they should find their models of a Christian lifestyle and Christian virtues. And in this society they should lose the feeling of coercion and servitude: "For when a servant considers that each home is a nursery for the Christian church and a mighty fortress against all the confusions of life outside he will feel honored and exalted to serve this home like one who is freed from bondage by calling."[57] The sense of *serving the common Lord* should make the two parties friends. This is the *new life* that ought to arise out of the relationship. Household prayers, or, if these cannot be restarted, common participation in public worship, ought to make this possible and natural on both sides.

Schleiermacher's second sermon on the subject[58] begins directly at this point (I, 652ff.): The difference between duty and inclination, between the important and the unimportant, must be dispelled in a *reverent sense of the sanctity of all life*. But only here does the conflict between spirit and flesh begin; we have still to reach an ordered insight into the total context of the matter. Servants must guard against the *sullenness* which does not do things from the heart ("nothing is more depressing than the constant sight of a sulky person who does nothing from the heart and therefore has no heart in anything"),[59] but also against the *obsequiousness* which knows nothing of true conviction or true loyalty, which characterizes a person as a servant, no matter how exalted his position, and which is rightly despised because it is not in any sense serious. Employers, however, must be on guard against arbitrary *caprice* and against *boasting* of their superiority, realizing that all superiority comes from the God of love and is thus granted only for love's sake, so that, where needed, love may be built up and augmented. When all this is taken into account, faults on the one side will no longer evoke faults on the other or vice versa, a fixed and general habit and order will replace individual idiosyncrasies, and truth and openness, along with security and reliability, will return in the relationship. Human society can be established only when it presents us with a picture of the whole relationship of men to God.

4. Hospitality (8th sermon, I, 665ff.).[60] According to modern usage this sermon would have been entitled "social life." Schleiermacher's aim is to speak about the Christian aspects of invitations and the social round. Like the individual Christian, the Christian household should not hide itself but as a part of God's city on his holy hill, sensing the richness of divine grace, it should be ready to extend this wealth to others. The text is Heb. 13:2: "Do not neglect

[57]I, 648; Schleiermacher has "to be helpful to" for "to serve."
[58]"On Christian Servants. Second Sermon"; text: Col. 3:22f. and 4:1.
[59]I, 657.
[60]"Christian Hospitality"; text: Heb. 13:2.

to show hospitality to strangers, for thereby some have entertained angels unawares." It is of "the essence of Christianity to spiritualize everything physical."[61] Hospitality, too, has a *physical* beginning, today when "Christian fathers, who are in some sense more closely linked, invite each other, with their families, to their homes," not so much to satisfy a true need as previously, though this element neither can nor should be totally absent: "For the compatibility of temperament would be suppressed or muffled out of which alone the freest and merriest spiritual enjoyment usually develops in social intercourse."[62] The physical and spiritual aspects must be properly related, of course, and it may "be said of our people that in all manifestations of hospitality the physical predominates more than is necessary."[63] But this danger did not stop Jesus from participating in the marriage at Cana and "giving a word of instruction and exercising an influence precisely where" there was plenty.[64] He never criticized excess. Only when no spiritual enjoyment is in view is the only worthwhile aim of social life missing from the start. When the spiritual element is crowded out by the physical, the angels of the Lord are certainly not entertained, or at any rate they do not carry words of promise on their lips. An unspiritual wasting of time stains the conscience of the true Christian and all customs must be gradually shaped in such a way that they harmonize with our spiritual life and serve to promote it. The second rule to be observed is that there must be spiritual *giving* and *receiving* in social life. First *giving*. Every Christian home should embody God's grace in a distinctive way and hence have something special to pass on. Cheerfulness and joy should not be expected from guests if these qualities are not already present in the home. One cannot try to create a wider circle if no satisfaction is found in the smaller. If this is the situation, then it is better to call a halt and to seek inner healing by repentance. We have to *show* to guests the peace of God and the blessedness of his children. Then *receiving*. In spiritual things this is just as blessed as giving. As the fathers did from angels, so we should receive promises and warnings from the like-minded guests who seek to refresh us in what is good and beautiful. And then we can and should go like God's angels to others to comfort and instruct and uplift them even in their lighter moments of social rest and joy, relaxing any confusion of feeling or condemnation by a suitable word, keeping jesting within pardonable limits by a light but sure phrase, maintaining in our cheerfulness fellowship with the higher content of life, and keeping spiritual aspiration alive in innocent enjoyment. When this is universal Christian practice, the ancient history of the tower of Babel will be reversed and there will increasingly spread out from little circles of Christians a beautiful spiritual understanding and free and helpful intercourse. "Understanding the *same* signs and speaking the *same* language, all will work with united force at the *same* common task, and coming and going together, giving and receiving as friends, they will meet as angels of the Lord in the merry but significant moments of life. Amen."[65]

[61] I, 667.
[62] I, 668.
[63] I, 669.
[64] *Loc. cit.*
[65] I, 676.

5. *Philanthropy*. The last household sermon deals with this (I, 677ff.).[66] As
we stated already in § 1, Schleiermacher perceived the rise of the modern
social question.[67] Philanthropy is a problem for the Christian household because each household stands within the modern development which, the more
vital it is, the more it creates inequality and therefore the need for philanthropy. Without modern sociological complexities we should not have most
of the amenities of life. We thus owe these indirectly to the fact that so many
of our brethren have too little. Seeking to give help and achieve more equity
is thus a simple matter of *justice*. Following Schleiermacher in this very vigorously worked-out train of thought could have saved Protestantism a good
deal of guilt and punishment. Why did his followers not listen to the master
precisely at this point? His text here is Eph. 4:28: "Let the thief no longer
steal, but rather let him labor, doing honest work with his hands, so that he
may be able to give to those in need." Stealing is a mode of acquisition which
is not grounded in the true and higher law which demands that all that we do
for our own welfare should be in harmony with the common welfare and that
of all the individuals concerned. God, of course, has made the poor as well as
the rich, and total equality is a well-meaning dream which neither can nor
should be realized. But if one person by enriching himself causes another to
sink into want, he *robs* him of "the noblest part of his existence"[68] even
though he undertakes to do all the good that the other obviously can no longer
do, and indeed *in this very way*. "*Before you think of being benevolent and
supporting the needy, be just*, set aside all injustice, however secret, which is
the main reason why others are in want. . . . A society from which all injustice
of this kind is not banished is not honored but shamed by even the most
generous philanthropy. For what are philanthropists of this type but . . . whited
sepulchres?"[69] Quite apart from the fact that even the most imposingly generous gifts are hardly worth noting in comparison with the wealth unjustly
acquired. Offerings made from such a source are not acceptable! Of course,
there has to be work and culture for philanthropy, but it is culture that pau-
perism threatens to overwhelm. After all, this philanthropy is nothing special
to boast about. It is simply a grateful certification that God has at least maintained us on this level. It is a *work of necessity* and in some sense of shame
which is not to be stressed more than the matter calls for. And by works of
necessity we are not righteous before God. And note finally that it does not
say that we should give to the needy but that we should *have* to give. Schleiermacher takes this to mean that we should not give directly but through the
community. "Those who acquire more in their occupations than they need for
their households should give to the community and the community should
share it."[70] To receive physical things from this, from which we should all
receive spiritual things, will not then be a burden on the poor, which is the
dark side of all private altruism. Because the *church* has not been on the scene
as a fresh and living entity, the *state* has had to take up what was once an

[66]"Christian Philanthropy"; text: Eph. 4:28.
[67]Cf. pp. 37ff.
[68]I, 681.
[69]I, 682.
[70]I, 687.

affair of the church and ought to be restored to it. We are summoned to redress this fault of an earlier generation. The reorganization of congregations must carry with it a reorganization of the church's giving to the poor along the lines indicated.

I am glad we could close this section, our survey of Schleiermacher's preaching, and the old year, with this sermon and what we have just heard. All kinds of detailed points might be raised, but you will know what I had in mind when I said at the outset that here we should get to know Schleiermacher at his *best*. He is at his best when thinking through the problem and problems of ethics on the assumption that Christianity is a present force which is at work in the sphere of history and nature as well as in the spiritual sphere. If we accept this presupposition, or if for a moment we close our eyes to the fact that from both a heavenly and an earthly standpoint nothing can really be for the best on it, we can only rejoice in the work, brilliant in its own way, which is done here. We can and should really respect it even though we are often almost too impatient to listen because of the presupposition. The problem and problems of ethics are there irrespective of the presupposition. No matter what else we may say about him, we have to allow that Schleiermacher has at least given us a sharp and serious indication of this. Sermons about the Christian home should in fact be the *last word* (but a *last* word that presupposes a rather more important *first* word) of Christian theology.

CHAPTER II
THE SCHOLAR

§ 4

THE ENCYCLOPEDIA

Schleiermacher made quite a name for himself in at least three branches of scholarship: in that of classical philology as a translator and interpreter, especially of Plato; in that of philosophy, including psychology and pedagogy, as a systematic and historical thinker who, even if he did not succeed in founding a school, at least went his own way with unmistakable originality in comparison with the philosophical leaders of the age, Kant, Fichte, Hegel, and Schelling, who was closest to him; and finally in that of theology, which will be the theme of the present chapter. In this third field his scholarly activity extended to all the relevant disciplines with the exception of the Old Testament, which he consistently avoided. If of his strictly theological works we mention only two, the Encyclopedia[1] and his main work *Der christliche Glaube,*[2] we find among his posthumously published lectures the parallel work *Die christliche Sitte,*[3] an Introduction to the New Testament,[4] a Hermeneutics,[5] a Life of Jesus,[6] a Church History,[7] a Practical Theology,[8] and various exegetical writings.[9] As concerns the breadth of his scholarly learning and accomplishments he must certainly rank among the great names in Christian theology and be mentioned alongside Origen, Augustine, and Calvin. No one since can be compared to him, nor soon will be. All that we can do is take a sample of this prodigious wealth and find decisive answers to some decisive questions.

Schleiermacher the theologian does not differ from Schleiermacher the preacher as we have already come to know him. Our task is to summarize,

[1]F. Schleiermacher, *Kurze Darstellung des theologischen Studiums* . . . (1811, 1830; Berlin, 1843) (*Sämmtliche Werke*, 1, *Zur Theologie*, I, 1ff.); *Brief Outline on the Study of Theology*, tr. T. N. Tice (Atlanta, 1966).

[2]Cf. under § 6; for the edition cf. p. xix, n. 24.

[3]Cf. p. 30, n. 88.

[4]F. Schleiermacher, *Einleitung ins Neue Testament*, ed. G. Wolde (Berlin, 1845) (*Sämmtliche Werke*, 1, *Zur Theologie*, Vol. VIII).

[5]Cf. under § 5.

[6]Cf. p. 101, n. 218.

[7]F. Schleiermacher, *Geschichte der christlichen Kirche*, ed. E. Bonnell (Berlin, 1840) (*Sämmtliche Werke*, 1, *Zur Theologie*, Vol. XI).

[8]Cf. p. 16, n. 69.

[9]Cf. *Sämmtliche Werke*, 1, *Zur Theologie*, Vol. II (Berlin, 1836).

elucidate, and make more precise what we have seen already, not to present esoteric mysteries which he pronounced only on the podium and not in the pulpit. In principle at least, there are in him no such mysteries. Or rather, the great and little heresies that he permitted himself may be heard, if we have ears to hear, *just as well* and perhaps even better in his sermons than in the carefully pondered and articulated expositions of, for example, *The Christian Faith*. In both cases he dealt with the *same* theme and spoke the *same* word, except that in the latter case he presented it as a *science*, that is, in his own view predominantly as *a system*, or as a construction of thought which aims at unity and totality, as full and coherent knowledge which is strictly formulated in detail. Our goal, then, is to achieve a second look at the *same* subject, but with sharper edges and fuller perspective than before. In § 9 of the Encyclopedia we read: "If one unites religious interest and the scholarly spirit to the highest degree and with the greatest possible balance of theory and practice, this is the concept of a prince of the church."[10] We can hardly deny to Schleiermacher himself this honorary title that he himself invented. I hope that we shall also come to see again the same essential relationship of identity between his theology and his philosophy.

Schleiermacher's scientific theology is in a particular way the theater of the *debate* between Christianity and modern culture which I called the true theme of his theology at the commencement of this series.[11] Like so many after him, Schleiermacher wanted to be both a Christian and a modern man, both a modern man and a Christian. In the sermons, where he seems to speak exclusively as a Christian, one can sometimes forget this, for his proclamation of Christianity seems to be understandable as a self-originated and self-contained entity developing according to its own law. The same applies to his philosophy, in which he seems to speak only as a modern man, unfolding the great dialectic of knowledge and being with no apparent regard for the Christian factor. But certain remarkable parallels between the sermons and the philosophy warn us at once against construing the relation between his Christianity and his modernity as that of a neutral contiguity. In both instances we find the same orientation to the two antithetical but not completely antithetical *poles* or *foci*. In both instances we find the same doctrine of the transcending of this antithesis in a third *nonqualitative* factor. In both instances we find the same concept of existence as a progressive approximation of antithetically determined life to this point of indifference. In both instances we find that the true agent of this movement (which can be called equally well the "kingdom of God" or the "supreme good") is *man*, the individual. This parallelism obviously points us to a place where the principial basis of its possibility and necessity, the secret identity of the two series, has to be discussed. This place is Schleiermacher's theology in the narrower sense, and the problem of how the two series meet in Schleiermacher will have to be the true problem of this chapter.

[10]Cf. p. 137, n. 1. Barth is using the critical edition of H. Scholz (Leipzig, 1910) (*Quellenschriften zur Geschichte des Protestantismus*, 10), pp. 3f.
[11]Cf. p. xix.

The Encyclopedia, with which we properly begin, is calculated to plunge us at once into the heart of the matter. It bears the title *Kurze Darstellung des theologischen Studiums zum Behuf einleitender Vorlesungen*. It arose, then, out of the need of the academic teacher to give his listeners a printed guide. That he lectured on this theme in his first academic courses (Halle, winter semester 1804/05) shows how strong was his desire to get down at once to what is basic and total in theology. And the fact that he had hardly begun teaching before he spoke about future publication in his letters (Scholz, p. X)[12] points in the same direction. Yet the origin of the work cannot be sought only in the technical academic need. There was something which in principle Schleiermacher had to do and say first to orient and organize theological scholarship. Because of circumstances relating to Napoleon, publication was delayed until 1811. In the meantime the author had finally settled in Berlin. The work made strikingly little impact on his contemporaries. In the nineteen years between the first and the second edition only one review seems to have been devoted to it, although this was a serious and penetrating one probably penned by the Heidelberger Schwarz. Apart from Schleiermacher himself, only his loyal friend Gass in Breslau seems actually to have used the guide in his academic lectures. And as regards its wider influence it is remarkable that only the Roman Catholic theological encyclopedia of J. S. Drey (Tübingen, 1819) saw some possibility of appropriating Schleiermacher's method at decisive points.[13] The enigmatic brevity of the first edition, which consists only of theses, may perhaps explain its meager impact. Schleiermacher began to exert a major influence on theology only with his *Glaubenslehre*, which first came out in 1820–1821, and only the second edition of the *Kurze Darstellung* made the contribution that was its due. This appeared in 1830, and it was altered a good deal in expression, though not in substance, and provided with some explanatory notes.

In this second version you will find it in Volume I of the *Theological Works* of Schleiermacher, in Hendel's *Library of Literature*, Nos. 833–834, in the Perthes *Library of Theological Classics*, Vol. 48, and finally in the definitive critical edition of Heinrich Scholz (Leipzig, 1810, in Stange's *Quellenschriften zur Geschichte des Protestantismus*, 10), which I shall be quoting.

Among critical evaluations of its content I may mention especially Wilhelm Bender, *Schleiermachers Theologie* (Nördlingen, 1876–1878), II, 299ff.,[14] and Alfred Eckert, *Einführung in die Prinzipien und Methoden der evangelischen Theologie* (Leipzig, 1909), pp. 52ff. (especially on pp. 23ff. the account of the impact of the *Kurze Darstellung* on the theological literature of the 19th century, which I regard as more meritorious than the somewhat dubiously based systematic appraisal and criticism). Also worth mentioning are the shorter accounts and evaluations by the younger Gass (*Geschichte der protestan-*

---

[12]The reference is to the introduction which H. Scholz wrote to his edition of the *Kurze Darstellung* (Leipzig, 1910; p. X of this is p. XIV in the new impression, Darmstadt, 1973).

[13]On F. H. C. Schwarz, J. C. Gass, and J. S. Drey cf. Scholz, pp. XIV–XVI (or XVIII–XX).

[14]W. Bender, *Schleiermachers Theologie mit ihren philosophischen Grundlagen*, Vol. I: *Die philosophischen Grundlagen der Theologie Schleiermachers* (Nördlingen, 1876); Vol. II: *Die positive Theologie Schleiermachers* (1878).

tischen Dogmatik; Berlin, 1867, IV, 532ff.), Frank (*Geschichte und Kritik der neueren Theologie*; Leipzig, 1894, § 7),[15] and Scholz ([Introduction], pp. XX[ff.]).[16]

The arrangement of Schleiermacher's work is simple: general introduction, then (1) philosophical, (2) historical, and (3) practical theology, an outline that we shall do best to follow unchanged.

1. Introduction [§§ 1–31]. In the very first sentence of the first section we come up against the momentous question in what sense theology is a science. Schleiermacher's definition is as follows: It is a positive science, that is, a sum of scientific elements united not so much in virtue of the idea of science *itself* but as the key to a *practical* task. It relates to a specific form of belief, to a specific shaping of the consciousness of God. Hence Christian theology relates to Christianity. "Relates"! In § 9 this relation is called a "religious interest" and in § 8 it is "interest in Christianity"! But the preceding sections §§ 3–7 give an unambiguous interpretation of this expression. Theology deals with the problem of the *impartation* of a specific mode of faith from some people to others by means of ideas. It deals with the *direction* or *government* of the church. The desire to take part in this activity is what makes knowledge that might be characterized differently into *theological* knowledge. It relates to this knowledge as the soul does to the body. Gass ([*Geschichte und Kritik . . .*], p. 534) lauds this definition on the ground that it expresses the natural relationship between theology and the church. In contrast Bender ([*Schleiermachers Theologie*], p. 299) complains that it does not evidence any very high opinion of theology as a science, that it pitilessly removes [it] from the list of sciences (p. 302), that it degrades it to the level of a science only in appearance on which a death sentence is pronounced if the distinction between clergy and laity is thought of as erased (p. 300). Frank, too, regarded the relating of theology to the church's task as a restriction and sought instead to find the goal of theology in the investigation and presentation of Christianity as it is understood by faith ([*Geschichte und Kritik . . .*], p. 84). Both the praise and the censure, into which we will not for the moment go, are understandable. What I do not find understandable is when Scholz ([Introduction], pp. XXVI[f.]),[17] relying on the passages which refer merely to an interest in Christianity, discovers a contradiction in the statements of Schleiermacher, and thinks he can ascribe to him an objective "understanding of Christianity," distinct from instruction for church leadership, as the final goal of theology, and that this makes it, in Scholz's words, an "objective science." We reply that this does not correspond to Schleiermacher's own intentions in the *Kurze Darstellung*. The word "interest" is obviously an unmistakable abbreviation for "active participation." According to the solemn declaration of § 5 Christian theology is "the sum of the scientific data and rules without whose possession and use there can be no harmonious direction of the Christian church, that is, no church government." According to § 2 any other form of belief will produce

[15]F. H. R. Frank, *Geschichte und Kritik der neueren Theologie, insbesondere der systematischen, seit Schleiermacher*, ed. P. Schaarschmidt (Erlangen/Leipzig, 1895²), pp. 82ff.

[16]Scholz, § 2.

[17]Pp. XXXf. in the new impression.

another theology. Fundamentally it is not a matter for everybody in the church but only for those who belong to its leadership (§ 3). (The direction or government of the church is primarily to be taken in the sense of its clergy or leaders in the most general sense.) When attained and possessed apart from the relation to this activity, the knowledge is not theological but is part of the science to which its content belongs, linguistics, history, psychology, or the philosophy of religion (§ 6). Without this desire for practical activity theology loses its soul, its unity, the very thing that makes it theology. On the other hand, *practical* interest in Christianity also needs the specific work of theological scholarship (§ 8).

In §§ 9–13 Schleiermacher offers a series of closer definitions of the vital identity of theological and ecclesiastical work as he perceives it. I have already quoted the famous passage about the "prince of the church"[18] who represents religious interest and the scholarly spirit to a supreme degree and in the best possible balance. Insofar as the scales tip on the one side or the other we have either the *theologian* in the narrower sense who is more concerned about learning than Christianity or the *cleric* who devotes more time to the work of church government. According to § 11 all theological work belongs to the sphere of leadership and all church work belongs to that of theology. An *inner vocation* is needed for both activities. Each must determine his own vocation according to the element that predominates in him (§ 13), but no one-sidedness must prevent any of us from uniting in ourselves both ecclesiastical interest and a scholarly spirit (§ 12).

It is in this sense, which in my view is perfectly clear and unequivocal, that Schleiermacher calls theology a *positive science*. In view of his thoroughly historical and psychological view of Christianity we shall not be surprised at this definition. Specifically it is also the result of a little debate with Schelling which we must briefly consider. In 1803, more than a year before Schleiermacher first undertook to lecture on the encyclopedia, Schelling had published his *Vorlesungen über die Methode des akademischen Studiums* (ed. Weiss, II, 537ff.).[19] In these lectures Schelling had defined positive sciences, in distinction from the *primal knowledge* reserved for philosophy and, in plastic form, art, as the temporal *differentiations* of this knowledge objectified by and in the *state*. Orientation to the point of indifference where the ideal and the real world are one in the absolute, and yet two, produces *theology* as the direct science of the absolute divine being. Orientation to the center of the real world, arising out of the remoteness of the real from the ideal, of the object from the subject, of the many from the one, produces the science of nature, or, more specifically, of the organism, *medicine*. Orientation to the center of the ideal world, arising out of the return of the real to the ideal, the object to the subject, the many to the one, produces the science of history, or, more specifically, *law, jurisprudence*. Schleiermacher in his review (*Jenaische Literaturzeitung* [1804], *Briefe*, IV, 579ff.) raised against this scheme the objection

[18]Cf. p. 138.
[19]F. W. J. von Schelling, *Vorlesungen über die Methode des akademischen Studiums* (Stuttgart/Tübingen, 1803) in *Werke. Auswahl in drei Bänden*, ed. O. Weiss (Leipzig, 1907), II, 537–682. (In the MS Barth mistakenly gives the name of the editor as Braun.)

that there can be no science of the point of indifference in the same sense as there is of nature or history. Such a science, that is, a science of the absolute divine being, would necessarily *divide* at once, in the nonabsoluteness of human knowledge, into real and ideal knowledge, or natural and historical knowledge. Hence theology cannot be a science in the same way as medicine and law. It must not try to prove kinship with these. It has a common *subject* with them but its *treatment* of this subject is a special one that cannot be grouped with theirs. Schleiermacher does not say, however, what this special feature is. He finally rejects Schelling's assertion of the significance of the state for the objectification of the sciences. From his 1808 work *Gelegentliche Gedanken über Universitäten in deutschem Sinn* (*Philosophische Werke*, I, 535ff.; also in Spranger, *Über das Wesen der Universität*, *Philosophische Bibliothek*, Vol. 120, 1919 [pp. 105ff.]) it appears that in the meantime Schleiermacher had grown a little closer to Schelling, if not in the main question regarding the character of theology in relation to the *subject* of all science, at least in the subsidiary question of the relation of science to the state. He, too, finds the essence of the true university as a scholarly union solely in the faculty of philosophy, in comparison with which the three other faculties are special schools "which the state has either founded or at least, because they stand in direct relation to its essential needs, . . . taken under its protection."[20] "The positive faculties arose individually through the need to give practice an indispensable basis in theory by a tradition of knowledge."[21] The faculty of law arose through the need to proceed from a state of anarchy to a state of law by means of a system of more consistent laws; that of medicine through the need to know and modify the physical state and through the obscure and mysterious sensing of the intimate relation of the human body to nature as a whole; and finally that of theology "developed in the *church* to maintain the wisdom of the fathers, so that what had happened in the past to distinguish truth and error should not be lost for the future, and in order to give to the further development of doctrine and the church a historical *foundation*, a sure and definite *direction*, and a common *spirit*; and as the state allied itself more closely with the church, it had to sanction these institutions too, and take them under its protection."[22]

[1/10/24] In this presentation Schleiermacher groups theology with medicine and jurisprudence, but this is now achieved[23] only by abandoning any speculative

[20]*Philosophische Werke*, I, 581.

[21]*Loc. cit.*

[22]I, 581f.

[23]In the margin Barth's MS contains the following sentences summarizing his previous lecture to make a smoother transition for his audience. They merge into the main text at this point.

"Schleiermacher views theology as a positive science constituted by its relation to the practical task of the Christian church. He rejects the speculative concept of positive theological science as Schelling taught it; for him a real science of the point of indifference along the same lines as the sciences of nature and spirit is impossible. In 1808 he grouped the faculty of theology with the faculties of medicine and law as special schools based on the practical needs of the state, and as such he contrasted them with the faculty of philosophy as representative of the true university. Hence Schleiermacher's equation of theology, medicine, and law, while outwardly similar to that of Schelling, is reached, at least in his work on the universities, only. . . ."

basis for *any* of them and basing and describing them as specialized sciences only in terms of their relation to the *state*. The title "positive sciences," which he now uses for theology too, does not mean for him, as it does for Schelling, that they are objectified differentiations of absolute knowledge but that as the basis of indispensable practical concerns and tasks they offer the corresponding theories under the blessing of the state, and it is in this light that he sees medicine and law as well as theology. The shift does not mean, then, that he now has a higher view of theology but rather that he has a lower view of the other two faculties. In this work on the universities Schleiermacher did not, of course, speak his last word on the question of knowledge. As we shall see, he recognizes a *speculative* branch of the two sciences of nature and spirit that for him constitute the totality of knowledge, and the term positive in the lower sense obviously does *not* apply to *speculative* physics and *speculative* ethics, since these are functions of the *true* science of philosophy. The decisive point, however, is that in distinction from Schelling he finds no place for any speculative theology. We must mention here a hitherto neglected statement from a comment on § 1 of the *Kurze Darstellung:* "If a *rational* theology has *previously* been introduced into the arrangement of knowledge (sc. the university, or learning in general), this undoubtedly relates to the God of our God-consciousness but as *speculative* knowledge it is totally *different* from our theology." How it is different we are not told. Note especially the "previously." For Schleiermacher *this* speculative theological science is no more than a historical fact. It has no place in his own view of knowledge. For him theology, in distinction from physics and ethics, is no more than a positive science in the sense depicted. If it can still exist as a science, if it is linked to pure science in the true sense, this is *not as* theology but only as it *borrows* from other sciences that are not just positive but speculative as well. In the section on "Philosophical Theology" we shall see that for Schleiermacher this science from which theology borrows is *ethics*. Our present task, however, is to establish that for Schleiermacher theology *itself* is left up in the air. The uneasy complaints of Bender and Frank and the attempt of Scholz to find a reinterpretation in the text of the *Kurze Darstellung*[24] are readily understandable. So, too, is the effort made by Alfred Eckert to console Schleiermacher, himself, and Schleiermacher's heirs with the thought that in contrast with Schleiermacher's opinion *all* sciences are in fact *no more* than positive sciences (including philosophy and mathematics!), that is, the "practical exercise of certain powers in the life of a people as these are to be found in the organism of the state."[25] There is reason enough to try to find in Schleiermacher a basis of theology that is not there. But the praise of Gass for Schleiermacher's happy uniting of theology and the church[26] is also understandable and justifiable, at least if what he calls the church, or the Christianity in which theology should take a daily interest, stands up to investigation and has the necessary weight to provide for up-in-the-air theology an equivalent alongside the other sciences. It will have to be a very powerful and superior truth that Schleier-

[24]Cf. p. 140.
[25]A. Eckert, *Einführung in die Prinzipien und Methoden der evangelischen Theologie* (Leipzig, 1909), p. 61.
[26]Cf. p. 140.

macher, rejecting the saving plank of speculation, thinks he has on board in the ship of the church if the homelessness of theology in the schema of the sciences signifies its being all the more solidly at home elsewhere. If not, rejection of that plank would be an act of desperation. "Otherwise it would not be worthwhile being a theologian," to use the words of Scholz (Christentum und Wissenschaft, p. 53).[27]

Let us look at the remaining contents of the Introduction. §§ 14–17 deal with the aims of theological education. Full mastery of all theological knowledge cannot be demanded of individuals because in virtue of its historical and practical character it is infinite in scope. But restriction of some to one part of theology and others to another would result in neither individuals nor all of them together dealing with the whole. The condition for dealing with even a single discipline in the true sense and spirit of theology is an acquaintance with the principles of all the theological disciplines in order that there may be unhindered communication between each and all. Possible specialization may be demanded by the special nature of individual talents or by the concept of the existing need of the church that someone has formed, and to a large extent the happy progress of theology depends on the right talents being found at each period for what is most needed at the time. The more dominant the orientation to the practical, as the first edition says more precisely than the second, the more general theological education must be, whereas virtuosity in a single field will produce the greater scholarly achievements. Specialization in a special discipline, then, must not aim at a full knowledge of the field but at a "purification and supplementation of what has already been achieved," that is, at independent research (§ 19).

Finally, §§ 18–31 deal with the division of theological knowledge. §§ 18–20 begin with the encyclopedia as such. Schleiermacher realizes that there can be different ideas of the encyclopedic task. One view focuses on "the interconnection of all the parts of theology and the distinctive value of each part in relation to the common goal" [§ 18]. Schleiermacher calls this formal, and he himself understood and handled the task in this way. It does not relate to the content but to what he calls the general and nexus-oriented organization of all theological knowledge in its individual disciplines, that is, the question of method in the broadest sense. Another view would be the material one (Wernle)[28] which focuses on the inner organization of each discipline and its essential parts. A third would be essentially interested in the aids that help toward a rapid mastery and would thus be in the main biographical and lexical (Hagenbach).[29] A fourth would be methodological, concentrating on the techniques of theological study (Kähler).[30] As far as the second, third, and fourth aims are concerned, we come away empty-handed from Schleiermacher's out-

---

[27]H. Scholz, Christentum und Wissenschaft in Schleiermachers Glaubenslehre (Berlin, 1909; Leipzig, 1911[2]).

[28]P. Wernle, Einführung in das theologische Studium (Tübingen, 1911[2]).

[29]K. R. Hagenbach, Enzyklopädie und Methodologie der theologischen Wissenschaften (Leipzig, 1880[10]).

[30]M. Kähler, Die Wissenschaft der christlichen Lehre von dem evangelischen Grundartikel aus dem Abrisse dargestellt (Leipzig, 1893[2]), pp. 3–42; cf. also Wie studiert man Theologie im ersten Semester? Briefe an einem Anfänger (Leipzig, 1892[2]).

line, as he himself is aware. There are some occasional material hints, some references to the literature, and some methodological and practical tips, but what it offers, and seeks to offer, are only the principles. |

The real construction of theological knowledge then begins with § 21. The true aim of the work is obviously to show that there is a structure, that theology is an organism and not an aggregate. In the first edition this was metaphorically indicated by the description of philosophical theology as the *root* (§ 26), historical theology as the *body* (§ 36), and practical theology as the *crown* (§ 31). §§ 21–25, which are the most important sections along with § 1 and § 5, first indicate the place and role of *philosophical theology*. This is neither rational theology such as one finds in medieval and the older Protestant scholasticism nor speculative theology in the sense of Schelling. We have seen that Schleiermacher did not regard the former as theology, insofar as it existed at all for him, and that he was unwilling to recognize the possibility of the latter. For him philosophical theology is the demonstration of the—indirect—*relationship* between theology as such, that is, theology as the *positive* science of Christianity, and *pure* science, that is, the science that in virtue of its speculative aspect has a *direct* share of its own in the *idea* of knowledge. A purely empirical assertion of the fact of the church or piety would not be enough for real knowledge of Christianity. The nature of Christianity in its distinction from other modes of belief has to be understood, and so, too, has the nature of piety "in connection with the other activities of the human spirit" [§ 21]. This is to say already that the pure science to which theology seeks attachment has to be *ethics*, and in Schleiermacher this means "the science of the principles of history" (§ 29), the science of the necessities in the development of the human spirit, including the resultant cultural sciences in the narrower sense, esthetics, politics, and the philosophy of religion, with which we may link history, law, and the like as empirical sciences of the second rank. Theology obviously belongs to *this* group. According to Schleiermacher, then, theology must borrow its scientific basis from ethics and its primary derivates.[31] To use the words of Scholz (*Christentum und Wissenschaft*, p. 53), it is "*a daughter of ethics*, as which it has to give religion and the church their spiritual place in the total life of humanity" as "necessary fruits of the human spirit that is ethically productive." It is first of all the task of *ethics itself* to show that the existence of such fellowships (i.e., religious) is a necessary element in the development of the human spirit. The concept of the church has to arise scientifically in concert with concepts of all the

---

[31]In the margin we find the following graph, adopted with some modifications from H. Scholz, *Christentum und Wissenschaft* . . . , p. 52:

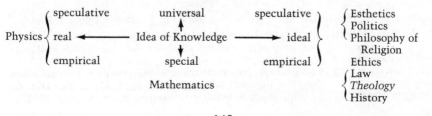

other organizations of common life that arise out of the idea of humanity (§ 22, cf. § 48). Otherwise religious societies would have to be seen as *aberrations*, as has often in fact been done. "Piety as seen thus is [indeed] the true atheism" (note on § 22).[32] This striking result (in which atheism is not a denial of God but of piety) shows that here we have at least come up against a vitally important part of Schleiermacher's basic position. It is a task of the philosophy of religion (which for him has fundamentally as little to do with theology as has esthetics with politics) to establish and elucidate in principle the differences between religious societies. The first edition says very generally: "A vital presentation of this idea (sc. that of the religious society) must also establish within it the element of the *variable* which contains the seeds of everything *individual*."[33] It is naturally in this light that we are to understand the concept of "borrowed principles" which plays such a big role in *The Christian Faith*. We shall see later how Schleiermacher viewed in detail the makeup of his philosophical theology as one of theological borrowing. § 25 formulates for the first time the task of *practical theology*. For an understanding of the whole work note that here where the organism of theology is being explained purely in terms of its inner law Schleiermacher puts *practical* theology *before* historical theology! It is defined by the purpose of church leadership. This consists extensively of the integration and increasing adaptation of the proper sphere of Christianity into human society (understood as people as well as customs and institutions), and intensively of the increasingly pure presentation of the idea of Christianity in this area. *Techniques* are needed for this. Presenting these is the job of practical theology. But church leadership also needs—and this brings us already in §§ 26–28 to *historical theology*—an acquaintance with the relevant totality in a *given state* which has to be regarded as the result of the *past*. As it presents a specific point in time, the present which has developed out of the past, in its true relation to the idea of Christianity, this establishes practical theology and verifies, or confirms, the concepts of philosophical theology which have been purely conceptually attained. Historical theology is the true *body* of theological study. By practical theology, which it contains within itself historically, this body is connected with the active Christian life, while philosophical theology links it to true science. In the concluding sections §§ 29–31 Schleiermacher discusses more closely the interrelations of the three parts. So long as *philosophical* theology is not fully worked out as a discipline, its individual elements can "be achieved only fragmentarily with the study of historical theology" [§ 29]. But always, even for this to happen, the study of *ethics* as "the science of the principles of history" [§ 29] must be the beginning of the whole. Without this the study of *historical* theology would be an incoherent exercise and would degenerate into lifeless tradition. *Practical* theology for its part is conditioned by the historical theology which has to be perfected by philosophical theology. "Overhasty preoccupation with techniques leads to superficiality in

---

[32]The term "note" relates here and in what follows to the elucidations added in the second edition and is to be distinguished from the term "footnote," which relates to the footnotes added by Scholz to the text of the first edition.

[33]§ 24 of the first edition (in the Scholz ed., p. 9, footnote 3).

practice and indifference to scholarly development" [§ 30]. An appropriate course of instruction will thus lead from philosophical theology by way of historical to practical. But no matter how we arrange the parts, much from the one will always be presupposed in the others in view of the essential relationships between them.

Bender ([*Schleiermachers Theologie*], p. 305) criticizes this whole schema- [1/14/24] tism on the ground that it leaves unclear the distinction between philosophical and historical theology. The force of this objection seems to me to be blunted somewhat by the fact that Schleiermacher himself obviously made it in the last sentence quoted. Naturally historical theology has to derive from philosophical theology some knowledge of the idea of Christianity whose relation to the various periods it has to deal with in its own discipline. And naturally philosophical theology has to derive from historical theology a view of the nature of Christianity and the forms of religious society. Schleiermacher later summarized this as follows (§ 65): "Philosophical theology undoubtedly presupposes that the data of historical theology are known but itself establishes for the first time the truly historical view of Christianity." Yet he would probably answer Bender by saying that this reciprocity does not alter the fact that we have in the two disciplines two fundamentally different ways of dealing with the same subject, that the one treatment—this is clear enough—is mainly *a priori* whereas the other is mainly *a posteriori*, and that we thus have two disciplines which are just as different as the various forms of human knowledge, which all meet in their subject, are (and again are not) different. The distinction between speculative and empirical knowledge as Schleiermacher understands it—and this is the issue in the distinction between philosophical and historical theology—can hardly be described as intrinsically unclear. Hence I should not take too tragic a view of *this* criticism. More difficult is another one that is hinted at in Bender, Eckert,[34] and others, yet oddly enough not very sharply or radically felt. This is directed against the absolute dependence of theology on ethics, which is obvious throughout the schema and which is mediated by the borrowed discipline called philosophical theology. Continuing our earlier metaphor, we must ask whether there is not still, then, a plank of salvation for theology when it is so severely threatened in the little ship of the church. May it be that Schleiermacher does not really think that he has on board the strong and superior truth which caused him to scorn Schelling's possibility? Does he still have to hold out the prospect of help from outside, of a superior truth *beyond* the church or Christian belief, if theology is to be even a positive science and if it is to be worthwhile to be a theologian? A superior truth *beyond* the church which makes the church's science truth? Where will this lead? What can it mean? If we were previously anxious about the strange homelessness of theology, we might have reason now to be even more anxious about its suddenly being guaranteed a home by the "science of the principles of history." Is this the secure place that theology wants and that we want for it? Is it so secure that under the protective patronage of ethics and the philosophy of religion the so-called "idea of Christianity" might not develop into something that will cause theology to pray

---

[34]Cf. Bender, *Schleiermachers Theologie*, p. 303; Eckert, *Einführung*, p. 66.

God to be delivered from its *friends*, and even more so, perhaps, than if it had entrusted itself speculatively to Schelling's point of indifference? Let us set aside these questions for the time being and consult in conclusion, with no more marginal glosses, what Scholz has to say in justification of Schleiermacher's way of integrating theology into the structure of learning. He refers (1) to the methodical root of the procedure, which is to be found in Schleiermacher's strict concept of scholarship in virtue of which each individual discipline must find a place on the scale of learning as the "living branch of a common trunk,"[35] the idea of knowledge. Then (2) there is in Schleiermacher an *anti-empiricist* motif: "a phenomenon like the primal one of piety and its objectification" in the church must be viewed "in terms of the spirit of intelligence . . . traced back to the source of all higher being, the contact of nature with reason . . . and regarded as an organic part of the general ethicizing process"; Christianity "for all its originality has to be connected in some way with the religious phenomenon as such" and through religion with the "universal source of life," "the fount of intelligence"—"the whole universe of the spirit is a single process of development."[36] (3) The third motif in Schleiermacher is to be sought, according to Scholz, in the "elemental feeling" with which he saw religion and Christianity "in their gritty individuality" yet also in their inner "contact with the motivating forces of the spirit in general."[37] The ultimate concern in all Schleiermacher's theology is simply to express conceptually his distinctive feeling for life as this is oriented to objective *syntheses*. Taking note of the elucidations of this undoubtedly legitimate interpreter and apologist for Schleiermacher, we pass on to the next section.

2. Philosophical Theology [§§ 32–68]. A special introduction to this section in §§ 32–42 first pinpoints the basic problems that Schleiermacher had already hinted at earlier (§ 24). It has been determined that Christianity cannot be constructed purely *scientifically* or speculatively but also that it cannot be conceived of purely empirically. Schleiermacher describes the third option that remains as the *critical* one. He means by this an evaluation of everything that is historically given in Christianity according to an idea of religion and the church that is determined by ethics, and determined in a way that is variable and capable of differentiation. "Hence philosophical theology"—he says expressly in § 33—can take "its starting-point only *beyond Christianity* in the logical sense of the term, that is, in the general sense of a religious society or a fellowship of faith." "Beyond . . . in the logical sense of the term." This phrase did not occur in the first edition, and he also had "standpoint" instead of "starting-point" in 1811. In 1830, then, he made his meaning more precise by showing that the priority of ethics, where philosophical theology must begin, over Christianity is to be understood only formally and methodologically and not as a material ranking or value judgment, and that only the start of philosophical theology is to be located at this point which is

---

[35]Cf. H. Scholz, Introduction to the *Kurze Darstellung*, p. XXXI (or p. XXXV); Scholz has "lebendige Verzweigung," Barth "lebendige Abzweigung."
[36]Scholz, p. XXXII (p. XXXVI).
[37]*Ibid.*, pp. XXXIIf. (pp. XXXVIf.).

logically superior to Christianity. In spite of these restrictions, one cannot fail to see that the decisive word is spoken here. To determine the nature of Christianity, one does not go to Christianity itself but to a court which stands over against both it and similar structures, and which quite apart from Christianity knows what is what in matters of religion and the church. The note to this important thesis then adds expressly that a specific faith or church can be properly understood only in its *relation to others alongside it or after it* (cf. § 21 on "understanding" the nature of Christianity)—that is, only in correlation—and that this critical starting-point will have to be the same for *all* the other forms of faith envisaged according to § 2. I need hardly say that we have here the methodological source of the modern study of religion. If on the one hand Schleiermacher rejected a direct deduction of Christianity and Christian theology from pure principles after the manner of Schelling, he substituted for this on the other hand the determining of its nature by a science that was at least partially speculative. Frank remonstrates with particular sharpness here that with this subsuming under a general concept of religion and the church that is constructed out of ethics, Christianity has to submit to a non-Christian, natural-philosophical judgment instead of vice versa.[38] In this regard it should be noted that one can hardly determine the rights and wrongs of Schleiermacher's procedure along the lines of a battle of prestige between theology and philosophy. Whether philosophical control of the definition of Christianity is helpful or fatal can be determined only on the basis of the detailed material execution. We shall have to come back to this in *The Christian Faith*. The first chapter on Schleiermacher's sermons, of course, has already made some input. But however that may be, according to § 35 it is at any rate only in the light of the historical distinction of the given state of Christianity from the point that is methodologically superior to it that we can decide what in its development may be regarded as a pure expression of its idea and what must be regarded as a deviation from this or as a state of sickness. Since this will be done *differently* from the standpoint of the different churches that call themselves Christian, it is obvious [that] philosophical theology will be different for each of them. Our own, then, is *Protestant*. The main problems of philosophical theology are defined herewith: the determination of the essence of Christianity and—on this basis—the establishment of the truth-content of the detailed and concrete forms of Christianity in their relation to this essence. Schleiermacher calls the first part of this *apologetics* and the second *polemics*. Both according to §§ 39–40 are inalienable concerns of the church's leadership. The common conviction which according to Schleiermacher lies at the basis of sharing in a church fellowship has to be given recognition: hence the need for research into the *distinctiveness* or *essence* of Christianity or Protestantism, that is, apologetics. Only in apologetics should one look outward from Christianity to other religions and from Protestantism to Roman Catholicism. But this common conviction carries with it an intrinsic distaste for sick deviations from it: hence the question of the *correctness* of what claims to be Christianity or Protestantism, that is, polemics. And this looks inward, dealing with the deviations of Christianity or Protestantism from its *own* idea

[38]Frank, *Geschichte und Kritik der neueren Theologie*, p. 88.

and not with those of *other* churches from this idea. In the first edition (I, 2, § 5)[39] Schleiermacher explains his meaning by adding that a plain contradiction of the essence of Christianity, for example, atheism or an antireligious society, cannot be the subject of theological polemics. Schleiermacher seeks to differentiate apologetics and polemics in philosophical theology from the activities that bear the same names in the sphere of practical theology. According to § 37 they belong "by the nature of their subject-matter to historical criticism." This does not mean, as Eckert thinks ([*Einführung* . . .], p. 80), that we are to call philosophical theology a "historical discipline" but is simply another reminder of the superior "science of the principles of history" which must provide the norm for evaluating historical phenomena.

We may be brief in our depiction of what Schleiermacher has to say about these two disciplines, for the details, which are shrewd and well considered, but remarkably wooden and artificial for the most part, differ from the basic principles by having had hardly any influence on theology, and indeed, except in the introductions to the *Christliche Glaube* and the *Christliche Sitte*, they were not further developed even by Schleiermacher himself. He made the conjecture in 1811 (Scholz, p. XIII)[40] that people would say of the work "that there are in it many ghosts . . . theological disciplines that never were and never will be." We are forced to say this of its apologetics and polemics. Nevertheless we can learn something about Schleiermacher even from these ghosts. What counts in the encyclopedic presentation of these disciplines is the working out of the *concepts* which according to Schleiermacher are their true material:[41] in apologetics (§§ 43–53) the dialectic of the *natural*, that is, that which expresses the general concept of the religious society, and the *positive*, that is, the distinctive or differentiated element within the complex of all religious societies, especially the positive from the Christian standpoint. The nature of Christianity is thus to be understood as regards its evolution by means of the concepts of revelation, miracle, and inspiration, as regards its continuous relationship to the Jewish and Gentile worlds by means of the concepts of prophecy and type (apropos of which Schleiermacher notes that a proper establishment and use of these concepts is perhaps the supreme task of apologetics), as regards the constancy perceptible in its historical development by means of the concepts of canon and sacrament, and as regards its peaceful coexistence with other organizations arising out of the concept of humanity by means of the concepts of hierarchy and church government. The basic concern of polemics (§§ 54–62) is with the concepts of the *sick* and the *alien*. A diseased weakness of Christian piety gives rise to indifferentism, a diseased weakness of the social impulse means separation, alien teachings lead to heresy, and alien elements in government produce schism. Both disciplines will naturally take different forms for different confessions. Hence Schleiermacher demands that special, that is, Protestant, *apologetics* should

---

[39]Here and in what follows I denotes the first part, 2 the second section, and § 5 the fifth sub section.

[40]In a letter dated December 29, 1810; cf. *F. Schleiermachers Briefwechsel mit J. C. Gass*, ed. W. Gass (Berlin, 1852), p. 87, quoted in Scholz, Introduction, p. XIII (or p. XVII).

[41]Barth has here a marginal note: "Apol[ogetics]: against Pag[anism] and Roman Cath[olicism]   Pol[emics]: against Roman Cath[olicism] and Errors"

refrain from calling only itself Christian and the rest non-Christian (§ 51 note), and he demands that special *polemics* should not describe as heretical or schismatic that which merely contradicts the distinctive nature of a specific and partial society (§ 61 note). Finally he demands of a fully articulated apologetics that, since all conflicts within Christianity are destined to disappear, while avoiding false attempts at union it should in a divinatory way present the forms of this disappearing (§ 53), and of a fully articulated polemics that it should provide the means whereby we may discern in the first seeds of a heresy whether we are dealing with a sickness of the church that is to be treated with tolerance or with a new differentiation that is to be recognized in freedom (§ 62). |

Even though we cannot enthusiastically adopt the total scheme, we cannot avoid acknowledging with admiration how well-thought-out it all is. I do not mean it ironically when I say that we are dealing here with theology in kid gloves. It is intellectually brilliant; read the sections on apologetics and polemics for yourselves and you will be quickly convinced. It is also consistent; there is no point in bringing detailed objections against Schleiermacher, for one thing leads on admirably to the next, and the apologetic and polemical systems are fully parallel even though each is developed in and for itself. In relation to the final points we can, of course, raise some *questions* for which we will find no answers in the text. No Christian society should pretend that it alone is Christian, we are taught by Schleiermacher's apologetics, obviously on the basis of a presupposed concept of religious societies in general. But on the basis of the same concept, one might ask, can Christianity as a whole pretend to be the *only true* religion? Again, Schleiermacher's polemics forbids us to use the terms heresy and schism unless they denote opposition to Christianity as a whole. But with what right, one might ask, may Christianity as a whole apply the term *error* to other modes of belief? Again, Schleiermacher's apologetics foresees a disappearance of all conflicts within Christianity. May one foresee a similar disappearance of all conflicts between Christianity and *other* religious societies? Finally, if what is regarded as sick from a Christian standpoint, a weakness of piety or fellowship, enjoys the protection of tolerance according to Schleiermacher's polemics, and if what is strange from a Christian standpoint, and leads to a new differentiation, enjoys the protection of freedom, how far has Christianity the right to experience what does not correspond to its own nature as anything more than a sickness or a foreign body, and how far does it have the right to engage in polemics against it? On the basis of ethics as the descriptive science of the actual principles of history, is not one religious society, whether Christian or not, just as *healthy*, and just as *justified* in its *individuality*, as any other? In sum, is Christianity right or wrong when it maintains that it is the truth? Schleiermacher's philosophical theology does not answer this question. It does not even put it. It seems not even to be aware of it. In the last resort, like its mother, Schleiermacher's ethics, it seems not to want to get beyond the question of Pilate: What is truth?

3. Historical Theology [§§ 69–256]. With its 188 theses this part makes up [1/15/24] in quantity more than half of the whole work (including the introduction), and materially it is not for nothing described as the true body of theology. To anticipate, Schleiermacher understands by "historical theology" (1) the exegesis of the New Testament as the history of primitive Christianity, (2) church history and the history of doctrine, and (3) dogmatics and statistics as information regarding the present-day church. Here again we have a special introduction which develops the general principles of historical theology and offers the material derivation or construction of the specific parts of this branch or trunk of theological science [§§ 69–102]. The first statement of § 69 discloses at once both the basic presupposition and the whole problem of this part of the work: "Historical theology (which according to § 26 is required for church leadership because the present state of the church can be understood only as a product of the past) is in content a portion of modern history," or, more specifically according to the note, it is "the inner side of history, the history of modern civilization and culture." When Schleiermacher speaks of modern history, he has in mind an era of at least two thousand years. In this Christianity has initiated a distinctive development; this is all that remains to be said of it in this context. We are thus on the empirical wing of ethics or intellectual history. All the natural branches of history, and obviously in the broader sense all the empirical sciences, are coordinated with historical theology insofar as it is simply history. Now, of course, it is not just history; it is also a theological discipline with a bearing on church leadership, and thus far the other branches of history are merely *ancillary sciences* in relation to it. The study and treatment of the same historical materials will be different according to one's purely historical or theological approach, but here, too, theological science obviously has to abide by *alien* norms that are not grounded in itself: the principles of historical research do not cease to be the same for both fields (both secular and theological history). Or, as we read at the end of the introduction (§ 102): "Historical criticism is the universal and indispensable instrument for historical theology as it is for the whole field of history." I repeat that, according to Schleiermacher, exegesis and dogmatics belong to historical theology as thus defined. According to him, therefore, there may not only be a secular church history but also a secular biblical exposition as a branch of general history, and even a secular historical dogmatics is not ruled out but strictly is demanded for the sake of scientific completeness. With this characterization of the most vital theological disciplines, namely, exegesis and dogmatics, the primacy of historians in theology, or theological historicism, is obviously established firmly and solidly and definitively. It is interesting to see how theology reacted to this in the 19th century. That church history could be something radically different from a bit of history more or less lit up by theology no reputable person would have dared to maintain any longer even before Schleiermacher. In this regard his program was accepted as more or less self-evident. Uniform applause greeted his belief that exegesis should be expressly regarded as one of the factors that makes up the historical character of Christianity; not to mention others, Frank and his disciple Eckert welcome it with full-scale jubilation: "It is perfectly correct," says Frank, "that exegetical theology should not be treated as a section on its own alongside historical theology. For it deals with the primitive history of Christianity and the Christian church, and the transition to the further history of the church is a fluid one" ([*Geschichte und Kritik* . . .], p. 87).[42] On the other hand, the integration of dogmatics into historical theology raised a general storm of protest. Although Schleiermacher stated all along the line that dogmatics is the science of Christian faith or experience, in an obscure feeling that there is something wrong about a full subsumption of dogmatics under history it was thought that it should be described as the "systematic" discipline, although Schleiermacher himself, rightly in terms of his own presuppositions, noted in § 97 that this grandiose description conceals to its material disadvantage both the historical character and the practical purpose of the discipline. Only two honest men, Richard Rothe and the Swede Reuterdahl, dared to remain loyal to the master in this regard.[43] What are we to say about this? I believe that if Schleiermacher is *right* to presuppose that the subject-matter of dogmatics is the given religious consciousness of the dogmatician, or the so-called faith of the Christian community, as well as the total consciousness of the community over two thousand years, then we have to admit that *he* and his two loyal disciples are *right* in their opinion that this science is a *historical* one with all the ambiguity that this means for a theological discipline. What is right for the apostle Paul and the reformers will be right in modern descriptions of the religious consciousness as well. I would even go so far as to say that Schleiermacher's very clear-cut and radical attempt first to bring all the biblical, historical, and didactic data of theology under a common historical denominator, and then dialectically to oppose to this a specific theological approach, could be regarded[44] as a very promising one were it not that the cloven hoof of the consistent validity of the historical method on both sides of the antithesis betrays the fact that the dialectic is not authentic, that there will not really be any true *theological* approach, and that under this sign theology will be secretly betrayed and sold to the methods of empirical scholarship even though its special sphere will be preserved. That this takes place, and that Schleiermacher and those who follow him consistently rightly saw that it *has to* take place, has its basis in the fact that for him the object of theology is a phenomenon, a spiritual phenomenon to be sure, yet a psychical entity like any other, namely, what is called piety. This being so, it is hard to see how the universal historical or descriptive method, suitably modified to fit the subject, can fail to win out and achieve predominance in the theological area as well. And it is even harder to see with what right dogmatics as the science of what the contemporary period recognizes to be the intellectual expression of its Christian piety can escape having a historical character.

But let us return to Schleiermacher's expositions. §§ 71–80 of the introduction to historical theology deal with the problem of the antithesis between *origin* and *development* in history, or, as one might put it, between *originality* and *continuity*, or, as Schleiermacher says in § 73, between *epochs* and *periods*.

[42]Cf. also Eckert, *Einführung*, pp. 89f.

[43]R. Rothe, *Theologische Enzyklopädie*, ed. H. Ruppelius (1880); H. Reuterdahl, *Inledning litt Theologien* (Lund, 1837). Cf. on this Eckert, *Einführung*, pp. 31f., 38f.; Scholz, Introduction, pp. XVIIIf. (XXIIf.).

[44]In the MS Barth has a second "oppose" (*gegenüberzustellen*) instead of "regarded" (*ansehen*); the editor has corrected the slip.

Schleiermacher hastens to explain (§ 71 note) that in history the two stand in only relative antithesis. Each historical totality runs its course as "a multiple alternation of elements of various kinds" (§ 72). With this antithesis, according to §§ 74–76, there intersect those of the elements of various parallel histories, that is, of ideas, institutions, movements, personalities, and peoples. §§ 78–80 apply these general principles of history to theology: "The whole course of human affairs . . . (and) *in* this the whole sequence of expressions of one and the same force" constitute a *totality*. Hence a smaller historical totality like Christianity must be regarded as the "development of a new thing, of something that was not there before," but also as "the outworking of something that was already there in some way" [§ 78]. Christianity as the rise of something new means according to § 79 that it is "a specific historical totality which . . . takes its own course through a series of periods divided by epochs." Seen as the outworking of something already present, however, it is a single period of one branch of religious development. As theology, historical theology chooses the first approach, for, says the note to § 80, Christian faith could not be what it is if its underlying reality were not posited exclusively as something original. This sounds promising. But unfortunately one should not overestimate the significance of this statement, for in terms of what precedes "original" can only refer to a specific totality whose development is an expression of the same force, a factor in one and the same history, in virtue of which it can also be the outworking of something already present.

§§ 81–85 present the derivation of the three "historical" disciplines from the constitutive principle of theology. The most immediate requirement for church leadership is a historical awareness of the present. Since the present can be understood only as a product of the past, there is needed a knowledge of all that has gone before. From the increasingly complex involvement of this in the interplay of other forces, there arises the question of the most primitive state as that which most purely presents the distinctive nature of Christianity. Academically, the order will be reversed: first a knowledge of primitive Christianity, then of the total course of Christianity, then of its present state. After a parenthetical reference (§ 86) to such *ancillary disciplines* as general history, geography, and philology, Schleiermacher proceeds to give a description of the basic features of the three disciplines in §§ 87–102. We shall allude to these later. I have already drawn attention to the important thesis § 102 (= § 70 note).[45]

Schleiermacher calls exegetical theology his first historical discipline. I have already remarked on the way in which he is universally praised for eliminating the distinction between the Bible and church history, for lowering the antithesis between primitive history and history to the level of an antithesis between beginning and continuation. The very first definitions show that this is *all* that is at issue, and can be at issue, in the study of primitive Christianity. For him "primitive" (in German the prefix "Ur-") has for him the totally innocuous significance of the first recognizable form of what is evolving. Primitive Christianity denotes the time "when doctrine and fellowship . . . first came into being and were not yet in fixed form" (§ 87), "emergent Chris-

---

[45]See above, p. 152.

tianity," as the first edition says. One can hardly describe as very convincing or impressive the attempt that is made in the note to § 87 to differentiate primitive Christianity from the ensuing period by means of the concept of the fluidity or fixity of the fellowship. Since knowledge of primitive Christianity can be achieved only through acquaintance with the documents of the period, which, as Schleiermacher admits, might be said of both church history and the Christian present, "in view of the distinctive nature of these writings" [§ 88 note] this discipline becomes in a special way exegetical theology. How Schleiermacher tries to establish the "distinctive worth" of primitive Christianity we have seen already (§ 83). It is hard to see, however, how its writings can have any special value compared to those of other periods or why they demand special exegesis. From an intellectual and Christian standpoint one must regard § 83 and §§ 87–88 as among the weak portions of the sketch. Schleiermacher obviously adopted the general theological custom of giving a special place to biblical exposition, but the point of this had long since become alien to himself and his disciples, it did not fit in with his scheme, and it thus caused an inconsistency without serving, or really being able to serve, the interests that it had formerly served in the theology of the Reformation period. § 89 is also very remarkable and not at all promising with its declaration that exposition is so closely related to philosophical theology that we must all work out our own exposition and essentially let ourselves be instructed by the masters, that is, the real specialists, only at the historical and philological level. A strange discipline, one might say, in which we need follow the experts only in the ancillary sciences, and strange experts or masters who are so strictly only in these sciences, like violin virtuosos who in fact have a knowledge only of the varnish and strings on their instruments! And it is even less a consolation for philosophical theology that all its efforts will lead only to the result that we must all work out our own schemes of biblical exposition!

The first concept to engage Schleiermacher's attention when he takes up exegetical theology is that of the *canon*. This shows that he was already aware of the problem of the place of the Bible and biblical scholarship in theology. The canon designates (§§ 103–104) the *object* of exegetical theology. This consists of the primitive Christian writings which are regarded as "being able to contribute to the original" and as such "normal depiction of Christianity" [§ 103], or, in content (§ 105), "the normal documents of the reality of Christ to and with his disciples" and of the disciples "in the establishment of Christianity"; in this definition Schleiermacher thinks he is recognizing the point of the ancient division of the canon into *euangelion* and *apostolos*. In the first edition (II, 1, § 7) he also found in these two components the antithesis of rise and continuation as regards the canon too. In the second edition (§ 105 note) he expressly dropped this idea on the ground that it might set up a distinction between the two parts relative to their "canonical dignity." But the distinction between the canon and the so-called apostolic fathers (or the apocrypha, § 109) is not a rigid one in respect of time or person (§§ 106–107). Even materially the concept of normal "canonical dignity" cannot be reduced to fixed formulas (§ 108).

Hence, second, the first and supreme task of exegetical theology is that of *higher criticism*, that is, the more precise defining of the canon (§ 110). The

Protestant church must lay claim to "ongoing engagement" in this task. The church's decision about the canon has no "authority which lifts it above investigation." In line with early vacillation we must start inquiries both (§ 111) into whether what is canonical is really uncanonical and into whether what is extracanonical ought really to be canonical, whole books (§ 112) as well as individual sections or verses being taken into consideration. Only approximately can it be established (§ 113) whether *external* signs suggest that a doubtful passage is *remote* from the "center of the church," by which he simply means its "fulness of mind and insight," or *inner* signs suggest that it may stand in a *looser* relation to the essential outlook of the canonical presentation. The boundary of the canonical is always relative and fluid; it is not staked out but remains an ideal entity; nor is it necessary that the canon should take any other form; it is permissible to have it in two editions, the traditional one and one that is constructed critically (§ 114), and, in deviation from the normal practice of the church, to abandon the uniting of the New Testament with the Old Testament (§ 115), which "does not contain a normal presentation of distinctively Christian beliefs" [§ 115 note]. The final point is made in the first edition much more briefly, incisively, and definitely at the climax of the whole section on exegetical theology (II, 1, § 3): "To bring the Jewish codex into the canon is to regard Christianity as a continuation of Judaism and is in conflict with the idea of the canon." Here then, at least verbally, Schleiermacher did moderate his well-known dislike for the Old Testament. On the other hand he is more critical in relation to the New Testament to the extent that in the first edition [II, 1, § 15] he could still say that as something that is historically given the canon must "remain as it is," the thought being inadmissible that the church was essentially in error in its decision regarding it. |

A third group of theses, §§ 116–124, deals with *lower criticism*, whose task is the same as that of philological textual criticism in other fields, namely, the ascertaining of the original (sc. oldest) readings and the establishing of a history of the New Testament text (§ 120). The theological aim of work on the canon produces here, too, a distinction between the expert, who can furnish correct texts with a critical apparatus—"purely philological tasks" [§ 124 note], as Schleiermacher himself puts it—and the ordinary theologian, who must know the principles of criticism and have a general knowledge of the sources. |

Apart from detailed matters such as the evaluation of the Old Testament, there is little to criticize in all this. On the presupposition, which Schleiermacher, of course, does not share, that there is a canon in the strict sense, it is good that the canon should be called the subject matter of biblical theology. One may even allow that Schleiermacher is right that according to the Protestant view the canon is not a given entity that was fixed once and for all by the decision of the early church and that its determination is in principle one of the tasks of biblical theology. Nevertheless one may ask whether this task makes any sense if it is not undertaken with the intention of preparing the ground for a decision, not of the academic world, but of the *church*, which will confirm or correct the decision of the early church. The very term itself shows that it is obviously the church which recognizes what the canon is, and that it does so *definitely* and *definitively* until it is better informed. Hence relative uncertainty about what is canonical and what is not can be the last word in this matter only if scholarship has the last word. If the concept of the canon is in correlation to *revelation*, this is naturally not so. For Schleiermacher it stands in correlation to the *beginning*, and this justifies and establishes the exclusion of the church in this matter and the "primacy of scholars" (Schlatter)[46] and hence also the resultant uncertainty and the possibility of a double canon.

This leads Schleiermacher fourth (§§ 125–131) to *languages*. Without a [1/17/24] knowledge of these no exposition is possible because no translation, however masterly, can replace the original. Aramaic is desirable as the basis of many passages in the New Testament, and so is Hebrew (though only) because of the relationship of the New Testament to the Old. Other Semitic languages are also valuable for a full understanding of the canon, but these are only for experts. |

The fifth theme which Schleiermacher addresses is *hermeneutics*, or the art of exposition (§§ 132–138), which according to § 138 is the true center of exegetical theology. Because of the importance of the theme I will deal with Schleiermacher's hermeneutics in a separate section, and hence I will refer here only to the most essential points. In the first edition (II, 1, § 31, omitted from the second) we find the excellent thought that "the goal of all exposition" is "to reconstruct the act of writing." Its *principles* should not form an aggregate but a system which rests on the nature of thought and speech [§ 133]. Note provisionally the important thesis § 134: "Protestant theology cannot accept an idea of the canon which in dealing with it rules out the use of this art," along with the note which discloses that what is particularly meant by this danger is the notion of "a miraculously inspired and perfect understanding" of the canon. The question will have to occupy us how far, after this rather brief dismissal of the older Protestant doctrine of the internal testimony of the Spirit, there is, *positively*, a *theological* hermeneutics. According to § 137 special New Testament hermeneutics is to be regarded provisionally only as a special instance of the general art of interpretation. According to § 136 the main *problem* of New Testament hermeneutics seems to have been for Schleiermacher that of the relation between the individual writings and the canon as a whole. Regarding the practice of the art he thinks (§ 138 note) that the basic principles have such a decisive influence on the handling of criticism and on the linguistic findings that no one (§ 139) should rely on others in this field but each should achieve the greatest possible personal mastery. |

In a sixth group of theses, §§ 140–146, he deals with what one would call today the historical background of the New Testament. To understand a work one needs a knowledge of the ideas which produced it and of the life-situations of the authors and readers, in this case of earlier and later Judaism and the cultural and political circumstances, and for these in turn one needs the knowledge and the correct use of a whole number of sources. The first edition (II, 1, § 33) says explicitly and correctly that "no view of the canon can declare

---

[46]Neither this phrase, nor one like it, has been found in the works of Schlatter; Barth was no doubt quoting from memory.

these conditions of understanding to be superfluous." According to § 143 all this material is related to apologetics, and according to § 144 it should be entitled "Jewish and Christian antiquities" and belongs to "Introduction to the New Testament,"[47] although Schleiermacher himself did not keep to this arrangement in his lectures on the subject.[48] |

The section concludes with two principles regarding the relationship between Christianity and scholarship in this whole discipline. According to § 147 work on the canon which manifests no interest in Christianity can only be directed *against* it. On the other hand work on the New Testament cannot be much help without philology, for, pretending to be theology but unable to achieve a pure and accurate understanding, it can only "cause confusion by a pseudodogmatic tendency" (§ 148). In other words, a non-Christian New Testament scholar would be an opponent of the canon or its content, but a non-scientific New Testament scholar would turn out to be something even worse, namely, a fatal friend. Positively, then, a "personal interest in Christianity" [§ 147] and a "philological spirit and skill" [§ 148] are the real criteria of biblical scholarship which is legitimately theological and scientific. In this or a similar fashion, culminating at least in this gentle both-and, the problem is still handled today, with emphasis as needed either on the one side or the other. But one might ask whether a third and much more important thing beyond these subjective conditions is not totally *forgotten* here, namely, what the older Protestant theology called "the inner testimony of the Holy Spirit." This is not exhaustively indicated either by "personal interest in Christianity" or by a "philological spirit and skill." It denotes materially a partnership between the expositor and the author that he is expounding, an understanding regarding the theme of the text, which neither the Christianity nor the scholarship of the expositor can provide, but which like the theme is a given, so that like the concept of the canon itself it has to stand in correlation with *revelation*, by which the expositor knows that he is confronted, and also with the *church*, which he knows is standing behind him with its mandate as the true subject of the knowledge and exposition of this text. In comparison with the older church, including the reformers, a gap opens up in Schleiermacher at this point, and this gap was not filled by the theology of the 19th century, zealously though it called for Christian experience on the one side and historical criticism on the other.

Schleiermacher calls the second historical discipline "historical theology in the narrower sense, or church history"[49] (sc. § 149: in the broader sense): "knowledge of the whole development of Christianity from the time that it established itself as a historical phenomenon" [§ 149]. According to § 90 this church history in the broader sense subdivides into real church history (the history of the community) and the history of dogma (or doctrine). In §§ 150–159 there is first developed a brief methodology of the general science of history. Historical study unites an *intuitively synthetic view* of a complex of facts in its own inwardness with a *discursively analytical consideration* and presen-

---

[47]Schleiermacher has "zum Neuen Testament," Barth "in das Neue Testament."
[48]Cf. p. 137, n. 4.
[49]This is the title of Part II, Section 2 of the *Kurze Darstellung*.

tation of the many facts into which this inner complex breaks down, a comparison being suggested in § 151 note with the relationship of soul and body. Real historical depiction, the "construction of a fact" by uniting the two functions, is a "free intellectual activity" which is to be distinguished as such from the "mechanical attainment of historical knowledge after the manner of a chronicle" [§ 152], but not in such a way that the talent for historical apprehension makes that mechanical skill superfluous [§ 155]. Church history, to which Schleiermacher turns in § 160, has as its subject everything "that proceeded from the unique power of Christianity" in distinction from that which merely "originates in the nature of the organs that are set in motion" or "the influence of alien principles" [§ 160]. It has first to note that a new Christian principle appeared with different and differentiated *functions* which in their *interconnection* at each period under review constitute a whole which is the subject of church history. The two main functions that call for notice in the development of Christianity are, according to § 166, (1) the "construction of doctrine," that is, "the pious consciousness clarifying itself," and [2.] the formation of community life, that is, the "community impulse which is to be satisfied in all through each."[50] Sometimes it will be the academic and especially the philosophical situation and sometimes the political and social circumstances that have an impact on these functions, and they may *possibly*, though not *necessarily*, be the cause of *"sick* conditions" (§ 167); in this regard it should be noted that the whole idea of the pious consciousness found its way into Schleiermacher's presentation only in the second edition, the first edition usually describing the same thing as Christian principle or the like. Church history in the narrower sense, that is, the history of the church's *life*, deals especially with the *cultus*, "the public impartation of elements in religious life" [§ 168], and *custom*, that is, the impress of Christian principle on action (§§ 168–176). Schleiermacher finds the movement of the history of dogma (§ 177) in two things: first, the self-contemplation of Christian self-consciousness, and second, the effort to give this self-consciousness increasingly agreed and accurate expression. The first edition (II, 2, § 28) stated more abstractly, but in a way that perhaps indicates Schleiermacher's purpose more clearly, that it deals with "the progressive consideration of the Christian principle" on the one hand and on the other with "the search for the place for statements of Christian feeling in the prevailing philosophical system." In § 178 we find a concept which was especially championed by the Hegelian school in theology, namely, that there is an order in the historical appearance of individual doctrines and dogmas, a sequence which is seen to be necessary in view of the nature of Christianity, whereas personal relations, or relations that lie outside the matter itself, have an influence on the development of doctrine only in periods when the church is in a sick condition (§ 179). In virtue of the twofold inner and outer movement of the history of dogma there arises (§ 180) on the one side a striving for *"deduction* from the canon," as the first edition put it (II, 2, § 29) (or for the agreement of statements with those of primitive Christianity, as the second edition says), and on the other side a striving for *agreement* with things that originated elsewhere and are not the

[50]Schleiermacher has "in each through all and all through each."

products of Christian faith, that is, *philosophical principles*. The first edition issues a warning here: "The attempt to bring philosophical systems into theology usually stands opposed to the use of proper biblical exegesis" (II, 2, § 32), but the second edition omits this. Instead we read in § 181 that it is just as unhealthy when some, hampering the development of doctrine, try to stay with the original statements of Christianity, as when others, disrupting and falsifying the principle of doctrine, try to introduce philosophical principles into Christian doctrine without any connection with the New Testament. § 183 draws attention to the problem of the history of Christian ethics when it is sundered in part at least from the history of dogma. |

Recommending that you read for yourselves the purely methodological theses §§ 184–194, I now turn at once to the third section of historical theology, which Schleiermacher entitled "Historical Knowledge of the Present State of Christendom." Under this title we have to do primarily with dogmatics, that is, with the presentation (§ 97) of Christian doctrine "as it is valid in a given age." In accordance with this definition we should conclude strictly that he has in mind a discipline which along the lines of symbolics presents and develops the doctrines of different Christian churches in their relationships and contradictions. But this is not his intent. He rejects the term "systematic theology" but still maintains that properly each church can deal dogmatically only with its own teaching (§ 98), the presentation of that of other churches being a part of the history of dogma (§ 195 note). For us, then, dogmatics can only be "knowledge of the doctrine that now obtains in the Evangelical Church" [§ 195]. Such a presentation is *dogmatic* as distinct from historical when the context of the doctrine is established by the personal view of the one who does the survey. For this *conviction* is necessary, but not the agreement of all contemporary experts. *Valid* doctrine consists of all "that is officially maintained and accepted without provoking official opposition" [§ 196 note]. Schleiermacher obviously means what an official representative of the church may teach as such without being officially referred back[51] to a higher authority (leaders or synods) (§ 196). The concept of dogmatics does not apply to a predominantly individual presentation which deviates from the common teaching or to one which simply expresses the common teaching at a particular time (§ 197). Why dogmatics? The leadership of the church needs insight into the general development of the principle of a period and the possibilities it contains for the future and it also needs a norm for the popular expression of doctrine which will avoid ancient and modern errors. According to Schleiermacher it was from the latter concern, and the task of preaching, that dogmatics originally developed (§ 198). What the church *decides* about doctrine is always provided by contact with the last *epoch* (for us the Reformation), while the *individuality* of the dogmatician has more impact on that which points to the future within it (§ 199). The dominating principle of a period, or the doctrine developed out of it, forms the coherent core of every dogmatic presentation. But it may be taken differently by different people, and there may be detailed or interrelated elements in it that are not connected

---

[51]Barth uses here the archaic word "koramieren" ("[ad] Koran nehmen"), which means "to take to task."

with that principle but intimate the development of a new one. A comprehensive dogmatics has to allow for both factors and it has thus to be *divinatory* as well as *assertive* (§§ 200–202). The theses that follow in §§ 203–208 have justly become famous. They deal with the terms *orthodoxy* and *heterodoxy*, which Schleiermacher boldly interprets in such a way that the former denotes those elements of teaching in which it is a matter of holding fast to something universally acknowledged, whereas the latter denotes those whose tendency is to keep doctrine mobile and open. Both are *equally important* for the historical development of Christianity and its individually significant elements; the former brings unity and the latter freedom. There are things that are *antiquated* in preaching and that have also lost their significance for the scientific totality of doctrine, thinks Schleiermacher, but he does not tell us what authority decides where and when this is to be regarded as the case. It is *false orthodoxy* to carry such elements forward in dogmatics. On the other hand, it is *false heterodoxy* to object to formulas which are current in the church's preaching and do not disturb the system as a whole. Dogmatics should avoid both; for all its mobility it must remain orthodox in the main heads of doctrine and for all its respect for accepted teaching it must introduce what is heterodox. A dogmatician who is either a one-sided innovator, "making everything mobile" (first edition [II, 3, § 14]), or a no less one-sided glorifier of what is old, is an imperfect instrument of the church.

§§ 209–231 again offer a series of methodological observations[52] which [1/21/24] this time I will not skip, for they are very important for Schleiermacher. He deals first with the *churchly character* of dogmatics. Dogmatic statements have *more* or *less* need of specific attestation. *Less* if the popular, biblical, and academic expressions of the same thought are almost identical, so that any believer can control them equally—this is Schleiermacher's criterion of truth— by the certainty of his own direct pious self-consciousness. These are the statements which on his view will replace in his day the so-called "fundamental articles" of older Protestant dogmatics that are now outdated. Specific attestation is more necessary when this congruence is lacking. It must then consist of the tracing back of the content of the relevant statements to the New Testament (in what was earlier called the scripture proof) and of a demonstration of their agreement with related, neighboring statements that have their own inner certainty. In the first edition we seem to find something different (II, 3, § 20), for he says there well and briefly: "Every element that is adopted in the presentation must test the way it is defined by the canon and by speculation." Did Schleiermacher really have anything different in view in the second edition? Compare § 209 with § 180, where relative to the history of dogma the second edition says expressly concerning these generally accepted statements with which there must be agreement that they are *not* statements originating in Christian faith but in philosophy. We shall see that in the second edition this is his view in dogmatics as well, but he now devotes a special discussion to it. For statements which define the character of a period, or for specifically Protestant statements, a proof from the confessional writings can replace the proof from scripture "if we can still accept the exposition

[52]§§ 223–231: Dogmatics and Ethics.

which was in vogue at the time" [§ 211]. Worked out dogmatically, such statements will necessarily express the antithesis to Roman Catholicism. |

From a second standpoint Schleiermacher discusses the question of the scientific character of dogmatics. Here he honors in the second edition what the first edition called the proof from speculation alongside the proof from the canon. "The strictly didactic expression," says § 213, which the "scientific attitude gives" to dogmatics "is dependent on the prevailing state of the philosophical disciplines," formally on logic, materially on psychology and ethics. Any philosophy but one that is materialistic, sensualistic, or atheistic can be linked to dogmatics, teaches § 214. Hence, according to the philosophy that a dogmatician accepts, there can be different versions of the same doctrine without altering its religious content. In the words of the first edition, there results "a differing expression of the individual doctrines without forfeiture of the original religious affections of the mind which are meant to be represented by the doctrine" (II, 3, § 26). Differences of terminology—and this is all that can be meant—can thus give rise to dogmatic controversy only through misunderstanding. On the other hand the formulas of two dogmaticians that academically sound much the same may conceal a very different religious content about which there then has to be dogmatic controversy (Schleiermacher has in mind some statements of Protestant and Roman Catholic dogmatics which sound much alike but whose agreement is only verbal and not material). |

A third series expands on another distinction that Schleiermacher makes, namely, between that which *everybody* ought to know about dogmatics and that which is required *only* of *experts*. A universal requirement for evangelical theologians is that they should form their own convictions about the central dogmatic loci or heads—central (or strict) to the extent that they are important and distinctive for the Reformation or the present-day church.[53] (It is the same swing of the pendulum between what has been and what is coming into being, what is already there and what is just emerging, the old and the new, that[54] always constitutes dogmatic knowledge for Schleiermacher.) The dogmatic expert or master, however, must also be acquainted with all contemporary approaches and controversies, with all "ventured opinions," by which we are to understand not only the "ephemeral phenomena of temperamental and disordered personalities" but also those ideas that proceed from antichristian or antievangelical impulses. The expert must be able to reach a sound judgment on all these without any loss of alert receptivity (§ 222 note)—a difficult task, one might say, for a harassed person. |

Fourth and last Schleiermacher discusses the important question of the relation between dogmatics and ethics [§§ 223–231]. He does not regard the distinction between the two as material or original. Christian rules of life are also theoretical and are statements of faith. A *union* of the two disciplines

---

[53]In § 219 Schleiermacher says: "It is required of all evangelical theologians that in forming their own convictions they should study all the strict loci of doctrine, not only as they developed out of the principles of the Reformation as such and in opposition to Roman Catholic dogmas, but also to the extent that something new has taken shape whose historical significance at least for the moment cannot be overlooked."

[54]The MS erroneously has a "das" for a "die" here.

would prevent the distortion of dogmatic statements into "spiritless formulas" and of ethical statements into "purely external precepts" [§ 244 note]. It would also dispel the deep-seated illusion that ethics can be understood and practiced independently alongside doctrine, and the possibility of basing dogmatics on some other philosophy than ethics. In favor of separation it may be argued—and since Schleiermacher himself stayed with this method he seems to have regarded this point as a cogent one—that dogmatics takes its vocabulary from the rational theology or metaphysics of the day, whereas ethics takes it from moral philosophy. All that has been said about the task of dogmatics, about orthodoxy and heterodoxy, and about the churchly and scientific character of dogmatic work, applies equally to ethics, and hints regarding the relations between the two are not neglected.

The picture that Schleiermacher has given of the scientific character of Christian doctrine can only be called unclear in the light of his expositions of the history of dogma and dogmatics. For him Christian doctrine was, is, and will be a product of the religious affections of the mind or the pious self-consciousness which—it is assumed—usually expresses its various states in this form (not in this form alone, but also in this form of doctrine, or religious thought). It is also assumed that this religious self-consciousness, and with it its doctrinal expression, goes through a process of historical development, and that every age has the right to explain this process in terms of its own state and the expressions of this state, regarding these as a (provisional) fulness of the times pointing forward to a distant and better future. In this sense the history of dogma reaches its climax in dogmatics as a branch of the church's knowledge of the present. If for the development of the discipline there is needed not only an acquaintance with the material, that is, prevailing Christian thought, but also the personal conviction that can give the necessary cement to the building made of this material, this is an accidental and subsidiary aspect of the historical method in its application to the present. But the method of dogmatics—Schleiermacher did in fact carry out this decisive point in the second part of his program with great brilliance—is still that of historical description. He never considers the possibility of relating dogmatics to the final truth of philosophy. Here the world has already been abandoned to the speculative sciences of nature and culture insofar as the dialectic that transcends them both does not prove that there is *no* final truth for them either. He also never considers basing dogmatics on *revelation*, whose truth would be different in principle from that of the coming and going emanations of the pious self-consciousness, and more than the endlessly self-renewing life which is the substratum of that process of development. He also never seems to consider the question of the *truth* of his dogmatic statements. They do not seek to be anything more or less than a faithful reflection of reality, namely, the reality of the expressions of the religious mind that are possible, permissible, and necessary in the given state of things. Schleiermacher does have certain *criteria* for establishing this reality. We have seen that he tries to elucidate the concept of what is valid at a given time with the help of the idea of what is official; that he characterizes the inner movement of the process of dogmatic learning as listening to the voice of religious experience on the one side and working to translate the language of this voice into clear ideas on the other; that he finds a corrective in scripture or the confessions on the one side and in the dominant philosophical concepts of contemporary scholarship on the other; that he does justice to the spirit of the current period and assigns it a duty over against the individuality of the dogmatic thinker; and that he makes out of the concepts of orthodoxy and heterodoxy friendly methodological frontiers that one should not cross but know how to walk between as a clever theologian who can unite them in himself and in a "dark thrust" know the right path.[55] It should also be said that Schleiermacher wanted coherent thinking in dogmatics and required all theologians to be engaged in building their own convictions. But one should not overlook the fact that, all told, these criteria and postulates have a more or less formal, relative, and technical character. There is no expectation of a decided Yes or a decided No, of an Either-Or, in all these methodological counsels and maxims. As a whole and in particular they have the character of laws of nature; they *describe* the *basic forms* in which the reality of which dogmatics speaks appears in thousandfold experience; but they are not authoritative courts which stand imperiously above the natural religious process, not merely as forms which it takes, but as presuppositions from which it derives. Schleiermacher knows of no such *presuppositions* in the strict sense, of no genetic principle, not in the biological but the transcendental sense. In him Kantian criticism became an agnostically enframed positivism. According to his account only *feeling*, which is finally identical with the self-consciousness, has genuine transcendence, the dignity of *truth*, and even this has it only with a complete lack of particularity or quality, with timeless inwardness. Christianity as a *specific* feeling, and Christian doctrine as a specific *expression* of this specific feeling, that is, as the subject of a positive science, and this positive science itself, have *no* part in this transcendence, in this dignity of truth. Theology no longer moves into or out of this light in the theology of Schleiermacher, nor dogmatics in his *Kurze Darstellung*.

Let us now conclude our survey of the Encyclopedia with a few swift strokes. The character of dogmatics in his system could not be more sharply clarified than by the fact that its closest neighbor is church statistics—the theme of §§ 232–250. Schleiermacher naturally does not mean by this the compiling of figures and the drawing of conclusions from these figures in the modern sense of the term. He is thinking of acquaintance with the inner and outer state of the church at a specific historical moment. In the form of symbolics, which is a subdivision of the discipline according to § 249, prevailing doctrine belongs to this sphere, except that it is now simply presented for reference and not tested and interrelated as in dogmatics. The task of statistics is to give an account of the state of *all* Christian churches. Schleiermacher has three objects in view. The innermost of these is the *content* of the church fellowship, its distinctive community spirit, the health or sickness of the religious life that fills it (whether indifferentism or separatism is a threat), how it may be known from the state of its doctrine, from the community's

---

[55]Cf. J. W. von Goethe, *Faust* I.v.328f. (Prologue in Heaven):
Ein guter Mensch, in seinem dunklen Drange,
Ist sich des rechten Weges wohl bewusst.

interest in this, from the influence of its community spirit on the other spheres of its life, from its manifestation in liturgical life. The second is the *form* in which this content manifests itself, that is, the constitution by whose determinations church life is ordered, the organization of its leadership, the clergy and their relation to the rest of the community. Statistics is all the better when it can give a more perspicacious account of the relation between content and form. The third consists of the *outward relations* or connections of the Christian fellowships both with non-Christians and with one another, but especially with the state and scholarship; in this regard it should be noted that these last relations can vacillate between two extremes: Either the church recognizes no scholarship or social order as the one that it can itself develop, or the objective consciousness may claim for itself the truth of the self-consciousness, scholarship swallowing up Christian doctrine and the state the church. It need hardly be said that by means of mutual concessions Schleiermacher's way leads between the two extremes. |

§§ 247–248 offer an interesting parallel to §§ 147–148. As the latter said of exegesis, so the former now say of church statistics that a scientific concern for the present state of Christianity that has no interest in the church can lead only to scepticism or to attacks on Christianity, but a purely religious interest with no scientific spirit can serve only the subjectivity of a person or party. |

These theses point to a problem that arises in this whole issue. They show that the discipline that Schleiermacher calls statistics might in some way become a criticism of the church as it is. It is certainly unhelpful that in the modern study of theology in the universities this discipline is almost universally neglected or treated as secondary, that hardly any specific courses are devoted to it, although Schleiermacher may well have been right when he equated it in importance with dogmatics. This would undoubtedly have been justifiable if it had really been a matter of criticizing the existing church, if theology, after presenting the church's doctrine with respectful objectivity in dogmatics, had done it the service of measuring its real life by the newly won or purified norm of the Christian truth which stands above both theology and church. Next to this service which only theology can render, what can be more valuable for the church than a friendly court which champions its cause but is still independent of it, and by which its actions and aspirations, its preaching, its worship, its community life, and its public activity or inactivity are all set in the light of its own origin and exposed to criticism in the freest and most ruthless way? If the doctrine and indeed the whole existence of the church were what it ought to be, the immanent criticism of the world, the prophetic voice of truth, the living conscience of society, would it not, or would not the Protestant church at least, which does not claim to have Christian truth in fee, have to postulate that it, too, is appropriately held in check, and truth, even Christian truth, is constantly told it to its face, by the world? And what can better be regarded here as the bearer of the Christian things that have to be said in criticism of the state of the church than an academic theology which has its seat as an instrument of the church in the very midst of the world, in the very citadel of secular learning? Should theology be content to serve the church without doing so also in the form of criticism? Will it not acquire a good conscience in its rendering of true and serious service to the church precisely and solely by constantly showing its leaders how their appearance and activity look to Christian eyes and also to secular eyes from a secular standpoint, what the voice of the people, viewed as the voice of God, has to say regarding and against the church, not against its origin, but, with a knowledge of its origin, against its actual form and reality?

These are, of course, thoughts that are remote from Schleiermacher's statistics, and inevitably so in view of the basic outline and character of his theology. The possibilities with which he reckons in §§ 247–248 are only academic scepticism on the one side and religious subjectivism and party spirit on the other, and he can only warn against these without considering that there might be a scepticism, a final scepticism, and a subjectivism, a supreme subjectivism, whose voice it would be best for the church to hear to its own salvation. But the presupposition of this final scepticism and supreme subjectivism is, of course, that there is a final and supreme truth. A theology which as dogmatics does not know the *latter* is understandably incapable of the *former* as statistics. Its statistics will be the exact opposite of prophecy, of Christian crisis, namely, an assembling of facts, just as its dogmatics will be nothing but an assembling of facts presented with conviction and arranged with perspicacity. One might object that Schleiermacher is well enough aware of this critical function of theology in relation to the church, namely, in his philosophical theology, which, as is expressly stated later (§ 257), "has to bring to clear awareness the feelings of pleasure and displeasure at the existing state of the church." But Schleiermacher's philosophical theology explicitly takes a standpoint or starting-point that lies *outside* Christianity. Hence one cannot expect any *Christian* criticism of the church from it. Yet its existence is, of course, the reason why Schleiermacher does *not* expect this function, which it discharges, from his statistics. That this discipline could have no future under these auspices, but would be a Cinderella of whose existence only 10 percent of theologians and 0 percent of the rest of humanity would have even an inkling, is also understandable. The essential irrelevance of a collection of facts about the churches can hardly be concealed even when the obsolete title of statistics is replaced by a modern one such as information about the churches or about popular religion.

[1/22/24]   Schleiermacher crowned his chapter on historical theology with some "concluding observations." § 251 develops a remarkable but characteristic special doctrine of the individual ("personality") and his[56] significance for historical theology. It is more fitting for historical theology than for other historical sciences to link its depiction of epoch-making times "to the lives of preeminently active individuals," and individuals are the more suitable for this purpose the more they correspond to the idea of "princes of the church." Even notable deviations in doctrine are often made most intelligible from the lives of their authors. But the dominant impact of individuals on the masses in the Christian churches is to be seen on the whole as a declining one. It was absolute in Christ but was later shared among many. The further we go, the less such princes of the church are to be expected. We shall now skip over a

---

[56]The "ihre" of the MS (probably referring to the fem. "Persönlichkeit") has been emended to a "seine."

number of theses which show how urgently necessary philosophical theology is as a safeguard against all false apriorism and empiricism, and move on at once to the fourth section.

4. Practical Theology [§§ 257–338]. We recall that in the first edition this was extolled as the "crown of theological study."[57] It is primarily set in relation to philosophical theology. With its question as to the nature and form of Christianity, the latter as the representative of ethics has brought to "clear awareness the feelings of pleasure and displeasure at the existing state of the church" [§ 257]. Though taking a standpoint or starting-point that lies outside Christianity, it has discharged the function of criticism about which we spoke a moment ago in relation to statistics, and it is now the task of practical theology "to order, and direct to its goal," the "considered activity" which results from the movements of the mind related to these feelings (1. feelings of pleasure and displeasure, 2. movements of the mind, 3. activity, 4. practical theology!). So § 257. Ordering and directing to the goal are the point of practical theology—§ 260: Establishing the right way to carry out all the tasks that come under the concept of church leadership—not establishing the correct understanding of these tasks. According to § 263 the "considered activity" which is the theme of practical theology consists of "influencing the church in such a way that Christianity may be more purely represented in it," that is, of spiritual direction. Since no other means are to be used than "certain influences on the mind, or again spiritual direction," it follows that the *means* and *end* that are discussed in practical theology are *identical*. |

In the rules that it seeks to give to those called upon to lead the church, what is at issue is a method, and indeed (§ 268) the "method of the circle whereby the (presupposedly increasing) power of leaders stimulates the masses and the masses in return evoke this (power)." According to § 267 church leadership is simply a special form of the general distinction between leaders and the masses. Its special feature is that it relates to the regulation of the circle of religious power, or, concretely, to "leadership in the cultus and the ordering of practice" [§ 269], an activity that can be viewed and adopted as either more clerical or more theological in the narrower sense, and considered from the standpoint of either the individual congregation or the church as an organic union of all such congregations. The latter distinction gives Schleiermacher (§ 271 and § 274) the principle by which he divides his practical theology into the doctrine of *ministry* in the church, that is, leadership in the local congregation, and the doctrine of *government* in the church, that is, leadership in the larger union. |

Let us look at ministry first (§§ 277–308). "The local congregation" is the "sum of the Christian households of the same confession living in the same place and united in common piety" [§ 277]. The cultus is first dealt with here under the title of the *edificatory* work of leadership in which the pastor joins with the congregation. This work rests "chiefly on the impartation of the religious self-consciousness expressed as thought" (§ 280). The science of practical theology has to determine what elements in the common teaching es-

[57]First ed., Introduction, § 31 (Scholz, p. 10, footnote 2); cf. p. 145.

tablished by dogmatics are suitable for this impartation, and in what way [§ 281]. Formally it has also to deal with religious style, and finally it must consider what innovations of form or content to command or forbid. Religious speech is the "true core of the cultus" (§ 284), but not necessarily in the form of the Protestant sermon. In this regard homiletics must be on the lookout for more and better forms. The other element in the cultus in which the parson is not a free author but an agent of the church authorities is liturgy. Since his activity as preacher and liturgist takes the form of direct impartation by "organic" (physical) operation, there has to be "a use of *miming* . . . in the field of religious presentation" [§ 288 note], and with regard to the influence of the ecclesiastical environment there has to be a similar use of the theory of *ornamentation* [§ 289 note]. From the standpoint of leadership in which the pastor is relatively distinct from individual members of his congregation as such, the main thing is *catechizing*. By the vitalizing of their religious consciousness in both thought and impulse the young should be put on equal terms with adults here as regards religious receptivity; this is, therefore, a special task in the general field of education. The same standpoint yields (§ 296) "a theory for treating converts" and another (§ 298) for missions. Because he introduced the latter into the theological encyclopedia Schleiermacher has always been highly regarded by the supporters of missions. The relative inequality of members of the congregation means that there is a task of *pastoral care* that aims to restore relative equality (§§ 299ff.), and naturally according to § 302 the spiritual care of the sick and social nurture of the weak, that is, edification and ordinary converse, are closely related to this. Within the context of discipline a final section (§§ 303ff.) deals with this insofar as it is not a matter for the whole church or for personal freedom and insofar as it can be done when Evangelical practice is still in process of emergence as compared with that of Roman Catholicism. |

Now let us listen to Schleiermacher on church government (§§ 309–334). "A historical unit can continue in being only through the same forces as those by which it arose," we read in § 312. Hence Evangelical church government consists of two elements, one of union and organization, that is, ecclesiastical authority, which essentially orders and restricts, and one which is unbound, the free power of the spirit, which in principle any member of the church can exercise, and which essentially stimulates and warns. In this section practical theology has to show how these two factors, without yielding anything or disrupting one another, can be in vital interaction. Ecclesiastical authority orders the relationship between pastor and congregation, seeks to regulate cultus and practice by balancing necessary uniformity with justifiable local customs, and in cases of dissension in the congregations gives final decisions as an expression of the common spirit. It recognizes (§ 323) that alterations in doctrine "should arise out of the research of individuals only when these are adopted into the conviction of the common body," but also seeks to maintain "the unity of the church in the basic principles of its origin." It has to work toward safeguarding the church either against "impotent independence of the state," and of the university in respect of its teaching, or against "ever so respectable servitude under it" [§ 325]. (Cf. §§ 325–326 with §§ 240–241.) Finally—a climax that is typical of Schleiermacher—the church authorities of the different Evangelical churches (Lutheran and Reformed!) all have the task of keeping themselves open to closer connections with one another and fostering these within their own fellowships, "so that no favorable opportunity for establishing them may be neglected" [§ 327], the task, in other words, of promoting union. This task marks the limit of church authority because its fulfilment depends not only on this authority but also on the activity of the free power of the spirit and because with this fulfilment the existing form of church government perishes. The second and unbound element in church government, the free power of the spirit, Schleiermacher finds represented chiefly in the vocation of academic theologians and ecclesiastical authors to the extent that these coincide with the frequently mentioned category of princes of the church. The problem of *academic theology* he discerns in the question how the scholarly spirit can be kindled in young theologians "without weakening the religious interest" [§ 330], how individual research can be encouraged[58] and yet a demand made for the faithful preservation of the legacy of previous theological work in the church. *Ecclesiastical authors* have also to consider that "all error arises only in relation to the truth, and everything bad only in relation to what is good," and that this principle is the basic condition of all controversy and all improvement [§ 332 note]; furthermore, if they want to secure recognition for something new, they must direct their full attention to the joint antithesis and connection between the old and the new. Finally they must orient their presentation in such a way that it can be understood only by those of whom it may be expected that they will use it properly—all of these being conditions in which Schleiermacher unmistakably offered a portrait of his own literary characteristics. |

In the concluding considerations which he also appends to his practical theology [§§ 335–338] he says among other things that he cannot speak specifically about *expertise* in this field because it rests on contingent personal limitations and in and for themselves those who are called upon to be church leaders can always be effective even if with different degrees of perfection. The better the grounding in philosophical theology, the more accurately will the tasks of practical theology be posed; the richer the historical education, the more correct will be the methods that are found; the higher the natural ability and general culture, the better the execution.

We ourselves may be brief in our final remarks on this last part of the book. Again I will not stop to consider how far this or that deduction or division is logically or practically tenable or possible. Here as in other parts of the system we must agree that even on Schleiermacher's own presuppositions many things are too brilliantly and hastily tossed off to be pedantically tested in detail or criticized specifically, although it should be noted that in his lectures on practical theology[59] Schleiermacher himself followed the main outlines of the program suggested here. Let us be content to state that his distinctive presuppositions and their consequences are everywhere visible here. Those who base their philosophical theology on an ethics which is itself only the description of a principle that actually holds sway in history, those who

---

[58]The MS has ". . . how encouragement for individual research can be encouraged."
[59]Cf. p. 16, n. 69.

apart from this borrowed science know only a historical theology, and a historical theology which ranges from what is elsewhere the exposition of holy scripture to what is usually called dogmatics, though it also has an "interest" in past and present facts, can only have a practical theology which is technical in nature when they finally leave the sphere of a higher science of nature (§ 25). As we have seen [§ 260], there is to be no precise discussion of the task. The means and end are identical. Spiritual direction is the self-oriented end which, sanctioned basically by philosophical ethics and illustrated in a Christian form by the picture book of history, occupies a holy place in the church. What happens in this holy place is a meaningless question. "It" *happens*. "Religious power" is in full operation. Only the *How* can be the object of renewed research and discussion. Again, as so often in the sermons, we get the impression that the Christian church is a gigantic body, growing throughout history and into the present, with all kinds of wonderful organs and suckers which reach out like polyps in every direction, or, to put it more elegantly, it is a river which, growing broader and shallower and flowing more slowly, moves with a mighty flow to the sea which is its goal but also its end. Try it out for yourselves whether you can get any clear idea of what Schleiermacher has in mind with other than naturalistic images, with images in which the spirit is really something specific, something truly and definitively different. It is in keeping with his biological understanding that he sees the congregation being built up through families that are united in common piety. Note that for him it is not the pious *individual*, as in English pioneers of the liberal view of the church,[60] but, under the plain influence of the concepts of natural science, it is the *family* which is the individual unit from which the congregation is formed, and then from the congregation the church. The final development is naturally a *Reformed* relic, but I would beg of you not, on account of this relic, to confuse his teaching, which rests on very different premises, with the Reformed doctrine of the church. It is in keeping with his total view that the pastor in his so-called edificatory activity is primarily the mouthpiece of the community itself and not the minister of the Word of God, that in his so-called pastoral care his aim is simply to remove the inequalities and imbalances that arise in the normal working of religious power, and that in children, let alone adults, his task is simply to vitalize the religious consciousness and impulse that is already present. Finally it is in keeping with this total view that there is in the last section the depicted play and counterplay between what is called church authority and what is called the free power of the spirit. How does it come about that this authority is called *authority* and that this power of the spirit, embodied in professors of theology and ecclesiastical authors, is called the power of the *spirit*? When the two mutually—not cancel one another out but (and here at a decisive point Schleiermacher's

---

[60]Cf. especially J. Locke, *A Letter concerning Toleration* (1689); also *Two Treatises of Government* (1690). According to E. Hirsch, *Geschichte der neuern evangelischen Theologie im Zusammenhang mit den allgemeinen Bewegungen des europäischen Denkens* (Gütersloh, 1949), I, 51, the church is for Locke a free union of believers in voluntary association. Hirsch finds in Locke the influence of John Milton (1608–1674) and Roger Williams (c. 1604–1683).

view is seen to be less spiritual than the opposing Roman Catholic view)—restrict and condition one another, when they confront one another as two entities struggling for equipoise! This quantitative evaluation and use of qualitative concepts like authority, subjection, spirit, and freedom, this, for all the verbal dialectics, very nondialectical and materialistic way of playing them off against one another, is the intellectual naturalism of Schleiermacher poking through again in a disruptive manner, and there is no comfort to be found for it in the many excellent observations that are made in detail because all these things—for example, the point that there can be error only in relation to truth—direct us to the naturalistic background when they are interpreted in context. It is no great testimony to the century of theology since Schleiermacher that so many of these concluding points sound just as up-to-date as if they had been written today, that we have not really, for example, moved beyond the idea that the barren contrast between an academic and a religious interest is the fundamental problem of academic theology, and that the pragmatically metaphysical way of handling spiritual entities as though they were building blocks can still in recent decades seem to be the triumph of a theological philosophy of history.

Let us try to conclude our investigation with a connected survey of the way [1/24/24] that we have taken. Following Schleiermacher's advice, we shall attempt to see how in him the *error*, or what seems to us to be the error, stands related to the *truth*.

1. We shall begin with a word on the whole. The enterprise and its execution give evidence of a passionate urge for theology as a *system*, as connected thought, as an integrated order both within itself and with all other learning. In this respect he brings to light an important and inalienable concern of theology. How can the discipline which claims to have and to present knowledge of the logos in the most comprehensive sense be wanting in logos in the subordinate and technical sense of an orderly account of its own desire and achievement? A theology which is inwardly chaotic and outwardly incapable of an encyclopedic orientation, of a definition of its place in learning, will be a poor theology no matter what excellent insights it may present in detail. Those who want to spare themselves trouble here should let Schleiermacher tell them that an earthly intellectual exercise, which is what theology is in spite of its subject, cannot escape the validity of earthly intellectual laws. Nevertheless, the laws which will have to be respected here are laws of the spirit. It causes alienation and mistrust when we find that in Schleiermacher's system we are obviously dealing with a kind of natural entity, an organism with a root, body, and crown; that all the deductions and distinctions proceed according to the principle of cell division; and that in the whole system there are, therefore, no sharp margins and contrasts or questions and answers. The opposite of chaos has to be the Spirit that broods over the deep [cf. Gen. 1:2]. But Schleiermacher obviously wants to give us *more* than a theology of the Holy Spirit, as though theology could and should be more than this. His theology seeks to be a part of the cosmic interconnection of spirit and nature. It is this, but as such it is *less* than theology could and should be. It is a bit of

the cosmos[61] which as such is impressive and can awaken astonished admiration, like a waterfall or a tropical creeper, but it has no deeply persuasive or convincing force. *Living* systematics is the Word, the *logos tēs zōēs* [1 Jn. 1:1], in its difference from life and supremacy over it. Schleiermacher's systematics itself seeks to be life. It has its wish, but in so doing it forfeits its birthright. And since his scientific system as a whole has this biotic and cosmic character, the encyclopedic integration of theology into this larger whole can only accentuate and sharpen the situation.

2. We called Schleiermacher's view of theology a positive or nonspeculative one which, in line with the concerns of the Christian church, is oriented to the historical facticity of the Christian revelation. We recognize the element of truth in this view. In contrast with the great idealists Schleiermacher tried to see that Christianity is not abstract universal truth which can be attained by abstraction; it is a contingent and highly specific thing. He was undoubtedly protecting a vital interest of theology when in 1804, in opposition to Schelling, he described "lofty caprice" as the key to Christianity.[62] But in rejecting the idealistic grounding of theology he had all the greater responsibility to see to it that justice should be done in some other way to the question of truth that was raised with salutary severity by idealism, namely, by a strict assertion of the revelatory character of that specific thing. He had to demonstrate a truth not merely equal to universal truth, but superior to it, in the "lofty caprice" of the contingent entity which with an appeal to the practical concerns of the church he exalted as the theme of theology. He did not do this, but like the theology itself, the theme of this theology, revelation in Christ and the related religious self-consciousness of his community, is a natural (though also a spiritual) organism, a datum, a fact and *nothing more,* reality and *only* reality. Neither the principial nor the historical criticism to which he then subjects this fact has anything whatever to do with the question of truth. Hence he does not do sufficient justice to this second vital interest of theology. Evading the Scylla of apriorism, he runs into the arms of the Charybdis of an empiricism masked by spiritualizing. In face of this one feels a true homesickness for the honest fanaticism for truth of the Enlightenment.

3. We have seen how Schleiermacher establishes a basis for theology as a science by borrowing from ethics. Ethics contributes the concept of piety and the pious fellowship, and in it theology finds the spectacles, as it were, to see and understand its theme. Here, too, one cannot escape the impression that it is very *proper* that theology can find no home of its own in the system of learning but as one earthly-intellectual entity among others, and more exposed than others to doubts about its scientific nature because of the unique-

---

[61]The sentences from "who broods over the deep" to this point replace an original text stroked through by Barth: ". . . who here is obviously the cosmos. This is to claim more than can be granted to man, and its result is obviously too little. Schleiermacher's theological system may be impressive but it is not convincing or compelling. And the integration of theology into all science should not mean subjection."

[62]In the review of Schelling's *Vorlesungen über die Methode des akademischen Studiums* (cf. p. 141, n. 19) in Br., IV, 586: "Again his speculative view of Christ cannot be united with his assertion that Christ is the boundary of two ages, and it erases somewhat the holy caprice which from this angle is the key to Christianity."

ness of its subject matter, it has to live as a lodger, as it were, in this area. The only point is that the place where theology borrows from ethics should not be inside but outside the smooth wall of the territory of the latter if it is true that theology is the science of revelation and that the boundary, the smooth *outside* wall of ethics (whether one defines its task with Kant or with Schleiermacher), is not the *concept* but the very critically posed *problem* of revelation. If in his view Schleiermacher had meant (1) the homelessness of theology in learning, and (2) this critically negative relation to ethics (not integration in it) that is denoted by an open question regarding the frontier, I should see no reason to contradict him. But he did not mean this. His theology is not the stranger within the gates of Israel who is sanctified as such but a full citizen and member of the family, even though one that is poor and timid.[63] With the assurance that piety and the pious fellowship are things that are envisaged by ethics, a little lodging is kindly provided for it within the academic whole when it for its part, obedient to the wishes of the master of the house, abandons its claim to be the science of revelation and is content with the theme of piety that is allotted to it instead. The situation is much the same as that of the army of Hanover at Langensalza (1866) when, having laid down its arms, it was allowed by Prussia to go home without further harassment. But one can hardly call this a proper procedure.

4. In discussing the so-called philosophical theology of Schleiermacher we noted that at the climax of apologetics, and also polemics, the express command goes out to the Christian denominations not to claim absolute truth for their own standpoint nor to engage in overzealous negation of that of others, and the question suggested itself whether the same applies to Christianity as a whole in relation to other religions. One could, and indeed should, unhesitatingly accept this relativizing of the confessions and even the religions if it meant the necessary relativizing of all Christian teaching, life, and being by its divine origin, subject, and object. Christian dogma in its Roman Catholic, Lutheran, and Reformed versions, and even the literally repeated word of scripture on the lips and in the use of Christians of any observance, and even Christianity itself in its historical manifestation, are not as such identical with the truth of Christian revelation; and measured by this, Christians in relation to one another and to non-Christians have in fact no reason to claim that their standpoint is absolute or to engage in absolute attacks against one another. If Schleiermacher had in view this relativity of all human and all Christian things before God, how could we not agree that he is right? But he clearly does not mean this. The crisis by which all the witness and message of revelation is relativized is not for him revelation itself but the philosophical ethicist's view of the totality of all pieties and pious fellowships within which *each* possibility can fundamentally be the highest one and there is no revelation unless the totality itself be called such. But this does not merely extirpate the arrogance of religious man confusing himself with God and trying to play the pope. It also eliminates all the seriousness of truth and all zeal for it. It eliminates meditation on the Word of God which has to be the transcendent meaning of the human words, the preaching and dogma, of a church that takes

[63]Barth has here "verschupfter" for "verschüchterter."

itself and its work seriously, not for its own sake, but for God's. It eliminates the possibility of proclamation, of a "Here I stand; I can do no other,"[64] not in a narrow-minded overestimation of one's own insight, but in confidence and with sighing that God will add his own confession to it. It eliminates the possibility of dialogue between the churches in which there can and must be a struggle to know God, in which not every sharp shot is removed from the cannon in advance on the theory that all and none are right. In place of this the only positive thing to emerge in Schleiermacher, the only thing to be affirmed with passion, is union, that is, a return to the totality of the one that is the same in all, and one can only be surprised that Schleiermacher did not already envisage the possibility of a religious union of humanity.[65]

5. We have seen how in Schleiermacher the true body of theology, namely, historical theology, becomes a part of history in general. This makes sense. The Bible and the church's present-day teaching are elements in history. It is not just an accidental and contingent and external task, but an inward and essential task of theological exegesis and the establishment of church doctrine, to see and recognize and pay heed to this fact always and everywhere, not just in passing, but all the time. But we only take up the theological task when we dialectically oppose to this fact the further fact that these elements of history are only witnesses to revelation or to the view of revelation which is offered in the church pending its better instruction. Without this dialectical inversion, if a little interest in Christianity or even "conviction" is the only thing demanded of the scholar, it is hard to see how this branch of historical learning can bear the name of theology. But the inversion is undoubtedly not present in Schleiermacher. For him the body of theology is absolutely historical. If in itself his organization is not the object of empiricism in the lower sense, if personal participation is needed for his understanding, and if the parts grow gigantically in places, it is still an optical illusion to think that eternal things are at issue at even a *single* point. This body does *not* have an immortal soul, nor is there *any* prospect of its resurrection. The integration of exegesis and dogmatics into history is suspicious because in spite of the antithesis between epochs and periods, and in spite of the differentiation of primitive Christianity, church history, and the church's present, history is for Schleiermacher a unity within which there are only relative contrasts, so that knowledge of it cannot in principle be anything like the knowledge of God, since no account is taken of anything that lies fundamentally outside or beyond this unity, of any critical *negation* of the totality of these relative contrasts. But if at least the knowledge of God is a contradiction in terms *without* such a critical negation, this means the end of exegesis and dogmatics as theological disciplines.

6. In surveying Schleiermacher's exegetical theology we have admiringly noted the occurrence of the concept of the "primitive" on which he tried to establish the normative character of the New Testament and especially the

[64]Luther is supposed to have concluded his speech at the Diet of Worms on April 18, 1521, with the words: "Here I stand; I can do no other. So help me, God! Amen."

[65]Rudolf Otto founded a "Religious Union of Humanity" in 1921. Cf. *Die Religion in Geschichte und Gegenwart*[3], IV, col. 876.

methodologically central concept of New Testament study, that of the canon. Here if anywhere we prick up our ears, for with this an element seems to be presented which, if it is taken seriously, will necessarily break through the great equation of unity and totality in history and hold out the prospect of real theology. I do not think that the apparent (!) inconsistency of which Schleiermacher is guilty here can be explained by saying that he still had too little knowledge or understanding of religious history and its unbroken continuity. He was as clear as any modern student of religion about the relationship in principle between primitive Christianity and religions before or outside Christianity. If nevertheless there is still in him this relative isolation of primitive Christianity and its writings, we obviously have before us the same disruptive phenomenon that in our first chapter we found already in his Christology, and that might perhaps be called the best and most typical feature of his whole theology, namely, the insistence on Christ's significance, with all the tenderness that one might desire, as the first link in Christian history, or at least as the author of the religious self-consciousness which constitutes the church. But unfortunately in both instances the disruption is not serious and the consistency of Schleiermacher's theology remains victorious even in the inconsistency. We have seen how wobbly are the reasons that he can present in §§ 83, 87–88 for that isolation of primitive Christianity. They made not the slightest impression on those who later followed in his tracks, and through his most congenial friend in the modern period (Troeltsch) the sun has brought it to light[66] that Schleiermacher himself would have done better to stop using the term "primitive" (in German the prefix *Ur-*).[67] This is shown by the fact that according to the *Kurze Darstellung* the New Testament expert is one who commands the ancillary New Testament disciplines, that the concept of the *canon* is not so much a presupposition that must be constantly affirmed as a simple object of research in historical theology and therefore an indefinite entity like all such objects, that Schleiermacher's hermeneutics not only has not enough idea but no idea at all what to make of the concept of *inspiration*, and that with ability in historical inquiry all that is required of a theologian is what is called an interest in Christianity. If that inconsistency as such shows that Schleiermacher could not altogether avoid the constitutive idea of the Reformation-Protestant school, its innocuous nature explains why the period that followed could so triumphantly stride over it. The Reformation attitude to the Bible was in fact destroyed at its very root in this science of

[66]Cf. A. von Chamisso's poem: "Die Sonne bringt es an den Tag" (1827).

[67]This enigmatic reference can mean that Troeltsch brought to light Schleiermacher's abandonment of the normativity of the canon either by his more unequivocal use of *Ur-* or by his refraining from its use. There is support for both possibilities in the texts of Troeltsch known to Barth. For the first cf. *Was heisst "Wesen des Christentums"?*, *Gesammelte Schriften*, Vol. II: *Zur religiösen Lage, Religionsphilosophie und Ethik* (Tübingen, 1913), pp. 386–451, esp. 411–423; for the seond cf. "Die Bedeutung der Geschichtlichkeit Jesu für den Glauben" (Address at a Student Conference at Aarau, 1910) (Tübingen, 1911), esp. pp. 14–16, 42–44. Barth's copy of the first work, with much underlining, is in the Karl Barth Archive at Basel, and he is known to have been at the Aarau Conference (cf. his *Theologie und die Kirche*, *Gesammelte Vorträge* [Munich, 1928], II, 8; ET *Theology and Church* [London, 1962], pp. 60f.).

primitive Christianity. It is in Schleiermacher's favor that he was unwilling to admit this, but from another angle it is regrettable that he did not do so.

7. As much can be said for the view that dogmatics is part of the study of the church's present as for the view that it is a historical discipline. Historicism as such is not objectionable; it is a justifiable agent of the knowledge of truth, of theological truth no less than any other kind. The same applies to the coordination of dogmatics with church statistics, strange though this may seem to be at a first glance. What the church has to say to the world and the world to the church can be—and more than appearances might suggest—coordinated and mutually conditioning complexes of knowledge. It would be worthwhile, then, at least to reconsider the suggestions of Schleiermacher in this regard which have been neglected up to our own time. But not, of course, without paying special regard to his initial presuppositions. Without having to deny the historical character of this study of the present [it is a good thing to realize that everything topical, no matter how passionately or profoundly it may be experienced and apprehended as present (and that perhaps most of all) belongs as such to history, to time][68]—the double question has to be put whether the church as such really has something serious to say and whether there is anything serious to say about it. What Schleiermacher's dogmatics and statistics have to say are not serious and might just as well be left unsaid. Might not the pious self-consciousness equally well, or even better, stay silent? If it is true that "if the soul speaks, then, alas! the soul no longer speaks,"[69] and if it is true that "feeling is everything, the name is sound and smoke, the encircling glow of heaven,"[70] and if Schleiermacher's view of the matter might well be summed up in these sayings of his great contemporaries Schiller and Goethe, why, then, speak, why produce sound and smoke? That the contributions of church statistics as Schleiermacher thought of it do not seem to be vitally necessary to the church is more than proved by the unconcerned and unpunished neglect of this part of his legacy. The world can very well do without *this dogmatics* and the church can very well do without *this statistics*, for neither the one nor the other has anything new or different or superior to say to its respective partner, not being an element in discussion with this partner nor directed to any true counterpart. Theology as monology is a triviality. Things would be different if the theological dogmatician and statistician were aware of exercising in their work the office of the prophet, not of the *bearer* of revelation but of its *herald*, whether from the church to the world or the world to the church. Prophecy is the proclamation of something new, of something that is not yet present but is coming, of something that stands supremely in contrast with what is, with the given, the real. Theology as prophecy would be no mean matter. It would not have to be afraid of the burden of its own historicity and relativity, of the inadequacy of all human words. The name of the *Lord* before which it would bow is not by any means sound and smoke, and the Word of the *Lord* by which it would live would not

---

[68]The brackets here are Barth's.
[69]Cf. F. von Schiller's epigram on "Speech" in *Tabulae Votivae*:
"Warum kann der lebendige Geist dem Geist nicht erscheinen?
Spricht die Seele, so spricht, ach! schon die Seele nicht mehr."
[70]Cf. J. W. von Goethe, *Faust*, I.v. 3457f.

return empty [cf. Isa. 55:11]. But these are possibilities which Schleiermacher's theology was fundamentally unable to allow for, and we can only state that it did not do so.

8. Practical theology is, we have seen, a matter of technique. It is as well that we should not be offended by this secular term. On the contrary, it is as well to let Schleiermacher tell us that the activity that he calls church leadership is in fact totally a matter of technique like any other. The Reformed legacy of Schleiermacher, which we have seen again, in part at least, in his soberly human view of the church with its orientation to the concept of the community, is one of the sounder parts of his system. But a technology in which means and end coincide, and which is thus an end in itself, is wholly secular, and even from a secular standpoint has no real substance, for if we ask how to do things without first putting the question which produces real *techne*, namely, what things we are to do, the question of the How is already an impractical one because it is pointless. And the sober objectivity of the Reformed view of the church is quickly abandoned when the dialectic between Christ and the church is dissolved and changed into identity. We saw last time[71] that all the objections to the historicism, psychologism, and naturalism of Schleiermacher's basic view come together in relation to practical theology in the question whether, when the course of religious power is presupposed, and the authority and freedom of the Spirit as that which is never given, but is always and everywhere possible only to God, is challenged, the technology whose basic principle is necessarily the denial of this possibility does not become pointless, and with it the discipline which deals with this technology. With this question we shall close.

[71]Cf. pp. 170f.

§ 5

HERMENEUTICS

As we turn from the whole to some of the details of Schleiermacher's work in academic theology, apart from *The Christian Faith*, which we shall naturally have to take as our main theme, I want to show you from at least one other example how he went about his task. I am choosing for this purpose his hermeneutics, partly because of the principial importance of the material, for if a theologian of this significance wants to explain to us from what standpoint he reads and understands other writings, and especially the Bible, will not this apparently specialized question be in a very special way the place where everything is decided?—and partly because here, as in the household sermons, we shall have the chance to get to know Schleiermacher at his best and most brilliant, in his natural strength, on his home ground, for, to use his own expression, he was a virtuoso in the field whose method hermeneutics describes. Another reason why we should not let this opportunity slip is that our objections to the general direction of his work will obviously be increased rather than diminished in the course of our lectures.

I am using as sources (1) two addresses which he gave in 1829 at the Berlin Akademie der Wissenschaften with the title "Über den Begriff der Hermeneutik," in which he took issue with the philologists Wolf and Ast on the subject (*Werke, Zur Philosophie*, III, 344ff.),[1] and (2) his lectures, edited by F. Lücke in 1838, on hermeneutics and criticism with special reference to the New Testament (*Werke, Zur Theologie*, Vol. VII).[2]

1. Let us attempt in a first subsection to see what Schleiermacher's basic principles of exposition were. Here we shall have to draw primarily on the two addresses at the Academy and the introduction to the lectures. For Schleiermacher hermeneutics is the *art of understanding*, that is, of the thoughts embodied in the words or writings of another. He wanted the term to be taken generally so as to be able to establish the more surely its special aspects. Wolf

---

[1]F. Schleiermacher, "Über den Begriff der Hermeneutik mit Bezug auf F. A. Wolfs Andeutungen und Asts Lehrbuch," *Sämmtliche Werke*, 3, *Zur Philosophie*, Vol. III, ed. L. Jonas (Berlin, 1835), pp. 344–386. New edition: *Hermeneutik*, ed. H. Kimmerle (Heidelberg, 1959), pp. 123–156 (ET *Hermeneutics*; Chico, CA, 1977).

[2]*Hermeneutik und Kritik mit besonderer Beziehung auf das Neue Testament*, from his written remains and transcribed lectures, ed. F. Lücke (Berlin, 1838) (*Sämmtliche Werke*, 1, *Zur Theologie*, Vol. VII).

and Ast had tried to make only the texts of classical antiquity the subject of the art. He reminds them that hermeneutics is also an essential tool of theology. It must be more embracing, therefore, than these special applications. Understanding something in another tongue would be too narrow a definition; texts in one's own language may need the art. Finally the written word does not form a boundary for it. Its use in the most direct dealings with others is a part of civilized life quite apart from philological or theological studies. It is an art. There is a *mechanical* understanding, for example, of the words that are bandied about in the marketplace and on the streets and in salons and at games, where one can almost guess in advance what others are saying. There is also an understanding which is more or less broadly and carefully based on *experience* and observation and which constitutes the secret and property of the person who understands. Finally, and this is where hermeneutics begins, there is an *art* of understanding which can be grasped and taught and learned according to specific rules. This art corresponds to the art of speaking, that is, rhetoric. Each act of understanding is the converse of an act of speaking. As the other has put his thoughts into speech, so I for my part must put his speech into thoughts. Understanding presupposes that we can equate ourselves with a speaker, that we can know what he has said, not just as his original readers or hearers took it, but as he himself spoke it, that we can know his inner and outer life, and that we are thus in a position—this is understanding—to reconstruct his speech, to think his thoughts after him without deviating from them and without ourselves ceasing to think. In this process— and this is the obstacle that hermeneutics seeks to overcome—there lurks the danger of *misunderstanding*. I can give to the words spoken by someone else a different meaning from that which they had as he spoke them. I can take irony seriously or vice versa. Schleiermacher calls this *qualitative* misunderstanding. But I can also, if it is factual, get a wrong impression from a sentence. He calls this *quantitative* misunderstanding. Both possibilities of misunderstanding are present in all speech. Even the term "God" is exposed to them. Where understanding is not an art, it proceeds on the assumption that understanding is natural and our only job is to avoid misunderstanding. Where it is an art, however, it proceeds on the assumption that misunderstanding is natural and the first concern is to seek understanding at every point. Is there some necessary and compelling insight into the expressed thoughts of someone else? No, replies Schleiermacher to the Homer scholar Wolf, who was influenced by the Enlightenment. In view of the multiplicity of historical and linguistic factors that have to be taken into account, and especially in view of the individuality of the author, where is there not the possibility of a *different* understanding from that which is the *most* likely? The art of hermeneutics, then, is an art of relative *approximation* to the goal of an absolutely certain understanding.

The basis of the art according to Schleiermacher is as follows. Every speech or writing of a person has a double character. It is on the one side an extract from the totality of speech, and therefore the person is simply the place where a given language takes form in a specific way. On the other side it is a fact in his individual life and to that extent the use that he makes of the language is one moment in a psychological and biographical series. Schleiermacher calls these two possible approaches the *grammatical* and the *psychological* aspects of a text. Not every text will be of equal interest to an expositor. On the grammatical side the interest is *classical* and on the psychological side it is *original.* The classical may not be original, for example, Cicero, and the original may not be classical, for example, Hamann. In the *Kurze Darstellung* we are told already that the New Testament on account of its poor Greek may not be very attractive to the linguistic scholar.[3] The union of the classical and the original produces a higher third—the category of *genius.* Understanding involves an integration of the two approaches, the grammatical and the psychological; an integration so close that a text cannot be understood psychologically unless it is also understood grammatically and vice versa. Both types of interpretation have fundamentally the *same dignity;* it is wrong to call the psychological a higher type. According to the subject the emphasis may be put more or less exclusively on the one side or the other. Purely historical texts, for example, demand a minimum of psychological interpretation and letters a maximum. The task of understanding is absolutely discharged when each method, pursued independently, leads to the same result as the other and thus renders the other superfluous, that is, encloses it, for example, by achieving a full psychological understanding of someone from his words. This demands on the one side a full knowledge of the language and on the other a full knowledge of the person. Since neither can be achieved, there will always be in practice an alternation between the two methods. Hence understanding presupposes two talents, a knowledge of languages and a knowledge of individuals. If either is lacking, the one who seeks understanding will be hampered, though in fact one or the other will always predominate. There are linguistic experts who hardly need to think about the psychological processes of the author and there are psychological experts who seldom take up a dictionary and hardly need to think about his relation to the language; they can still achieve a correct understanding. If we want to be good expositors, however, it is advisable to work at both skills. Then if we do not become experts in either one or the other, we will not be complete failures in either the one or the other. An expositor who bungles on the grammatical side (and for Schleiermacher this means the literary side in the broader sense), no matter how profoundly he may think that he understands the author, no matter how strenuously he tries not to read anything in, has to be called a hermeneutical *nebulist.* On the other hand someone who is just a grammatical and literary expert, who does not see the whole man in his work and cannot enter into his life, has all the marks of a hermeneutical *pedant.* The ideal of the expositor—and some will be closer to it on the one side and others on the other, but in principle they should all be close on both sides—is thus to be found, though it is not attainable in reality, in the middle between the two opposing and one-sided exegetical ideals, or the two corresponding poles called scarecrows. If the ideal of exposition, like that of the expositor, is out of reach, the feasible exegetical task is that of not fully perceiving an author in the context of his

[3]*Kurze Darstellung*, § 124 note.

words and personality, yet understanding him just as well and *even better* than he could make himself understood, that is, give an account of himself.

Yet in pointing to the dialectic of the grammatical and psychological approaches we have not said all that there is to say about the basis of Schleiermacher's theory of understanding. The speech or writing of a person has a double character in another respect. On the one hand it is something individual, alongside other individual things, in a series or nexus, whether considered grammatically or psychologically. On the other hand it is itself a totality, unique and complete, again from both angles, in language and in the author's life. Understanding has to mean grasping it on both sides. Here too, then, it will divide into two distinct functions. The first, which relates to the individual side in the context of a grammatical or psychological whole, Schleiermacher calls the *comparative*, historical, or extensive interpretation. The second, which relates to the whole in the individual, he calls the *divinatory* or intensive interpretation. Again the equal validity and necessity of *both* methods is strongly urged. Direct understanding of a text would denote an absolute mastery and coincidence of both that is hardly possible in time. In reality neither can replace the other; they are always in correlation, and understanding is in constant *transition* from the one to the other. Again there is a distinction of talents corresponding to that of functions, and justice must be done to both, as both must also be reminded of their dangers. The concept of *divinatory*, or, as it is once called, prophetic interpretation was the new thing which Schleiermacher espoused in his addresses, especially against Wolf, but also in careful demarcation from the speculative exegesis of Ast. The soul "senses" things. Our understanding of another's speech, as in children, always begins with a bold divinatory stroke, with a sensing of the totality in a work. Where does this come from? From the title? From the author's preface? From the table of contents? From the editor's introduction? All this can help, but can also be a source of error. Schleiermacher speaks comparatively most favorably of the "otherwise apparently reprehensible tendency to leaf through a book before one reads it properly."[4] With luck and skill this can be of "significant value."[5] But antiquity did not know all these aids. In fact divinatory exposition, which aims at the understanding of the individual element in terms of the whole, could only go by the tone and form and progression of thought in the text or speech and then draw from this conclusions about the whole in terms of which alone the individual features may be understood. It thus turns on its point, as it were, and becomes comparative even though the root from which it springs does not cease to be a different one. Schleiermacher himself conceded that what we finally have is a circle. A cursory reading, "a more regular and complete leafing,"[6] must come first, and here, too, there must be divinatory understanding to be any understanding at all. More exact comparative exposition of the individual parts then follows, and if this does not take place, the understanding is *no* understanding at all.

[4]Barth has "ordentlich," Schleiermacher "ernstlich."
[5]"Über den Begriff . . . ," *Zur Philosophie*, p. 370; Kimmerle, *Hermeneutik*, p. 144.
[6]*Ibid*., p. 372; Kimmerle, p. 146.

The two types[7] of understanding, the grammatical-psychological and the comparative-divinatory, are *related* to one another according to Schleiermacher, and in such a way that each pole of the one group relates to the two poles of the other. As so often with Schleiermacher, we thus have crosswires. At the precise point where the two groups (which may be traced back to the original antithesis of thought and being) intersect, there is to be found ideally the understanding that is sought in hermeneutics. In this regard it should be noted that here as in similar constructions in Schleiermacher the balance is not perfect, for divinatory exposition naturally has a closer affinity to *psychological* than it has to grammatical, and comparative exposition has a closer affinity to *grammatical* than to psychological, just as dialectics and ethics on the one side, and mathematics and physics on the other, have a closer affinity to one another in the main system. But this difference is only relative; there are plenty of fields or instances where grammatical exposition cannot get along without *divinatory*, or psychological without *comparative*, and fundamentally any one is always to be thought of as cooperating with the others. In correct interpretation the various aspects must always come together in one and the same result.

Apart from this fourfold expository method, which is one even in its fourfoldness, there is *no* other. The possibilities of general hermeneutics that are united in this system are all that there are. Both the lectures at the Academy and the introduction to the lectures culminate in this momentous declaration. If Ast's speculative philology demanded a threefold hermeneutics of letter, meaning, and spirit, Schleiermacher incisively observes that what Ast calls spirit coincides with meaning and that the hermeneutics of letter, having no reality of its own, also coincides with this one hermeneutics of sense.[8] Schleiermacher disposes even more rapidly of allegorical exposition. It is justified where the passage itself is allegorical, and that is all.[9] But how about the dogmatic exposition that arises in relation to the Bible? "Here the question obtrudes upon us in passing whether the holy books of the Holy Spirit have to be treated differently."[10] A pressing question indeed! But Schleiermacher's system proves a match for the Holy Spirit. Whether inspiration is present is a result and not a presupposition of exposition. Were not the biblical writings the utterances of individuals to other individuals, occasional writings? With

[7]Next to the paragraph beginning here the following diagram may be found in the margin of the MS:

Hermeneutics:		divinatory	
	grammatical ——————————+—————————— psychological		
		comparative	
Philosophy:		dialectics	
	physics ——————————+—————————— ethics		
		mathematics	
Ethics:		individual	
	organizing ——————————+—————————— symbolizing		
		identical	

[8]"Über den Begriff . . . ," *Zur Philosophie*, pp. 382ff.; Kimmerle, pp. 153ff.
[9]*Ibid.*, pp. 385ff.; Kimmerle, p. 155.
[10]*Hermeneutik und Kritik*, p. 22.

what right does one substitute the Holy Spirit as the author and the whole of Christianity as the recipient? Could even the Holy Spirit speak in any other way through them than as if they spoke without him? Is the reality of the Holy Spirit in them any other reality than that of "inner impulse"?[11] Grammatically and psychologically, then, we are to deal with everything at a purely human level, and here, too, everything must be according to the universal rules.

But is there not a *special* New Testament hermeneutics? Certainly, replies Schleiermacher, but special simply means individual, or appropriate to this language and these people. The special character of New Testament hermeneutics is thus based on the "Hebraicizing character" of the Greek in which the New Testament spirit, "the new Christian spirit," expresses itself,[12] and on the special constitution of the biographical action with which this special linguistic constitution is connected.

This, then, is how Schleiermacher very simply and triumphantly deals with the ancient doctrine of inspiration. He seems not to have known, considered, or at any rate understood it except in the very crude form that the biblical authors were recording instruments of the Holy Spirit. It is eliminated along with poor allegorizing and the spirit-theory of Ast, and Schleiermacher's system prevails. How remarkable that he does not seem to have considered the possibility that the thought which I understand in what is said by someone else, whether with or without his system or any other hermeneutics, might be contingently, without any qualitative or quantitative possibilities of misunderstanding, the truth or Word of God, and that I should then have good reason to treat this address more specifically and more seriously than any other as the bearer of *this* content, a reference to *this* subject. What if special New Testament hermeneutics, whether gratefully employing Schleiermacher's method or any other general method, were to consist quite simply of taking these texts more seriously in this specific sense? Why should not God have spoken to man in a way that is necessarily and compellingly understandable? And why should not human speech be necessarily and compellingly understandable as God makes it so? If God is God? But here we come up against the frontier beyond which we do not pass in Schleiermacher or in his tracks.

2. *Grammatical Exposition*   }
3. *Psychological Exposition*   }   Dropped[13]

---

[11]*Ibid.*, p. 24.

[12]*Ibid.*, p. 27.

[13]The two headings are the titles of the first and second parts of Schleiermacher's *Hermeneutik und Kritik*, pp. 41 and 143. The term "dropped" indicates that Barth originally planned to deal with these topics but had to drop the subsections due to lack of time.

§ 6

THE CHRISTIAN FAITH

Prepared to some extent, it is hoped, by our previous lectures for the things that await us, we now come to Schleiermacher's chief theological work, the book on which, above all the other achievements of his richly gifted mind, his reputation and decisive influence on the theology and church of the 19th century were deservedly established. If thus far I have intentionally led you to more remote and infrequently quoted or discussed tracts of his life's work on which we could quietly observe the man and get to know him, we now enter upon soil that has been turned over by all kinds of deeply and less deeply digging spades, so that, if we were to try to listen to all that has been written about the book and its parts over the last hundred years by way of reference, commentary, agreement, and repudiation, we could spend the rest of the semester exegeting only the first ten sections. But I will remain true to our previous method of not only letting Schleiermacher speak for himself but also letting him explain and criticize himself, for I believe that here, too, this is best suited to the material and best adapted to give us an understanding of the man, and that in what we have done thus far we have sufficiently studied the ecclesiastical and academic aspects of his theology to enable us, now that we are confronted by his *magnum opus,* to rely essentially upon what we see with our own eyes. Schleiermacher himself once said (*Sendschreiben an Lücke,* p. 52) that he wrote his book in such a way that it should be understandable in and for itself and would not need elucidation by any other works, either by others or himself, apart from his Encyclopedia.[1]

He published the work in two volumes in 1821 and 1822 when he was fifty-three years of age, and brought out the second edition, which is normative for his historical influence, nine years later in 1830 and 1831 (*Theologische*

---

[1]*Schleiermachers Sendschreiben über seine Glaubenslehre an Lücke* (ET *On the Glaubenslehre: Two Letters to Dr. Lücke;* Chico, CA, 1981), ed. H. Mulert (Giessen, 1908), p. 52: "The book must be at least as understandable in and for itself as now. Do not laugh at me, that this is not said very sincerely; I simply mean that to make plain what is said no reference to any other book, whether by others or myself, is necessary. I naturally exempt my Encyclopedia. . . ."

Werke, in Reimer and Hendel, *Bibliothek theologischer Klassiker*).[2] Yet in spite of what Schleiermacher says, the little work from which I have quoted is also indispensable to a proper understanding. Schleiermacher published it in 1829, under the title *Dr. Schleiermachers Sendschreiben über seine Glaubenslehre an Dr. Lücke,* at the very time when he was setting about the preparation of the second edition of *The Christian Faith.* Lücke was with Gass, Jonas, Sydow, and some others one of Schleiermacher's most intimate theological friends. He was at this time professor of systematic theology here in Göttingen and editor of Parts 2 [and 3] of *Studien und Kritiken* [1829], which had been founded in 1828. You will find the *Sendschreiben* in the second volume of the *Theological Works*[3] and also in a critical edition, with introduction and notes by H. Mulert (Giessen, 1908), which is one of the series *Studien zur Geschichte des neueren Protestantismus* by Hoffmann and Zscharnack. It contains an incisive debate with an impressive array of reviewers and other literary friends and opponents of the first edition. Schleiermacher did not want to burden the book itself with this material, which helped to "lighten his heart," as he himself put it.[4] Among the critics addressed by Lücke we find F. C. Baur, then at the beginning of his illustrious career, K. I. Nitzsch, and J. F. Fries the philosopher. A particularly lively opponent, though also a personal friend, was F. Delbrück, professor of philosophy at Bonn. Others included K. H. Sack, a Bonn theologian and the author of apologetics and polemics, the chief leaders of rationalism, Bretschneider and Röhr, the supernaturalist Steudel in Tübingen, Tzschirner in Leipzig, who vacillated between rationalism and supernaturalism, and the speculatively oriented Braniss in Breslau. |

From this response on all sides we can see what an impression the book immediately made in distinction from the Encyclopedia. It could now be seen where Schleiermacher was heading, as it obviously could not when only the runic markings of the Encyclopedia were visible. One cannot say that contemporary theology welcomed the work; on the contrary, we find Schleiermacher "lightening his heart" in the *Sendschreiben* as though beset by a swarm of gadflies. But the tone of triumph and assurance in his answer is unmistakable. He obviously did not believe that he had met with any powerful or overwhelming criticism that would give him serious pause to think. He comes out in the letters as a man who is misunderstood, the distinctiveness and totality of whose will has not been perceived, who is ready to discuss details, who declares that at more than one point he might take a different course, but who is conscious of being right in his main contentions, and that he will have the future, if not the present, on his side. At any rate the book has been read (or at least skimmed through) by many people. The lapse of time between the two editions might cause surprise, but it should be borne in mind that in addition to the legitimate edition there had been two other printings, one in Reutlingen and the other in Halle. The *Glaubenslehre* seems to have been

[2]On this edition see p. xix, n. 24; for other editions see Hendel's *Bibliothek der Gessamtliteratur,* Vols. 1027–1038 (Halle, 1897) and *Bibliothek theologischer Klassiker,* Vols. 13–16 (Gotha, 1889).

[3]*Über seine Glaubenslehre, an Herrn Dr. Lücke, Sämmtliche Werke,* 1: *Zur Theologie* (Berlin, 1836), II, 575ff.

[4]Mulert ed., p. 36.

studied with particular diligence in Württemberg. Furthermore, the list of those who expressed themselves on the matter between 1822 and 1830 is much longer than that of those mentioned in the *Sendschreiben*, whether because Schleiermacher, as he himself says, did not know all that was written, or because he preferred to react to some of the utterances with silence. Among these is the most violent and malicious attack that had been made on *The Christian Faith* thus far. Its author was none other than Schleiermacher's Berlin colleague Hegel, who in 1822, obviously fresh from reading the work, made statements like the following: In this work spirit, in the most dreadful contrast to religion, which finds man's salvation and honor in knowing God, descends to the level of the beasts, except that it has unfortunately the advantage of an awareness of its own ignorance. If feeling constitutes the basic determination of man where the substantial encounters spirit and the eternal comes to it, then it is put on an equality with animals. It is then logical to seek religion in the feeling of dependence and "the dog is the best Christian, for it has this most strongly. . . . The dog also has feelings of redemption when its hunger is appeased by a bone."[5] "What is theology without a knowledge of God? Sounding brass and a tinkling cymbal."[6] Humanly speaking it is understandable that Schleiermacher should not reply to statements such as these. But this crude criticism, if any, must have given him pause to think, and perhaps did in fact do so. Among the reviewers and opponents one misses altogether any representative from the pietist camp which was then becoming so powerful and would be everywhere victorious twenty years later, the only exception being the song writer A. Knapp, who belonged to the Hofacker circle, and who in 1828 wrote a work against Schleiermacher,[7] though the latter disregarded this in his open letters. That Hengstenberg's *Evangelische Kirchenzeitung* refrained from debating with Schleiermacher does no credit to this influential organ of the party or to the spiritual capacity and intellectual alertness of its leaders, but is rather a symptom that in spite of its claims the movement of awakening had no solution that might have prevented the mounting theological problems of the 19th century. This silence was not golden. We may conclude this account of the reception of the first edition of *The Christian Faith* with a bit of poetry. One of Schleiermacher's Romantic friends, A. W. Schlegel, elder brother of the author of *Lucinde*, penned the following verse under the title "A Significant Name":

> Der nackten Wahrheit Schleier machen,
> Ist kluger Theologen Amt,
> Und Schleiermacher sind bei so bewandten Sachen
> Die Meister der Dogmatik insgesamt.[8]

[5]G. W. F. Hegel, *Vorrede zu Hinrichs' Religionsphilosophie* [H. F. W. Hinrichs, *Die Religion im inneren Verhältnisse zur Wissenschaft* (1822)], *Sämmtliche Werke*, ed. H. Glockner (Stuttgart, 1930), XX, 19.

[6]*Ibid.*, pp. 26f.

[7]A. Knapp, "Ist die Verschiedenheit der dogmatischen Systeme kein Hinderniss des Zwecks der Kirche?" in *Studien der evangelischen Geistlichkeit Wirtembergs*, ed. C. B. Klaiber (Stuttgart, 1828), pp. 35–151.

[8]A. W. von Schlegel, *Sämmtliche Werke*, ed. E. Böcking (Leipzig, 1846/47), II, 233.

You will find these and similar items collected in the two essays by H. Mulert, "Die Aufnahme der Glaubenslehre Schleiermachers," *Zeitschrift für Theologie und Kirche* (1908), pp. 107ff.; (1909), pp. 243ff. But now to business!

The Christian Faith is the title I have used in my heading for the section. Not *Glaubenslehre* (Doctrine of the Faith), which is most commonly used, which Schleiermacher himself quotes, and which is what the work is in practice. In this brief form one must always bear in mind how much more complicated and revealing the real title is: *The Christian Faith Systematically Presented according to the Basic Tenets of the Evangelical Church.* Those who are familiar with the contents of the book, and who know the letters to Lücke, can attach significance to almost every word in this title. It would not be a futile exercise to try to do this. "The Christian Faith"—not, then, dogmatics? No, deliberately not, although the book undoubtedly occupies the place in the encyclopedia which is reserved for dogmatics and in the book itself there is no pedantic dodging of the term "dogmatic." "Christian Faith" denotes programmatically the change in contents that we have already noted in the *Brief Outline* and for which we were prepared after the sermons. Revelation is not reflected in dogma nor is it in this refraction the subject matter of dogmatics. But *Christian faith,* a specific form of religious self-consciousness, is reflected in the basic tenets of a particular church (here the Evangelical), and this refraction is the subject matter, not of a dogmatics, but of a presentation of the Christian faith according to the basic tenets, and so on. This is the great Copernican revolution with which Schleiermacher has drawn the undoubtedly correct and unavoidable conclusion from the history of Protestant theology since the Reformation and with which he has made and still makes disciples in spite of all the attempts of positive theologians to kick against the pricks. So long and so far as we do not perceive this revolution to be a mistake and reverse it; so long as the opinion rules intact that with it (1) Schleiermacher has honored the true legacy of Luther in theology, and (2) he has naturalized theology on the soil of Kant's critical philosophy (of which Schleiermacher all his life spoke with sovereign disdain); so long as the title is felt at a first glance to be right and not wrong (and who of us does not feel this?)—Schleiermacher is in fact the master and enjoys no less authority than Melanchthon and Calvin did in the 16th and 17th centuries. In attaching this significance to the title I am not reading anything in but engaging in "comparative" and "divinatory" exegesis in the best tradition of Schleiermacher. In his letters he himself leaves us in no doubt that he regarded the changing of dogmatics into an analysis of religious self-consciousness as the decisive and characteristic feature of his work. In them he defends himself on the one hand against those who contend that his theology is speculative, that he replaces Christian truth with a knowledge of God that is attained *a priori* by transcendental critical abstraction, and he defends himself on the other hand against those who, like Hegel, find no speculative basis at all in his theology. He responds to critics on both the right and the left with the same decisiveness: Not so! You must believe me, he

---

Schlegel, who is best remembered for his translations of Shakespeare, is playing on the word Schleiermacher ("veil-maker"): "To make veils for the naked truth is the job of clever theologians; all masters of dogmatics are Schleiermachers ("makers of veils")."

writes almost with entreaty, the analysis of self-consciousness in the *Glau-benslehre* is not meant to be anything but "simply and honestly empirical." When he speaks of the consciousness of sin, "of the need of redemption and the satisfaction that we find in Christ. . . ," he has in view "real facts of experience and not facts of the consciousness preceding experience" ([*Send-schreiben*, ed. Mulert], p. 21). The true aim of the book is indeed "the presentation of the distinctively Christian consciousness" (p. 33). He constantly wants to evoke in his book an "awareness that the tenets are merely inferred" and that "the inner state of mind is original. I wanted to do things in such a way that it would be as clear as possible to the reader at every point that the saying in Jn. 1:14 is the basic text of dogmatics" (p. 34). In both form and content his dogmatics "is wholly conditioned by the presupposition that the concept of God to be developed in it is not original (= *a priori*) . . . but has simply arisen in reflection on this higher self-consciousness" (p. 64). The question of truth that might be put to such reflection is simply suppressed. It is enough that it is real. He wants "to clarify and affirm piety" for men "without proof or ideas by means of the ancient *logos anapodeiktos*" (p. 18). "For the Christian doctrine of faith the presentation is also the foundation; for everything in it is established only as it is presented as a correct statement of the Christian self-consciousness. For those who do not find it in their self-consciousness, no foundation is possible" (p. 56). He is also clear about the historical connection of this teaching with the older pietism from which he himself derived. Piety as a determination of the self-consciousness precedes pious ideas. Religion is *not* the daughter of theology. "I draw this contrast, and in so doing—even if my way of putting it is not always the same as theirs—I am simply doing what a numerous school has constantly done for more than a century" (pp. 15f.). It is symptomatic, not of Schleiermacher, but of the state of theology in the time that he came to the fore, that he should have to defend himself both against the suspicion that his theology was *speculative* and against the reproach that it was not. That Hegel's objection that the honor and salvation of man lie in his knowing God, which involuntarily reminds experts of the beginning of Calvin's *Catechism*,[9] could also arise as *the Christian* objection; that there might be an original which is not an Apriori but revelation and therefore something very different from the fact of consciousness which Schleiermacher reads into Jn. 1:14 and in whose manifestations he finds the stuff of dogmatics—this possibility lay outside both his own field of vision and that of his critics. The discussion in the *Open Letters* moves monotonously around the poles of religious psychology and metaphysical speculation, and Schleiermacher chose his vantage-point within *this* antithesis.

Apart from this main point in the title of the book we should note two other things if we are to achieve an understanding. The first is the expression "systematically." This is no mere phrase but an intention. Why does Schleiermacher's dogmatics have to be a system? Schleiermacher provides his own

---

[9]*Catechism of the Church of Geneva* (1545): "Minister: What is the chief end of human life? Scholar: To know God by whom men were created." Cf. *John Calvin's Tracts and Treatises* (Grand Rapids, 1958), II, 37.

commentary on this when he says that he has set himself the task of taking the God-consciousness that is developed in the Christian church, and that we all bear within us, and so presenting it in all its expressions ... that the individual determinations that arise in this way may be seen together and strive to be one as feeling itself is always one and the same, no matter whether it relates to the sense of our freedom of will, or our link with nature, or historical development (p. 28), or when he says in another place that his systematic art has nothing whatever to do with principles and deductions but consists solely of an "aptitude to find formulas of division which will make it possible for us to be convinced that the presentation is complete" and enable us "indirectly, if not directly, to be led back from each dogmatic tenet to the direct self-consciousness represented by it" (p. 47). The word "systematically" is thus to be put in dialectical relationship to the words "according to the basic tenets"; the latter denote the breathing out, the transition from religious immediacy to reflection, the former denotes the breathing in, the return from thoughts to pure feeling, and all of them together offer a complete survey of the vital process that Schleiermacher seeks to describe in his title. Dogmatics must be a system, then, in order to restore the balance that is temporarily upset by the existence of basic tenets of the Christian faith. |

Another term in the title can and must be exegeted: "the Evangelical Church." What does this mean? As we gather from the preface to the second edition, it means the church that is no longer Lutheran or Reformed but united. And concerning this Schleiermacher remarks: "As it must be regarded as a basic condition of the union that has now been accomplished in these territories that there is no longer any need of a dogmatic adjustment of the two parts, and even less of a new symbol," he has felt it to be his duty "not only to start with this presupposition but to practice it to the best of his powers as an established dogmatic tenet by a free and conciliatory treatment" of the confessions concerned.[10] In other words, now that the strife between Lutherans and Reformed, having become pointless, is obsolete and at rest, it is my task to make a basic principle out of the pointlessness of the two church teachings that have now been effortlessly united into one, and in this basic principle of the indifference of all dogmatics, which is so far-reaching that not even an adjustment is necessary, to give a confirmatory blessing to the peace of the new Evangelical Church. It is thus a springlike prospect that the very title of the work holds out on every side.

1. Survey. (I here recommend the summary by M. Rade, *Die Leitsätze der* [1/31/24] *ersten und [der] zweiten Auflage von Schleiermachers Glaubenslehre* [Tübingen [and Leipzig], 1904] in Krüger's *Kirchen- und dogmengeschichtliche Quellenschriften,* Series 2, No. 5, though this does not excuse one from reading the whole work.) The incontestable greatness of the *Glaubenslehre* consists in good part of the fact that in spite of its bulk of over a thousand pages it can be easily surveyed because it is well arranged, and it is well arranged because it simply develops a single thought. Older dogmatic works like Augustine's

[10]Redeker ed. (cf. p. xix n. 24), I, 4f.

Enchiridion, Bonaventura's *Breviloquium,* Aquinas' *Summa,* Calvin's *Institutes,* and Zwingli's *Commentary on True and False Religion,* not to speak of Melanchthon's *Loci,* cannot even remotely compare with it in this regard. In them the material constantly bursts with invisible force out of the confines of the system that no doubt the authors had before them as an ideal. The adopted order, even if it is skillfully worked out as in the Scholastics, is more or less accidental, and there is a constant need to show the reader why this or that part of the material is necessary. The closest to the *Glaubenslehre* in this regard is a small but famous work from the Reformation period, namely, the *Heidelberg Catechism* with its three sections on man's misery, redemption, and gratitude, but even here the four main catechetical materials which, with more or less justification, are introduced unaltered and undivided into the three divisions see to it that anything that might be called a system is not in fact present. But a system is present in Schleiermacher, and it is so in almost *suspiciously* brilliant fashion, one might say, if one compares it with the unsuccessful efforts of the older masters. The material is forced into a mold. We now *know* why we must speak about this and this and this in dogmatics, and why we must do so in precisely *this* context; this is the charm of the work. There is no place for anything contingent, strange, or indigestible in the statements of the Bible or the dogmas of the church. A sizable dwelling in early Victorian style has been erected on the meadow that was strewn with erratic blocks, and it has been built of the very same stones, but now trimmed and shaped. Spirit has looked at nature, and invaded, conquered, and subordinated it. But is it not suspicious that this could be done so completely, or almost completely? Are the statements of the Bible and the church no more than natural forces which like steam and electricity were simply waiting for the research and reflection and the shaping hand of men to serve their destiny, that is, that of men? Was this triumph possible without all kinds of reinterpretations, truncations, wrestings, and jugglings? Does not the waxlike pliability which those statements that were so hard in the hands of the ancients have now suddenly acquired indicate that, while their wording remains the same, they have undergone a change of substance which has made them different from what they once were? Was the lack of success in the systems of the ancients only a sign of their lack of skill and not perhaps a sign of their greater objectivity relative to the material? The difference is this. To get to know the content of their dogmatics we have to travel with them up and down across all kinds of clefts and racing streams through a wilderness of forest or mountain, whereas with Schleiermacher we have only to look around for a panoramic view and we can see everything, even if only, unfortunately, in succession—and he suggests at times that we should be able to do it with a single, comprehensive, *central* look.

I shall now try to give you a very brief survey of the composition of the work. Along the lines that one would expect from the Encyclopedia, and also, as we saw last time, from the title, an introduction of thirty-one sections explains the concept and method of dogmatics. The conclusion is that dogmatics attempts the most precise and systematic possible presentation of the teaching which is currently valid in a specific (here the Evanglical) church, that is, of the epitome of the religious (here Christian) disposition translated into speech (cf. §§ 15f., 18f.). If the specifically Christian determination of the pious consciousness is summed up in the concept of redemption, this determination obviously involves an antithesis; sin on the one side and grace on the other are the determinative factors, or the names which religious or dogmatic speech gives to these factors. In this Christian religious self-consciousness a general religious self-consciousness is presupposed and contained. From the distinction between "presupposed and contained in the concept of redemption" and "determined by the concept of redemption" Schleiermacher derives his main division (§ 29) of *The Christian Faith* into Part I and Part II, and Part II subdivides into the consciousness of sin and the consciousness of grace.[11] This first division is intersected by a second, for the teachings that are to be expounded in Christian doctrine may be viewed as descriptions of human states, as concepts relative to God's qualities and acts, or as statements about the characteristics of the world [§ 30]. From this second differentiation, which has three sections in view, Schleiermacher derives the subdivisions which are to be worked out in Part I and the two divisions of Part II: the state of man, the constitution of the world, and the qualities of God relative to the universal religious consciousness (Part I), to the consciousness of sin (Part II,1), and to the consciousness of grace (Part II,2). It should be noted in this regard that Schleiermacher himself describes the statements about God and the world as "secondary forms" (more about this later) and finds the true body of doctrine in the first form of the statements about man. This produces the following graph:

by the Christian antithesis

presupposed   determined

Sin   Grace

God	Eternity	Omnipresence	Omnipotence	Omniscience	Holiness	Righteousness	Love		Wisdom	
Man	Creation		Preservation		Angels and Devils	Original Sin	Sin	Christ: Person Work		Christian New Birth | Sanctification
World	Perfection of World		Perfection of Man			Evil		Church: Rise	Church: Perseverance	Church: Consummation

Specifically the work is developed as follows. In Part I, under the heading of the universal religious consciousness which is already presupposed in the Christian experience of contradiction, (1) as a description of this consciousness itself it deals with creation (including angels and devils) and preservation; (2) in relation to the qualities of God it deals with his eternity, omnipresence,

---

[11]Cf. Redeker ed., I, 171, 341, 353; II, 11.

omnipotence, and omniscience; and (3) in an account of the constitution of the world as this is indicated in the universal religious consciousness it maintains the perfection of both the world and man. In Part II,1 (the consciousness of sin) it deals (1) with sin as the state of man both original and actual; (2) with evil as the constitution of the world as seen from this angle; and (3) with holiness and righteousness as the divine attributes. In Part II,2 (the consciousness of grace) complications arise, but they hardly disrupt the arrangement. The division deals (1) with the state of the Christian, which covers the whole of Christology, i.e. Christ's person and work and then what would earlier have been called soteriology, summed up here in the doctrines of new birth and sanctification. It then turns (2) to the constitution of the world from the standpoint of the church, to which 270 pages are devoted and which is seen (1) in its rise (naturally in principle and not historically in the narrower sense), (2) its perseverance, and (3) its consummation. Under "rise" the doctrines of election and the imparting of the Holy Spirit are developed, under "perseverance" (relative to what does not change), the statements about scripture, the sacraments, and the office of the keys, and (relative to what does) the statements about the visible and the invisible church, and finally under "consummation" no more and no less than the whole of eschatology to the extent that anything is left of this in Schleiermacher. The only remaining task (3) is to present the divine qualities of love and wisdom as these relate to grace and to crown the whole development of the consciousness of grace (I am not sure whether this is an instance of perplexity, genius, or extreme systematizing power) with a rather sparse exposition of the trinity, in which Schleiermacher does not find a true statement of Christian consciousness but a combination of several such statements to the extent that it expresses the fact that no less than the divine being itself was in Christ and indwells the church through its common Spirit (II, 528).[12] This ends the account of the expressions of the Christian consciousness. I must not neglect to point out at least some peculiarities of Schleiermacher's system which may be seen already from the survey and which we shall have to discuss more thoroughly later. I have in mind three points in particular: (1) the placing of the doctrines of creation and preservation under the heading "Description of Our Pious Self-Consciousness";[13] (2) the coordination of Christology and soteriology under the heading "The State of the Christian insofar as He is Conscious of Divine Grace";[14] and (3) the treatment of eschatology under the heading "The Constitution of the World Relative to Redemption,"[15] and especially as an annex to the doctrine of the church. This arrangement will give some idea of how the work disposes of the erratic blocks to which I referred earlier.

Before entering into details we should also take note of some general problems that are posed by the survey, not, of course, in order to solve them, but so that we may recognize them in our broader investigation. They are as follows.

---

[12]§ 170; Redeker ed., II, 458f.
[13]Redeker ed., I, 185.
[14]Redeker ed., II, 29.
[15]Redeker ed., II, 207; pp. 408ff. for the eschatology.

a. The Relation of the Introduction to the Whole. From the first edition onward the Introduction has claimed the interest of readers in a disproportionate way. Attention has been paid to the introductory sections of Part I. There has been ongoing work on the Christology. Individual investigations have naturally been devoted to all parts of the structure. On the whole, however, one might say that what follows § 31 is dutifully studied by many, more or less attentively noted by more, but not read at all by most. What has always interested people about Schleiermacher's *Christian Faith* is the Introduction, in which they have found and find—what? a basis for Christianity, a derivation of its truth from universal truth, an *a priori* demonstration which provides a sure foundation for *a posteriori* dogmatizing, in short, a substitute for the lost proofs of God and for other proofs of the possibility and truth of the statements of the Bible and the church. It was and is unavoidable that we children of an age whose theology suffers from a chronic lack of objectivity, who do not know what we are talking about when we talk about God, but who still want to talk about him—that we cannot escape the question whether there might not be in these foundations, derivations, and proofs something that can restore a good conscience to us, especially to us theologians, without compelling us to believe in God with that realistic objectivity or to know about him as the Middle Ages and the age of the Reformation did. This question, the embarrassed question how one can be a modern man and still be a Christian, is what has made the Introduction to the *Glaubenslehre* interesting, because something like an answer to the question has been obstinately detected in it.

Schleiermacher himself, of course, would have started back from such readers of his Introduction with every sign of horror. He was incensed by the idea that the "main point" or "core" of the whole work was to be found in it (*Sendschreiben an Lücke,* p. 31). It was not meant to be anything but a "preliminary orientation" which strictly speaking lay outside the discipline itself. Its only point was to determine the proper place for Christianity among the various modifications of the general religious consciousness (p. 54) and to provide a formula for "what is valid in all the modifications of the Christian self-consciousness but not present outside it." It was meant to deal with the concept of revelation as this is common to many or all religions and then with the relation of this concept to Christ with the idea that the relation of the general concept to the redemption accomplished by Jesus of Nazareth is, purely substantively, Christianity (p. 57). He had no intention of using these introductory researches into religion, the religions, and the Christian religion to provide a basis or an *a priori* demonstration for the last of these (pp. 55f.). As we saw last time,[16] the only basis for the Christian doctrine of faith is its presentation (p. 56). It is against this background that we must understand what is said in I²,[17] namely, that the only purpose of the Introduction is partly to provide an exposition of dogmatics (or the concept of dogmatics) which underlies the whole work, and partly to supply a preface for the method and arrangement adopted in it. We must also set against the same background the later statement that what precedes the exposition of science cannot be part of

[16]Cf. pp. 188.
[17]Here and in what follows the raised figure denotes the edition.

it. These preliminary propositions are not themselves dogmatic, or, in other words, there can be no question in this Introduction of the answer after which the hungry are snatching, namely, the answer to the question of truth.

If we have understood what Schleiermacher said about philosophical theology in the Encyclopedia,[18] it should not be too hard for us to understand this repudiation of his. And a quick glance at the Introduction, especially the much considered first chapter, confirms the fact that Schleiermacher was simply using borrowed statements, first from ethics regarding the nature of the pious self-consciousness in general, then from the philosophy of religion regarding the ladder of religions, then from apologetics regarding the character of Christianity, and that he then concluded the whole with a presentation of the relation between dogmatics and piety which has no bearing on the question at issue. Was he not right to warn off those whose interest is apologetic and to point them to the presentation itself as the true basis? A tragic destiny overtook him, one might say, when the final 840 pages that were meant to be the basis had so little effect as such that there has constantly been a stubborn return to the first 160 pages, or, strictly speaking, the first 100 pages,[19] to seek there the philosophers' stone where according to Schleiermacher's own protestations it is not to be found. But is it really hard to understand this? One has only to consider that in § 3 we find the term "immediate self-consciousness," that § 4 says that in our piety we are conscious of being "absolutely dependent," or, which is the same thing, "conscious of being in relation with God," that § 6 calls the religious self-consciousness "an essential element in human nature," and that in § 8 the class of religion to which Christianity belongs, the monotheistic class, is put at the top of the ladder of historical religions. All this has the remarkable smack of truth, of almost or completely absolute things. Immediate, absolutely dependent, relation with God, essential element in human nature, highest step in religion—whatever these terms may mean, are they not more than descriptive? Do they not involve ultimate decisions? Can we, or Schleiermacher, blame anxious theologians if they see the flush of dawn here, if they detect solid ground? How formal is the disclaimer that these statements are not part of dogmatics, that they are only borrowed from other and secular disciplines! No matter where they come from, those who come upon them seem at any rate to recognize their truth. All the better, indeed, if they come from some secular discipline, whether ethics or whatever! All the more surely does the substitute beckon us! All the more surely are we spared the bitter choice between the Scylla of modern scepticism and the Charybdis of medieval objectivity! Does not all this indicate that Schleiermacher himself is well aware that he has another foundation for his structure apart from the presentation itself to which he so impatiently points his readers and with which, strangely enough, no one will be put off, that he himself really starts with this different foundation, and that various by no means indifferent matters are settled there behind the scenes, for instance, that piety is neither knowledge nor action but a determination of feeling (§ 3), that there

[18]Cf. pp. 146–151, esp. pp. 146–148.
[19]The reference is to the 160 pages of the Introduction, or 100 pages if one excludes Chapter I, iv, and Chapter II.

is such a thing as absolute dependence and that this is the same thing as a relation with *God* (§ 4), yet an essential element in *human nature* (§ 6), or the interesting thesis (§ 13) that the appearance of the Redeemer in history, as divine revelation, is neither something completely supernatural nor something completely suprarational? Consider what it means that all these things, before real dogmatics has begun, have already been expressly decided with an appeal to truth that is established in *some other way*. Is it not clear that in these circumstances the place of such mighty events is no mere overture that one might neglect, but that it is perhaps more interesting than the whole opera that is performed after it? No, Schleiermacher has no reason to complain if we inquisitively focus especially on these first thirty-one sections. Ethics and the philosophy of religion these may be, but it is obviously here that the cat that we are later to buy is put in the bag, that the meal that we are to eat is cooked. It is here that the decision is made what is at issue in the Christian religious consciousness, what may be said and what may not be said. Here, then, we must cautiously stop for a while before we move on to the whole which is here so harmlessly introduced.

b. *The So-called "Antithesis" of the Second Main Part.* The lever with [2/4/24] which Schleiermacher put the second main part of his dogmatic material in motion is the concept of antithesis, namely, between sin and grace. He arranges this second part within the two "sides" of the antithesis, whereas, in contrast, the first part deals with the religious self-consciousness which is not determined but presupposed by the antithesis, and which is still included in this antithesis even when it is determined by it. See the headings of the two parts.[20] But to understand the point of the distinction we must first have understood the concept of antithesis and therefore the arrangement of the second part.[21] The texts that should be read here are especially §§ 11,2; 62,1; 63,2–3; 64,1. How does Schleiermacher arrive at the antithesis of sin and grace and what does he understand by it? He gives a first answer, especially in relation to sin, although without expressly using the terms,[22] in his definition of the *the nature of Christianity* in the Introduction (§ 11,2) when he takes it to be an admitted fact that the term "redemption" denotes what is common to all Christians even if in different ways. This term obviously denotes passively the *transition* from a bad state, presented as bondage, to a better one, and actively the *help* which is provided for this by another. What is this presupposed worse state when it is a matter of piety (note the tacitly accepted restriction of the concept of redemption to the sphere of piety)? Obviously "that the vitality of the higher self-consciousness is hampered or destroyed so that its union with the various determinations of the sensory self-consciousness, and therefore the religious elements in life, occur less or not at all." In its extreme form one can call this state one of "ungodliness, or, better, forgetfulness of God," but in no case are we to think of a "total impossibility of reviving the consciousness of God." How else could we experience it as an evil?—and to remove the lack we would then have to think in terms of a

[20]Cf. pp. 191, n. 11.
[21]Marginal note in the MS: "§ 5!"—followed by the thesis of § 5.
[22]Barth means "sin" and "grace."

"transformation in the strict sense," and "this idea is not contained in the concept of redemption," decrees Schleiermacher, without batting an eyelid. After this broad attack on the New Testament concept of redemption he can easily say that it remains only to describe that state "as a missing facility in introducing and maintaining the God-consciousness into the context of real moments of life." The difference between the two states is viewed as simply one of more or less, that is, as a quantitative one. The worse state involves more activity of the sensory self-consciousness, or less of the higher self-consciousness, and under these conditions "a satisfaction of the orientation to the God-consciousness" is not possible; the feeling of absolute dependence is in bondage and stands in need of redemption. It is not non-existent in every respect but it is also not dominant in any respect. This is Schleiermacher's view of sin. |

In contrast the better state (§ 63,2) is "the facility with which we can assimilate the God-consciousness to the various sensory stimulations of the self-consciousness." If we are conscious of *sin* as an *act* because even in its bondage the sense of absolute dependence is not nullified, we are conscious of *grace*, grounded in the experience of redemption, as an *impartation*, though impartation and act are not mutually exclusive, for even sin and grace are not kept apart in the same self-consciousness as [totally] *irreconcilable* (§ 63,3). The energy of the God-consciousness is never maximum or constant in relation to the sensory consciousness; a restrictive lack of force is always posited as well. Similarly the link with redemption can never be total in a Christian consciousness; it is always posited as the act of the Redeemer along with sin as *our* act. Dividing up the treatment of sin and grace is thus done only "arbitrarily" for the sake of clarity (§ 64,1). A separate description of either one is no description of a real Christian consciousness. As an exclusive consciousness of sin would be no Christian consciousness even in relation to certain parts of life, so it is with the consciousness of grace apart from a recollection or recognition of one's need of redemption, that is, a consciousness of sin. |

I need hardly draw your attention to the fact that this teaching is poles apart from that of Romans 6 on the same subject. The explanation is simple. If sin and grace are quantities, and mutually limiting and therefore *relative* quantities, this is because what is called "redemption" is only a state of consciousness, a given factor. In the second edition Schleiermacher avoided the term "relative" so far as I can see. But not in the first, where he says expressly in § 33: "Christian piety rests on the experienced antithesis between one's own incapacity and the capacity that is imparted by redemption to actualize the pious consciousness; but this antithesis is only a *relative* one." Exclusiveness, the exclusiveness of the antithesis of life and death as the New Testament posits the antithesis between sin and grace, is proper only to *truth* and not to reality, only to *spirit* and not to nature, not even psychical nature, only to *God* and not to the human consciousness of God. An experienced antithesis cannot be an absolute one. Only a believed and known antithesis can be this. Schleiermacher was right here. Sin is in fact a part of the Christian *consciousness* of grace no less than grace itself, and grace will always in fact be present a little with even the worst *consciousness* of sin. But the insight into this relativism did not work like dynamite on Schleiermacher's basic view of the subject of the doctrine of faith. It did not force him to consider whether apart from our consciousness there might be a sin that reigns exclusively and a grace that triumphs exclusively, whether *this* antithesis ought not to be the theme of a presentation of Christianity that is informed by the New Testament. Instead he comfortably made this relativism the cornerstone of his dogmatics. If we light the fuse, if we say what should be said, namely, that sin as a part or quantity is not sin against *God,* and grace of the same kind is not *God's* grace, then the whole building collapses. Schleiermacher did *not* say this. His whole theology lives by reason of the fact that he did not say it. The antithesis of his second part is a psychological one and therefore it falls short of the *Christian* antithesis at least in the New Testament and Reformation sense. This is what holds his system together. Note in this regard the remarkable passage (§ 62,1) at the beginning of the second part. Here Schleiermacher considers the possibility whether there might not be, even if to the value of something infinitely small,[23] a constant positing of the relation of man to God *beyond* the antithesis psychologically regarded as a hampering or promoting of the God-consciousness. This might be conceivable, he thinks, either as constant suppression, as the obtuse uniformity of the God-consciousness in a being in which only the rest of the content of the consciousness is really alive, or as the blessed uniformity of a constant supremacy of the God-consciousness in a being in which the whole consciousness can continually become God-consciousness with absolute ease and strength. Obviously in describing these states Schleiermacher has in view something of what the pietist vocabulary used to call "spiritual death" and "spiritual life." In this form, then, he tried at least to *conceptualize* an absolute relation to God, either negative or positive, in which there would be no antithesis. The absolute New Testament dialectic of sin and grace puts in an appearance here, even if only at a distance and in a fairly horrible cramped psychological form. But only to disappear again at once. That the one might be an ungodly impossibility and the other a divine impossibility—but both higher than reason—Schleiermacher did not perceive. On the other hand he was too perspicacious and his taste was too good for him to adopt those two artificially contrived possibilities seriously. He thus goes on to say that obviously our religious self-consciousness is not one in which no more or less is posited, but it *vacillates* between the two extremes as it shares in the heterogeneities of human life. Is not this more or less merely a "fluid distinction," asks Schleiermacher himself, rather than an antithesis? At any rate it is the latter only as we have free development or restriction, desire or the lack of desire, and these are not to be regarded as so different in this field that strictly the one can always or anywhere be present without the other. This antithesis, which according to Schleiermacher might also be called a fluid distinction, this vacillation between two extremes as he himself also puts it, is thus the content and the principle of division in Part II, and it is consequently the real subject of the Christian faith. I was grasping the real intent of Schleiermacher and not maliciously misunderstanding him when in the heading I expressly spoke of the *so-called* "antithesis."

c. *The Relationship between the Two Parts.* The Christian consciousness as it is determined by the antithesis in the manner described forms the theme

[23]Schleiermacher: ". . . the infinitely small."

of the second main part. The situation would be simple if Schleiermacher had allotted to the first main part the universal religious consciousness which does not, or does not yet, contain this antithesis and which is to be thought of empirically or transcendentally. Obviously we would then be dealing with a religious philosophy either along the lines of pre-Kantian natural theology or along critical Kantian lines. Something of this sort might be read out of the title of Part I in the first edition, which runs: "Development of the Religious Self-Consciousness as One that Indwells Human Nature and Whose Contrary Relations to the Sensory Self-Consciousness (i.e., its antithetical determinations) Have Yet to be Developed." But § 39[1], which specifically claims that this self-determination is Christian, rules out any possible misunderstanding to the effect that we are dealing merely with something universal as distinct from specifically Christian, with an earlier state as distinct from the later Christian state, with a transcendental *a priori* as distinct from a Christian reality. The misunderstandings which nevertheless arose caused Schleiermacher to make his title more precise in the second edition in the familiar form: "Development of the Religious Self-Consciousness as It is Already Always Presupposed, but also Always Contained, in Every Christian Movement of the Religious Spirit." The task of understanding what Schleiermacher was after is not made easier, of course, by these circumstances. The texts that we have to compare are § 11,3; § 29; § 32; § 62,2–3 and the presentation in the second letter to Lücke, pp. 30–47 in Mulert.

In continuation of the definition of the nature of Christianity previously mentioned, § 11,3 says that what distinguishes Christianity from other religious societies to which the concept of redemption is not alien is (1) that this and the antithesis posited with it are not just one individual religious element like others but that all other pious movements relate to them (a genuinely Pietist-Moravian statement), and (2) that redemption is posited as something that has been accomplished universally and completely by Jesus of Nazareth; the two points cannot be separated from one another but belong essentially together. Let us leave on one side for the moment the relationship between them. The decisive point is the one that follows. This definition of the nature of Christianity is not to be taken to mean that the Christian religious consciousness can have no other content than Jesus and redemption, but that all the elements of religion are posited by it, or (to the extent that the sense of absolute dependence is still in bondage in them) are posited as in need of it. These other aspects of religion that are also posited may be stronger or weaker without jeopardizing their Christian character. Only elements that bear no relation at all to redemption and do not present the figure of the Redeemer have no place in Christianity. |

But what do we mean by these other contents that are everywhere posited as well? § 29,1 gives the express answer: The antithesis between the bound and the liberated feeling of absolute dependence plainly presupposes the feeling itself and a knowledge of it. This is the first point. Little can be said against it. But one might ask what kind of presupposition or knowledge this is, and how far what is presupposed and known is a feeling. Yet Schleiermacher evades this question with two elegant leaps. For, he explains, the feeling of absolute dependence occurs only in man, and we can know it only insofar as it is in ourselves. Might not the presupposition of sin and grace, which is what he is really investigating, be also quite different from something that is present in man, for example, the judgment and mercy of the electing God, or the fall and reconciliation of man? Might not the presupposed knowledge of this presupposition be the knowledge of God himself? But then the sense of absolute dependence would be a very questionable expression for what is presupposed and it could not be confidently maintained that this presupposition is in ourselves. Schleiermacher preferred to base his first statement on a second, on the confident assertion of the most obscure element in the first. And now he makes the second leap. Because what is presupposed in man is a given, the state which virtually precedes the antithesis is neither complete forgetfulness of God nor a mere striving after God-consciousness that is devoid of content, but God-consciousness itself must somehow be a given in self-consciousness. He has reached his goal. A presupposition that is in us but not in our *self-consciousness* could not be a given. If this something is God-consciousness, this might still be regarded *subjectively* even in us: God's *own* consciousness, to be distinguished from our self-consciousness, and as such never a given. But with the help of the notorious theological "somehow" Schleiermacher preferred to make a further affirmation, again underlining the weakest side of the second statement as he had done with the first, and so God-consciousness is presented as a given, as something in his consciousness that man knows, and in this way Schleiermacher proves the presence of that other content in the Christian elements in religion which is also posited, of that presupposition of the religious experience governed by the Christian antithesis. And with the proof derived from this second mortal leap he has already reached the peak that he had to climb. |

In § 32, with which Part I opens, one looks in vain for any explanation of this procedure. Indeed, the thesis simply reinforces the impression of something miraculous when it states that the sense of absolute dependence is always presupposed and *therefore(!) also contained* in the Christian religious consciousness, and that it is so as the only way in which one's own being and the infinite being of God are generally one in the self-consciousness. Not only do we here again come up with astonishment against the argument that the feeling of absolute dependence, because it is presupposed in the Christian consciousness, is also contained in it, but even more we are told that this presupposed and contained factor is not just the God-consciousness that is somehow a given in the self-consciousness, but that it also claims to represent the unity of one's own being and the infinite divine being in the self-consciousness. |

All else—we return to § 29—is now easy to understand. This other content of the elements in religion which is presupposed and therefore co-posited, but not determined by the antithesis, does not fade away when the mind is grasped in a Christian sense. On the contrary, the corresponding state of mind is eased and favored thereby; it now becomes a part of the Christian religious consciousness as the accompanying component which is *not changed* by the sense of sin and grace. On the other hand, one must also say that it does not independently constitute a real religious element but only as a component in combination with that positive determination (cf. § 32,1). Thus the sphere of [2/5/24]

Christian piety is to be found in both components together, the presupposition being related to the determination as in life as a whole the individual's (self-) positing as an I relates to the detailed elements in his existence (§ 32,1). It may be that the distinctively Christian factor is less pronounced in the borrowed theses that make up the presupposition and that these are close in expression to what may be said in other religions, yet the statements about the religious self-consciousness are genuinely dogmatic statements, and in their connection with the other components they are specifically Christian statements, and not just—Schleiermacher lays the greatest stress on this—"constituent parts of a general or so-called natural theology" [§ 29,2]. The sphere of dogmatics is strictly confined to the period of the Christian development of the antithesis (including what is presupposed and also contained in this development); what is before this period or *beyond* it, when the antithesis of sin and grace has already been overcome again, does not belong to the doctrine of faith, or does so only in connection with pious states of mind within the antithesis [§ 29,3]. There are no elements in the religious life (§ 32,3) whose content is the God-consciousness in and for itself, not even in the Jewish or Mohammedan religion where the determined component is not redemption in Christ but either the legislation of Moses or the prophecy of Mohammed. In the sphere of Christian piety, then, there is no general God-consciousness unrelated to Christ. The statements of Part I are not overestimated as though we had there an original natural theology that is universally valid. On the other hand, there are no statements in Part II that do not go back to the presupposition of the antithesis, the sense of absolute dependence. The statements of Part I are not underestimated as though they were simply the reflection of a sorry monotheistic God-consciousness when they are in fact merely abstractions of the Christian God-consciousness. The measure of the relationship to Christ is the constancy of the God-consciousness produced thereby, whereas—and here Schleiermacher marks himself off from Zinzendorf—a relationship to Christ by which the God-consciousness is pushed in the background or outdated may be a very inward one but strictly speaking it is not religious [§ 62,3].

To recapitulate, the Christian consciousness in the narrower sense has a presupposition, the consciousness of dependence, or God-consciousness in general. We find this in ourselves (the first leap), in our self-consciousness (the second leap). This God-consciousness, then, is not merely presupposed but also contained in the Christian consciousness. Hence the statements of both parts together form the totality of the necessary dogmatic theses. The problems in this train of thought obviously arise at the leaps. We shall have to come back to them when we review the Introduction. Our concern here is simply to answer the question what Schleiermacher was really after with this whole complicated process. Not to give a natural theology, he again assures us. But why then these frantic efforts to bring God-consciousness into the self-consciousness via Christian experience as its presupposition, and thereby to posit the I in relation to which the whole of positive Christianity is simply one aspect of existence alongside others? And all this, as we have seen, when the same path has been taken already in the Introduction, but in the reverse direction, immediate self-consciousness being shown to be consciousness of absolute dependence or God-consciousness. Is the real point in Part I anything other than to establish the connection between the *predicates* that will be developed in Part II and[24] the *subject* of the dogmatic statements that is already brought to light in the Introduction, and in this way to anchor Christianity, not in its Christian determination, but in the necessary presupposition of this, namely, in the universally valid theses of ethics and the philosophy of religion? To be sure, Part I of *The Christian Faith* is not a natural theology. But what does Schleiermacher himself say in the thesis of § 33: "The recognition that this sense of absolute dependence is not something accidental, nor a distinctively personal thing, but a universal element in life, completely replaces for the doctrine of faith all the so-called proofs of the existence of God." Thus Part II develops specifically Christian dogmatics, Part I its presupposition. The Introduction recognizes this presupposition to be a universal element in life which "indwells human nature," as the title of Part I in the first edition revealingly puts it. And according to § 33 this recognition replaces the proofs for the existence of God. Thus the Introduction is at least a substitute for a natural theology, which is in full agreement with what we have seen about its relation to the whole work, and Part I is to be viewed as in fact a two-way bridge between this substitute natural theology and the dogmatics proper. |

Let us now see from the expositions in the second letter to Lücke whether this was in fact what Schleiermacher had in mind. He expressly tells us there that he considered the possibility of *reversing* the order of the two parts, what the reasons for this were, and what finally persuaded him to preserve the present order. The idea occupied him as early as the first edition. "Would it not have been natural and fitting for a theologian who is of the *Reformed* school, and who even in the present state of the union does not think he should deny this, to have followed the *Heidelberg Catechism* more closely?"[25] He means by this that with a reversal of the order of the parts he would have begun *The Christian Faith* with the doctrine of the plight of man. "The Father would have been seen first in Christ. The two definite statements about God would have been that he renews the human race by the sending of Christ and that he founds his spiritual kingdom in him."[26] Part I would not then have been misunderstood as it unfortunately has been, namely, as the speculative and more important part from which Schleiermacher descends in the form of an anticlimax to the less important part, to the positive dogmatics, namely, to Part II, whereas on his own view Part I, although it belongs to the main structure, is merely a vestibule or narthex, an unfilled space, which receives its content only from what is presented later. How much clearer this understanding would have been if this whole complex of statements had been put where its full significance could have been perceived! How much more definitely, for example, could omnipotence have been presented if there had been a sense of the new spiritual creation, or omnipresence if there had been a sense of the omnicausality of the divine Spirit, or omniscience if there had been a

---

[24]The MS has "with."
[25]*Sendschreiben an Lücke*, ed. Mulert, p. 30.
[26]*Ibid.*, p. 31.

sense of divine grace and the divine good-pleasure![27] Placed after the Christology, the doctrine of the church, and the like, all these propositions of Part I would have taken on a "warmer hue" and appeared "in the distinctively Christian light"[28] that Schleiermacher had in mind. "No one could then have failed to see that the depiction of the distinctively Christian consciousness is really and truly the proper purpose of the book,"[29] for it would then have been much more necessary to go back at each point to the Christian center of the self-consciousness. The academic and religious concerns of the *Glaubenslehre* would then have been seen to be much more closely related.

One might say that all this, on Schleiermacher's own assumptions, constituted a sound argument, and it is surprising to hear that he consoled himself with the thought that sooner or later someone else would come who would happily and successfully adopt this far superior arrangement.[30] Why did not he himself do it? Two reasons, he says, restrained him with invincible force; he calls the first a *whim* and the second an *inability*. |

1. The "whim" is his aversion to the form of the anticlimax. An academic work is not a meal in which one can count on a certain measure of intoxication if the best drink is produced first (p. 32). As he saw it, the best should not be brought out too soon but left for the end; with that reversal, however, the so-called natural qualities of God (omnipotence, etc.) would have come last. He felt that this would have supported the charge of pantheism that was often leveled against him. But a second consideration was even more important. In the form of the anticlimax, he could have handled the teachings of the present Part II only very briefly. This would have been a disadvantage, not, of course, for the book in itself and as such, nor as an expression of his personal convictions, but "relative to the present needs of our church."[31] There follows the most famous passage from the letters to Lücke with reference to which Mulert thinks he must even extol Schleiermacher as a prophet.[32] He asks Lücke what he senses for the future, not of theology, but of evangelical Christianity,[33] in view of the advances in science and history. How long can the concept of creation (apart from the six days and the like) "hold out against the pressure of a cosmology that is formed from one of the scientific combinations that none of us can escape?"[34] How long will it be before the New Testament miracles (not to speak of those of the Old Testament) are again confronted with the dilemma, and this time on more solid presuppositions than those of the 18th century, either that they are fables, with all the background that is in-

[27]*Ibid.*, p. 33.
[28]*Loc. cit.*
[29]*Loc. cit.*
[30]*Ibid.*, p. 35.
[31]*Ibid.*, pp. 35f.
[32]Cf. Mulert's Introduction (p. 3): "In his letters to Lücke some of the basic ideas of his theology emerge more clearly than in any of his other writings and they are expressed in the light of coming developments that he foresaw in theology, the church, and intellectual life in general. ... That he became a prophet, and that he prophesied correctly, one may see for oneself on pp. 36ff. and 41ff."
[33]*Ibid.*, p. 36.
[34]*Loc. cit.*

separable from them, or that they are facts but can be explained by natural analogies? What will be the final judgment of historical criticism on the Pentateuch or on the Old Testament canon as a whole? Will our talk about the types and prophecies of the Old Testament be able much longer to achieve credibility among those who have formed a sound and vital appreciation of historical matters? What new things will criticism bring relative to the New Testament canon?[35] "What will happen then, my dear friend? I shall not experience this age, but can go quietly to sleep. But you, my dear friend, and your contemporaries who are like-minded with us, what do you think you will do? . . . Will the knot of history come loose, so that we have an equation of *Christianity with barbarism* and *science with unbelief*? Many, of course, will take this path, there will be many predispositions in this direction, and the ground is already quaking under our feet from which these sorry masks will come creeping out of tightly closed religious circles that declare all research to be satanic apart from entrenchments of the ancient letter. But such people cannot be elected to keep watch over the holy sepulchre" (p. 37). For "if the reformation from which the first beginnings of our church emerged did not have the aim of establishing an eternal compact between a vital Christian faith and independent scholarly research that is open on every side, so that neither hampers the other, it cannot do justice to the needs of our age, and we need another reformation, no matter what form it may take or what conflicts may shape it. My firm conviction, however, is that the basis for such a compact was established and we only need a clearer sense of the task to be able to fulfil it" (p. 40). The rationalistic possibility is *not* taken into account that the rise of Christianity can be put in the unending collection of ordinary experience, that we can accept a Jesus who after a considerable span can be given due honor as "the sage of Nazareth or a simple country rabbi,"[36] and that we should continue the work of culture and ethics along this line because there is little hope of finding a "new central figure" or a "new book of aphorisms."[37] *Not* considered either is the possibility of a speculative theology that with all its profundity can derive faith in Christ in a rather sophisticated way only from learning or philosophy, thus defending itself against natural science but plunging itself instead into an impossible antithesis between esoteric and exoteric teaching, and introducing "a hierarchy of speculation that verges on the Roman," although Schleiermacher makes no secret of the fact that at a pinch he personally would prefer the second of these two evils.[38] In opposition to these two rejected possibilities Schleiermacher sees it as the task that has been set for us by the Reformation that we should understand "every dogma that truly presents itself as an element of our Christian consciousness" in such a way that it does not entangle us with scholarship.[39] He thinks that he has fulfilled this task in his Part II. He hopes that he has presented, not just miracles in general, but especially "the miracle of all miracles," the coming of the Redeemer, in such a way that, "without prejudice to faith," "scholarship

---

[35]*Ibid.*, pp. 36–43.
[36]*Ibid.*, p. 37.
[37]*Ibid.*, p. 38.
[38]*Ibid.*, pp. 38–40.
[39]*Ibid.*, p. 40.

does not have to declare war on us," relationships to the Old Testament and similar secondary matters having been cast off, and within the realm of the factual no line having been drawn "between the natural and the absolute supernatural."[40] He thinks that scientists, faced by his Christology, will have to concede that there is in the sphere of the spiritual life a phenomenon which we can explain only as a new creation, as the pure beginning of a higher spiritual development, just as matter condenses and begins to rotate in infinite space. Part I prepared the ground for the discharge of this task, and this is why he kept the order. These are the extensive and not always clear or cogent explanations of the whim—the aversion to an anticlimax—which influenced him. |

2. We now turn to the "inability" of which Schleiermacher complains. Of what does this consist? He presupposes that Lücke will understand his statement that it is neither Christian nor good "to force so-called rationalists, even if in a good and friendly way, out of the fellowship of our church."[41] Since that is the tendency which is strongly asserting itself at the time, "it is my own, I do not know whether to say good or bad habit, that out of natural fear that the little ship in which we are all sailing might overturn, to lean to the other side as strongly as is possible with my slight weight." And he wanted to *show* and not just to declare that the worthy people who are thus styled might remain in the church *by right*. The task that he set himself in this regard was to demonstrate that heresy and heterodoxy are not the same thing and to indicate how much friendly agreement is possible within the space inhabited in common by the orthodox and the heterodox. He did not succeed in this as he would have liked in the first edition—it is here that he finds his "inability"—for in his definition of Christianity there, under the influence of Question 15 of the *Heidelberg Catechism*, he understood the concept of redemption almost too strictly; he promised to amend this in the second edition, and this is what he did. But he could not do it, he thought, if he began his exposition in the strict sense with that central point and thus allowed the place of the peace of God between the rationalists and the orthodox to go unoccupied too long.[42]

What does all this amount too? Obviously Schleiermacher has been confirming with his own mouth what we earlier suspected. Part I of *The Christian Faith* is in fact a bridge on which not only rationalists and orthodox but also scholarship and faith can find themselves together. On *this* side of the bridge, denoted by the Introduction, is the territory where Christianity, while acknowledged to be the best, is one religious possibility among others, and the direct self-consciousness that lies at the basis of religion is recognized as God-consciousness. On the *far* side of the bridge, denoted by Part II, is the territory that is specifically allotted to Christianity, marked off by the idea of the Christian antithesis (discussed yesterday) in such a way that no contradiction can arise between the consciousness of sin and grace which is its theme and the God-consciousness as such. *On* the bridge it takes place that the God-

[40]*Loc. cit.*
[41]For this quotation and those that follow, see *ibid.*, p. 44.
[42]*Ibid.*, p. 45.

consciousness as such, not the Christian consciousness of sin and grace but its abstraction, not without some difficulty—for how could there fail to be difficulty in this reversal of birth?—returns to the mother's womb of the direct self-consciousness from which it emerges in the Introduction. Here, then, justice is in fact done to all parties. For *faith* the consciousness of God arises out of Christian experience. For *scholarship* it is grounded in our universal nature. *Orthodoxy* finds the various heads of the church's doctrine of God more or less complete and with the further guarantee—something that the older Protestant dogmatics failed to give—that this doctrine could not be presented apart from Christ. *Rationalism* finds its beloved minimum of universal religion and it can also rejoice in the promise that precisely on the basis of this minimum it, too, can be a full-fledged member of the Christian church. The eternal compact which was the goal of the Reformation, though without meeting the needs of our own time, has been sealed. Christianity need *not* accompany barbarism nor scholarship unbelief. Natural science and biblical criticism can come. Empiricism and speculation have become superfluous and can go. The little ship of the church in which we are all voyaging is protected against overturning. No war will be declared and no one will be shut out. Is not all this very remarkable? There are only two mourners, the Bible and the Reformation, inasmuch as their goal was a different one from that assigned to them by Schleiermacher. From their standpoint the fact that the statements about sin and grace relate to those about the God-consciousness as *predicates* to *subject*, the fact that the God-consciousness, abstracted away from the experience of sin and grace, finds a place in man's direct self-consciousness as this can be a subject of psychology, the fact that a universal element of life resident in human nature is to be a substitute for the proofs of God that are now largely unusable, the fact that there is no absolute antithesis between the natural and the absolutely supernatural, and that *mutatis mutandis* the coming of Christ is similar to the formation of a new nebula—from their standpoint all these things are great and incredible novelties. And it is finally these novelties that make possible building of Schleiermacher's famous bridge.

   d. The Three Forms of Dogmatic Statements. We recall that according to [2/7/24] § 30 dogmatic statements may be formulated either as descriptions of human states, as concepts of divine properties or modes of action, or as statements about circumstances in the world. The arrangement according to the vertical sections discussed thus far unquestionably reminds us of the normal schema of Christian doctrine which was already valid for Augustine: doctrine of God, anthropology, Christology, and so forth. The originality of Schleiermacher emerges only when one inquires, as we have tried to do, into the reasons and purpose that these vertical sections have for him. On the other hand, the horizontal division denoted by the three forms is as original and typical at a first glance as is the tower of St. James for the city of Göttingen. Related successively to Part I and the two antitheses of Part II, these make up a totality of 3 × 3 = 9 sections. We must now ask what purpose they serve. To this end you should read §§ 15, 16, 31, 35, 50, and 64,2, and pp. 47ff. of the second letter to Lücke in the Mulert edition.

   In §§ 15 and 16 of the Introduction we find Schleiermacher's theory of statements of faith and dogmatic statements in general. Christian statements of this kind are verbal expressions of Christian religious states.[43] Like all modifications of the excited self-consciousness, religious affections, when they reach a certain degree of strength and definiteness, communicate themselves externally, originally in mimic form by facial expressions, movements, sounds, and gestures. A whole system of sacred *signs* and *symbolic* actions in which a society unites is quite conceivable apart from any noticeable intervention of thought. But inevitably with time will come reflection on the circumstances in which people find themselves engaged in such things, and an attempt will then be made to conceptualize them and preserve them in the form of thought. For a long time this attempt may be a purely inward one: thought is a form of speech which does not have the concepts whereby to communicate itself. Only when it does do we get the spoken statement or the statement of faith either in the strict sense or in a figurative one.[44] Christianity presupposes that this stage of development has been reached. Each element in proclamation is a statement of faith, that is, an attestation of the Christian determination of the religious consciousness as inner certainty. But proclamation subdivides into three linguistic forms: poetic, oratorical, and didactic. The relationship between these three possibilities, like the earlier transition from symbolical action to speech, is a *cultural* question. Relative to all three it is to be maintained (1) that communication as such is something different from piety itself, though the latter cannot be conceived of without communication, and (2) that it has its basis exclusively in the affections of the religious self-consciousness and cannot arise without them.[45] *Dogmatic statements* belong to the third possibility. They are didactic statements of faith which aim at "the highest degree of precision."[46] If poetic expression rests purely inwardly on an enhanced moment of life, "a moment of inspiration," if "oratorical expression rests on a . . . moment of excited interest which achieves a specific result,"[47] and if both have their particular perfection in their lawful participation in proclamation, the issue in the didactic expression is the linguistic apprehension and appropriation of what is originally given in the first two forms independently of the moments that are normative for them, so that it is less a matter of *kerygma* than of *homologia* (confession).[48] (For Schleiermacher "Christ's self-proclamation" is unique relative to all three possibilities and cannot be more precisely defined.)[49] The nature of the dogmatic or didactic statement in contrast to the poetic or oratorical is that it aims at consistency with itself and with similar statements, whereas the poetic expression changes into or is explained by precise ones and what is oratorical keeps its own particular measure. Normative here is the scholarly interest, the interest in language from the standpoint of (purely) formal logic. Logically ordered reflection, proceeding dialectically, focuses on the direct expressions of the re-

---

[43]Cf. § 15.
[44]Cf. § 15,1.
[45]Cf. § 15,2.
[46]§ 16.
[47]§ 16,1.
[48]*Loc. cit.*
[49]Cf. § 16,2.

ligious self-consciousness and directs their impact.[50] Schleiermacher stresses the formal character of the union of religion and scholarship achieved thereby. Indeed, he thinks that even philosophy, if it is not to disintegrate, must either begin or end with statements about the supreme being, statements which can hardly be distinguished from those that derive from pious reflection but are dialectically shaped, yet have to be kept clearly apart. Fundamentally only the latter are dogmatic statements.[51]

§ 31 *applies* this theory. According to the general definitions of the sense of absolute dependence, this feeling must combine with another and lower form of self-consciousness if it is to be a real consciousness in time. Any formula for it must also be a formula for a specific state of mind, and all the statements of the doctrine of faith must be capable of being presented as formulas of this kind. But every lower and sensory determination of the self-consciousness points back to a determinative factor *outside* it. To know a specific modification of the sense of absolute dependence that is united with this, there is thus needed a description of the element in the totality on which the state concerned is based, that is, a statement about some circumstance in the *world* that shows itself to be active in relation to the sense of absolute dependence in its combination with the sensory self-consciousness. Finally the feeling of absolute dependence, in terms of which the totality is comprised from which the determinations of the self-consciousness proceed, is "in and for itself a co-positing of God in the self-consciousness," so that all the modifications of the self-consciousness united with it can also take the form of statements about *God* as the author of this union.[52] The three forms of dogmatic statements result. But a distinction follows. Statements of the first form, "descriptions of human states of mind," can obviously be derived "only from the sphere of inner experience." Hence under this form, Schleiermacher thinks, "nothing alien can steal into the Christian doctrine of faith." This form, then, is to be called the "basic dogmatic form."[53] The statements about the circumstances of the world and the attributes and action of God are different. The former might be scientific and the latter metaphysically speculative. Hence they have no guarantee of being genuinely dogmatic. They are the statements of subsidiary forms and they are reliable as such only to the degree that they can be explained by those of the first form. Would it not be logical to offer only those of the first and basic form in dogmatics and omit those about the world and God as superfluous? Schleiermacher himself raises this objection. But no, he answers, for work along such lines would be "isolated, without historical basis," and lacking any true churchly character, so that it could not fulfil the purpose of a dogmatics. Dogmatic language has been shaped gradually on the basis of the other public utterances of religion—the poetic and oratorical. From these, and out of a need to establish the relationship between the kingdom of God and the world, the statements of the second and third forms arose. Hence dogmatics, even if it wants things to be different, has

[50]Cf. § 16,3.
[51]Cf. § 16 Appendix.
[52]Cf. § 30,1.
[53]Cf. § 30,2.

to take their presence into account if only to achieve the necessary clarification and purification.[54]

I will not give an express analysis of the other sections mentioned—which are all introductory to individual divisions—for they involve a good deal of repetition. Instead I will simply pick out certain things that might serve to elucidate the basic idea as we have thus far presented it. In § 31,2 Schleiermacher points out that in his presentation the doctrine of God with which dogmatics usually begins, and which entails a depiction of "the totality of the divine attributes," will achieve completion only with the completion of the whole. He finds this procedure to be an advantage rather than a disadvantage, for it brings clearly to light the connection between this doctrine and the facts of religion, and thus averts any appearance of speculative theory. § 35,2 speaks about the dangers of the second and third forms, "which no longer reproduce the pious self-consciousness directly" but "make God and . . . the world the subject of their statements." The danger arises that they might say something about this subject which "goes beyond the immediate content of that self-consciousness." Statements about God's attributes, Schleiermacher instructs us, have their nearest basis in poetic and homiletical descriptions and can easily make God seem to be finite in a way that does not harmonize with the sense of absolute dependence. On the other hand, since a world-view and a religious world-view are the same thing for simple people, statements that purport to be objectively scientific can easily find their way into statements about the world. On both sides, then, there can be deviations from true dogmatics, and these will be all the worse if they encroach on statements of the first form (§ 35,3). § 50 offers a clear-cut view of Schleiermacher's thinking when it says that "all the qualities that we attribute to God are *not* meant to denote anything specific in God himself but only something specific in the way of relating the sense of absolute dependence to him." These statements of the second form do not originally derive from dogmatic or didactic interest. They are not meant to establish knowledge but, as we have seen, they simply reproduce the *direct impression* poetically or rhetorically in its various manifestations. If we forget their religious rather than philosophical origin, they will often be taken up into what is called natural theology. Over against this one must affirm that they do not have a speculative content.[55] For in God, as in the feeling of absolute independence, there is *no* real multiplicity of functions, *no* antithesis, *no* differentiation. Hence a presentation of the divine attributes can and should only explain the feeling of absolute dependence by a reference back to the divine causality. In so doing, when it notes the distinctions it will not be saying anything real about God, just as there are no real distinctions in the feeling of absolute dependence in and for itself, apart from its determinations. The completeness of the divine attributes after which we seek is no other than the completeness of the self-consciousness in its various modifications.[56] The method of achieving these statements can only be that of applying the category of causality: What is the origin of the sense

[54]Cf. § 30,3.
[55]§ 50,1.
[56]Cf. § 50,2.

of absolute dependence? Finally the statements will subdivide into original statements that deal with the feeling as such (Part I) and derived statements that relate to the antithesis (Part II).[57] § 64,2 tells us regarding the secondary forms that the circumstances of the world that are at issue here are naturally those that relate to man. They will differ according to whether the God-consciousness is impaired or dominant. We have seen already that rather oddly Schleiermacher deals at this point with the doctrine of evil on the one side and that of the church on the other.[58] The question of the divine attributes, which here, then, are derived and not original, will thus run as follows: What divine qualities may be discerned in the state of sin, not, of course inasmuch as it is apostasy from God, but inasmuch as redemption is awaited and pre-pared in it, and to what divine qualities does the dominance of the God-consciousness point insofar as it is fashioned by redemption out of the state of sin?

The question of division which arises here was much more important for Schleiermacher (and is in fact much more important) than might at first ap-pear. In the second letter to Lücke he makes it plain that here, too, he seriously considered reconstructing his work. If he had done this, the revision would have been far more comprehensive and momentous than the reversal of the two parts that he also, as we have seen, considered. He had in view no more and no less than a complete exclusion of the two so-called secondary forms in favor of the first and basic form. "If it is true that they say nothing that is not already contained in its essential content in the statements of the basic form,[59] the two others might not be missed. And that is in fact my conviction, with which is linked the further conviction that our doctrine of faith will one day learn to get along without them. If someone is more advanced than I am in his course, what is more natural, if he sees clearly what shape his work must take when completed, than that he should try to complete it as quickly as possible?"[60] By no means arbitrarily these lines remind us of Moses on Mt. Nebo [cf. Dt. 34]. But Schleiermacher has to give up the idea of entering the promised land in person. He admits that it would be "no small satisfac-tion" for him to present his dogmatics in the unique way that he has in view. Over against the criticism of F. C. Baur he thought he could maintain that full justice could then be done to the historical Christ in his *Christian Faith.* Yet he argues, as in § 30 of the book itself, that he could have undertaken this alteration only at the risk of his book becoming "in this form a purely private book," "a museum piece in theological literature," which might edify and instruct many people, but could not be the public expression of Christian doctrine that it ought to be. Nevertheless, precisely because of the criticism of certain false dogmatic statements, which were especially numerous in the second and third forms, it was necessary to begin with what he had, on the one hand "going back to the direct self-consciousness of the Christian in the first form" but then accepting formulas that belong to a time long since past

[57]Cf. § 50,3.
[58]Cf. p. 192.
[59]Schleiermacher: ". . . in statements which carry the basic form. . . ."
[60]*Sendschreiben an Lücke,* pp. 47f.

in the third form, the criticism being correct.[61] Hence he remained true to the complicated method chosen in the first edition and left to a future day what he would have liked to have done himself. "I rejoice at least in the conviction that at least from a distance I have seen the form of a more free and living way of handling our doctrine of faith."[62]

Let us now clarify what all this means. Obviously a comprehensive characterization of what remained (or did not remain) of the older concept of the Word in Schleiermacher. To anticipate, nothing remained of the belief that the Word or statement is as such the bearer, bringer, and proclaimer of truth, that there might be such a thing as the Word of God. Schleiermacher knows the concept of the *kerygma*, but naturally a kerygma that only *depicts* and does not *bring*, that only *states* or *expresses* and does not *declare*. Truth does not come in the spoken Word; it comes in speaking feeling. And the most original expression of feeling is not the Word but the mime, and when the Word comes it first takes the form of poetry and rhetoric, and when we reach dogmatics logic only determines the form and does not pose the question of truth. And when feeling speaks and even teaches, its subject is no other than itself, its determinations and source, God as its cause and the cause of its determinations. And even when, indirectly, we have the statements of feeling about God and the world, its statements about itself are still the *basic* dogmatic form, and Schleiermacher would have preferred a dogmatics confined to such statements. External historical reasons hamper him in this regard, and he cannot let the opportunity slip, even as he seems to be making statements about God and the world which are meant to be anything other than statements *of* feeling *about* feeling, to engage in attacks upon them, and to trace back to the *subjective* sphere that which the Bible and the church are saying objectively in this regard. All that they say here is suspect and even dangerous. Poetry and preaching must discharge their office but only by way of expression and depiction, not with the idea that they are pronouncing truth. Dogmatics knows that truth resides, and will always reside, in feeling. It is *strictly* only what feeling says about itself. And it can speak the truth even about itself only approximately and inadequately. It can speak, but truth cannot be put in words. For feeling is nonqualitative and indifferent as regards its truth; it has no words, nor has the God who is its causality. "If the soul speaks. . . ."[63] To be sure, it has to speak, but its esthetic self-depiction is nearer the mark than its verbal self-depiction. We now understand why in *Christmas Eve* music is rated *above* speech and silent devotion above both.[64] All expressions of feeling are simply depiction and may be omitted. And if they are not, speech has less right and worth. And if there is speech, we do not have anything more than an attempt of feeling to depict *itself*. As I see it, what we have in this doctrine of the three forms is Schleiermacher's mystical agnosticism. In this light we can understand what was said earlier about the character of the Introduction as a place where proof is advanced for the truth, not of Christianity, but of

[61]*Ibid.*, pp. 49f.
[62]*Ibid.*, p. 51.
[63]Cf. Schiller's verse, p. 176, n. 69.
[64]Cf. pp. 70f.

feeling, about the character of Part II with its relativism of sin and grace, and about the character of Part I with its proof that specifically Christian feeling is at one with the feeling that is shown to be true or actual in the Introduction. If the proposition that the relation of man to God consists exclusively of feeling is the cardinal proposition of Schleiermacher's theology, we recognize in this doctrine of the three forms the key to the whole of the *Glaubenslehre*.

2. The Introduction. I do not intend to discuss all the thirty-one sections of [2/11/24] this famous prelude to Schleiermacher's work. Some, like §§ 14–15 and §§ 29–31, have been dealt with in detail already. The rest of the second half of the Introduction from which these come I must leave to your own study, which should not be too difficult presupposing what has been said and what has now to be said about the first half. When people speak about the Introduction to *The Christian Faith*, they usually have in mind §§ 3–14, or the first three parts of the first chapter. Not disclosing to novices what important things will occur, this chapter bears the innocuous title "In Explanation of Dogmatics." We have seen already[65] that as things are it is quite impossible to accept Schleiermacher's assurances (to Lücke and in § 1) that these 3 × 4 sections are to be regarded only as entrance steps that have nothing to do with the real content of dogmatics. On the contrary, as the whole of the 19th century rightly perceived, we have here the true *content* of dogmatics in relation to which all that follows is only an analysis after the fact, as it were, with something new to say only to those who have not noticed or understood what is going on here. To use the vivid comparison of E. Brunner,[66] the thought-warriors are here received under the cover of night into the roomy body of the Trojan horse, so that when the horse has crossed the bridge into the holy city (if we may expand the metaphor), and the great day of true dogmatics has dawned, they may emerge from it in battle array. It is as well therefore, if we are not to be surprised later, to pay full attention to what our Odysseus is doing at this point. What dogmatics is, according to § 2, is explained by a discussion of what the Christian church is. But what the Christian church is, according to the general academic presuppositions familiar to us from the Encyclopedia, we have to learn first from ethics, then from the philosophy of religion, and finally from apologetics as a discipline on the border line of theology and philosophy. According to § 33 of the *Kurze Darstellung* philosophical theology starts at a point beyond Christianity and theology as a positive science has its initial basis, both in general and in detail, in borrowings from the superior science of history. This is now worked out by Schleiermacher. All the sections that concern us consist of statements that are borrowed from ethics, the philosophy of religion, and apologetics, that is, disciplines that openly view Christianity from outside. According to § 2,2 ethics, as the speculative presentation of reason running parallel to natural science, has to declare itself regarding the concept of the church in general. The philosophy of religion is a critical account of the different churches insofar as in their totality they are the complete manifestation of piety in human nature. Its

---

[65]Cf. pp. 194f.
[66]E. Brunner, *Die Mystik und das Wort*, p. 66.

function is thus to show the Christian church what its particular place is within this totality. Finally apologetics, which with one foot at least is already a specifically theological discipline, examines and defines the distinctive nature of Christianity in its own context. Thus the announcement of § 2 that what follows will be a discussion of the concept of the Christian church, and the related headings of the three parts, are somewhat misleading to the extent that the true theme of these presentations is more the *piety* that constitutes the church, and Schleiermacher in the first part, apart from the first sentences of § 3, deals with the concept of the fellowship of piety, of which we think first in relation to the term "church," only in § 6, while in the second part he does not deal with it at all, and in the third part only in § 14, and even then more incidentally. What we really have is an investigation of *religion, religions,* and the *Christian* religion, and a second and more important thing that is not made plain in § 2 or by the titles, but only by the actual discussions, is that even this is not so much an investigation of the *reality* as of the *necessity* of at least the *basic fact* that is at issue here as "an essential element in human nature" [§ 6]. Instead of the innocuous heading of the first chapter, "In Explanation of Dogmatics," one might easily substitute in thought the alternative, "An Attempt at a Scientific Demonstration of the Object of Dogmatics." But let us turn to the material itself.

a. Religion (§§ 3–6). I solemnly draw your attention to the fact that we are now entering the holy of holies of Schleiermacher's theology. "On the Concept of the Church" is his own title for the section. But its theme is really what he himself—an ardent translator of all foreign terms in his later years—describes as *piety*. A society related to piety, to its maintenance, ordering, and promotion, is a church. With this explanation in § 3,1 he thinks he has earned the right to deal exclusively with *piety* under this heading, and then in § 6, as we have seen, to speak about *fellowship* in piety, having already stated quite incidentally in § 2,2 that the church is a fellowship or society "which arises only by free human acts and can continue only by the same." If this latter statement is true—and Schleiermacher does not regard it as necessary to adduce or establish it specifically from ethics—then the presupposition is laid down whereby under the heading of the church he may speak about piety as "the basis of all ecclesiastical societies," as the thesis of § 3 puts it, as the meaning and basis of the human activities from which they arise. And this statement is undoubtedly true if the other statement is true that philosophical theology begins at a point *beyond* or *above* Christianity and all other religions, so that if the above concept of the church stands, its concern is solely with the relevant human function and nothing else. I need hardly point out how momentous this presupposition that precedes the first step necessarily is. |

Let us first try to understand the famous definition of § 3 from Schleiermacher's own explanations. "Considered purely in and for itself, piety," he says, "is neither *knowledge* nor *action* but a determination of *feeling* or of *direct self-consciousness.*"[67] For him "feeling" does not mean unconscious states but self-consciousness. By it, he explains in § 3,5, we are not to think

---

[67]§ 3, Thesis.

of something confused or inactive. It is "strongest in the most vital (= the most conscious) moments." It can share in all the expressions of the will or even underlie them. Schleiermacher leaves us in no doubt that it is real consciousness. Indeed, it is *self*-consciousness, that is (as § 3,3 explains), consciousness of "the nature of the subject itself" as the unity in the alternation of remaining within itself and moving outside itself" in which its life consists. Additionally, it is *direct* self-consciousness in contrast to all objective conceptions. It is *the* self-consciousness behind which "all thought and will" sometimes retire [§ 3,2] and which with the same distinctness persists through series of acts of thought and will, either way distinguishing itself from these. This feeling or direct self-consciousness cannot be a transcendental concept or *a priori* in the sense of Kant. This is decided already by this first explanation in § 3,2. How could a transcendental concept be so distinct on the one hand and how could it sometimes suppress thought and feeling on the other, yet also more or less persistently accompany them? § 3,3 affirms instead that feeling is a *third thing* along with *thought* and *action*. It is the subject's total remaining within itself. Alongside it stands *knowledge*, which as a having known is the subject's remaining within itself and as a knowing is its moving out of itself. In contrast to feeling *action* is a total moving out of the self. The only fourth thing to be named alongside these three is the "nature" or "essence" of the subject itself. Feeling is direct consciousness of this. But this is a third thing alongside a first and a second, except that in contrast to these, as the *total* remaining of the subject within itself, it is not caused by this but simply comes to pass in it, being *receptivity*, not activity. We observe without completely understanding it the peculiarity of a purely passive yet not, as we have seen, inactive consciousness that is asserted here, and we turn to the famous definition of § 3,4: Piety is *neither* knowledge *nor* action. Not as though religion were not linked to these as to all other functions of the mind or spirit; every pious moment includes the seed of either the one or the other or both. But religion is not knowledge, not even knowledge of the doctrine of faith, not even essential knowledge of this doctrine or knowledge with conviction. Piety is the *object* of this knowledge and presupposes it, but it is not itself this knowledge. *Nor* is it action. May its content or form or result be characterized as an action? In the doing of a pious act does not everything depend upon its determinative impulse being emotionally aroused feeling? And are there not states of feeling like remorse, contrition, confidence, or joy in God which—and it is Schleiermacher's secret how far this is legitimate—"we call pious without regard to any ensuing knowledge or action"? Conclusion: There is a knowledge and an action that belong to piety but neither constitutes it. Or is piety a combination (§ 3,5) of knowledge, feeling, and action? There are such combinations, for example, the feeling of satisfaction and assurance when there is relative harmony between an act and a healthy purpose, or the feeling of confident certainty when an operation of thought is successfully concluded. But such moments of feeling are not specifically *pious* and they are only *accidentally* moments of feeling, being essentially either action or knowledge; the element of piety in them is always *essentially* a state of feeling and something different from knowledge and action. Finally, may piety be a knowledge that issues in action, or an action based on knowledge, to the exclusion of feeling? But if so, which? And how can action result from knowledge without an intervening determination of the self-consciousness? Is it not true that the knowledge concerned is *not yet* piety, and the action concerned is *no longer* piety, but it is this intervening determination of the self-consciousness that is piety? In fact, does one not have to say that if the knowledge of the *truth* and the doing of the *good* that are presupposed here obviously cannot be considered as being the true nature of piety either in general or in terms of a purely transcendental concept of faith, if the reference is only to possible *acts* of knowledge and action, then piety is indeed to be sought in a third act which latently but no less immanently confronts these two, which raises the question, of course, whether this third act called feeling is not uncannily related to, and perhaps even identical with, the function that is elsewhere described as *esthetic*.

Piety is a *determination* of feeling. What is meant by this is obviously the problem which, if we postpone our doubts for the moment, still remains after the elucidations of § 3. § 4 gives the answer. What distinguishes piety from other feelings, the thesis says, "is this, that we are conscious of ourselves as being absolutely dependent, or, which is the same thing, of being in relationship with God." Taking up the thread,[68] Schleiermacher says that all true feeling is a determined self-consciousness, determined by *something other* (note the neutral, neuter, impersonal characterization with which this decisive factor enters the stage for the first time). In other words, in all real self-consciousness "there are two elements, a . . . self-positing and a not-having-posited-the-self-thus, . . . a being and a having come into being in some way," the I and something else. But this other is not objectified in the immediate self-consciousness. Since we never exist except in company with others, the element of *receptivity* in the real self-consciousness is always the *first* one. Even the self-consciousness that accompanies action or cognition goes back to an earlier moment of receptivity. "Agreement with these statements," Schleiermacher thinks, "can be unconditionally demanded of anyone, and no one who is capable of self-observation will deny them." He should have added: and no one who thinks he can unconditionally answer this question of the priority of receptivity or activity by means of self-observation, that is, descriptive psychology. Piety, or our relationship with God, is to be defined in the categories of cause, effect, and interaction, that is, the typical categories of natural science. It is obviously by means of this undeclared presupposition and not otherwise that this statement regarding passivity as the first element in the self-consciousness, regarding the primacy of the object, is achieved—a statement on which all else is based. With quick and sure step the climax is now reached. The self-consciousness is determined by something other, and *this*, not the fact that it is *self*-consciousness, is the primary one of the two elements of which it is composed. Determined by something other, we feel *dependent* (§ 4,2). Determined by ourselves, which also occurs, we feel *free*, and we ourselves are then active in relation to the other. Hence the total consciousness is an "alternating action of the subject with the co-posited

[68]§ 4,1.

other." We are with the other, and this means our receptivity as well as our own activity. We ascribe receptivity as well as activity to the other as well as to us. In its togetherness with us, and ours with it, we posit it as the *world*. Our self-consciousness is "consciousness of our being in the world or our being together with" it. As the world it is a sequence of the shared feeling of freedom and dependence. The feeling of *absolute* freedom or *absolute* dependence (Schleiermacher's "schlechthinig" is used for absolute=without any counterpart) does not arise, then, insofar as the self-consciousness relates to the world. On Schleiermacher's view we can say of natural forces, and even of terrestrial bodies, that in the same way as they influence us we can exert "a minimum of counterpressure" on them, and naturally the impossibility of a feeling of absolute dependence in relation to the world does not, he thinks, need any special proof. There can be for us no feeling at all of absolute freedom, he argues in § 4,3, in our being in time. Our own activity has to have an object, and this cannot exist for us without having an impact on our receptivity. But a purely inward feeling of absolute freedom is impossible because our being, even our inner being, cannot come to consciousness except as it proceeds from our activity. Yet there is, he maintains, a feeling of *absolute dependence*. This does not arise from the impact of a given object on which we can have an impact in return. Nor, strictly speaking, does it exist in any individual moment as such, since each such moment is determined by a given in relation to which we might also have a feeling of freedom. (This is a remarkable statement, for "strictly speaking" it lifts this feeling of absolute dependence out of time, and therefore out of the consciousness, and therefore out of the realm of descriptive psychology! Prudently Schleiermacher did not take this statement strictly!) But if the feeling of absolute dependence has no object, as we have learned from Schleiermacher's own lips, where and how is it to be found? We know that receptivity is basic to the human consciousness, yet this priority does not mean exclusiveness? Nevertheless, as Schleiermacher maintains (the end of § 4,3) with an unheard-of leap, our self-consciousness, which accompanies all our activity, and therefore all our existence, since our activity never ceases, "is already in and for itself a consciousness of absolute dependence." It *negates* absolute freedom, the obvious meaning being that this is because, as the union of freedom and receptivity, it *conditions* both; because it is no the *far* side of relative freedom and receptivity. "It is the consciousness that all our activity has its origin outside us, just as the consciousness in relation to which we might have a feeling of absolute freedom would have to have its origin in us." |

Two questions must be put here, the one material and the other formal, both equally important. (1) How far does the maintaining of absolute dependence follow from the denial of absolute freedom? If the self-consciousness— and otherwise it is hard to make sense of the denial—is the boundary or the far side of freedom and dependence, the first result is simply the relativity of all the freedom and dependence of which we are aware in time. A consciousness of absolute dependence on the far side of this boundary, and as a *positive* determination of this far side, would have to be demonstrated in some very different way. Presupposing or maintaining that it results from the negation is a "sleight of hand" (K. Heim)[69] which can be explained only by the way in which Schleiermacher naturalistically takes it for granted that the passive element in the consciousness has priority (§ 4,1) and the naivety with which he equates what is psychologically first with the absolute. He introduces the absolute here, and in so doing he can posit the feeling of absolute dependence where he ought only to have put a question mark. (2) The subject of the denial or the assertion is the direct self-consciousness or feeling. But if receptivity is the first and decisive element in feeling, if feeling according to the rather different reading of § 3,3 is wholly receptivity, and if it has no object according to § 3,2, then how can one achieve or conceive of that denial and assertion and imagine such complicated things (cf. again the concluding sentences of § 4,3) in relation to them? Is there not allotted to poor feeling a function which, if it is not to forfeit what has hitherto been its most important determination, it cannot fulfil? One might add to these two questions the further consideration that in order to assert positively a consciousness of *absolute dependence* Schleiermacher could not dispense with passivity of feeling viewed as either primary or exclusive. But the more he maintained this, the more improbable it became that feeling could *assert* itself as a sense of absolute dependence. Indeed, the more he ascribed activity or the character of real *self-consciousness* to it, the more he ascribed to it, therefore, the ability to execute this logical operation and to *assert* that it is a consciousness of absolute dependence, the less it could really be the *absolute dependence* that it claimed to be, and the more evident it became that no more could be expected of it than the knowledge of *relative* freedom and dependence, the knowledge of its frontier. We must conclude, therefore, that at the climax of this train of thought, logically considered, an impasse is reached from which there is no exit. The consciousness of absolute dependence is asserted—that is clear—and from a comparison with the previously described consciousness of partial dependence on the world it is clear what is meant. But how this is achieved is by no means apparent.

[2/12/24]   Absolute dependence is next equated (§ 4,4) with relationship with God. The *source* of our active and passive existence which is denoted by the expression "absolute dependence" and co-posited in the self-consciousness, Schleiermacher calls *God.* Not the world or some part of it—in relation to which we feel ourselves to be, even if only relatively, *free*—but God. The original meaning of the word "God" is that which is "co-determinative" in the feeling of absolute dependence—that "to which we ascribe the way we are." In this regard it should be noted that the feeling of absolute dependence is not conditioned by "any preceding knowledge of God." There may be an original knowledge of God—but *The Christian Faith* uses the term "God" only as an expression of the feeling of absolute dependence, "the most immediate reflection on this feeling . . . quite independently of that original knowledge, and conditioned only by the feeling[70] of absolute dependence." The consciousness of God is *included* in this direct self-consciousness. It is originally *given* and

---

[69]K. Heim, *Gewissheitsproblem in der systematischen Theologie bis zu Schleiermacher* (Leipzig, 1911), p. 370.
[70]Schleiermacher: "by our feeling."

originally *revealed* in it. To man, who shares absolute dependence with all being, there is given with this a self-consciousness of it which becomes the consciousness of God and clarifies itself in the concept of God. To the degree that this takes place we ascribe piety to the individual. One can say that "God is given to us in an original way in feeling," but naturally no external givenness of God comes into consideration. |

Need I draw attention to the riddles and contradictions with which this section teems? The "something other" of § 4,1, first boldly characterized as neuter, now turns out to be God, *the* origin of our existence. Is this neuter really God, the God of piety, the God of which the doctrine of faith treats, the God of whom Hegel claims to have original knowledge?[71] Schleiermacher never tires of assuring us that this is so. But should not this assurance harden at once into very different statements about God? Along the same lines, this source is said to be "co-posited" in the self-consciousness (not just consciousness of it, but the source itself). God is *given* to us in feeling. Not given to us externally, as Schleiermacher assures us at length. But surely a neuter that is posited and given is obviously not Spirit, not God, but, no matter how abstract, a thing. Brunner[72] is undoubtedly right when in face of this situation he points out that it is quite impossible to conceive of Schleiermacher's feeling of absolute dependence as unconditional *reverence* or the like. The inducing and paying of reverence would imply a spiritual relationship appropriate to the relation between God and man. But this is not at issue here. What we have instead is the brutal *making* and *receiving* of the impact of a monstrous fact. One cannot equate this relationship with the older Reformed view of God or the general Christian concept of the omnipotence of God. It is one thing to call God omnipotent and quite another to call omnipotence God. But this is by the way. We have also to ask: How does this source come in? How does there come to be a *co-posited* and *co-determinative* factor in the feeling of absolute dependence? Were we not told in § 4,3 that the feeling of absolute dependence is not due to the effect of any object that is given in any way? Or is that which makes the impact the very fact that the feeling has no object? The supposed correlative of the self-consciousness as its own *reflection* projected into the absolute? Do not the statements in the section about the secondary character of reflection (compared to feeling) point suspiciously in this direction? But in this case we should be in the most fatal proximity to Feuerbach, and this feeling which is not oriented to any object but still objectifies itself freely in certain ideas could hardly be anything other than the divine power of the imagination, as we conjectured yesterday.[73] Conversely, how does the feeling of absolute dependence come to posit a *source* of our being, and to trace back the way we are to this other, when it is said on the other hand that the consciousness of God is included in it, that God is originally given and revealed? Which really holds true? The first? Then it is obviously not the feeling of absolute dependence, for this can have no counterpart. It is

---

[71]Hegel is not expressly mentioned in *The Christian Faith* but from marginal notes in his copy Barth obviously viewed many of Schleiermacher's statements as aimed at Hegel, for example, § 5 Appendix.

[72]Brunner, *Die Mystik und das Wort*, p. 73.

[73]Barth is perhaps referring to an oral aside in his previous lecture.

the *presence* of God, of the source, of all-crushing causality, in the consciousness; a consciousness which can differentiate itself from its source, which can
push back to this, is not the consciousness of absolute dependence. Or the
second? God originally given or revealed in feeling itself, the feeling of absolute
dependence as the real presence of God, then obviously the God who can be
objectively differentiated from this can only be its *reflection,* the *predicate* of
this subject.

§ 4, as we have seen, leaves us at a loss. We note with astonishment and
concern that Schleiermacher tries to describe the determination of the self-
consciousness as piety wholly within the schema of cause and effect. We do
not understand how feeling, when it is predominantly or totally presented as
receptive, is suddenly supposed to think of itself, or, even less, with what
right it can think of itself, as the feeling of absolute dependence. We suddenly
hear the word "God" pronounced, but the content of the word, and the relation
to man, are wholly impersonal. We are told that this God is co-posited in the
self-consciousness and we are plunged into despair by the fact that either this
vessel makes these contents impossible or these contents make this vessel
impossible. In this mood, then, we follow the master to § 5. This deals with
the relation of the direct self-consciousness as thus determined to other stages
of human self-consciousness. The sense of absolute dependence, the place
where God is given to us originally, is thus one stage among others? Yes, the
thesis tells us. It is the highest stage, but when it is reached it is never separate
from the one immediately below it, and in virtue of this link it participates
in the antithesis of pleasure and pain. Schleiermacher postulates three stages
of the self-consciousness (§ 5,1): (1) The first is the confused animal-like stage
which, as its name suggests, is that of animals, small children, and adults in
the pleasant state just before falling asleep. At this stage remaining within the
self and moving out from it, or feeling and perception, are still undivided. (2)
The second is the sensory stage at which feeling and perception part company.
The co-posited and co-determinative other in these feelings or the corresponding perceptions belongs to the sphere of reciprocity, that is, to the world (§ 4,2).
There can be no question of absolute dependence here. Social and moral feelings are included as well as those that are definitely self-centered. (3) The third
stage is that of the feeling of absolute dependence. We negate absolute freedom
(as shown in § 4,3). Like the world, we are a single finite being. Hence the
antithesis of the middle stage vanishes. The feeling subject views itself as
identical with that which was previously seen to be in opposition. But, one
might interject, what has this ascent from day-dreaming by way of objective
consciousness to the mystical feeling of solitariness—what has all this to do
with the relation to God? And this evolutionary psychologism is not meant
to be a philosophy of identity, a speculatively apologetic substructure for the
doctrine of faith, a weighty anticipation of the actual content of this doctrine?
But let us listen to more. According to § 5,2 a supreme knowledge is conceivable in which all lesser knowledge is summed up, and so is a supreme activity
in the form of a resolve that embraces all self-activity. But both presuppose
an antithesis, and the self-consciousness that accompanies them also stands
within this antithesis. In other words, this supreme knowledge and supreme
activity belong to the second stage. Only the feeling of absolute dependence'

is *above* and beyond the antithesis. This alone constitutes the third and highest stage. Certainly, one may note, if between the third and first stages, between mystical ecstasy—and this is how the feeling of absolute dependence is presented in this context—and animal-like confusion there is a clear mark of distinction. But if there is not, obviously one might just as well conclude that this feeling stands *beneath* rather than above the antithesis of the objective consciousness. |

There now follows the remarkable paragraph § 5,3. It deals with the rise or genesis of the feeling of absolute dependence. This, in which God is originally given according to § 4,4, is not present at first and like all else that does not exist in nature it cannot develop at first. Then it does develop (i.e., when a certain stage is reached in the development of the total consciousness, the biological possibility for it being already there). There takes place a kind of *symbiosis* with the middle stage of consciousness. It finally comes to *completion* in perfect union with this, with the sensory self-consciousness. Nor is this remarkable plant supposed to wilt or die, though notoriously this does not usually interest natural science as such. The course of events is thus as follows. So long as the lowest, animal-like stage does not vanish, the highest one cannot develop. The orientation to the union of subject and object which is native to the human soul cannot break through in the self-consciousness so long as the antithesis is still resolved in animal-like confusion. Things improve when the antithesis emerges in the sensorily perspicuous self-consciousness. The feeling of absolute dependence wills to exist like any living creature and to come forth in its own time. In this respect it needs the sensory self-consciousness, our perceiving and doing, just as the latter needs it, for otherwise it would be without any real self-consciousness. There is thus a simultaneity and interrelation of the two. A moment of purely sensory self-consciousness would be a deficient and imperfect state. But the same would be true of a moment whose content were merely the feeling of absolute dependence, for this would lack the definition and clarity which result from its relation to a definite sensory self-consciousness. Perfection, then, is to be found in the moment of union in which the two are mutually related. One can say that the more the subject, at every moment of its sensory, active and passive self-consciousness, along with its activity and passivity, posits itself as also absolutely dependent, *"the more pious it is."* Or, conversely, the more the orientation whose expression is the feeling of absolute dependence includes at every moment a definite sensory self-consciousness (a weaver's loom!), so that along with its activity and passivity the subject feels itself to be absolutely dependent, *"the more pious it is."* The more pious it is! The more gloriously it develops and the plant flourishes! I intentionally say the plant rather than the child, for if we did not already know, would we really think that the process described in § 5,3 concerns living people in their relation to the living God? |

Two questions arise. (1) How does the feeling of absolute dependence come to develop? What does absolute mean? What becomes of its passivity if it can develop? Is it not natural that we should ask (with Brunner) whether what Schleiermacher has in mind would not be better described as productive imagination,[74] or even more as nonqualitative and nonquantitative *life* which is nowhere alone but floods with hidden omnipotence through everything and has supreme cognitive value as such, rather along the lines of life in J. Müller?[75] (2) What becomes of the givenness of God in this feeling if this can develop? Is it, then, a biotic, quantitative entity linked to the correlation with the sensory? Obviously, but what are we then to think of this kind of God? God as "life"? Or as an objectification and personification of life? |

§ 5,4 brings further disclosures. In and for itself the consciousness of absolute dependence remains always the same. But as such it can be either no real consciousness in time or it must sound out in union with the sensory self-consciousness that rises and falls in multiple alternation (the opening chorus of *St. Matthew's Passion!*) even though it has no connection with it. But now things are different (for this Schleiermacher in § 5,3 simply appeals to experience). Our pious consciousness *follows* the sequence of moments of sensory self-consciousness that differ in content, now becoming this pious movement and now that, but remaining *the same* "throughout the whole series" [§ 5,4]. A soothing reassurance, one might say, and one worthy of the feeling of absolute dependence and of the God who is given to us in it. It may already be heard in passing at the beginning of § 5,3. The divine as such, then, takes no part in the vacillations of the sensory consciousness, but remains its superior self even though it follows them? Or is this reassurance not so soothing on Schleiermacher's lips? Is it saying that the divine as such is not capable of any antithesis or movement, that it can engage in such, *not* in virtue of its own power and superiority, but only in virtue of its symbiosis with the human? Let us see. The thesis in its second part speaks about the antithesis of pleasure and pain, that is, about what will emerge, under the terms grace and sin, as the great antithesis in Part II of the dogmatics (§ 64). We thus have every reason to take note. Where the pious consciousness is real, we are told, it is subject to *alternation* as some of its motions are nearer to joy and others to pain. It is not as though absolute freedom were coincident with the one and absolute dependence with the other, and even less as though what is pleasant or unpleasant to the senses shared the same character as the feeling of absolute dependence. But the antithesis, insofar as it applies to the feeling of absolute dependence, is connected with the *relation* of the two upper stages of consciousness at a specific moment. The emergence of the higher self-consciousness is an enhancement of life in general. Its easy emergence means easy enhancement and will have the "stamp of joy" whether or not the determination of the self-consciousness at issue is pleasant or unpleasant. The disappearing of the higher consciousness (!) means a diminution of life, and its difficult emergence is much the same as its absence, and can thus "be felt only as a hampering of the higher life." Thus far the pious consciousness and its antithesis. |

We are astounded by the relativism of all this. We are even more astounded by the optimism with which the author in good naturalistic terms again counts

---

[74]Brunner, *Die Mystik und das Wort*, p. 70.
[75]Cf. J. Müller (1864–1949), *Von den Quellen des Lebens* (Munich, 1919[5]) (e.g., pp. 36f.). For Barth's opinion of Müller cf. *Church Dogmatics* II,1, pp. 634f.; III,4, p. 386.

upon an enhancement of life that is either facilitated or hampered. But even more urgent for the moment is the question where and how the antithesis really arises. And Schleiermacher gives a wholly unambiguous answer. The higher self-consciousness does *not* carry this antithesis within itself. The bliss of the finite as the supreme climax of its perfection is "the unalterable evenness of life." The harsh actual antithesis of the hampering or smoothness creates "an unsteadiness in the pious life" "which we cannot regard as its supreme achievement" [§ 5,4]. The strongest feeling-content of the higher stage of life is the almost complete disappearance of the antithesis. What does this mean? It means in fact what we feared earlier. The assured superiority of the divine over the velleity of the sensory self-consciousness means neutrality in relation to the antithesis to which, according to Schleiermacher's own construction, the whole of Christian thought is oriented, the antithesis of sin and grace. This antithesis exists only in the pious consciousness. In this dogmatics, as is decided already on the thirties of its thousand pages, sin *against God* and the grace *of God* occur only in an improper metonymic sense. This antithesis consists only of the incompleteness of the process of the union of the higher and middle self-consciousness. Its overcoming is a matter of time, of progress, as we heard so often in the sermons. As is fixed already in § 4, this dogmatics knows nothing of any sickness unto *death*[76] or of any *unfathomable* mercy.

For the rest, the relation between § 3 and § 4 is very remarkable. In the one, which deals with the unimportant question of the genesis of the pious consciousness, the sense of absolute dependence and the God who is posited in it are severely compromised. In the other, where the truly critical question is put to the pious consciousness, that of the meaning of its individual moments, the same authority is boldly neutral, as though the overcoming of the antithesis that is raised by this question could take place by itself like the running down of a clock. But let us listen to the rest of § 5. § 5,5 deals with the continuity of the pious self-consciousness. Pious emotions can and should follow in an unbroken series. Those who bewail a moment that is totally empty of God-consciousness obviously mourn for something that is known to be *possible*, not impossible. But the possibility of unbroken God-consciousness can *vary* in strength. Its new emergence at any given moment shows that it was not previously dead (just as Christ was only apparently dead according to Schleiermacher). No determination of the sensory self-consciousness is totally incompatible with the higher self-consciousness. Either the one or the other always has to be interrupted except when both retreat behind the supervening confusion of consciousness. Thus Schleiermacher would deny any relationship with God to one who is sick in soul, or ascribe it to such a person only as it may be ascribed to one who is dead. As a pastor he actually comforted the relatives of the dead (or failed to comfort them) with the argument that with the entry into unconsciousness and its painful consequences the access of the dead to God takes place as all subjective determination drops away,[77]

[76] A reference to the title of Kierkegaard's work *Sickness Unto Death* (1849), which is itself based on Jn. 11:4.

[77] It has not been possible to document this, but cf. his letter to Henriette von Willich on February 12, 1809: "I simply console myself . . . with what I said in a sermon, that the last moment of full consciousness is the last moment of life" (Br., II, 225).

and according to an autograph under one of his portraits he himself said it was his supreme wish to be allowed to die in full possession of his faculties.[78] Strange, rather whimsical, and certainly very intellectualistic ideas! What has the continuity of the divine to do with that of the possession of our faculties if it is really in the feeling of absolute dependence that we have dealings with the divine? But whether that is so is the question that forces itself upon us increasingly with every page of every section.

The appendix to § 5 elucidates § 4,4. The consciousness of God is the direct inward expression of the feeling of absolute dependence. But this expression is always linked to a sensory self-consciousness. Hence the consciousness of God in all its forms bears determinations that belong to the sphere of the antithesis. This is the source of the unavoidable anthropomorphism in all the statements about God on which the criticism of those who have no experience of piety usually seizes. "But the pious are conscious that it is only in speech that they cannot avoid the anthropomorphic, while in the immediate consciousness they keep the object apart from the mode of presentation." We must answer such critics, then, with the question why they do not prefer to keep silent instead of claiming God's name in a most inappropriate way and enlightening their fellows with the products of their immediate consciousness, or, to put it more plainly, their imagination!

[2/14/24]   § 6 finally justifies the title with its reference to the church. "The pious self-consciousness becomes ... fellowship too," says the thesis, the reason being that it is "an essential element in human nature." As such it necessarily develops into a fellowship that is fluid on the one side but limited on the other. This fellowship is the *church*. These are the points that must now be elucidated. We turn first to the presupposition in § 6,1 that the pious self-consciousness is *an essential element in human nature*. We have seen already[79] that according to § 33 this presupposition is supposed to offer a perfect substitute for the so-called proofs of God's existence. We have also met in § 4 the assertion[80] that all thinking people can be unconditionally called upon to accept the principle of the predominant or exclusive passivity of the immediate self-consciousness. In accordance with this a small plea is now made for the presupposition. It might be objected that we all know a time in our lives when the feeling of absolute dependence is *not yet* present. Certainly, replies Schleiermacher, but that was the time of the imperfect life that was partly animal-like and confused, and partly sensory. One might point (though this would not be done today) to peoples *without religion*. But in the main such peoples represent only this "undeveloped state of human nature" in this as in other functions of life. One might also point to individuals who have *no religion*. But even these cannot deny that they are sometimes gripped by a feeling of a religious type even though they might call it superstition or the like. The presupposition can be refuted only by proof that this feeling does not have "higher value than the sensory feeling or that apart from it there might be

[78]Cf. *Aus Schleiermachers Hause. Jugenderinnerungen seines Stiefsohnes Ehren-fried von Willich* (Berlin, 1909), opposite the title page. According to J. Bauer, *Schleiermachers letzte Predigt*, p. 12, n. 2, the portrait was by A. Hüssener.

[79]Cf. p. 201.

[80]Cf. p. 214.

another of equal worth." As the *highest* stage of the self-consciousness it is also an *essential* element in human nature. But why as the *highest* stage? one might ask. Is the highest stage as such the highest *value*, and is the highest value as such the *essence* of a thing? Might not the piety of human nature be just as essential if the relation between the three stages of consciousness were presented in the form of a circle instead of an ascending line, so that the feeling of absolute dependence would stand alongside that of animal-like confusion? An essential *element*, says Schleiermacher himself, not the *essence*. But then the statement says no more than might be said of the elements of the second or even the first stage, namely, that at their own stages they are all part of the perfection of human nature. Obviously piety cannot be maintained or shown to be an essential element in human nature in any sense that is different in principle from what might be said of, for instance, sexuality. But this is concealed by the combination of the concepts of development and value which Schleiermacher proposes here. § 6,2 tries to show that the feeling of absolute dependence, as an essential element in human nature, is the *basis of a fellowship*. Again everyone is expected to recognize this conclusion. The consciousness of belonging to a species finds satisfaction only as one crosses the boundaries of one's own personality and accepts the fact of other personalities. Then with some degree of strength or maturity everything inward becomes outward and can be perceived by others. This happens to feeling, too, by means of expressions, gestures, and sounds, and directly by words. These first awaken in the other only an idea of the state of mind that is expressed, but by means of the sense of species (we see ourselves in others) it then becomes living imitation. All must agree that they are always in this fellowship of feeling with others as a natural state, and if they were not they would themselves create it. The feeling of absolute dependence is kindled in us all in the same way. This, then, is the schema under which the Christian church will later be considered. First comes the satisfaction of the sense of species. The feeling arises, is understood, and is awakened in others, and the fellowship, the pious fellowship, is there—no, not quite there, § 6,3 teaches us. It is at first uneven and fluid. The relationship and possibility of transferring pious feeling between people can vary greatly; there is always some fellowship between the pious, but they can be at opposite poles in respect of the strength and purity of their feeling, and so on. How does it come about that from this fluid and, strictly, unlimited fellowship there develop strong relationships and steadfast fellowship? § 6,4 provides the answer with the astonishing communication that this occurs first through the *family* as a natural, cohesive fellowship of the pious self-consciousness, and then through groups of families that are united by common language and customs and know or suspect a common derivation, whether in democratic equality or aristocratically under the guidance of some of the families. "Every such relatively closed pious fellowship" in which the pious self-consciousness takes its course in a certain way and in which pious emotions are propagated in an ordered and integrated way—and both so characteristically that adherents and nonadherents can be so distinguished in some way—"we designate by the term *church*." With this assertion, namely, that for the constitution of a church there is needed, apart from pious feeling itself, (1) the family, and (2) a plurality of related families or a clan, Schleiermacher's ethics makes the basic pronouncements which are borrowed to form the basis of his dogmatics.

I will try to summarize briefly the real content of this section, the psychological definition of the feeling of absolute dependence. This feeling is a real consciousness in time, not a transcendental concept. From the standpoint of *descriptive* psychology, it stands alongside or amid the two other vital functions of knowledge and action, while from the standpoint of *genetic* psychology it stands as the third and highest stage above the dawning and the objectively aware consciousness, being the specifically mystical act of consciousness. But it differs from a spiritual act such as reverence by reason of its lack of an object, for, strictly speaking, it *is* simply an object, pure passivity, receptivity, effect, dependence—hence its name. Nevertheless, there is co-posited *in* it that which *makes* it what it is, the absolutely active element, the superior cause that stands over against it, the other. It has the ability to separate its own origin from itself, its own presence from the posited presence of that wholly other; and man, in whom it has its locus, anthropomorphically, distinguishing the thing from the word, using the word only as an inadequate expression, calls this other *God.* In spite of this presence within it of the absolute cause or operation that seems to exclude all differentiation, it is able to develop quantitatively. It demands symbiosis with the sensory self-consciousness. In this marriage even to the point of merger, it finds what it lacks, namely, the possibility of existing in time. But in so doing it causes its partner to be confronted by the critical question of the promotion or restriction of life, of pleasure or pain, of grace or sin. Being itself neutral in relation to this question, however, it sees to it that the question is only relatively critical, a happy answer being present from the very outset. In a soothing way, it is an element that belongs universally and inalienably to human nature, following the natural laws of the development of society. By way of the family and clan, within a fluid consensus of pious feeling, it develops into the church, that is, the fellowship of a specific pious feeling.

I think we have learned what we wanted to know. § 6 Appendix with its definitions of the term religion and its variations—natural, specific, subjective, objective religion, religiosity, and the rest—I will leave for your own perusal and move on to the next section.

b. The Religions (§§ 7–10). Statements borrowed from the philosophy of religion form the next part of the *Glaubenslehre.* The philosophy of religion, which is itself a speculative daughter-science of ethics, seeks to understand and arrange critically the various historical forms of piety and pious fellowship. The investigation of this topic, then, moves over from the field of psychology to that of *history.* It deals in § 7 with the differences in religions as such, in § 8 with their differences in rank, in § 9 with their differences in type, and finally in § 10 with the relationship of the historical continuity of each religion to its character as this is determined by its rank and type. The section offers so much further material for an understanding of Schleiermacher's foundation that we must scrutinize it closely. I will be as brief as possible, however, in relation to everything that is not of basic significance. |

According to the previous definitions of the subject, obscure and contradictory though they were, we should expect in relation to the differences in religions the declaration that there can be differences only in external form and extent. Materially and in content, according to the definition given in §§ 3–4, is not piety itself the same in all of them? But in relation to this question we receive in §§ 7–10 the remarkable answer: Yes and No. No, we are first told in § 7,1. The differences relate not only to the form and extent of pious fellowships but also to "the constitution of the actual states of mind that underlie them," that is, their ability to achieve clarity in their relation to the sensory self-consciousness. Hence it is stated unequivocally that the feeling of absolute dependence is itself capable of historical differentiation. There is ascribed to it, indeed, the ability sometimes to *develop* independently of the general development of intellectual powers, to go its own way, not merely in the individual, but as the experience of a pious fellowship in history. But since religions of the same stage (Schleiermacher cites as an example the polytheism of India and ancient Greece) can still be fundamentally differentiated from one another, the concept of species or type has also to be taken into account as a principle of division (§ 9 will speak about this). Even more plainly than in the first section it is now terminologically clear that here, as everywhere latently in Schleiermacher, we are dealing with a kind of natural science of the spirit, except that, as we learn from § 7,2, we do not have in history unchangeable and recurrent forms, but at every stage we find transitions from one species to another, and within each species we have to expect ascents to higher stages, though this does not prejudice the applicability of the general schema. § 7,3 advances the rather bold thesis that the presupposition (on this view) of forms of piety that are coordinated with Christianity does not contradict the Christian "conviction of the exclusive excellence of Christianity." For, the astonishing reason runs, even in nature one can distinguish "perfect and imperfect animals" in the same species. Hence "Christianity, even if several species of piety share the same stage with it, can still be more perfect than any of them." The only thing is that we cannot on this assumption take the view that to most other forms of piety Christian piety is related "as the true to the false." For if this were so, how could they have so much that is similar to Christianity, and how would it be possible to move over from them to Christianity? Receptivity to Christianity cannot be based upon something false but only upon something true—a dazzling bit of sophistry, as though non-Christian religion *as such* were receptivity to Christianity! Schleiermacher then repeats a principle that is already familiar to us from the *Brief Outline*, § 332, namely, that error never exists alone, but only in relation to the truth, and that it is never fully understood until one has discovered its connection with the truth to which it is related.[81] With this fine and thoughtful thesis, which fits the context, however, only if the issue in the exclusiveness of Christianity is Christianity itself, the problem is intimated which governs what follows, namely, that of the exclusiveness of Christianity. |

§ 8,1, in an obvious parallel to the ladder of § 5, advances the evolutionary sequence: fetishism, polytheism, monotheism. Fetishism, which is idolatry, knows nothing of the totality of dependence. Only a limited area is put under the influence of the divine. In polytheism the dependence of everything finite

[81]§ 7,3. On *Kurze Darstellung*, § 332 cf. p. 169.

is recognized, yet not on a supreme being, but on a higher plurality of gods, though with some inkling of their unity. Monotheism expresses the dependence of everything finite on a supreme and infinite being. It thus occupies the highest rung to which the others are only transitional rungs. But, Schleiermacher himself interjects in § 8,2, is not this difference merely one of approach, a difference in the sensory consciousness? Indeed, one might ask, what remains here of the doctrine of the secondary character of all religious *concepts* and *ideas*? Can the feeling of absolute dependence itself not be one and the same in a worshiper of fetishes and a Christian? No, Schleiermacher tells himself and us—one is constantly surprised when he thus addresses his reader—no, it is not just a matter of a difference in ideas, but a difference in the direct self-consciousness. There is a difference in the feeling of dependence, which seeks and finds its source in the one case in a sensorily perceptible individual object, in the second in a plurality of natural forces, and in the third in the infinite. Only in monotheism does there take place what ought to take place by definition in the feeling of absolute dependence, namely, that in our finitude we are conscious of being absolutely dependent, and that we include everything finite, the whole world, in this consciousness. The latter point is decisive. As with the puzzling modifications of the feeling of absolute dependence in general, the issue is that of the varied relations to the sensory self-consciousness. The more this "expands into a general consciousness of finitude" in its relation to the latter, the more it becomes a world-consciousness, so much the purer the latter obviously is, and so much the more authentic is the monotheism. So convinced is Schleiermacher of the natural necessity of this process that in § 8,3 he thinks he can even speak about the irresistible progress and victory of montheism. Only in § 8,4 is the purpose of this whole exercise disclosed. At the highest stage, as monotheistic religions, are the Jewish, Christian, and Mohammedan religions. The Christian religion is "the purest form of monotheism that has appeared in history," for Judaism, as shown by its exclusiveness and its open relapses into idolatry, is still thought to be akin to fetishism, while Mohammedanism with its passionate nature and the strong sensory content of its ideas carries reminiscences of polytheism. I need hardly refer expressly to the historical dilettantism of the expositions in this paragraph; indeed, the whole schema of development which is used here finds no support in modern religious scholarship. I will also refer only in passing to the increasing obscurity of the fundamental principle; it is only with serious unwillingness that one can follow the evolutions of the chameleon known as the sense of absolute dependence. What concerns us is the question what Schleiermacher is really after here. Obviously in the light of the demonstration of the facticity and universality of the sense of absolute dependence in §§ 3–6 he wants to prove that in the historical world of this mysterious basic factor Christianity takes one of the highest places, indeed, the very highest place. He does this by postulating a series in which monotheism as its climax is secretly declared to be Christian monotheism and is shown to be the irresistible result of a consistent natural development of the religious spirit or feeling that has already been proved to be present and universal. Christianity "represents the highest stage in the development of religion because in it the whole world is understood as the effect of one cause, this again deriving simply from the natural expansion of the self-consciousness into a world-consciousness" (Bender, II, 358).[82] |

And this is not supposed to be a construction of Christianity *a priori*? one might ask—Schleiermacher having rejected any such idea with every sign of horror.[83] So far Christianity itself has not been discussed in a single word. On the basis of religio-philosophical, or, better, metaphysical discussions of finitude and infinity, freedom and dependence, and so forth, its "exclusive excellence" has been established and so, too, have certain material things, for example, the decree, notwithstanding this predicate, that it must not oppose itself as the truth to false religions, or the promotion of the ideal of the highest possible expansion of religious feeling into a general consciousness of finitude or a general world-consciousness; not to speak of the very naturalistic connection into which Christianity is brought from the very first lines of § 7 onward without any investigation whether it should really be combined with reflections on the family, the clan, and the like, let alone understood in the light of such things. Is it not true that all the dangers of a construction of Christianity *a priori* do not merely threaten but are really knocking at the door and indeed have already entered?—the only point being that in keeping with the character of Schleiermacher's thinking this construction is not transcendental but historical, philosophical, and naturalistic.

But let us listen to the rest of the section. Schleiermacher has two inter- [2/18/24] esting appendixes to § 8. The first again adds something new to the feeling of absolute dependence. This may be refracted in favor of the poor worshipers of fetishes who thus far have been treated rather unkindly but are now assured that they too will go to heaven inasmuch as the same *root* may be recognized in their spiritual products, in these "lower potencies" of the sense of absolute dependence. Schleiermacher's proof of this is so striking that I must share it with you. Christianity itself teaches in 1 Jn. 4:18 that *only* perfect love casts out *all* fear!! Hence imperfect love is never fully free from fear. Hence the fear of fetish worshipers, if only they do not worship the devil, "is only a refraction of the feeling of absolute dependence in coordination with imperfect love." There can, of course, be no refuting this. The second appendix to § 8 deals with pantheism, a delicate theme, since after the appearance of his letters to Lücke,[84] and even after the publication of the *Speeches*, Schleiermacher often had this "rude nickname," as he himself called it, hurled against his own theology. He does not handle the subject with perfect elegance. It arises in this context only because of a verbal similarity (he is dealing with -isms). Pantheism has never been "the confession of a pious society that has emerged historically." It has no part in the history of religion. It has arisen only "by way of speculation or simple reasoning." The only question is whether it is compatible with piety, and we have to say unhesitatingly that it is, so long as it does not mean a materialistic denial of theism. Are there not all kinds of confusions of God and the world in fetishism? Did not platonic philosophy

[82]W. Bender, *Schleiermachers Theologie*, p. 358, though Bender has "depending on" for "deriving from."
[83]Cf. pp. 193f.
[84]Cf. *Sendschreiben an Lücke*, pp. 23ff.

lead Greek polytheists to a similar equation? Even in monotheism does not the possibility exist of regarding oneself as part of the world and feeling dependent with all things upon that which is the one to the all, so that God and the world *remain* distinct in function if not in substance? And all this without altering piety itself? The distinction between a God inside the world and a God outside it is in any case strange and crude and "does not particularly fit the facts." How can one speak about God in terms of the antithesis of inside and outside without in some way jeopardizing the divine omnipotence and omnipresence?

All this smacks of virtuosity. First comes the declaration that the critical statement is so incidental that it need be touched on only in passing. Then it is said to be neutral: what we have is only speculation. Then it is shown to be really very close to every stage of religion. Then comes the assurance that it has nothing whatever to do with piety itself. Then it is shown to be impossible to refute. Then in conclusion we have the gentle hint that one cannot contradict it without subverting the divine omnipotence and omnipresence, with the purely incidental suggestion that the precise issue in pantheism is what *divine* omnipotence and omnipresence really signify.

Coming now to § 9,1, we find that the question of the distinctiveness of Christianity has not been fully answered by postulating different stages in monotheism and by trying to show that within the general category it is monotheism in the supreme sense. In transverse relation to this distinction a distinction of type or species is postulated too. At the monotheistic stage, although *mutatis mutandis* it is obviously meant that the same would apply to every stage, a twofold possibility exists—in the first edition (§ 16, [quoted in] Bender, II, 360) Schleiermacher says expressly that this twofoldness is "grounded in the innermost relations of the self-consciousness." The first possibility is that the consciousness of absolute dependence, which according to § 8,2 expands into a general consciousness of finitude or world-consciousness, will relate wholly to *activity* in the sensory self-consciousness. The passivity posited in it relative to the world becomes a total impulse for action; it tells us that something is to be done, and what this is. Schleiermacher calls this—in a not very enlightening way—the *teleological* type of piety. In contrast, the second possibility is that the feeling of absolute dependence will become in the sensory self-consciousness a consciousness of our *passivity* in both passion *and* action. The whole life of the subject is now viewed as the result of the operation of all things on it according to the ordination of the supreme being, all of which may be beautiful or ugly according to the pleasure or pain of the moment concerned—this is the *esthetic* type of piety.[85] Can we have any doubts but that Schleiermacher will decide for the latter as the higher form and introduce Christianity in connection with it? Does it not have the logic of his whole construction on its side? Is not the understanding of the

[85]Barth has a mark here referring to the following diagram in the margin:

Teleology		Aesthetics
	Monotheism	
	Polytheism	
	Fetishism	

feeling of absolute dependence as an impulse for a teleological movement of the will decidedly *more remote* from the nature of religion as Schleiermacher has defined it, and is not the esthetic enjoyment of the unity of the world experienced in absolute determination decidedly *closer* to it? Might one not ask whether there really can be any disposition for action, any development of activity, in terms of the feeling of absolute dependence? If there can be such as the characteristic feature of some religions, what relation can these religions have to the feeling of absolute dependence except a very indirect one, and if the nature or essence of religion is rightly found in the feeling of absolute dependence, how can the opposite, esthetic type of piety fail to be a higher one (Bender, I, 282f.)?[86] But Schleiermacher constantly has new surprises for us. No, he replies to these considerations, declaring in § 9,2 that Christianity is a *teleological* religion. Are we simply to regard this as a historical observation, not seeking behind it an evaluation which is strictly impossible, as stated, on Schleiermacher's own presuppositions? In fact we look in vain in § 9 for any sign that teleological piety is superior or of greater worth. It is simply different, and it includes Christianity. The proof of the greater worth of Christianity is given in § 8 with the assertion that it is the highest stage of monotheism (we saw in § 8,4 what a mortal leap this involved, from the standpoint of the history of religion, to the detriment of Judaism and Islam). With this the *a priori* construction breaks off, and § 9 offers another form of differentiation but with no attempt or achievement of any further proof along these lines, and the question is left open whether teleological religion is regarded as superior (in terms of the feeling of absolute dependence it would be hard to make this understandable) or whether we do not have in it, as in fetishism, the refracting of the feeling of absolute dependence into another form that is not really appropriate to it, or at least a *secondary* form of this feeling. That Schleiermacher did not try to remain true to his construction and complete his proof by declaring Christianity to be an esthetic religion does honor to his historical conscientiousness, and that he still set about to write a Christian dogmatics does honor to his personal belief in the truth of Christianity. Here as in his Christology we have an instance where the contingent reality of Christianity is as hard as a flint and remains undigested in the stomach of the serpent. But the fact that, content with the results at which he aimed in § 8, he bases Christian dogmatics on the feeling of absolute dependence when it so obviously points in a different direction does not give to his enterprise any more credibility than it has on other grounds. |

§ 9,2, then, tries to show that Christianity is a teleological religion. Obviously in contrast to the Jewish and Islamic religions which occupy the same rung with it? No again, or only secondarily. But—and this seems to us to be odd seeing that the distinction between "teleological" and "esthetic" supposedly characterizes this highest stage—the *sharp antithesis* to Christianity is found by Schleiermacher in a religious phenomenon on the second stage, namely, *Greek polytheism* with its idea of the beauty of the soul, which as a result of natural and cosmic operations is thus viewed as a purely passive influencing of the subject by the deity. In contrast the feeling of absolute

---

[86]W. Bender takes a similar line to Barth's on the issues raised here.

dependence in Christianity is related to "the totality of states of activity in the idea of a kingdom of God." All pain and all joy are pious here only insofar as "they are related to activity in the kingdom of God." The kingdom of God, then, is the telos, obviously as the epitome of all the *telē* of individual human activity? The same as the highest good in Schleiermacher's ethics? And only Christianity is the form of the feeling of absolute dependence in which, related to the sensory self-consciousness, this becomes a striving for this highest of all that is the same in everything high? Undoubtedly the essence of modern Protestantism is excellently described in this way, including the conscious but accepted inconsistency of the presupposition. Mystical quietism at root, it also seeks to be cultural religion, the trigger, ferment, and goal of all human activity, of all joy and all pain. We have seen in Schleiermacher's sermons how this Christianity looks concretely, and how he lived and acted in the ideals of this Christianity more than one might expect from his scholarly theological writings. All this helps to explain the refracting of the sense of absolute dependence in favor of a teleological orientation. But it also produces the all-obscuring ambiguity of the basic concept, which is passive to the point of unconsciousness when it has to be, but is then suddenly presented in both thought and action as active, creative, and capable of development. What is this concept but a reflection, an only too faithful reflection of man with his contradiction,[87] who cannot always be working but must also pray, yet cannot always be praying but must also work, except that there is in *him* no solution of this paradox? If only the paradox were recognized and stated to be such by Schleiermacher! A theology of man is not an impossibility as such, though by itself it would not fulfil the task of *Christian* theology. But it would have to be the story of the "sickness unto death"[88] from which man suffers in relation to God. Schleiermacher's theology, however, is even further afield from the task of Christian theology than Kierkegaard's, for under the pretext of Christian theology it raises a *song of triumph* to man, celebrating both his union with God and his own cultural activity, and necessarily coming to grief in so doing. Recollection of the cultural activity which is necessary for man disturbs and interrupts the presentation of his sense of absolute dependence, so that there can be no real *resting* in God—how can the depicted passivity be rest in *God?* At the same time the cultural significance of Christianity is bound to appear suspicious to real promoters of culture, who work without illusions, because of the inconsistent recollection of its passive religious background. The right to say *both* things: Pray *and* work, has obviously to be sought in God, or, rather, given by God, not as an analysis of the human self-consciousness and its components but as a synthetic pronouncement of God to man. To formulate this pronouncement is the task of Christian theology. Hence we have to supplement as follows the thinking of § 9,2 with its mention of Christianity. The Christianity of Schleiermacher and modern Protestantism, having taken a deep but not entirely happy drink from the intoxicating cup of mys-

[87]From C. F. Meyer's poem "Homo sum" in *Huttens letzte Tage* (1872):
... Ich bin kein ausgeklügelt Buch,
Ich bin ein Mensch mit seinem Widerspruch.
[88]Cf. p. 221, n. 76.

ticism, (1) is honest enough to admit that even on historical grounds it cannot go further along these lines in the name of *Christianity*; (2) being bound as by invisible hands to the contingent reality of Christianity, it is unwilling to proceed on its proposed course without the name of Christianity; and (3) it is aware of the dilemma that modern man cannot make anything of mysticism, and the time has thus come to think of a complement. This is how Christianity achieves the rank of a teleological religion, and if, as shown, its truth and value can no longer be proved apologetically as a result, this is no great loss in a dogmatics that deals with the mystical side, with the feeling of absolute dependence. All in all, the motto of § 9 is: "Incidit in Scyllam, qui vult vitare Charybdin."[89] I leave it to you to read how Schleiermacher at the end tries to take issue with Judaism and Islam. In a parallel to the oddities of § 8,4 he puts the former on the teleological side and the latter on the esthetic. Because of its theory of retribution he gives to Judaism only a "fairly good" in terms of its cultural capacity, so that in conclusion he can state, if not too forcefully, that the teleological type is "best expressed" in Christianity.

The final paragraph (§ 10) concludes the whole train of thought. A specific religion or church is not only a locus characterized by stage and type. It is also a distinct entity, just as the systems of natural science can finally denote only the various loci where this or that individual is to be found as their true subject. Individual here, however, means a historical conjunction of constancy and change; *change* takes place in something constant, and there is always something *constant* in change. This produces a distinct entity, an individual, or here, an individual form of piety (underline the references to constancy and change in the thesis). § 10,1 explains that what is called constant is the external factor, in the case of Christianity the "impulse" that was given by Christ. Without this outward characteristic there can be no inward one. What is called changeable is the internal factor, in the case of Christianity the consciousness of redemption according to § 11. Without this inward characteristic there cannot be an outward one bound to the name of a founder and finding representation in time and space. § 10,2 after a brief side-glance at the first half of the sentence,[90] devotes its main concern to the second. What is the *inner* factor in a religious fellowship that is described as changeable? The feeling of absolute dependence as it is characterized by stage and type. This receives its distinctive constancy from the first and outer element, that is, Christ. All pious societies of the same type will represent the sense of absolute dependence in the same external form but—this is the second, *internal* element—in a specific *modification*, so that it is the same in all of them, but in a different way in each. Schleiermacher explains his meaning in antithesis to the rationalistic view of religious history whereby the differences between Judaism, Islam, and Christianity are only a matter of addition and subtraction: the belief in God is the same but + Moses or + Christ or + Mohammed. On this view there could be no question of a belief in Christ, either because Christ

---

[89]Barth seems to be quoting loosely from Gualterus ab Insulis (Walter de Lille or de Châtillon), *Alexandreis* (1178–1182), V. 301:
Incidis in Scyllam, cupiens vitare Charybdin.
The point is that one is wrecked on the former in seeking to escape the latter.
[90]The thesis.

is obviously not constitutive for piety or because he is only an individual object of it that is important only in certain connections. "In every truly distinctive pious society," however, "the self-consciousness itself is differently determined," and it is "only an illusion" that in one mode of faith "there is something that is totally missing in others." Thus the incarnation of God and the impartation of the Spirit are found in other religions, and how much more so less important elements in the Christian faith. Apart from its distinctive self-consciousness, then, Christianity cannot be anything absolutely new in its relation to Christ. § 10,3 repeats the same thought, applied, as Schleiermacher himself admits, to a clearer conception of the pious individual. "Each has all that the other has, but determines it all differently," is the formula here. Finding what is individually distinctive and differentiating oneself from others is, of course, a task that can be only approximately fulfilled. It can be stated as a general rule that the same God-consciousness unites itself now with this and now with that relation of the sensory self-consciousness in such a dominant way that this one relation can become the channel for all the others, so that they are all subordinate to it and take on its tone and color. A distinctive type of faith arises in this way. In the Christian this *one* relation is experientially *Christ,* and this relation becomes the condition of all the rest, imparts its tone and color to them, and is thus relatively *superior* to them insofar as his God-consciousness on the one side and its relations to the sensory self-consciousness on the other become intrinsically different. The *tone* and *color,* not the *content* and *substance,* make Christianity what it is in contrast to other religions.

§ 10 undoubtedly suffers from an obscurity that is surprising in Schleiermacher. Perhaps this is connected with the deployment of a very complicated apparatus to say something very simple, so that this is not simply expressed but merely suggested in the concealment of a thicket of dialectic. Cannot this simple thing be summed up in the thesis that Christianity is a *historically conditioned religion*? A *religion:* it thus participates in the established fundamental fact of religion in general; it has an inner aspect, the feeling of absolute dependence, which has here a special form on the highest monotheistic stage as the consciousness of redemption; but thus far it is not a specific entity manifested and operative in history. A *historically conditioned* religion: thus far it takes on shape and extension among historical things; it has an outer side, the person of its founder, which gives it tone and color and with which its specific expression is indissolubly connected; but thus far it is also a relative entity, and with its special crystallization of everywhere identical elements it stands alongside others of the same kind. Perhaps Schleiermacher is best understood if the following point is considered. The two decisive principles, first, that everything is the same in all but is so in a different way in each, and, second, that each has all that the other has but it is all differently determined, can be applied equally well to different specimens of the same plant or animal species, or, to put it more plainly, to the thousands of leaves on one and the same tree. Is the distinctiveness ascribed to the various forms of religion anything other than the uniqueness that is to be found everywhere in nature, a uniqueness which involves a copy and reflection of one and the same thing, so that while it is *unique* it is *only* a copy and reflection and not truly singular? If Schleiermacher is understood in this way, then the darkness of this paragraph is illumined. And from all our previous researches he is unquestionably to be understood in this way. A theology that has chosen piety as its theme—even though this be Christian piety—may not and cannot reach any other conclusion than that of the relativism which finds revelation in the individual *as such* and therefore in principle in *every* individual.

Let us now see whether this interpretation is backed up by the appendix [2/19/24] on the terms "positive" and "revealed." This is one of the most important texts in Schleiermacher's theology inasmuch as here—characteristically in the corner of an "appendix" as though it only needed to be said in parenthesis—a little deduction is secretly and violently drawn from what precedes which in fact not only contains but also expresses a most momentous decision. The term "positive" is first defined in relation to the term "natural." Natural religion (*mutatis mutandis* like natural law) is that which can be abstracted equally from the teachings of all pious societies of the top stage as the common element in all of them even if in different determinations. What is differently determined, the individual element, is the positive element in a religion. The content of all the individual aspects of a religion, its doctrines, commandments, and the like, is dependent on the "original fact," on the determination of the sensory self-consciousness which according to § 10,3 gives tone and color to the whole and in virtue of which it is a historical entity. In the light of this specific content it is a positive religion. Thus far the appendix is obviously only a summary of the content of § 10 in the form of a definition. The positive element is simply what is unique in a religion as a result of the intersecting of constancy and change. All the more tensely, then, do we wait to see what new aspect the term "revelation" will bring to light. Revelation, in distinction from what is gained from experience or reflection, and communicated to others as such, is "a *divine* impartation and communication." All the religions and many *states* trace back their existence to something of this kind. Hence a "divine causality" is predicated which works outside the nexus of human affairs to seek and promote the salvation of men. A revelation denotes the fact that underlies a religion and conditions the individual content of its pious emotions but cannot itself be explained in terms of an earlier historical relationship. One thing, however, revelation is *not* according to Schleiermacher, namely, "a work . . . on man as a knowing being," for then it would be "originally and essentially teaching." If it may be this secondarily, its propositions can be viewed only as parts of a totality that is not itself teaching, namely, as "moments in the life of another thinking being" which works on us "as a distinctive existence by its total impress," and does so on our self-consciousness, on our *existence*. This factor which comes forward and works existentially is revelation. But it is still not possible to define revelation more closely than by saying that every prototype of a fact or a work of art that enters the soul and is a real prototype, not a copy, not excited or induced from outside, and acting not merely as the determination of a single aspect of the self-consciousness of the recipient but as a determination of its *existence*, is revelation. Examples are the oracles and heroes of paganism and the *world* of Rom. 1:19. But this "again can lead us to the further point that nothing individual that belongs to the world can *in itself* be regarded as divine revelation." Even though it has no source in a psychological nexus, "the rise of a prototype in an individual soul" is historically conditioned by the "total state of the society to which each individual belongs," just as the heroes and supposed sons of God are to be "understood in their existence in terms of the total power of the people." The relationship of the positive aspect of a religion to revelation is disputed by all the other religions and assertion of it cannot be made within the antithesis of true and false. "For part of the fulness of truth would be that God made himself known as he is *in* and *for himself.*" But how can a direct communication of God himself "proceed externally from any fact, and if it comes incomprehensibly into a human soul, how can it be grasped and understood by this soul, and if it is neither perceptible nor apprehensible, how can it be at work? A *working* revelation cannot communicate God in and for himself but only "God in his relation to us." This is "the essence of human limitation" in connection with God—not "subhuman ignorance," Schleiermacher observes in clear allusion to Hegel's criticism of the first edition.[91] In relation, then, to the origins of imperfect religions according to the above definition it can and must be said that they rest on revelation.

Does this add anything new to what was said about the positive aspect? Obviously not. What the five pages offer on revelation is a discussion of what Schleiermacher calls the "original fact" of a religion, the original influence on the sensory self-consciousness by which the slumbering religious feeling is awakened in us. This, however, is one of the factors that make up positive religion and does not take us beyond this. But positive religion—and we should never forget this—is a given entity, a part of the world, one of the many objects of Schleiermacher's great study of spirit-nature and nature-spirit, and in no sense more than this. It, too, is nature, world, part of the present order, even in the element which is common to all of us, let alone in its individuality, that is, in that which makes it a positive religion as distinct from the abstraction "natural religion." And the basis or causality of this individuality is the original fact which the term revelation is meant to denote. How much less may one expect of this that its determination will be on a radically different level. No, on exactly the same level as the second object it denotes a first object—somewhat further back—which must be mentioned at least in an appendix for the sake of completeness: the cause or condition of the second object, or positive religion, the thing A which is necessarily followed by B and gives it tone and color, yet a thing, no more, conditioned as well as conditioning in spite of the predicate of originality that is often ascribed to it, just as God himself according to § 4,4 is the source of the feeling of absolute dependence and no more than that. |

I have already on previous occasions[92] warned you not to be misled by Schleiermacher's use of the prefix "Ur"—Christ as a *proto*type, the New Testament as a document of *primitive* Christianity, and now a supposed *original* fact. These "Urs" are made of gypsum, not granite. Schleiermacher has no place for the concept of a beginning by creation to which the prefix invites our thinking. This is true here too. None of the different definitions of the

[91]For this cf. p. 186, nn. 5 and 6.
[92]Cf. p. 175f., n. 67.

concept of revelation holds up, impressive though they may sound at first. When he calls revelation a *divine* impartation and communication, this has a hopeful ring, but it is only by way of summary. Greeks, Egyptians, and Indians all claim to have such a communication, and the only thing that seriously remains is the "fact" underlying the religion. A fact, not a *teaching.* This noble anti-intellectualism would be gladly heard by the 19th century. But we must not overlook what lies behind it both here and everywhere. Divine communication as a fact sounds adequate, but what follows shows that it is no real communication but part of a series of facts already present, that is, of the world. Teaching would obviously disturb this peace. It would mean word, thought, spirit. But Spirit stands in uncanny correlation with Creator. In Schleiermacher, however, revelation must be in correlation with cause. Hence fact or life, not teaching! In this regard Schleiermacher differentiates himself from the innumerable theological dilettantes who have babbled on about his *knowing* what he was about. |

The occurrence and operation of this fact, as we have seen, are necessarily *existential.* Again a hopeful definition! But what razor-sharp dialectic is needed for a right use of this term here. Divine and human existence are the partners who meet. Read for yourselves how innocuous, not to say bourgeois, this meeting is in Schleiermacher. That alien existence enters into the circle of our lives, makes a total impression on our self-consciousness, and in this way our existence is determined in its totality. Nothing is simpler than that. But nothing is clearer than that in this depiction Schleiermacher is not thinking about the encounter between God and man but the encounter—he specifically recalls his hermeneutics—between those who teach and those who are taught, in which according to his theory it can be a matter only of direct (personal) impact and not of the communication of thoughts and words. Hence the appearance of the term existence gives a false signal. When he says on the one side that revelation is *not* a fact which can be *thought of* or *explained* in terms of a historical context, even though he at once ascribes a revelational character in this sense to the origin of certain acts and works of art, one might at first suppose that we were getting somewhere—but then he himself removes the bullet from the barrel by assuring us on the other side that such primal images are of historical, if not psychological, derivation, and even extraordinary divine personages can be explained in terms of the total power of a people. And on the last page of this classical passage the fairly orderly retreat becomes a headlong rout. The objection that the *truth* of the revelation of one religion is known to be *disputed* by all other religions—this theological bogyman is accepted without any attempt at a refutation, and the truth of what remains of so-called revelation is totally abandoned. |

Purely wraithlike is the possibility that *true revelation* might mean that God communicates himself as he is in and for himself; we do not have the organs that are necessary to receive such a communication. All revelation is simply "God in relation to us," that is, a modification of our self-consciousness. But what such modification is in principle *more* of a revelation than any other? Did not Paul call the *world* itself a revelation of God? Hence *all* religions rest on revelation. And why only religions? Along the lines of Schleiermacher, this is the further question that arises. Are not specific religions individual parts of the world? Rightly understood, is not *everything* revelation, and, again rightly understood, *nothing?* But we need not follow the final logic to see the importance of this conclusion of the second section on the religions. What is its result? Christianity is viewed as one of the manifestations of the feeling of absolute dependence. By means of its integration into a schema of development from fetishism to supreme monotheism, it is shown to be of "exclusive excellence," although somewhat laboriously at the decisive point. Contrary to the logic of the matter, and with no further attempt at *a priori* demonstration, it is then shown to be a teleological religion oriented totally to activity in the kingdom of God. There then crops up the problem of pure facticity in the individual religions as such with their dialectic of constancy and changeability, the external and the internal, the primal fact and its operation. The solution to this is the concept of uniqueness, the one leaf among a thousand that is this particular leaf. Finally as the arched vault over the temple comes the teaching that the existence and nature of this leaf among a thousand is the positive element in a religion, and the mysterious cause that determines why its existence and nature, the positive element, should be this and not something else is the *revelation* that underlies it. Wherever there is religion, then, there is also revelation. But all these statements, of course, are borrowed from the philosophy of religion and they are only academic sitings. They should not be used in apologetics nor as true statements of the Christian faith. Schleiermacher can write another 800 pages without bothering about this introduction. He does not bewail the fact that from the standpoint of the philosophy of religion he stands somewhere in the middle between mysticism and cultural religion, or that revelation in the true sense is denied in passing even before he can begin to speak about it.

It is under these auspices that we now turn to the third section.

c. The Christian Religion (§§ 11–14). The discipline of Schleiermacher's apologetics, which is on the border between theology and philosophy, holds the floor here with its borrowed statements. The speaker is not the self-consciousness of Christian piety, as from § 32 onward. Nor is it the task to systematize and formulate the direct statements of this speaker, which is at its best when it is silent. Hence we should not expect to hear Christianity express itself in its own context. Christianity is still discussed from outside in an impartial and comparative manner. Yet the real specialist, the theologian, albeit the philosophical theologian, now takes up the theme. He does not come on the stage as the hero, of course, but as the producer and master of ceremonies who awakens confidence by giving factual information. Christianity is discussed now, not from the watchtower of the philosophy of religion *above* the series of religions, but from the standpoint of Christianity itself as this has been established by the philosophical deliberations of the second section.[93] We already gained an acquaintance with the most important parts of § 11, the *magna carta* of Schleiermacher's theology, when we examined the total structure of the work, the decisive points whose architectural plans are

[93]In the margin Barth has a question mark against this sentence.

to be sought here. [Cf. 1 b [and] c].⁹⁴ We may thus give only a brief summary here. |

Now that the character of Christianity has been established in the second section as a monotheistic religion with a teleological orientation, the issue in § 11,1 is to define its nature by examining its basic fact and constructing from it the common content of the various Christian fellowships and parties. According to § 11,2 Schleiermacher thinks he has found this common content in the concept of redemption, which—I will not give all the details again—is to be viewed, not as "re-creation in the true sense," but as an increasing fusion of the sensory self-consciousness with the God-consciousness. But the concept of redemption (§ 11,3) is to be found in all religions. What distinguishes Christianity is (1) the relation of all pious affections to the antithesis denoted by this thought, (2) the viewing of redemption as the work of Jesus of Nazareth, and (3) the indissoluble connection between the former, the Christian content, and the latter, the basic Christian fact. To a stronger or weaker degree all pious moments are a consciousness of redemption, or of the *need* for it, accompanied by the image of the Redeemer. § 11,4—and here we enter territory that we have not so far traversed—is an attempt to establish the originality of Christianity specifically in relation to the second point, that is, its basic fact, the *personality of its founder.* The other monotheistic religions have founders too. The difference is not just that in Christianity this is Christ. It is rather (1) that in the others the function of the founders is simply to found the fellowship as such and redemption takes place only through the fellowship, whereas in Christianity the basic thing is the redemptive activity of the founder and the fellowship exists only on this presupposition as a communication and propagation of that redemptive activity. The difference is then (2) that in the other religions the founder seems to be taken arbitrarily and accidentally out of the common mass—he could just as well be someone other than Moses or Mohammed—and he himself is the first object of the divine teaching and order received and imparted by him, whereas in Christianity Christ is originally different from all others, is set over against all others, and cannot be thought of in any sense as himself in need of redemption. Any doctrine can still be regarded as Christian—Schleiermacher obviously has the rationalists in view here—so long as Christ is not regarded merely as the proclaimer of a teaching and an order of life, so long as *some* redemptive power is granted to his person, and so long as people do not claim to be redeemed from the Redeemer, that is, without any need for a special relationship with Christ. § 11,5 takes another [2/21/24] look at the task of the philosophy of religion from the standpoint of the nature of Christianity as it has just been established. It envisages a structure of the discipline in which the definition of Christianity achieved by theological apologetics is presupposed, and in which the concept of redemption, and the coming of a liberating fact that is necessary to accomplish it, are seen to be basic in a system of the chief moments in the pious self-consciousness, so that "Christianity is established and in some sense constructed as a distinctive form of faith." This is not a proof of Christianity because it does not force people to accept redemption into their self-consciousness as a central element

⁹⁴The brackets here are Barth's.

or to recognize precisely *this* redemptive fact. Even less is this the point and purpose of the present apologetic undertaking. Its aim is simply to offer an introduction that will enable us to judge whether the statements of the pious self-consciousness are Christian, and whether they are more strongly or more weakly Christian.

The marginal gloss that I have to make on § 11 can begin at the last point. How can the introduction, the apologetics, serve as a criterion whether a religious statement is Christian or not, or more strongly or weakly Christian, before the Christian statement has been made? What is it trying to accomplish? one might seriously ask. Not to force anyone to accept Christianity, Schleiermacher assures us with suspicious assiduity. But what does "force" mean? Given Schleiermacher's anti-intellectualistic view of the concept of faith, his disparagement of the logos, of the question of truth in religion, there can plainly be no question of forcing upon Mohammedans a conviction of the truth of Christianity with logical compulsion, any more than there could be any question of a view of the state grounded in the same descriptive ethics being able to convince a Prussian legitimist of the higher truth of French liberalism. This concession, then, is no concession at all; the point is self-evident. What we obviously have in principle—Schleiermacher is not quite satisfied with his exposition along these lines and is postulating a better one—is a demonstration that the distinctiveness of Christianity is "established and in some sense constructed" by the philosophy of religion, that the doctrine of the Christian faith, as an empirical or applied science, is thus built up on speculative ethics. This—and not, therefore, the conversion of unbelievers, but the demonstration of the integration of this faith or its teaching into the system of culture—was the concern that Schleiermacher tried to satisfy in the introduction and especially in the borrowings from apologetics. For the sake of this concern, however, he had to *anticipate* a summary definition of this faith and its teaching, for if the demonstration were postponed until the end of the book, if the faith were simply allowed to speak for itself without regard for this purpose, who could tell whether the demonstration would later be possible? Conversely, however, the apologetic that is worked out in full connection with the philosophy of religion or ethics or culture defines in advance what the teaching of this faith will *be*, or will *have* to be, in relation to that concern, and the doctrine of the faith itself will be the later thing, the unpackaging of that which is secretly and forcefully packaged here. |

What is its result? is the second question that we have to put. Schleiermacher's answer has already been given earlier with reference to the concept of redemption.[95] But only now do we have a full outbreak of the sickness of the feeling of absolute dependence presupposed as a basic systematic concept. Its natural quantitative and material ambiguity may be fully seen in the fact that there is no strictly dialectical antithesis of sin and grace within the concept of redemption but only the amphiboly of the greater or lesser ease with which the God-consciousness can develop and come to dominance in the sensory self-consciousness. Wedged in by the two possibilities of either defining the basic systematic concept of the doctrine of faith in terms of Chris-

[95]Cf. pp. 195–197.

tianity or Christianity in terms of the basic systematic concept, Schleiermacher chose the second route and thus transferred the ambiguity of his basic concept to the concept of Christianity which is normative for all that follows. The consequence of the purpose of the apologetic as we have sketched it may be seen as soon as it opens its mouth to utter the first borrowed statement; it is the dreadful heresy of § 11,2, which is enough by itself to make the whole of Schleiermacher's Christian faith completely unacceptable. |

By way of excuse and appeasement reference has been made to §§ 11,3–4, to the extraordinary significance that is ascribed there to Christ as the Redeemer.[96] An effort has even been made to find in the presentation and analysis of the founder-concept which is attempted there the epoch-making merit of Schleiermacher's *Christian Faith*.[97] In reply I must repeat what I said at the end of our own § 2 about the Christology of Schleiermacher's sermons. It is certainly remarkable and instructive that at the *heart* of his concept of the Christian faith Schleiermacher with some *vehemence* developed a *Christology*, both in the sermons and here. It is as if in his doctrine of the Redeemer, where he is not hampered by the basic systematic concept, he is trying to make up with almost convulsive Christian devotion for what is missing in this regard in his doctrine of redemption. But he himself assures us loudly enough that these two doctrines are not to be separated from on another. The dignity of his Redeemer, then, stands or falls with the content of what he calls redemption; that redeeming is his main business and not a secondary by-product of his teachings and injunctions; that he stands over against all others as the Redeemer; that he himself does not need redemption—these are the essential christological definitions that are developed here. But if redemption is that amphibolic more or less, what, then, is the Redeemer? Where is the originality of the *founder* if the *foundation* is not original? Do we not have to expect in advance—as the sermons have in fact shown—that on closer inspection the apparent absoluteness of the christological definitions will prove to be no more than apparent?

But let us conclude our analysis of the third section. § 12 deals with the relation between Christianity and Judaism. "Judaism," says Schleiermacher, not "Israel" or the "Old Testament." He puts Judaism, as one religion among others, *alongside* Christianity, and tells us in advance that we need not expect him to accept the patristic principle that there is one revelation in the two testaments. There can be only a continuity of the history of religion within which Christianity and Judaism both have a place, but the same may logically be said of Christianity and paganism. According to § 12,1 Judaism was infiltrated after the exile by all kinds of non-Jewish elements, while the pagan world for its part was prepared in different ways for monotheism. According to § 12,2 Christianity is not a "reconstruction or renewal" of Judaism, not even of the Judaism of Abraham, any more than it is reconstruction or renewal of paganism. According to Paul both Jews and Gentiles are "equally far from

---

[96]Cf. F. H. R. von Frank, *Geschichte und Kritik der neueren Theologie* . . . , p. 97; W. Elert, *Der Kampf um das Christentum*, pp. 58ff.

[97]Cf. A. Ritschl, *Die christliche Lehre von der Rechtfertigung und Versöhnung* (Bonn, 1870), I, 476ff. (ET *The Christian Doctrine of Justification and Reconciliation* [1900]); H. Scholz, *Christentum und Wissenschaft* . . . , p. 189.

God and . . . in need of Christ." In matters of piety both must be made new. The promise of Abraham has a reference to Christ only in the divine counsel but not in Abraham's religious self-consciousness, which is what really matters for Schleiermacher. According to § 12,3, if we want to support the thesis that there has been one church of God from the beginning of the world, then "according to reliable Christian teachers" (Clement of Alexandria) we shall have to include Hellenic philosophy in it as well as the Mosaic law. *General* expressions which can be understood as Christian piety may be found in the statements of a nobler and purer paganism just as clearly as in those of the Old Testament.

Like all that Schleiermacher wrote on this theme, § 12 betrays an extraordinary rashness and superficiality. The way in which he equates the spermatic logos of the Greek fathers and Reformed theology[98] with the Old Testament revelation makes no sense, whereas the equation of the Old Testament revelation with the New serves the well-considered purpose of protecting the *divinely* and absolutely new thing in Christ against confusion with something that is only historically and relatively new. Those who know and confess the revelation in Christ know that it does not begin with him, that according to Heb. 1:1 God "in many and various ways . . . spoke of old"—but did so "to the *fathers* by the *prophets*"—whether this includes some pagans is another question—and therefore spoke to *faith* and spoke through *revelation*. That this was possible fundamentally even outside Israel is stated by the doctrine of the *logos spermatikos* but not by a meaningless elimination of all distinctions between Jews and Gentiles. The whole concept is rendered pointless by the denial of anything specific or distinctive. But this is what happens in Schleiermacher, who with an objectless Christian piety knows only an objectless Jewish and Gentile piety and therefore can see between them only a general and uniform continuity, not a specific or particular identity which cannot be referred equally to the whole history of religion. In this regard his well-known private dislike for the uncomfortable God of Moses and Elijah offers some explanation but cannot be regarded as decisive. As in the doctrine of biblical inspiration[99] we are appalled by the fact that Schleiermacher seems not to have seriously considered at all the meaning of the church's dogma before replacing it with his own substitute.

§ 13—and everything now develops with sinister consistency—advances the thesis that the historical revelation in Christ is neither "something absolutely supernatural nor something absolutely suprarational." Naturally not: In § 13,1 revelation is not, of course, "the product of a spiritual rotation." It transcends the nature of the historical cycle in which it comes. Otherwise it would not be, as § 10 Appendix affirms, a starting-point. Nevertheless, it is "an effect of a power of development that dwells in our nature as a type." If we want to "portray human nature in its higher significance," then we must "regard as normal" the appearance from time to time of specially gifted in-

[98]For this concept, which derives from Stoic philosophy, cf. Justin Martyr, and for examples from Reformed orthodoxy cf. H. Heppe, *Reformed Dogmatics*, revised and edited by Ernst Bizer (London: Allen and Unwin, 1950; Grand Rapids: Baker, 1978), Locus 1: "Natural and Revealed Theology."

[99]Cf. pp. 182f.

dividuals or heroes; such gifts, which are grounded in hidden divine laws, may be assumed in the founders of religions. If only Christ is "appointed gradually to raise the whole human race to a higher life," his incarnation, that of the Son of God, is "something natural" in the sense not only that there must be ascribed to human nature at least the possibility of assuming the divine into itself but also that the temporal act is to be regarded as an act that is based upon an original orientation of human nature and prepared by all that has gone before, and therefore as "the supreme development of its spiritual power," for it would be most improper to call it divine caprice that this act took place in Jesus and not someone else. But nothing absolutely supernatural. Nor anything absolutely suprarational according to § 13,2. There is indeed something above reason in the Redeemer and the redeemed, namely, that whereby he accomplished redemption and accomplished it in them, but even this is *not* absolutely suprarational. The supreme goal of redemption is a human state in which human reason and the divine Spirit mutually know one another and can no longer be distinguished, so that the divine Spirit takes the form of "the supreme enhancement of human reason." Again, that which is to be achieved by the divine Spirit is from the very first co-posited in some way in human reason, for what contradicts this Spirit contradicts reason too, and the consciousness of the need for redemption bears witness to it. The rationalists are a proof that Christ is to be understood and extolled rationally too.[100] What is the origin, then, of this whole problem of the supernatural and suprarational in Christianity? asks § 13 Appendix. Its source is obviously the experience that underlies Christian statements, the distinctive fellowship of the Redeemer and the redeemed. The Christian self-consciousness as such cannot be produced by reason; this is the suprarational element. But "the whole of nature is also suprarational in the same sense as the Christian self-consciousness." As some are "affected" by nature, so are others by the Redeemer. Why, then, should not statements about the one kind of affecting be just as purely rational as statements about the other? All Christian statements are suprarational in one connection and rational in another: *suprarational* in the way in which all statements resting on experience are this inasmuch as they are based on a given and not on universal principles, so that they can be appropriated only as one has the corresponding experience; and *rational* insofar as they are subject to the same laws of conceptual construction and relationship as everything that is said.

It will be seen that we simply have in § 13 an application of the definition of revelation given in § 10 Appendix. The most surprising thing is the openness with which Schleiermacher says it all, unless we are more surprised by the 19th century when in spite of this candor it believed him. Fundamentally there is nothing super*natural* here—Christ, too, is an act of nature, a final development of its spiritual power. The Christian self-consciousness is supra*rational*, but only in the sense that throughout nature anything given cannot as such be constructed rationally. In the last resort even the divine Spirit is only a supreme enhancement of human reason. Thus revelation is

---

[100]Barth wrote "prove" rather than "are a proof." He is referring to the last sentence of § 13,2.

neither absolutely supernatural nor absolutely suprarational. This is the as-
tonishingly simple content of the paragraph. Concepts like that of a *fallen*
nature that *needs redemption* and is *not* finally capable of spiritual acts like
revelation, or *darkened* reason that cannot finally experience its supreme enhancement in the divine Spirit, seem not to exist at all for our master.

§ 14, the last of the apologetic borrowings, deals with the way in which
one does and does not become a Christian. "Through faith in Jesus as the
Redeemer," is the positive part of the answer. In § 14,1 being a Christian
means seeking in the Christian church (naturally by way of approximation)
the "absolute easiness and steadfastness of pious affections." *Resolving* to do
this is the preceding *certainty* "that by the work of Christ the state of need
of redemption will be set aside and the other ushered in." This preceding
certainty is faith in Christ. As faith in God according to § 4,4 is simply "certainty about the feeling of absolute dependence as such," that is, as one that
is caused by a being outside us, so faith in Christ is a beginning, infinitely
small perhaps, and posited only as a "real sensing," yet posited, "of the removal of the state of need of redemption," which as an effect is related to
Christ as the cause. In other words it is experience, which by depicting Christ
and his work is the one and only means to propagate faith, that is, "to evoke
the same inner experience in others." Christian proclamation is "witness to
one's own experience which should arouse in others a desire to have the same
experience." Every impression that is sought in this way is the same as the
contemporaries of Christ received directly from him. Those who can resist it
necessarily lack self-knowledge. This certainty and its mediation are enough
according to § 14,2. The necessity of redemption and the uniqueness of Christ
as Redeemer cannot be proved. Even if it sometimes adduces messianic prophecies, this is the view of the New Testament too (§ 14,3). This brings us to the
negative thesis for the sake of which the section is obviously written. As in
§ 10 it is to be found in an appendix which merits attention even by its length
(2 to 1). It deals with the concepts of miracle, prophecy, and inspiration, and
says in sum that these are not necessary for, and do not help to bring about,
the emergence of faith, that is, the initial experience of the meeting of spiritual
need by Christ. They presuppose faith and cannot, therefore, initiate it. *Miracle*: Does not scripture itself speak of devilish miracles? Where does it base
faith or even attention to Christ on miracles? What is the difference between
a miracle and any other inexplicable event? Is not the assessment of miracles
determined by faith? Where a new starting-point of spiritual life is postulated,
corresponding phenomena in physical nature are accepted. "It is natural to
expect miracles from someone who is the supreme divine revelation." Hence
Christ performed miracles like other founders of religions. But miracle is a
relative concept; a beginning of faith has to be present if it is to be accepted.
To the degree that a revelation, that is, a new beginning, organizes itself and
becomes nature, the supernatural phenomena that accompany it will fade into
the background again. *Prophecy*: Is it not possible to accept the relation of the
Old Testament prophecies to Jesus without believing in the true sense, that
is, experientially? Does not such acceptance presuppose already faith in what
is prophesied and those who make the prophecies? Can it be proved that the
prophets really foresaw Christ? Did not others prophesy too? Schleiermacher

refers here to Jesus' own eschatological addresses. Does one have to find in these a proof of his divine dignity? Did not prophecy, too, fade into the background the more the new order of salvation established itself as a historical phenomenon (nature!)? Would not faith be impregnable as experience "even if Christianity could produce neither prophecies nor miracles"? Finally *inspiration*: A concept that "has a very subordinate significance in Christianity"! The Spirit is what Christ gives his disciples by his teaching. No faith in Christ comes from accepting the inspiration of the prophets. We believe in it only because of the use that Christ and the apostles make of the prophets. Again it is not faith in the inspiration of the New Testament that awakens faith in Christ, but the "total impress of Christ" himself.

Hence we do not *need* these things, says § 14. With no sharpening of the negation, it might just as well be said that there *are* no such things. For Schleiermacher, indeed, there is only faith. By faith alone!—one could hardly imagine a stranger travesty of this Reformation principle than that of § 14 of *The Christian Faith*. Yes, faith alone, that is, the infinitely small beginning (a real sensing) of actual redemption with Christ as its cause; inner experience. What need is there of miracle, prophecy, or an inspired scripture? This experience already knows and has and is on the way to the absolute easiness and steadfastness of pious affections, and even in faith, or precisely in faith if it is faith in revelation, any recollection of the transcendence of God suggested in those concepts can only be disruptive and annoying to it if it does not want to be this. Hence it has to be said that faith has no interest in these things, with the happy result for dogmatics that with a single elegant jerk it is free of the irksome grip that was so hampering to it as a science. All that is usually so troublesome for a modern theologian is accomplished here at a stroke. Is not this astonishingly good apologetics? |

Let us look back at what has happened since § 11. There the essence of Christianity was found—with reservations—in redemption and the Redeemer. In § 12 the Old Testament was then detached from the New. § 13 juggles away the absolutely other in revelation. § 14 restricts faith to the inner emotion of real sensing and sets aside miracles, prophecy, and inspiration. This is quite a lot all at once, but naturally all of it is only introduction in the form of apologetic borrowings!

I break off here. Do you not agree that it is really worthwhile to read this introduction sentence by sentence before turning overcredulously and over-docilely to *The Christian Faith*? And might it not be that we can find consolation for being forced to stop here in the confidence that in these twelve sections we have perhaps in some sense come to know the whole of this version of the Christian faith?

§ 7

THE SPEECHES ON RELIGION

Apart from the four editions prepared by Schleiermacher himself in 1799, 1806, 1821, and 1831, you will find this work in the theological writings,[1] in the Pünjer edition of 1879[2] which compares the sharply divergent originals,[2] and in R. Otto's reproduction of the second edition.[3] Background material may be found in Dilthey's *Leben Schleiermachers,*[4] Haym's *Romantische Schule,*[5] and the Otto edition.[6] Because time is short, permit me on this occasion to omit any introduction and turn at once to the text. Coming from the introduction to *The Christian Faith,* we shall be testing the total picture that we found there of Schleiermacher's basic conception of religion and Christianity by its *original historical* form—which is what will concern us in the *Speeches.* I shall be keeping to the first edition of 1799 for this purpose.

Again because of the pressure of time, in this attempt to lead you into the content of this first and basic essay of Schleiermacher in academic theology I shall not try to analyze the text but draw some diagonals across it by means of which you can orient yourselves to it in Schleiermacher's own context. Let us start with the fact that Schleiermacher introduced himself here, not as a thinker or historian or writer or preacher, but as an *orator.* This is no literary whimsy, but is closely connected with the matter itself. As an orator! This means for one thing that the one who styles himself thus is incomparably more aware than if he had chosen some other category that he has a partner in the discussion, that he is addressing someone. Those who are addressed are the cultured among the despisers of religion, modern people who are completely engrossed in the earthly ideals of humanity, art, and science, and have no more time for the eternal and holy being above the present world (p. 2) because they are frightened off by the form in which they know religion (p. 175), but who in the author's opinion, because of their education, ought to be more capable than others of entering upon "the laborious path into the

---

[1]F. Schleiermacher, *Sämmtliche Werke,* 1, *Zur Theologie* (Berlin, 1843), I, 133–460.
[2]Ed. G. C. B. Pünjer (Brunswick, 1879).
[3]See p. xvii, n. 18. The references are to the original pagination of 1799 as given by Otto. The English translation (New York, 1958) follows the Otto edition.
[4]Cf. p. xiii, n. 3 (2nd ed. pp. 407ff.).
[5]Cf. p. 119, n. 31 (pp. 412ff.).
[6]Cf. pp. V–XLV (for pp. V–XVIII see ET pp. vii–xx).

inner depths of human nature" in order to find there the basis of thought and action, namely, that eternal and holy being (p. 20). He wants to present to them the essence of the religion that they despise because they do not know it (p. 22). He wants to show them that it necessarily wells up from within every better soul *of itself*, and that it is worthy to move the best and noblest by its inner force, and to be known by them according to its inner nature (p. 37). He wants to make it clear to them that we are born with a *religious disposition* as with any other, and that if nothing comes violently in its path this will infallibly have to develop in us in its own way (p. 144). Finally he wants to draw their attention unmistakably to the fact that among the religions that are commended the only one for them in practice is the Christian religion, which is relatively, though not absolutely, the highest and noblest and purest (pp. 235ff.). He considers the historical situation of his audience and on the one hand finds it hard for them "in these times of general confusion and revolution" to respond to his summons to them to plunge deeply into the infinite (p. 136), but on the other hand thinks that "the age is no more unfavorable for religion than any other," and that the aspirations of cultured people, their aversion to the moralism and intellectualism of the Enlightenment, their individualism, their investigation of the inner workings of nature, their desire for a total world-view, and their profound appreciation of culture can all "help a little toward the rebirth of religion" (pp. 161f.). "Your exertions can produce this result, and I honor you as, even if unintentionally, the saviors and cherishers of religion" (pp. 170f.). He hopes that even if all his speeches fail, those whom he addresses will at least be brought to the point of not resisting himself and those like-minded with him, of worshiping "the God that is in you" (p. 312).

An attempt to persuade, to convince, to win over, to defend, to commend, to achieve agreement—*this*, then, is what the *Speeches* are. But the agreement concerns the value of religion in general, and Christianity in particular, as a value of life which is not just possible but necessary alongside, no, above all others, which is even demanded by them, which is more or less latently present already, and which only needs to be recognized and set in motion. The situation into which Schleiermacher enters with his first step as a theologian is that of apologetics. Not simply following the logic of the matter itself like a Thomas Aquinas, he does not seek to say what Christianity is and ought to be in its own context, let the world say what it will about it. Nor does he resemble the reformers in contending for one view over against others. The orator does not proclaim religion itself; he speaks about it. What concerns him is not the substance but the form, not the inner dialectic of Christian truth but the *phenomenon* of religion, Christianity as such, and the place that it occupies, or does not occupy, in culture, or concretely in the judgment of the representatives of contemporary culture. On the point of proclaiming Christianity, he is struck by the fact that modern people do not listen, or shake their heads as they do, and so he first comes down from the pulpit to parley with them, to make the proclamation initially plausible as such (quite apart from its content), to make them willing to listen more favorably. They need to see that Christianity and the church are not so absurd as they think. Strictly, if only they will understand themselves correctly, they will have to acknowledge that the phenomenon as such is necessary and worth welcoming. The rest will then follow. This is obviously exactly the same situation as Schleiermacher finds himself in in the introduction to *The Christian Faith*. The trains of thought which we have just considered are speeches *about* religion, addresses to the cultured among its despisers, parleyings with a white flag in the hand, and if, with the whole of the 19th century, we are right in finding the center and true content of Schleiermacher's main writing at this point, we discover from the *Speeches* that this concern was from the very first characteristic and determinative, only too determinative, for his theological work. But Schleiermacher's self-description as an orator, or *rhetor*, tells us something else. The form in which he is expressing himself differs from that of the thinker and teacher whose only ambition is to be that, so that he is simply governed by his material, by the laws of logic, and by his natural gifts of speech and self-expression. It differs also from that of the preacher, who is governed by two further points—the practical aim of the address, and regard for the ability of his hearers to understand it. The form of the orator is controlled not only by material, logic, and purpose, but also by the aim to speak artistically or beautifully, to achieve perfection of form. The impression that something is not only said but finely said is one of the first that any impartial reader of the book receives on the very first page, and this impression is intended. The speaker himself assures us that religion must be communicated in a lofty style. It is appropriate to reach the very summit of what is possible in speech, to use all the fulness and majesty of human oratory. It is impossible to express and communicate religion otherwise than rhetorically (p. 49), using all the power and art of speech, and willingly adding to these the service of all the arts that can assist fleeting and volatile speech (p. 181). And shortly thereafter he tells us that the most definite and understandable expression of the heart of this matter is speech *without* words, that is, music (p. 183). What, then, is the phenomenon about which he is speaking if this is how it is with speech about it? By no means arbitrarily we draw attention to the fact that on p. 3 Schleiermacher, instead of calling himself a theologian, styles himself an expert (or virtuoso) in religion. Is this only a part of the fulness and majesty of human oratory? No, for we are told that in human life in general the aim is to achieve virtuosity, whether in morals, philosophy, or art (pp. 112f.). In exactly the same sense, but in a way which surpasses and supplements this general virtuosity, he thinks that there should be virtuosos and artists in religion (pp. 158, 205, 220, 223), naturally in religion itself and not just in religious expression. Indeed, God himself can sometimes be called a virtuoso, and a moody one, as befits the virtuoso (p. 91), while religion can be described as the noblest of all human works of art (pp. 33f.), and the whole world is called a gallery of religious scenes (p. 141). |

Where are we, and what is it all about, if these pictures, if the recollection of a Paganini or a Böcklin that the orator kindles in us, are supposed to lead us to the matter? Schleiermacher does, of course, describe in other words as well his position and task as a speaker on religion. He says at the very beginning, for example, that he is speaking about what has been the innermost spring of his being ever since he began to think and live. It is his *divine calling* to speak about the irresistible inner necessity of his nature. This is his place in the universe and what makes him what he is (p. 5). He says about himself what he says about religion. He never heard it but had it. Little of it is to be had in sacred writings (p. 15). He is under a constraint to communicate himself. Religion was the mother's womb in whose sacred darkness his young life was nurtured and prepared for a world still concealed from it. In it his spirit breathed before finding its outward objects, experience and knowledge (pp. 14f.). We are obviously reminded here, not of Paganini, but—who is not astonished at this personal union?—of Jeremiah [cf. Jer. 1:5]. Yet Schleiermacher knows even more about his own mission. In a formal train of thought in the first speech (pp. 5ff.) he develops out of the original antithesis of the real and the ideal the concept of the *mediator* who, sent by the deity, maintains a balance between a sensory orientation and enthusiasm, and thus builds the necessary bridge between finite man and infinite humanity. Endowed with a sensory impulse that is mystical and creative, his spirit aspires to the infinite in order to find there words and images with which to return to the finite as a poet, seer, orator, or artist. According to the ancient prophecy [cf. Jer. 31:34] such mediators will one day become superfluous; only the "soft stillness of holy virgins" will then be needed to maintain the sacred fire [p. 13]. But for the time being all of us apart from a few elect need such a mediator or leader to awaken our feeling for religion from its first slumbers (p. 121). In the fifth speech Christ himself is presented as the embodied idea of this provisionally necessary mediation (pp. 301ff.). But at the beginning of the first speech Schleiermacher puts himself in this category in virtue of his office as an orator. In another place, at the beginning and then again at the end of the fourth speech, unmistakably in expression of what he took to be his own function, we find the concept of *priesthood*. "The priest steps forward to present his own view as an object for the rest in order to lead them into the sphere of religion where he is at home and to infect them with his own holy feelings; he expresses the universum, and in sacred silence the congregation follows his inspired speech . . . and when he returns to himself from his wanderings through the universum, his heart and the hearts of all are the common site of the same feeling" (pp. 182f.). His whole life becomes a "work of priestly art" (p. 228). Not without some reference to his own work, the speaker discusses also the *heroes* of religion. "Certain lofty thoughts flash through their souls as these are kindled by ethereal fire, and the mighty thunder of a magical speech accompanies the lofty phenomenon and proclaims to the worshiping mortal that the deity has spoken. . . . It is for these heavenly sparks that you must seek (not for theological systems, is the meaning) when a holy soul is touched by the universum" (pp. 29f.). Is it not clear that if the being that speaks is a mixture of virtuoso, prophet, mediator, priest, and hero, then in fact all we can have is speaking about religion, speaking in the sense of the express statement: "I have struck up the music of my religion" [p. 135]? What is meant by the speech of such a being? Certainly not the communication of truth, nor speech that establishes knowledge, nor logos, but only, no matter how it may be defined in detail, the expression of something inexpressible, the symbol of a reality that is not perceived, the inadequate echo of a voice that is not heard, sound and smoke compared to the feeling about which it speaks.[7] It is with this kind of speech that the cultured among the despisers of religion are addressed.

But much more urgent is the question: What is it that is to be spoken about in this way? As we try to answer this question, we first come across passages that suggest that by this What we are to understand something specific in *human nature* that is overlooked by the despisers. "As a man I speak to you about the sacred mysteries of humanity" (p. 5). Mediation is to take place here between limited man and infinite humanity (p. 10). Religion has its source in the dispositions of humanity, and it is to the pinnacles of the temple of humanity that the orator wants to lead us (p. 20). Humanity could be angry with us if we failed to see that religion is part of human nature (p. 23). It is expressly stated—obviously so that one should not think of what is described in 1 Cor. 2 [v. 9]—that religion has been able to arise in the human heart (p. 47) on the far side of speculation and practice (p. 52). It belongs to the true life of man and must come forth out of "the innermost core of his organization" and be a continuum in his human disposition (pp. 139, 298). We are born with a religious disposition like any other (p. 144), and this is connected with everything "excellent and divine" that is otherwise imparted to our nature (p. 237). It means that the deity builds up as its own holy of holies "the part of the soul in which it prefers to dwell and in which it manifests and contemplates itself in its own direct operations," separating it "from everything else that is formed and built up in man" (p. 269). According to the famous passage at the end of the first speech (p. 37) there belongs to it "a province of its own in the mind" in which it holds unrestricted sway. |

All this points us unquestionably to something that can be understood psychologically. If we inquire as carefully as possible into its universal character, our astonished gaze falls in the very first speech (pp. 16ff.) on an ethnological discussion of the better or less good[8] aptitude for religion of the English, French, and Germans in which (as is natural in such discussions) things go badly for the English and French and the palm is given to the Germans. "Here in my native land is the favored clime that never completely fails to produce fruit. Here you will find everything scattered that adorns humanity, and everything that grows attains somewhere, in individuals at least, its finest form; here is wanting neither wise moderation nor quiet reflection. Here it (religion) must find a refuge from the coarse barbarism (the English) and cold worldly mind (the French) of the age" (p. 18). We may ignore the content of this assertion. Is it not remarkable that Schleiermacher can even think of opening up the problem of nationality when speaking about this *something*? What is the point? To the same category belongs his remarkable view of the *family*:[9] "In the happy time when each can freely exercise and use his own mind, at the first awakening of higher powers in holy youth under the care of paternal wisdom, each will share in the religion of which he is capable; all one-sided communication will then cease, and the rewarded father will lead the strong son not only into a more cheerful world and easier life but also directly into the holy, more numerous, and more industrious assem-

[7]Cf. p. 176, n. 70.
[8]The MS has "better or less better."
[9]Cf. pp. 61ff., 109.

bly of worshipers of the Eternal" (p. 232), as we read in the remarkable eschatology of the fourth speech. What are we to think, then, when in a famous passage in the second speech the innermost secret of religion is described as a kind of *marriage* between man and the universum: "I lie on the bosom of the infinite world; at this moment I am its soul; for I feel all its powers and its infinite life as my own; at this moment it is my body, for I permeate its muscles and members as my own, and its innermost nerves move according to my mind and feeling as my own" (p. 74). At the moment of the decisive breakthrough of that higher something into the inner life, man thus feels himself to be the *world, nature*? "Spiritual nature" (p. 102) is meant, of course, yet nature; and impulse, function, disposition, force, instinct, and the like are recurrent terms for the mystery, its operation being preferably described as a process of a chemical or vegetable nature. The *antithesis* asserted by the concept of spirit is deliberately removed. All who have religion believe in only one world, we are categorically told already in the first speech (p. 34). Religion "is a product of human nature grounded in one of its necessary modes of action or impulses or whatever you want to call them" (p. 22). A passage like the [2/26/24] following obviously has to be meant *physiologically* in some sense: "To protect the mind in some way against the encroachments of other powers an individual impulse is implanted in everyone to allow that other activity to rest and to open *all* the organs to the impact of all impressions; and by a secret and most helpful sympathy this impulse is strongest when life in general reveals itself most clearly in our own breast and in the world around us" (p. 147), a passage which cannot be misunderstood when we remember the feeling of absolute dependence of *The Christian Faith*, reminding us as it does that the feeling of absolute dependence, or faith, can be rightly understood only from a physiological standpoint. "Religion lives its whole life in nature, but in the infinite nature of the whole, the one and all." It breathes "where freedom itself has become nature again," as Schleiermacher puts it quite unambiguously (p. 51). That the eloquent metaphor of the marriage of the infinite and the finite (p. 267) was not just a metaphor for him but that the real marriage of man and wife is ultimately and most profoundly linked to the realization of this mystery, we know already from our own § 3, and we find this confirmed in the *Speeches* when Schleiermacher bluntly calls marriage "the fusion of two persons" "whereby they become tools of the creative universum" (p. 215). He obviously has intuitions of this kind in view when, marking off his own approach from that of idealism, he calls it a "higher realism" (p. 54).

We are right, then, to deduce from these symptoms that the *human* is part of the *natural*. The multiple obscurity of the idea of *speaking* about religion is not thereby illumined but its obscurity becomes more understandable. But I want to put a third preliminary question regarding the emergence of this partly human and partly natural factor. "At all times only a few have understood anything of religion," we read at once on p. 1, and similar aristocratic-sounding statements occur frequently (e.g., pp. 18f., 194f.). We must try to evaluate them in connection with what is said about virtuosity in religion. From the human standpoint it is not self-evident that this thing can actually emerge, that the relevant disposition is strongly enough developed for a person to have the necessary experiences or for an *understanding* of what is taking place within to be present. But we must set alongside these statements others which say that religion is an integral part of human nature. When we do this, we realize that the limitation of religion to a few is to be understood in the same way as the rarity of the flowers or fruits of an exotic plant which shows what it can do only on the right soil, in the right climate, and with the right care, not in any kitchen garden. Nevertheless, from the standpoint of the side of the religious relation which confronts man, we have here a "continuum," just as even the most unusual natural phenomenon is an exponent of one and the same natural force which is always and everywhere at work in other forms. "The universum is engaged in unbroken activity and reveals itself every moment" (p. 56). "To see all happenings in the world as actions of a God—that is religion" (p. 57). "Miracle is merely the religious name for an event; every event, even the most natural [and usual],[10] is a miracle once the religious view of it can be the dominant one. To me everything is a miracle" (p. 118). "The whole world is a gallery of religious scenes" (p. 141). Of the church it is said: "This society is a priestly nation, a perfect republic, where each is alternately leader and people, following in others the same power that he feels in himself and by which he also rules others" (pp. 184f.). The same approach is adopted to the various religions and their mutual relationship. "I see nothing but that all is one" (p. 185). Only ideally are there antitheses and contradictions, but in reality everything merges (p. 185). The more one progresses in religion, the more the whole religious world must seem to be an indivisible whole. "Only in the lower domains may a certain divisive impulse be perceived. . . . Mystics and physicists in religion, theists and pantheists, those who have risen to a systematic view of the universum and those who see it only in its elements or in dark chaos, all shall still be one" (p. 187). All these things (Fourth Speech) are "the glorious branches . . . into which the heavenly tree of priestly art divides its crown" (p. 221). Nothing (end of Fifth Speech) "is more irreligious than to demand uniformity in humanity at large," and similarly "nothing is more unchristian than to seek uniformity in religion." "The universum wants to be contemplated and worshiped in every way. Innumerable forms of religion are possible; and if it is necessary that each should be actualized in its own time, it is to be desired that there should be a sense of many at every time" (pp. 310f.). "It is an irreligious view"—Paul is to be blamed—that God "prepared some vessels for honor and some for dishonor [cf. Rom. 9:21]; you must not view anything in isolation but see each in the place where it is" (pp. 91f.). Hence one should have not only one approach to all things but all approaches to each (p. 153). "For each one, and everything in each, (is) a work of the universum, and only thus can religion view man" (p. 143). What I call a religious roller is the instrument with which I see Schleiermacher treating religious virtuosity here. One radically forgets that in these statements about such matters as revelation and miracle, or about the world, man, and the religions *God* is supposed to be the subject in some meaningful way. A human-natural something is put in his place. Or, conversely, we radically forget that in a meaningful statement about God, God can only be thought of as the *subject* and not the predicate. Instead we operate here with a concept of God

---

[10]"and usual" is missing in Barth's MS.

as the ineffable infinite relationship of everything finite. Thus the roller is ready, and the virtuosity with which it is used is not as great as it seems because once the basic exchanges are accepted one thing ineluctably follows another. We may quietly answer our question as follows: What is called religion does not really *emerge at all* in Schleiermacher because according to its own statement it is always and everywhere present from the outset.

But after these preliminary questions let us now turn to the material definitions. For the sake of brevity and clarity I will let you study for yourselves the polemical passages, especially the famous negative explanations in the second speech that religion is not metaphysics or morals, or the battle against Enlightenment pedagogy in the third speech, and keep to the positive side. Let us begin with the statement that religion is a distinctive movement of the heart (p. 26), its orientation to the Eternal (p. 31), and as such a continuum within it (p. 139) inhabiting its own special province (p. 37). If it is asked what this province is, the chief answer is given in the word "mind." "Religion is a mind and taste for the infinite" (p. 53), we are told in a famous passage. We can for the moment ignore the second term and find for the former the following definition: It is a striving to get "an undivided impression of a whole; what and how something is for itself is what it wants to see, and to know everything in its unique character" (p. 149). Three directions of its activity are perceived: outwardly toward a world-view, inwardly toward a view of self, and the two together as an artistic view (pp. 165f.). All this in the special sense of a view of the part in the whole and the whole in the part. If we are not deceived, we have here the same thing as Schleiermacher would later call direct self-consciousness. And as he would later define religion as a determination of the self-consciousness, so here we are told about a *way* from all those three directions to religion, that is, to a feeling for the universum. A strict viewing of the self leads negatively to the denial of the self by a feeling for the infinite and therefore to contemplation of the universum. Essential viewing of the world leads similarly to the removing of the finite outside us and the finding of the universum. And more than anything else surveying majestic works of art in which the two unite can accomplish this miracle, so that the fusing of religion and art, which now stand side by side like two friendly souls, can become a serious postulate (pp. 166f.). It is in terms of this supreme value of art above the two antitheses that the striking phrase "mind and taste for the infinite" is chiefly to be understood, but it seems that the concept of religious virtuosos is also to be understood along these lines. The word "mind," however, gives us only the setting or the province or, one might say, the organ of religion. |

We now ask what *happens* in this province, how it comes about that the human mind is a mind for the infinite. The answer is to be taken especially from the second speech. The essence of religion is "neither thinking nor action but contemplation and feeling," is the almost canonical thesis (p. 50). Religion views man neither as a *finite* being as in metaphysics nor as one that is *striving* after the infinite as in morals but as a participant in the infinite even *in* his finitude (p. 51). In quiet resignation it watches and senses how with everything else man is constantly plunged "in the eternal ferment of individual forms and essences"; it sees how he "must become what he is whether he wants to or not" (pp. 51f.). Obviously what we have here is the later feeling of absolute dependence except that Schleiermacher now separates what he later put together in a single concept, a more objective and a more subjective element, contemplation and feeling. Contemplation is the receiving, fusing, and understanding of the influence exerted on us by the totality of things. If we view it as the influence of the *whole*, the *infinite* totality, the *universum*, we have religion. But contemplation itself is always something individual, separate, and independent. In its individuality, beside which there are other individualities and which can affect other people differently—in the infinite everything finite stands undisturbedly side by side, everything being *one* and *everything* true—in one part of the whole to find the whole, or, which is the same thing, to view it as an action of the one God—that is religion (pp. 55ff.). In nature, then, the object of religious contemplation is not, for example, the power of nature as such, nor the beauty of nature, nor the infinity of its masses, all of which might have no religious significance for scientifically educated people, but *regularity* in nature, and even more so the apparent *anomalies* in its course which stimulate the imagination, the transitions from death to life, and finally and above all the miracle of *individuality*. To see the spirit of the world in all these things—that is religion (pp. 78ff.). And even beyond all that, contemplation of *mind* in the humanity around us, humanity in the world but the whole of undivided humanity in which each individual has a certain radiance,[11] is a supplementary part of the universum, and is not, therefore, to be seen and understood individually, but even in his individuality only within the whole. One should look around to see if one might not find one of those mediators in whose light the rest of humanity is bright. And then one should return to oneself to find that one is oneself a compendium of humanity, that with one's personality one embraces in some sense the whole of human nature, and that this in all its manifestations is no other than one's own manifold, plainly delineated, and in all its changes eternalized I, so that no mediator is needed but one is oneself a mediator for many (pp. 87ff.). There is also observation of *progress* in the history of humanity and its development. This, too, is a shaping of the universum, the coming and going of national individualities, the smiling march of the lofty world-spirit over everything that opposes and hampers him, and the nemesis that follows in his train. World history—it, too, is a clear triumph of life over death, the great, ongoing redemptive work of eternal love!! (pp. 99ff.). |

Over against contemplation on the subjective side stands *feeling*, the changes brought about in the inner consciousness by contemplation, the new relation to mind and circumstance created by the acts of the universum. As the sun blinds us so that for a moment we see nothing and then everywhere a black point, so, produced by contemplation, feeling accompanies us in our acts, not causing them, not making us do certain things, but still accompanying them like sacred music. "To have religion in quiet action that ineluctably springs forth from its own source is the goal of the pious" (p. 71). All those feelings are religion in which the universum is one point and your own I is in some way the other point between which the mind hovers, namely,

[11]Barth here uses the word "Silberblick" in a poetic sense.

reverence, humility, love, gratitude, all that the ancients called *eusebeia*. Religion steps forth here as the spokesman and mediator of morality among men, yet also as the representative of universality over against one-sided ethical virtuosity, and therefore an indispensable supplementation in this regard too (pp. 108ff.). But then Schleiermacher asks us expressly to pardon him if he laments for a moment the fact that he can speak of contemplation and feeling only in isolation. "Because of this I cannot express the finest spirit of religion" (p. 72). For us who have just come from the mysteries of *The Christian Faith* this is fortunately not so; we understand him very well when he says: "Contemplation without feeling is nothing and can have neither a right origin nor true power; feeling without contemplation is also nothing; the two are something only when and because they are originally one and undivided" (p. 73). Throughout this long winter, when and where have we ever found in Schleiermacher even a single tiny antithesis which is not sooner or later arched over by this rainbow of peace and original unity? And so we fully understand the passage—a classical one for all his admirers—in which contemplation and feeling are presented in this original *union* of theirs, the "first mysterious moment": "If only I could express it, or at least hint at it, without desecrating it! It is fleeting and transparent like the first breath of dew on awakened flowers, bashful and tender like a maiden's kiss, holy and fruitful like a nuptial embrace; nor is it merely like these things, it is all these things. Quickly and magically a phenomenon, a circumstance, develops into a picture of the universum" (pp. 73f.). |

Please pay attention to the footnote that R. Otto, an unimpeachable witness, has appended here. "This statement," he says, "is the key to Schleiermacher's ideas about experiencing the Eternal. By this he does not mean ecstatic raptures or visionary contemplation, but the interiorizing of the infinite in the finite, that is, of the eternal being, content, and basis prior to all being and occurrence around us, which in infinitely varied individual ways comes with appropriating force to the contemplative mind in direct experience and feeling. In this regard, however, he very obviously presupposes a genuinely mystical predisposition of the human soul, namely, a native power to detect the Eternal, the Divine, in temporal things, and thus to be its own prophet and to experience its own miracles, its own revelations."[12] I think this is true, and I would only add that this mystical unity of contemplation and feeling in which the human soul, mystically predisposed as it is, becomes its own prophet, is later called the feeling of absolute dependence and will become the basic principle of the supposed doctrine of the Christian faith. Hence we have not really heard anything new when we have been told in broad strokes what kind of happening it is in virtue of which the human mind becomes a mind for the infinite, that is, for religion. Action and reaction, object and subject, the external and the internal, the operation of the whole and openness to it, both meeting at an indifferent point which is defined as an individual circumstance that represents the universum and which is made possible by the mystical predisposition of the human soul—we can hardly penetrate deeper than this into the

[12]Cf. R. Otto's edition, p. 47.

fount of Schleiermacher's theology. The most that we can now do is to elucidate some of the concepts. |

[2/28/24]   Note the term *universum*. We must not think that we can create ourselves (p. 2). No less than all else that is finite, we are simply a *copy* and representation of it (p. 51). We can only *accept* ourselves and all else that is finite as a depiction of the infinite (p. 56). We can only love the world-spirit and joyfully watch his working [p. 80]; even in history we can only perceive and accept. I know no passage which shows that Schleiermacher's universum—like the source of the feeling of absolute dependence—is anything other than omnipotent *causality*. There is no fear in love [1 Jn. 4:18] for this God, Schleiermacher assures us [p. 80]. Nor any Spirit either, one might add. For if it were a matter of Spirit in this relation, it would certainly involve more than observing. Schleiermacher himself emphasized strongly that one cannot think of his universum except in supremely powerful action. An "original and independent action" of what is contemplated forms the beginning of contemplation (p. 55). If only Schleiermacher had given a more precise definition of the terms "original" and "independent," or made it clear elsewhere that they are meant seriously! But all we have is the assurance that God *acts* (p. 57) (or are we to say: *God* acts!). The Spirit of the world reveals itself (p. 86). "Eternal humanity is tirelessly at work" (p. 92). "The universum forms its own observers and admirers" (p. 143). All this is very beautiful, but when the last passage goes on to say: " . . . and how this takes place we can only see so far as it may be seen," what really distinguishes the divine action from a waterfall, projected into infinity, which sets in motion at one and the same time a very actual and possible turbine in this poor vale of earth? Does this powerful being have to be called God then? And if it does not on Schleiermacher's view, how is it that the speeches are on *religion*? Should they not perhaps—but Schleiermacher would not concede this—be called something else? |

The observers and admirers thus fashioned by the universum see and feel the infinite in the finite. In the finite! Schleiermacher puts the whole stress on this. It would be a theft (p. 52), a deception (p. 146), to try to find the infinite directly apart from the finite. We cannot perceive the nature of things, the substance of the whole, only its action on us (p. 56), and this only in detached individual contemplation (p. 58). "An individual religion such as we seek can be brought into being only when by free choice—for it cannot occur otherwise, since every view would have similar claims—one specific view of the universum is made the central point of the whole religion, and all else is related to it" (pp. 259f.). Religion begins with an "inconceivable fact," a "miracle-story" (pp. 267f.), a memorable occurrence (p. 274), whose point is always that amid the finite and specific there develops in man a consciousness of the infinite and the whole. Not as though this involved an irrevocable restriction to a particular number and selection of views and feelings. But (cf. *Christian Faith*, § 10,3) the fact, the state, in which our spirit is "first greeted and embraced by the universum" determines the character and tone of the whole succeeding series of our religious insights and emotions no matter how far we may advance in our view of the universum "beyond what the first childhood of our religion offers" (p. 267).

There follows from all this Schleiermacher's teaching on specific religions. "Where have I seen all these forms? In the true sphere of religion, in its specific forms, in the positive religions ... among the heroes and martyrs of a particular faith, among the zealots for particular feelings, among the worshipers of a particular light and individual revelations. . . . As no one can come into existence as an individual without being placed by the same act in a world, in a specific order of things and among specific objects, so a religious person cannot achieve individuality without inhabiting by the same act some definite form of religion" (p. 271). The vaunted freedom of natural religion is only the freedom to remain uncultured, free of the need to "be, see, and experience something definite" (p. 272). Natural religion is for Schleiermacher too weak, too little different from moralism and sentimentality. He compares its drift toward the uniform and universal to that of sectarians, except that what we have in it is a uniformity in the indefinite (p. 273). It does not have the "memorable occurrence" with which real religion must begin (p. 274). It is properly only a waiting for existence, its nature being "negation of everything positive and characteristic," and aversion for the extraordinary and for schooling (p. 277). Its adherents want to be "self-produced and self-taught in religion, but they are rough and uncultured, having neither the power nor the will to produce anything distinctive" (pp. 277f.). We already know where Schleiermacher is moving with this attack: "To have religion is to contemplate the universum, and the worth of a religion rests on the way you contemplate it and the *principle* which you find in its actions" (p. 126). Way, principle—this should not be confused with the quantity of religious *matter* that differentiates it outwardly from others (pp. 250ff.). Even the fetishistic, polytheistic, or philosophically theistic *character* of a religion does not constitute its particularity (p. 255, cf. pp. 126ff.), and even less so the antithesis between personalism and pantheism (p. 256). We have a positive religion "where everything is seen and felt in relation to a central view, no matter where or how this is formed or what the preferred view may be" (p. 260). Only those who pitch their camp in one such view have "any fixed abode," any "right of active citizenship in the religious world" (p. 261), though the present positive religions will not be the only ones, and those that now exist give the freest play to the individuality of everybody: "The harvest is great and the workers are few [cf. Mt. 9:37]. An endless field is open in each of these religions in which thousands may disperse" (pp. 263f.). The only point is that we must not be led astray by the fact that the adherents and the heroes and holy writings of a specific religion often speak impressively about the fact that underlies it, as though it were one and the same as its basic view—which is not at all the case. The basic view of a religion can be nothing other than "some view of the infinite in the finite, some universal element of religion which may also occur in all others, and which must do so if they are to be complete, the only thing being that it is not put at the center [in][13] them" (pp. 282ff. [quotation from p. 284]). No "frigid uniformity," then, must be allowed to destroy the divine superabundance (p. 64); there must be no attempt "to force one's religion" on others (p. 136), but "reciprocal communication ... between those who already have religion" (p. 188). All these are thoughts that in rather more

[13]The Otto edition omits the "in."

systematized form are already familiar to us from *The Christian Faith*, the only difference being that the natural contingency of the so-called central view which underlies a positive religion, the impossibility of differentiating it from the totality of all other central views and thus claiming it as a specific one, is even more clearly presented.

In line with this concept of positive religion is that of the *church*. "If there is religion at all, it must necessarily be social; this lies not only in the nature of man, but also and especially in its own nature" (p. 177). We want witnesses for that which stirs our feelings. We cannot keep the impact of the universum to ourselves. Impelled by his very nature, the religious person speaks, and the same nature creates hearers for him. Every expression of religion is of interest to others, who listen to its notes because they recognize in them their own. In this way reciprocal communication is organized, speaking and hearing are indispensable, and there arises "the rich, superabundant life in this city of God when its citizens assemble, each full of a native force that seeks free expression, and full of a holy desire to apprehend and appropriate all that the others can offer"!! The depiction that one gives in the name of all represents the universum and inoculates them with its sacred feelings, as I have already shown[14] (pp. 177ff. [quotation from p. 181]). The true church according to Schleiermacher, as we have seen already in the sermons, is the church of possessors, the fellowship of those who already *have* religion. Read for yourselves the peroration at the end of the fourth speech in which he extols the academy of priests, the chorus of friends, the band of brothers, in which each knows that he, too, is a part and work of the universum and thus a worthy object for the contemplation of all the rest, so that with sacred modesty yet ready openness he discloses himself to them that each may enter in and see. "All that is human is holy, for all is divine" (pp. 233f.). Only accidentally alongside this true church may there also be an institution for the benefit of students and apprentices in the art, but the two ought not to be mixed, nor should the majesty of the state and its concerns be extended to the church. Personal communities ought to be founded in place of local congregations, grouped around real virtuosos in religion. The distinction between priests and laity ought increasingly to vanish along with every other distinction. "The external religious society will be brought closer to the universal freedom and majestic unity of the true church only as it becomes a fluid mass, with no confines, in which each part may now be found here and now there, and all the parts intermingle peacefully," so that "no one can feel any longer that he belongs to a particular circle and those who believe differently to another" (pp. 206–230 [quotation from p. 226]). "Those who contemplate the Eternal have always been quiet souls, either alone with themselves and the Infinite or, if they look around them, grudging to no one his own way so long as he understands the mighty word" (p. 64). In this either/or from the second speech we already have the whole ambivalence of the concept of the church in the fourth speech: *Either* an esoteric fellowship *or* a tolerant negation of all boundaries; in reality, of course, a both/and, and indeed the one by way of the other: the infinite in the *finite*, but in the finite the *infinite*.

[14]Cf. pp. 247.

But how about the communications that circulate around everything in this church? How about *theology*?—insofar as there can be any speech about God and the things of God alongside the sacred music. Obviously theology does not fare too well if it is true, as we have already been told in the first speech, that the spirit is usually *damped down* on the way from the first mouth to the first ear (p. 28)! Dogmas and principles are obviously not the content of religion. The *content* of reflection differs from the act itself (p. 116). Words are only the *shadows* of contemplation and feeling (p. 140). Nevertheless, those who think comparatively about their religion inevitably find certain basic theological concepts on their path and are unable to avoid them. Let us see what becomes of the most important of these. What is meant, for example, by *revelation*? Answer: "Every original and new view of the universum is a revelation, and each knows best what is original and new to *him*, and if something that is original and new in *him* is also new for you, his revelation is also a revelation for you, and I would advise you to weigh it well" (pp. 118f.)! As regards the process, Schleiermacher expresses himself more vividly in the first speech when he talks about the heroes of religion: "An atom begotten by some supraterrestrial power fell into their minds, made itself kin to everything there, extended itself with almighty force, and then broke up as by divine destiny in a world whose atmosphere offered it too little resistance, and in its last moments produced one of those heavenly meteors, those momentous signs of the times, whose origin no one knows, and which fill all the dwellers on earth with awe. You must seek out these heavenly sparks which arise when a holy soul is touched by the universum" (p. 30). In content, or materially, revelation is obviously no different from what is elsewhere described as the beginning of the religious life in an individual on the basis of a specific insight. Is there an *absolute, true, eternal* religion? Answer: "The basic view of each positive religion is eternal in itself because it is a part that helps to make up the infinite whole in which everything is necessarily eternal"; since, however, the central position of this or that basic view is historically and psychologically conditioned, the religion itself, each religion, is transitory. Other historical situations bring other basic views, and religion can no longer exist in the previous form. It is thus a historically relative judgment when Schleiermacher says about Christianity that it "still has a long history ahead of it." Furthermore, Christ himself spoke about the time when there would be no more question of a mediator but the Father would be all in all [cf. 1 Cor. 15:28]; he thus acknowledged the transitoriness of Christianity (pp. 307f.).

Schleiermacher is no better when he talks about the concept of *holy scripture*. As "dead letter" this is mentioned for the most part only in an unfavorable context. "Every sacred writing is only a mausoleum of religion, a monument that a great spirit was there who is there no longer; for if he still lived and worked, how could he attach such great value to the dead letter which can only be a weak impress of himself? A person does not have religion who believes in a sacred writing, but one who has no need of such and could very well make his own" (pp. 121f.)!! "Religious communication is not to be sought in books. . . . Too much of the original impression is lost in this medium." Only when the original effect "is chased out of the society of the living does it have to conceal its varied life in the dead letter" (pp. 179f.).

Finally, "the holy scriptures became a Bible by their own force, but they do not forbid other books to be or become Bibles, and they would be glad to associate with whatever is written with the same power" (p. 305). The way in which the Bible is quoted forms a chapter of its own, and a remarkable one at that. |

Then the concept of *miracles*. We have seen already[15] that miracle is simply a religious term for event. "To me all is miracle. . . . The more religious you are, the more miracle you will see everywhere" (p. 118). "Those who do not see miracles of their own from the standpoint from which they contemplate the world . . . have no religion" (p. 120). |

We receive especially astonishing communications about a concept which is not, for that matter, an essential one, the concept of *God.* "For me the deity can be no other . . . than a specific religious way of looking at things." We should not be content merely to worship in God the genius of humanity. The universum is more than humanity. But religion is also independent of the idea of a supreme being that rules the universum with freedom and understanding. "To have religion is to contemplate the universum." How? On *this* its value depends, so that "a religion without God can be better than one with God" (pp. 124–126). Whether people have a fetishistic, polytheistic, or "systematic" view of the universum depends on their feeling for it, "and this is the measure of their religiosity; whether they have a God in their view depends on the direction of their imagination," concerning which we are now told incidentally that it is "the highest and most original thing in man, and that everything outside it is only reflection on it" [pp. 128f.]. Thus "the person who has it in his nature to personify the universum is in essentials, in the substance of religion, no different from the one who does not, and there will never be lacking those who can easily think themselves even into the opposite form" (p. 186). "In religion, then, the idea of God is not so exalted as you think, and among the truly religious there have never been zealots, enthusiasts, or fanatics for the existence of God." God is present in religion only in the active sense; it has no place for the existing and commanding God, who is simply a misunderstanding of the physicists and moralists (p. 130). Hence "God is not everything in religion, but one thing, and the universum is more" (pp. 132f.). |

Finally *immortality.* One should be on guard lest the desire for this betray an aversion to the true goal of religion. With our contemplation of the universum, should we not become as much united with it as possible, thus losing ourselves in the infinite, but instead we want to remain isolated and not forfeit our individuality? Does not death offer us a unique opportunity to transcend humanity, but instead we want to take it with us into the world to come? "But the universum tells them, as it is written: Whosoever loses his life for my sake will keep it, and whosoever wants to keep it will lose it" [cf. Mt. 16:25]. "Try, then, to give up your life out of love for the universum. Seek here already to destroy your individuality and to live in the one and all; seek to be more than yourselves so that you may lose little when you lose yourselves. . . . Immortality should not be a desire unless it be first a task that you have

[15]Cf. p. 250.

solved. In the midst of the finite to become one with the infinite, and to be eternal in a moment, is the immortality of religion" (pp. 131–133).

Let me conclude this survey and series with these famous passages on God and immortality at the end of the second speech. Apart from the depiction of Christianity in the fifth address, which I will leave to your own reading, I have now touched at least on all the essential ideas of the book. Of the other works of Schleiermacher that I would like to have included, there remain only the *Christliche Sitte* and the philosophical works, especially on dialectics and philosophical ethics. From my acquaintance with these writings, however, I can assure you that they might enrich in many ways the picture of Schleiermacher's theology that we have won—for his was a very fertile mind—but they definitely would not give to it any different character.

For me the results of this study are fairly shattering. When I embarked with you on this material, which I had not examined closely for many years, I was prepared for something bad. But I was not prepared to find that the *distortion* of Protestant theology—and we have to speak of such in view of the historical importance of the man—was as deep, extensive, and palpable as it has shown itself to be, especially in the last quarter of an hour, though I have not expressly said so. I hope that you have not regarded it as mere talk if in spite of everything I have occasionally remarked that Schleiermacher's achievement fills me with *respect* and *admiration*. I now know better than I did before that he was a great and gifted and pious man, that among all who came after him, whether they followed in his tracks or tried to kick against the pricks, there was and is none to hold a candle to him. Protestantism has not in fact had any greater theologian since the days of the reformers. But this theologian has led us all into this *dead end*! This is an oppressive and almost intolerable thought. How can it really be reconciled with confidence in Protestantism's power of truth? Or should we in fact say that this was and is the normal and legitimate continuation of the Reformation, the completion of the work of Luther and Calvin: this doctrine of the feeling of absolute dependence or of the universum and all that is connected with it? If it were, for me the right thing to do would be to become a Roman Catholic again. But at an even higher level, how can it be reconciled with the providence of God ruling over his church? Or should we reverently say that it is the inscrutable way of God on which we have been put and which we have to tread as children of our time? But disobedience to history has sometimes been better obedience to God's governance than obediently following a path that has been entered. Nevertheless, in view of the results of our study, these two questions, that of the truth of Protestantism and that of the divine guidance of the church, are very serious ones. And the more we ponder them, the more serious the situation becomes. If we reject the two suggestions above, if we cannot find in Schleiermacher a legitimate heir or successor of the reformers, if we cannot see in the indubitable domination of his thinking the gracious guidance of God but the very opposite, a wrathful judgment on Protestantism which invites it to repentance and conversion instead of continuation, then the only possibility that remains—and I do not see how one can avoid this—is obviously that of a *theological revolution*, a basic No to the whole of Schleiermacher's doctrine of religion and Christianity, and an attempted reconstruction at the *very* point which we have constantly seen him hurry past with astonishing stubbornness, skill, and audacity. The higher one values Schleiermacher's achievement in and for itself, and the better one sees with what historical necessity it had to come and how well—how only too well—it fitted the whole spirit of Christianity in the 19th and 20th centuries, the more clearly one perceives how easy it is to say No in word but how hard it is to say it in deed, namely, with a positive counterachievement. Schleiermacher undoubtedly did a good job. It is not enough to know that another job has to be done; what is needed is the ability to do it at least as well as he did his.[16] This is the serious and humbling concern with which I take leave of Schleiermacher; and if you agree with my assessment, I hope you will share this concern. There is no occasion for triumphant superiority at this tomb, but there is occasion for fear and trembling at the seriousness of the moment and in face of our own inadequacy.

[16]The last two sentences are an addition in pencil in the margin. They replace the original ending of the preceding sentence: " . . . namely, with a positive counterachievement, with better work than Schleiermacher's as a *doctor ecclesiae,* a teacher of the church." Barth may have made this alteration later, perhaps when preparing his essay "Brunners Schleiermacherbuch" (*Zwischen den Zeiten,* VIII [1924], 49–64), in which he takes up and develops (esp. pp. 61ff.) the same ideas, and for the concept of a *counterachievement* quotes H. Scholz, *Christentum und Wissenschaft* . . . , p. 201.

CONCLUDING UNSCIENTIFIC POSTSCRIPT
ON SCHLEIERMACHER

Having been invited to write an "Introduction" to this selection from Schleiermacher's writings, I have decided (after initial hesitations) that I could most conscientiously contribute, in the form of an "Afterword," a brief overview of the history of my own relationship to this "church father of the nineteenth (and also the twentieth?!) century"—or, if you will, an "unscientific postscript." What follows thus somewhat presumptuously describes a not unimportant segment in the course of my own life.

The temptation for some thus might not be slight to begin reading this book here, whereas it would be more meaningful for them to take in and digest the selection from Schleiermacher's expressions of his own life which has been so capably and creatively compiled by H. Bolli (without any involvement on my part). So, the curious are warned! Whoever takes a different view from the one here solemnly advised does so with my express disapproval. *Dixi et salvavi animam meam*.

There was once a time, so I must begin, in my youthful occupation with theology when—after first having worked through Immanual Kant's *Critique of Practical Reason* several times and (only then, but equally intensively) his *Critique of Pure Reason*—I knew how to swear no higher than by the man, Daniel Ernst Friedrich Schleiermacher.

I had highly respected my father, Professor Fritz Barth in Bern—his picture still hangs directly before me today—as a sound scholar, quite apart from all personal and spiritual ties. But I myself could not adopt, as one said at that time, his (moderately) "positive" theological attitude and direction, determined in his youth through J. T. Beck. Neither my first New Testament teacher, Rudolf Steck, with his amiable but rather tediously exact analyses (he considered even Galatians to be "inauthentic") nor my first dogmatics teacher, Hermann Lüdemann, with his ever ill-tempered systematic acuity (he was, like Steck, a direct pupil of F. C. Bauer's), was able to make a deeper and enduring impression on me. The same was true of the Old Testament scholar Karl Marti, who was also a greatly learned man; what he (a pupil of Wellhausen's) had to say about Israel's history and religion was a hopelessly dry kind of wisdom. That the Old Testament was concerned with something exciting I did not begin to discover until Berlin under Gunkel. What I owe despite everything to those Bern masters is that I learned to forget any fears I might have had. They gave me such a thorough grounding in the earlier form of the "historical-critical" school that the remarks of their later and contemporary successors could no longer get under my skin or even touch my heart—they could only get on my nerves, as is only too well known.

In Berlin, where by the way I learned to esteem Harnack even higher than Gunkel, I then bought myself, along with Wilhelm Herrmann's *Ethics*, a copy of Schleiermacher's *Speeches on Religion to its Cultured Despisers*, in the edition by R. Otto, which I still use. Eureka! Having apparently sought for "The Immediate," I had now found it, not through Hermann Kutter, who wrote his first book under that title, but through Schleiermacher. That those *Speeches* were the most important and correct writings to appear since the closing of the New Testament canon was a fact from which I did not allow my great Marburg teacher [Herrmann] to detract—just as little as I did his denigration of Schleiermacher's later and late writings. I did not see, yet I sensed, the line of continuity which runs through Schleiermacher's life's work from the *Speeches* to the so-called *Glaubenslehre*[1] (a rather un-Schleiermacherian designation), and was implicitly inclined to give him credit all down the line. Anyway, as was certainly quite in order, I also loved Eichendorff and was especially fond of Novalis. Was I (am I!) a bit of a romantic myself? (By the way, what I wrote in the first edition of my *Romans* on pp. 195–204 about the evils of romanticism with explicit reference to the young Schleiermacher is something of which I "repent and suffer in my heart," just as in my holy zeal at that time I did not really do justice to pietism.) One thing, however, is certain, that even before 1910 I was a stranger in my innermost being to the bourgeois world of Ritschl and his pupils. In the year when the first edition of *Romans* appeared (1919), I could still produce the provocative sentence: "We can afford to be more romantic than the romantics." But even the "historicism" by which Ernst Troeltsch and the historians of religion of that time thought they could outbid the Ritschlians (and thus also the teacher whom I still regard so highly, Wilhelm Herrmann) struck me as being too sterile, and at any rate was not what I was looking for. I had just now (not without direct and indirect instruction from Schleiermacher) tasted something of what "religion" itself was supposed to be. And the pallid "Schleiermacher renaissance" which began to emerge around 1910 was also a more literary affair which did not take me any further, nor could it take me any further. The only one of its representatives who made any impression on me as an interpreter of Schleiermacher, and who gave me something lasting to think about, was Heinrich Scholz, who then later became my close friend. At any rate, that Schleiermacher renaissance was superseded a few years later by a Luther renaissance, which, at least in its beginnings (around the anniversary celebrations of 1917), despite and because of Karl Holl, struck me as rather unfortunate.

Now, as to what concerned me, in 1909 I moved from Marburg to Geneva, and in 1911 to Safenwil. At both places the relatively few writings of Schleiermacher's which I owned received a special place of honor on my still rather modest bookshelves. But then came certain turning points which also touched my relationship to him.

---

[1]The term *Glaubenslehre*, which is commonly used to refer to Schleiermacher's *The Christian Faith*, carries the connotation of received church doctrine.—TRANS.

Although in Geneva I had still lived completely and utterly in the religious atmosphere which I brought with me from Marburg, and especially from the circle of the *Christliche Welt* and its friends, when I moved to the industrial village of Safenwil, my interest in theology as such had to step back noticeably into second place (even though it continued to be nourished by my eager reading in the *Christliche Welt*, the *Zeitschrift für Theologie und Kirche*, and even in the works of Troeltsch, etc.). Because of the situation I found in my community, I became passionately involved with socialism and especially with the trade union movement. At that time I did not yet know that, in his later years, Schleiermacher also had become involved in the beginnings of these things, at least on the periphery—even though here and there I might have gathered that from his sermons! Those now came into my possession, along with his letters, his *Christian Morals*, and other of his writings—after a foray I conducted into my maternal grandfather's estate in Basel. This grandfather had studied in Berlin during the forties of the nineteenth century under, among others, the later Schelling, and afterwards in Heidelberg under R. Rothe; thus, he had still been able to take in something of Schleiermacher's atmosphere, but then in the following period had gone over, like so many of his contemporaries, to a rather primitive theological conservatism, which was softened only by the mild pietism of my good grandmother. He had indeed purchased Schleiermacher (good for me that he did!), but had hardly read him seriously, and, judging from a few biting notes in the margins, had not loved him. So now those books had landed in my lap. But then, I had to read Sombart and Herkner, I had to read the Swiss trade union newspaper and the *Textilarbeiter*. Indeed, I also had to prepare my weekly sermon and my confirmation classes. Although in these pastoral activities I was decisively stimulated by Schleiermacher, it goes without saying that, like Schleiermacher himself as he proceeded, I did not exactly express myself in the language, or even exclusively in the original sense, of the *Speeches*. Even so, I really had neither the time nor the desire to pursue further research into his work.

Then came the beginning of my friendship with Eduard Thurneysen. He was committed to what was then the "modern" theology of his Basel teachers, P. Wernle and B. Duhm; beyond that, however, he was connected with Hermann Kutter and, further back, with Christoph Blumhardt. He made them both better known to me; before that my knowledge of them had only been cursory. From Kutter I simply learned to speak the great word "God" once again seriously, responsibly, and forcibly. From Blumhardt I learned just as simply (at least at the beginning) what it meant to speak of Christian hope. Ragaz and his "religious socialists" interested Thurneysen, and they interested me too, but only from a certain distance. The concept of "God's kingdom" was portrayed in various ways (sometimes more transcendently, sometimes more immanently)—but certainly no longer in the form familiar to us from Ritschl and his followers. The question lay in wait for me at the door: Had not even "my" Schleiermacher perhaps used that concept in a way which to me was now becoming increasingly strange?

And then the First World War broke out and brought something which for me was almost even worse than the violation of Belgian neutrality—the horrible manifesto of the ninety-three German intellectuals who identified themselves before all the world with the war policy of Kaiser Wilhelm II and Chancellor Bethmann-Hollweg. And to my dismay, among the signatories I discovered the names of almost all my German teachers (with the honorable exception of Martin Rade). An entire world of theological exegesis, ethics, dogmatics, and preaching, which up to that point I had accepted as basically credible, was thereby shaken to the foundations, and with it everything which flowed at that time from the pens of the German theologians. And Schleiermacher? Had not even he in the first of his *Speeches* from 1799 written impossible things about the British and the French? Had he not also been a leading Prussion patriot from 1806 to 1814? Would he also perhaps have signed that manifesto? Fichte certainly, perhaps Hegel too, but Schleiermacher? According to what I know of his letters from the period after 1815, I remain convinced that, no, he would not have done that. Nevertheless, it was still the case that the entire theology which had unmasked itself in that manifesto, and everything which followed after it (even in the *Christliche Welt*), was grounded, determined, and influenced decisively by him.

"My child, what are we now to speak?" These well-known words from *The Magic Flute* continue: "The truth, the truth, lest she also be complicit." But that was easier said than done. It was Thurneysen who once whispered the key phrase to me, half aloud, when we were alone together: what we needed for preaching, instruction, and pastoral care was a "wholly other" theological foundation. It seemed impossible to proceed any further on the basis of Schleiermacher. I can still see Thurneysen's contemptuous gesture to my Schleiermacher books in Safenwil. But where else could we turn? Kutter was also impossible, because he, like Ragaz later on, would have nothing to do with theology, but wanted only to know and to preach the "living God." He was also impossible for me, because, with all due respect for him and his starting point, his "living God" had become extremely suspicious to me after his wartime book *Reden an die deutsche Nation* [Speeches to the German Nation]. During that period Thurneysen once even broached the strange question of whether we shouldn't study Hegel. But nothing came of that then. We did not even reach for the Reformers at first, although in Geneva I had worked through Calvin's *Institutes* closely and from an earlier period had come to know (or thought I had come to know) the chief writings of Luther. The "old orthodoxy" was present to us only in the caricatures in which it had been taught to us at the university. In fact and in practice, as is well known, something much closer at hand forced itself upon us. We made a fresh attempt to learn our theological ABCs all over again. More reflectively than ever before, we began reading and expounding the writings of the Old and New Testaments. And behold, they began to speak to us—very differently than we had supposed we were obliged to hear them speak in the school of what was then called "modern" theology. The morning after Thurneysen had whispered to me our commonly held conviction, I sat down under an apple tree and began, with all the tools at my disposal, to apply myself to the Epistle to the Romans. That was the text which as early as my own confirmation classes (1901–1902) I had heard was supposed to be concerned with something central. I began to read it as if I had never read it before—and not without deliberately writing out the things which I was discovering. Only now did I begin to regard my father, who had died in 1912, with, as I put it in the preface to the first edition of *Romans*, "respect and gratitude" theologically as well. He belonged to those who were disregarded and slightly disdained in the theological lecture halls and seminar rooms of his time. And regardless of the warning at the end of Mozart's *Seraglio* that "Nothing is so hateful as revenge," I will not conceal the fact that for a moment the thought raced through my head that I could and would now exact a kind of reprisal from those who had placed my father in the shadows, even though he had been just as learned as they (only from a different point of view). Be that as it may, I read and read and wrote and wrote. Meanwhile, we published a bundle of sermons. True, among the books I had inherited from my father, I found many by J. T. Beck which were fruitful to use. True, at that time we also read huge amounts of Dostoevsky (here again at Thurneysen's prompting) as well as Spittler, Kierkegaard, and even Overbeck—who had not been "disposed of" and whom one merely needed to mention in Basel at that time to make everyone's hair bristle. My philosopher brother, Heinrich, took care that I should once again seriously confront the wisdom of Plato as well. And Father Kant, who had provided the initial spark for me once before, also spoke in a remarkably new and direct way to me in those years. Even Kutter, despite everything, doubtless continued to speak to me. So at that time (and indeed later), I read the biblical text with many different kinds of spectacles, as I unhesitatingly made known. But by using all those different kinds of spectacles, what I honestly wanted to express (and was convinced I was expressing) was the word of the Apostle Paul. That is how *The Epistle to the Romans* originated and appeared, in a first, and then immediately in a second edition, in which, at the beginning of a long and pugnacious preface, I at once confessed that "no stone" of the first edition was left "standing upon the other." During the time when I was at work on the second edition, our eldest daughter, today an energetic grandmother, but then a little girl of six years, explained to anyone who was willing to listen that Daddy was now working on "a much better Epistle to the Romans"! What the angels might have been saying to themselves on this occasion is another matter. At any rate, the second edition, the one which became "famous," thus came into being. Whoever might want to pursue further the beginnings and progress of the so-called dialectical theology may turn to the volumes prepared by J. Moltmann and W. Fürst.[2]

However, in this whole story what about my relationship to—Schleiermacher? It is certain, for one thing, that neither in his youth nor in his maturity could he have preached a sermon like the one I preached and then published in 1916 under the title, "The Pastor Who Does Right by the People." It is also certain that what I thought, said, and wrote from that year on, I simply did without him, and that his spectacles were not sitting on my nose as I was expounding the Epistle to the Romans. He was no longer a "church father" for me. It is further certain, however, that this "without him" implied

---

[2]*Anfänge der dialektischen Theologie*, 2 vols., ed. J. Moltmann (Munich: Chr. Kaiser Verlag, 1962); ET, *The Beginnings of Dialectic Theology*, ed. James M. Robinson (Richmond, VA: John Knox Press, 1968); *"Dialektische Theologie" in Scheidung und Bewährung, 1933–1936*, ed. W. Fürst (Munich: Chr. Kaiser Verlag, 1966).

a rather sharp "against him." On occasion, I intentionally made that explicit. Yet I really did not do it—since "old love never fades"—without a deep inner regret that it could not be otherwise.

But then it came about in the course of this change, which my friend Emil Brunner also made, that in his book *Die Mystikund das Wort* (1924) he gave very drastic expression to our departure (which was unavoidable) from Schleiermacher. I had to review the book in *Zwischen den Zeiten*, and found myself in something of a quandary over it. Although it contained a great deal which I also held in my heart against Schleiermacher, I was not very happy with the way in which Brunner presented his case. I did not regard the term "mysticism" as an adequate designation of Schleiermacher's intentions. Moreover, in his fight against Schleiermacher and his victory over him (and here there were already some first indications of my later conflict with Brunner), I saw him relying just as forcefully on F. Ebner's anti-idealistic logology (a forerunner of contemporary linguistic philosophy) as on the validity of the "Word" (of God). (It is not without reason that J. Moltmann has so happily stressed this in his edition of the writings of "dialectical theology."[3]) Above all, although certainly "against" Schleiermacher in my own way, I for my part was neither so certain nor so completely finished with him as Brunner undoubtedly was after he had completed that book.

I owe to his book, nonetheless, that it had an extraordinarily stimulating effect on me in the new and comprehensive study of Schleiermacher which I had meanwhile undertaken. For almost overnight in 1921 I found myself transposed into a newly founded chair for Reformed theology at Göttingen. I had now cheerfully decided—Ragaz and Kutter gave me no applause for this decision—in my own way and style to pursue theological research and teaching with grim seriousness. To carry out this task I was of course only very partially equipped. And so, before venturing on dogmatics, I announced some purely historical lectures—essentially for my own instruction, but not without a considerable influx of students. First I offered a two-hour course on the Heidelberg Catechism, then some four-hour courses on Calvin, on the Reformed confessions, on Zwingli, and finally on Schleiermacher! As far as I know, no one either before or since has attempted to interpret Schleiermacher in the light of his sermons. That was precisely what I first tried to do in my lectures, moving on from there to his *Speeches*, to the *Soliloquies*, to the *Dialogue on Christmas*, to the *Brief Outline on the Study of Theology*, to his *Hermeneutics*, and finally, as far as time allowed, to *The Christian Faith*. Certainly it did not remain hidden that I was not exactly satisfied with the things which were appearing before our wondering eyes. But I attained the main purpose toward which I strove: I now understood Schleiermacher a little better than before (as I hope my students did as well). So without presupposing that I could pronounce an anathema over him, I was then in a position during my last three semesters at Göttingen to begin working out, and lecturing on, my own dogmatics. However, the posture of the Göttingen theological faculty was so Lutheran at that time that I was only allowed to teach that topic under the completely different heading of "Instruction in the Christian Religion."

[3] J. Moltmann, *Anfänge der dialektischen Theologie*, Vol. 1, xviif.

Laughing up my sleeve, I carried out this charade for three semesters. In the period which followed I then wrote various essays on Schleiermacher—for example, on "Schleiermacher's *Celebration of Christmas*" (1924)—in part with a certain irony, but on the whole with a straightforward respect for his achievement, for his humanity and spirituality, and for the greatness of his historical impact. Indeed, with all the distance I had gained from him, I was not without a certain love for this person who had evidently perceived "human nature" in its totality. Through my probings into Schleiermacher, I also learned to appreciate from afar certain matters where I stood (or again came?) much closer to him theologically than I had ever supposed could be the case after 1916. Has not Paul Seifert even gone so far as to assert that my growing, and increasingly noticeable, interest in Schleiermacher's theology was "certainly indicated by the surprisingly positive evaluation" of him in my *Protestant Theology in the Nineteenth Century*?[4] "Positive" is no doubt somewhat too strong a term for what I really said there. Nevertheless, when faced with such a slight exaggeration, I do not want to deny that for all my opposition to Schleiermacher, I could never think of him without feeling what Doctor Bartolo so well articulated in *The Marriage of Figaro*: "An inner voice always spoke to his advantage"; or at least, never without confirming the rather coarse popular expression, "A criminal always returns to the scene of the crime." And did I not even openly boast in 1947 that on the basis of my presuppositions I was actually in a much better position to illuminate Schleiermacher than, say, Horst Stephan (who, by the way, was among my teachers at Marburg)? However, it must not be overlooked that after praising everything worthy of praise in my writings on Schleiermacher, I still had ringing in my ears the venerable "Apostles' " and Nicene Creeds. Theologically speaking, I could not revert to Schleiermacher.

This phase in my relationship to him is noteworthy for the following reason: it was determined not only by a much better knowledge of his work, but also by a conscious distancing of myself from him which could no longer be reversed.

Then a further and presumably final phase unexpectedly developed. That is, it came to pass that we "old fighters" from the second and third decades of our rather eventful century suddenly saw ourselves overtaken and overwhelmed by a new theological movement. "Demythologization" and "existentialization" of theological language were its catchwords. And the one who had inaugurated it was none other than our erstwhile companion of old, Rudolf Bultmann.

As far as *demythologizing* was concerned, the enterprise left me cold. For one thing, it was only too well known to me—not the term but the matter itself—from my theological beginnings. Furthermore, I found it much too humorless. Finally, after my experiences with modern man, who was after all the object of the exercise, I could not regard it as a fruitful instrument for conversation with this creature. Apologetics is something of which I am deeply

---

[4]Paul Seifert, *Die Theologie des jungen Schleiermacher* (Gütersloh: G. Mohn Verlag, 1960), 11.

suspicious, something alien to me in all its forms, and therefore also in this reductionist approach.

However, I certainly listened to the other news, so vigorously presented, that theological language was supposed to need *existentializing*. For I had indeed known for a long time, and had even said myself in the first and then especially in the second edition of *Romans* (occasionally even with the use of the term), that genuinely theological language could not talk about its object in merely intellectual terms, but could only express what it had to say *existentially*, that is, in terms which directly and unavoidably confronted persons in their human existence. Even before I read Kierkegaard, that had been thoroughly pounded into me by Wilhelm Herrmann, and in fact had not been entirely unknown to me before that. For me that belonged to the obvious formal conditions, to the moral presuppositions of my "theological existence," to which in one way or another I tried to do justice and to which I tried to adhere. But now I was receiving what at first (but only at first) glance seemed to be fabulously new tidings, that theology had to be *existential* theology in a material, technical, and fundamental sense as well. Apart from his knowledge and confession as a baptized member of the Christian community, thus apart from the way he was engaged in his own human existence, the theologian was first supposed to orient himself toward and clarify that which was supposed to be at stake for human existence and human engagement in general and as such. Only then, in that context, and according to the standards of such "existential" instruction, might he consider and articulate the Christian engagement of his existence, and thus his Christian faith. His task as a theologian was supposed to be to understand and proclaim precisely the faith which had become credible in this way. Tertullian's dictum that *Deus non est in genere* was in error: *Deus est in genere*. That was what struck me as something really novel in my first encounter with this most recent theology. One of the most unforgettable experiences of my life was the time when Bultmann (it may have been around 1922—he was still amiably disposed toward me in view of the second edition of *Romans*) once visited me in Göttingen in order to read to me for more than an hour over coffee and almond-cake from the lectures of Martin Heidegger which he had attended and transcribed. The purpose of this exercise: just as we had to apply ourselves to any great spiritual achievement in precisely this ("existential") direction, so we also had to apply ourselves to the gospel documented in the New Testament. Delighted by this basic systematic teaching of his, as well as by the "historical-critical" method which he himself so masterfully represented (in this respect a true pupil of his Marburg predecessor, Jülicher), many older and younger students gathered themselves around him. Instead of orienting oneself to Heidegger, or Jaspers, or M. Buber, or finally even to fifty pages of D. Bonhoeffer, one could most recently even as a Roman Catholic theologian become a Bultmannian. And, as many from the younger generation in particular experienced (in connection with the general spiritual exhaustion after the Second World War), to a certain extent one could even concur with him (the master) instinctively or intuitively. Among themselves Bultmann's pupils then became a rather various and even splintered group. But on the basis of Bultmann's systematic starting point, they remained a group and a school. On the basis of that starting point, they can no doubt be brought together under a common denominator.

What is that common denominator? Now I must speak of the impression which the whole phenomenon made on me from the beginning and which has only increased with time: the common denominator was and is indeed Schleiermacher—not the very image of him, but certainly in a new form which accommodated itself to the "contemporary spiritual situation" or "linguistic situation" and to the contemporary (or rather one contemporary) vocabulary. Unmistakably, my old friend and enemy, Schleiermacher! Once again, the Christian exhortation relegated to that cozy nook where the comtemporary society and world pretend to their authoritative claim! Once again, the symbiosis of theology and philosophy so characteristic of Schleiermacher! Once again, an anthropologizing of theology, just as obviously as in Schleiermacher, who had thereby simultaneously brought the theological learning of the eighteenth century to completion while establishing that of the nineteenth century! Once again, the tension-in-unity between subject and object which he had so masterfully described in the second of his *Speeches*! And once again, the original and ultimate unity of both which he there so triumphantly proclaimed, the glorious elimination of the "subject-object schema." Once again, the move found in *The Christian Faith* of granting supremacy to "feeling," in whose place of course one could then set "faith" in order to move somewhat closer to the Bible or the Reformation; "faith" on which was conferred sovereignty over everything which might be its ground, object, and content. So that is more or less (the list could easily be extended) how, in attentively considering its rise and development, I supposed and suppose that this most recent "modern" theology ought to be understood—as a new and vigorous Schleiermacher renaissance!

Now, allow me one more citation from *The Marriage of Figaro*: "What I said about the noble youth was only a suspicion, it was only a matter of distrust." Was it in this case only a matter of suspicion and distrust? Yet I found it remarkably confirmed by the fact that I occasionally ran across utterances from the representatives of this (for the present) new direction in which they openly enough acknowledge precisely the same kinds of parallels. Consider what Martin Redeker writes in the introduction to his excellent reissue of *Der christliche Glaube* (1961):

> The feeling of absolute dependence thus means being engaged by the transcendent as something infinite and unconditioned. If one wanted to interpret the concept of feeling and of immediate self-consciousness in contemporary terms so as to rule out psychologistic misunderstandings, then perhaps this primal act of human existence could be characterized through modern existentialist philosophy in terms of care for being, for the foundation and meaningfulness of existence, as Tillich has already suggested in his dogmatics. The theology of the experience of faith thus means connecting all theological utterances to these basic questions of human existence.[5]

[5]Martin Redeker, in the introduction to Schleiermacher's *Der christliche Glaube* (Berlin: W. de Gruyter, 1961), xxxi.

Or consider carefully what Friedrich Hertel writes in the preface to his recent book on Schleiermacher's theology (dedicated to G. Ebeling): "If theology and proclamation are to be guided today by the task of a 'non-religious' interpretation, and thus if nothing else is to be considered as speaking humanly, then one may not forget that it was Schleiermacher—despite his employment of the concept of religion—who paved the way for this striving!"[6] Or consider just as carefully the disposition and conceptuality with which Hertel analyzes Schleiermacher's first two and decisive *Speeches*.[7] And what had I already run across in 1922, the time of the "beginnings of dialectical theology," from the pen of Bultmann himself in the very year he had discovered Heidegger, at the outset of his long review of the second edition of *Romans*?

> Karl Barth's *Epistle to the Romans* may be characterized by one sentence, the phraseology of which he would disagree with, but which would still be valid in terms of the usage that has been prevalent in the present time: the book attempts to prove the autonomy and absoluteness of religion. It thus takes its place ... in the same line with such works as Schleiermacher's *Speeches on Religion* and Otto's *Idea of the Holy*, with modern attempts to demonstrate a religious a priori, and finally with the Epistle to the Romans itself, which ... basically has no other intention than this. However different all these attempts may be in detail, they seek to give verbal expression to the consciousness of the uniqueness and absoluteness of religion.[8]

The disposition and conceptuality in this review were also noteworthy. It was "faith," again and again it was "faith," which was at the center of those things which Bultmann found interesting and now praiseworthy in my book (whose first edition two years before he had rejected rather contemptuously). What (according to him) I had expressed about faith, he supposed he could effortlessly place in a series with what Schleiermacher, R. Otto, and E. Troeltsch had treated under the heading of "religion." Then in this very same series he even dared to place Paul's Epistle to the Romans itself! At that time he had not yet learned to use the language of Heidegger. But what does it matter? In that book review the outlines of the whole Bultmann, even the later and the latest Bultmann, can clearly be recognized. No wonder that the closeness, and even the alliance, which once supposedly existed between us, could only be something apparent and transitory, as later became painfully evident: Bultmann was and is a continuator of the great tradition of the nineteenth century, and thus in new guise, a genuine pupil of Schleiermacher.

And this is precisely the common denominator under which I see him as well as his followers, who are otherwise so diverse among themselves: what connects them with him, and with each other, is the consciously and consistently executed anthropological starting point which is evident as the focus

---

[6]Friedrich Hertel, *Das theologische Denken Schleiermachers untersucht an der ersten Auflage seiner Reden "über die Religion"* (Zürich-Stuttgart: Zwingli Verlag, 1965), 9.

[7]Ibid., 87–124.

[8]Rudolf Bultmann, "Karl Barth's *Epistle to the Romans* in its Second Edition," in *The Beginnings of Dialectic Theology* (see no. 3 above), 100 (translation slightly revised).

of their thought and utterances. And that was and is precisely a clear recurrence of Schleiermacher. Was it not Schleiermacher who had already made the distinction, so remarkable in the second "speech" even though it was capable of supersession [aufhebbar], between "intuition" and "feeling"—a distinction which later disappeared in favor of the "feeling" which incorporated "intuition" within itself (absolute dependence!)? Had he not already described the Christian faith as a particular form of this "feeling," in which all objectivity, and all contents characteristic of it, were supposed to be sublated [aufgehoben] and supplied? Hadn't he already known nothing of the Old Testament as an indispensable positive presupposition of the New? Hadn't he already reduced the function and meaning of Jesus to that of a great prototype of faith, and thus of that feeling? Hadn't he already reduced the proper relationship postulated between Christians and Jesus to that which today is proclaimed as the "discipleship" owed him? Wasn't his eschatology as devoid of all concrete content as that which today is known as the "theology of hope"?

Certainly many existentialist theologians (as Wilhelm Herrmann had already done) ardently appealed to Luther, to whom Schleiermacher appealed only seldom or not at all (having found him too rough-hewn and contradictory). Still others reverted more to Kierkegaard, to whom of course Schleiermacher could not yet have appealed. As to Luther, no doubt out of the Weimar Edition of his works, that great Pandora's box, one can extract a theologically existentialist, and thus indirectly Schleiermacherian, thread! But how many other threads one must then leave unconsidered or must even decisively cut off! And as to Kierkegaard, I must confess that the appeal of the existentialist theologians to him as their great and direct forerunner has made me a little reserved toward him. Why did he actually delimit himself—in his original manner, but yet also in conformity to the spirit of the middle of the nineteenth century—so sharply against Hegel, but hardly at all, to my knowledge, against Schleiermacher? In short, despite the fact that the vocabulary of his recent theology included concepts which Schleiermacher certainly would not have cherished—such as Word, encounter, occurrence, cross, decision, limit, judgment, etc.—I could not allow myself to be deceived that within their own context they did not break with the narrowness of Schleiermacher's anthropological horizon, that there under the pretext of being so correctly "human," in that certainly unromantic sobriety, his path was once again traversed. That Schleiermacher made the christianly pious person into the criterion and content of his theology, while, after the "death of God" and the state-funeral dedicated to him, one now jubilantly wants to make the christianly impious person into its object and theme, these certainly are two different things. In the end and in principle, however, they probably amount to the same thing. And because, despite all remaining admiration, I for my part had decisively departed from Schleiermacher's path, it was not possible to join with those multitudes who, openly or secretly, consciously or unconsciously, were following in his train. Rather, as it says in the song, I had to "make my wayward path through the woods, a mangy little sheep"—I, the poor neo-orthodox theologian, the supernaturalist, the revelational positivist, as I had to hear from so many quarters on both sides of the Atlantic. Until better instructed, I can see no way from Schleiermacher, or from his contemporary epigones, to the chroniclers, prophets, and wise ones of Israel, to those who narrate the story of the life, death, and resurrection of Jesus Christ, to the word of the apostles— no way to the God of Abraham, Isaac, and Jacob and the Father of Jesus Christ, no way to the great tradition of the Christian church. For the present I can see nothing here but a choice. And for me there can be no question as to how that choice is to be made.

So, just as I finally could not hold fast to the old Marburg, so could I catch hold of the new Marburg even less. Even less? Yes, for at the risk of seeming malicious, I must here add something else—a "merely" humanistic, or if you will, a "merely" aesthetic question, which irresistibly pressed itself upon me in the course of comparing Schleiermacher with his contemporary followers. Given the fact that I might be able to attach myself to Schleiermacher theologically (something I cannot now do) on some kind of grounds (which are not now visible to me) and then of course join forces with those who follow him in our own day, nonetheless I would still remain deeply alarmed at the simple contrast between the stature, the weight, and the quality of Schleiermacher's personality and achievements—human, Christian, and academic—and those corresponding qualities which have so far appeared in the framework of the new Schleiermacher renaissance. To cite a tolerably similar example at least for the sake of clarity: what a shockingly different niveau between Schleiermacher's definition of God, still impressive in its own way, as the "source of the feeling of absolute dependence," and the definition from one of his contemporary epigones, at first glance so similar and apparently dependent on Schleiermacher's, but then so terribly wretched and banal by comparison: God as the supposed "source of my involvement with my fellow humans"! To this example could easily be added a multitude which are similar and even worse. But no, I will resist the malicious desire to characterize Schleiermacher by comparing him in any further detail with his contemporary pupils. Rather, setting aside everything which I have *in petto* [in private] against the being, acting, and stirring in the sphere of today's swaggering theologians, I want to turn now to something positive, in the form of a little song of praise for the human greatness of Schleiermacher and his work, and thus without in any way referring too closely to the greatness or smallness of our own day.

"Small of stature" like Zaccheus, and beyond that, after his sister Charlotte (who later became so close to him) had once dropped him as a small child, somewhat misshapen, Schleiermacher was an open, expansive, and truly comprehensive spirit. Pressing beyond all mere "diagnosis" and analysis, he aimed toward synthesis. He had the freedom to take part with hearty affirmation in the style, the language, and the ideals of his contemporaries, or just as freely to step back from them, or even decisively to oppose his special knowledge to them as something novel. He was inclined toward peace, even when he became very cutting. Many things troubled and angered him which he saw and heard and read, but I can recall no passage in his letters or even in his books where he expressed himself peevishly, acidly, or poisonously with regard to them. That was certainly related to the fact that at every stage of his life, and in all the branches of his life's work, he had something positive to say. His youthful writings (the *Speeches* and the *Soliloquies*) served, of course, as a prelude, but one which established the melody. When he spoke and wrote he was thus not experimenting, but was proceeding on the basis of well-considered tenets and themes, which he never styled or formulated stiffly, but in which he displayed, rather, an astonishing suppleness of thought. If his style often approached the limits of the tolerable, especially in his earlier years, yet he never became tasteless. He discovered and represented in personal union a consistent philosophy and just as consistent a theology. And in both fields he worked out a remarkable coherence between the whole and the parts, as well as between his earlier and later writings. Beyond that, he was also in a position to produce, with his left hand as it were, a complete translation of Plato with introductions to all of the dialogues. And, after listening to a flute concert, he was able to depict the most difficult point in his dogmatics in the form of a short novel.

There was, in addition, his humanity in the stricter sense: he knew the meaning of friendship and love. And although he was not spared disappointments here (Friedrich Schlegel!) and there (Eleonore Grunow and the rather immature, dependent, and opaque young widow who then became his spouse), he endured them with manly forbearance and dignity—refined and gallant, a gentleman to the end. In those two fields [philosophy and theology], he was acquainted with more than mere play. He displayed a similar humanity toward the two colleagues in Berlin who so spitefully fought him: Hegel the philosopher, and Marheineke the Lutheran dogmatician. Furthermore, in the *Sendschrieben an Lücke* [Open Letter to Lücke] and in the notes and supplements to the later editions of the *Speeches*, it may be observed how capable he was of self-criticism and of unfolding new and corrective aspects of his previous work (even if one must admit that, had he really put that into practice, then—such was indeed precisely his strength!—he would have remained terribly true to himself). At any rate, according to K. A. Varnhagen von Ense's *Denkwürdigkeiten* (1848), which are generally so illuminating for that period, Schleiermacher also possessed the wonderful ability to laugh, above all at himself.[9] He was an ethicist on the basis of a profound ethos which did not restrict him either to the philosophical or (even less) to the theological sphere in formal and methodological questions (which he wonderfully mastered!), but rather which permitted and demanded (happily or unhappily) that he dare to take up the most difficult particular problems of human and Christian, individual and social existence.

And now we come to the center of his humanity, which must be kept firmly in mind in any consideration of the range of issues which he represented, when we go on to say that Schleiermacher was outspokenly a man of the church. Throughout the course of his life, he thought, spoke, and acted in the consciousness of his concrete responsibility precisely on that front. It drove him, from his youth to the days of his old age, irresistibly to the pulpit. And whatever one may think of it theologically, he not only talked about the "feeling of absolute dependence," but had that feeling himself—rather, it had him. He himself was one of those who were moved by what he said about it in the pulpit (as well as in the podium and in the salon!), carried away at times to the point of tears. And that no doubt hangs together with the fact that

---

[9]K. A. Varnhagen von Ense, *Denkwürdigkeiten*, Vol. 4 (1848), 274.

while he certainly conceded to the "worthy men called rationalists" those things which at that time were to be conceded, he himself—no pietist, but certainly a "Moravian of a higher order"—had a personal relationship to Jesus which might well be characterized as love. Although constantly engaged with the question of John the Baptist, "Are you he who is to come, or shall we look for another?," he never broke free from Jesus, but had to return to him again and again. I suspect that on that basis (and contrary to the malign appearance in particular of his christology), and only on that basis, was it given to him to depict the "Christian faith" not only in aphoristic excurses, but also "in its context."

As this particular man—thinker, preacher, teacher, and writer—Schleiermacher determined the nineteenth century. Not in the field of philosophy! In those textbooks, as is well known, he figures only as an "also ran." Certainly, however—and precisely this will be drawn in as a positive point in any evaluation of his scholarly intention—in the field of theology. Here his influence has survived. It has survived not only his being badly compromised by Feuerbach, and then his being compromised even worse by Ritschl and his followers, but also that catastrophe which broke out in 1914 for the whole theology which followed him, and even the onslaught of "our" so-called dialectical theology. Here, even in the middle of our century, he was able to produce, as shown, those "existentialist" epigones. Truly a great man and a great achievement!

That, then, is the song of praise from one who is able to concur with Schleiermacher *rebus sic stantibus* in *no* fundamental sense whatsoever. Nor, therefore, with the liberal, mediating, and conservative theology of the nineteenth century. And thus especially not, and even less, with the Schleiermacher-epigones of the present. At this point, on the same purely humanistic level, let me pose a brief question to them: Where and when among you, in your school and in what you have produced, has a personality and a life's work emerged whose caliber and stature would be worthy of mention in the same breath with those of Schleiermacher, even if only from afar? In this respect I place myself among you, but the question pertains to you especially who are in a particular way to be measured against him. Perhaps I have overlooked someone or something up to now. Perhaps those who and that which are here missed are still to come. If it can be shown to me in good time, then I would also want to praise you, if not your theology, on a similarly humanistic plane. Until then, I will think of you in terms of what is written in Psalm 2:4, whereas despite everything I could not think of Schleiermacher in such terms. Schleiermacher impresses me (I notice that here I am involuntarily lapsing into the style of the ironic-polemical passages of the *Speeches*), whereas you— although and because I am sincerely striving to love even you as myself— impress me not at all.

It may be surprising that I have declared myself to be at odds with Schleiermacher only with reservations: *rebus sic stantibus*, "for the present," "until better instructed." Something like a reservation, a genuine uncertainty, may rightly be detected here. The door is in fact not latched. I am actually to the present day not finished with him. Not even with regard to his point of view. As I have understood him up to now, I have supposed and continued to suppose that I must take a completely different tack from those who follow him. I am certain of my course and of my point of view. I am, however, not so certain of them that I can confidently say that my "Yes" necessarily implies a "No" to Schleiermacher's point of view. For have I indeed understood him correctly? Could he not perhaps be understood differently so that I would not have to reject his theology, but might rather be joyfully conscious of proceeding in fundamental agreement with him?

In what follows I will attempt to formulate and ventilate two questions four times in order to make my perplexity known. By answering them dialectically, perhaps my history with Schleiermacher can now go further.

1. Is Schleiermacher's enterprise concerned (a) necessarily, intrinsically, and authentically with a Christian *theology* oriented toward worship, preaching, instruction, and pastoral care? Does it only accidentally, extrinsically, and inauthentically wear the dress of a philosophy accommodated to the person of his time? It is clear that in that case—regardless of details—I would at least have to entertain the possibility of affirming the enterprise. But would I then have understood it correctly? Up to now I have supposed that Schleiermacher cannot be understood in this way, thus finding myself materially at odds with him.

Or is his enterprise concerned (b) primarily, intrinsically, and authentically with a *philosophy* which turns away from Aristotle, Kant, and Fichte in order to locate itself in the vicinity of Plato, Spinoza, and Schelling, mediating between logos and eros while aesthetically surmounting both, a philosophy indifferent as to Christianity and which would have wrapped itself only accidentally, extrinsically, and inauthentically in the garments of a particular theology, which here happens to be Christian? It is clear that in that case I could only take and maintain my distance from Schleiermacher. But in this way have I understood him correctly? And if in this way I have not understood him correctly, then am I acting properly by distancing myself from him and his enterprise?

2. In Schleiermacher's theology or philosophy, do persons feel, think, and speak (a) in relationship to an indispensable [*unaufhebbar*] Other, in accordance with an *object* which is superior to their own being, feeling, perceiving, willing, and acting, an object toward which adoration, gratitude, repentance, and supplication are concretely possible and even imperative? Were that the case, then I would prick up my ears and be joyfully prepared to hear further things about this Other, in the hopes of finding myself fundamentally at one with Schleiermacher. But then, if I supposed I could find such things in him—perhaps in the dark passages of the *Speeches* where he expresses an "intimation of something apart from and beyond humanity" or in that later, famous definition of God as "the source of the feeling of absolute dependence"—would I have understood him correctly? Up to now I have supposed I had to understand him differently, thus not being able to attach myself to him. Was and is that supposition foolish or indeed quite wise?

Or, for Schleiermacher, do persons feel, think, and speak (b) in and from a sovereign consciousness that their own beings are conjoined, and are indeed essentially *united*, with everything which might possibly come into question as something or even someone distinct from them? If that were the case, then the door between him and me would indeed be latched, and substantial communication would then be impossible. But have I understood him correctly if up to now I have supposed that I ought to understand him in this way? Would I need to understand him in a completely different way in order to regard substantial communication between him and me as something which is not impossible?

3. According to Schleiermacher, do persons feel, think, and speak (a) primarily in relationship to a reality which is *particular* and concrete, and thus determinate and determinable, and about which, in view of its nature and meaning, they can abstract and generalize only secondarily? In that case Schleiermacher and I would be in profound agreement. But have I understood him correctly here when I interpret him in this way? How wonderful and hopeful that would be! However, if I would then have attributed something to him which does not at all accord with his own outlook and intention, then how could my outlook and intention, which would not at all be in concordance, to say nothing of coincidence, possibly be reconciled with his?

Or, according to Schleiermacher, do human feeling, thinking, and acting occur (b) primarily in relationship to a *general* reality whose nature and meaning have already been derived and established in advance, so that on that basis only secondary attention is paid to its particular, concrete, determinable, and determinate form? In that case, of course, I would immediately have to issue a protest. In that case Schleiermacher and my humble self would be completely separated from the outset. But in that case—having so understood him up to now—would I have understood him correctly? If he could be understood in some other way, then my protest would be left hanging in the air. I would then have to meet him with a *Pater, peccavi!* and to accept modestly the instruction he would have to impart to me. Oh, if only I were in such a position!

4. Is the spirit which moves feeling, speaking, and thinking persons, when things come about properly, (b) an absolutely *particular* and specific Spirit, which not only distinguishes itself again and again from all other spirits, but which is seriously to be called "holy"? If this is the correct way to understand Schleiermacher, that is, if it accords with his own standpoint, then—instead of disputing with him—what is to prevent me from joining him and deliberating further with him about its basic content and consequences? But then, in this way have I understood him correctly? Could I, as a conscientious interpreter, be responsible for this understanding of Schleiermacher's position?

Or, according to Schleiermacher, is the spirit which moves feeling, thinking, and speaking persons rather (b) a *universally effective* spiritual power, one which, while individually differentiated, basically remains diffuse? In that case we would be and remain—he, the great, and I, the little, man—separated from each other. But in this way have I understood him correctly, i.e., congenially? Or have I burdened him with an alien point of view? If I could dispense with this viewpoint, would I not have to recognize and confess that he and I are not quite so far apart?

Whoever has followed carefully this fourfold explication of my two questions will not fail to recognize that in each case I would greatly prefer to have understood Schleiermacher in terms of the first question, and just as greatly to have misunderstood him in terms of the second. When my life is over I would certainly like to live at peace with Schleiermacher with regard to these issues. Yet in all four cases I had to end each question with a question! And that means that all along the line I am not finished with Schleiermacher, that I have not made up my mind, whether on the positive or even on the negative side! Even though and because I find myself embarked upon a course, clear as day to myself and others, which certainly is not his. With regard to this man's basic standpoint, I find myself in a great, and for me very painful, perplexity. And to illuminate it even more sharply, I will not fail to pose a final pair of questions:

5. Are the two questions which I posed four times (a) *correctly* formulated as such, i.e., so as to correspond to Schleiermacher's intentions? Would the possible answers to these questions be sufficient for a substantive judgment (positive, negative or critical) about the standpoint he represented? Do these questions provide a basis for a meaningful and relevant discussion about the way he worked out the details of his position?

Or are all the questions I have posed (b) *incorrectly* formulated, i.e., so as not to correspond to Schleiermacher's intentions? Thus, would their possible answers be insufficient for a substantive judgment about his point of view? Do they fail to provide a basis for a substantial and relevant discussion of the particular tenets and themes by which Schleiermacher worked out his position?

The only certain consolation which remains for me is to rejoice that in the kingdom of heaven I will be able to discuss all these questions with Schleiermacher extensively—above all, of course, the fifth—for, let us say, a couple of centuries. "Then I will see clearly *that*—along with so many other things, also that—which on earth I saw through a glass darkly." I can imagine that that will be a very serious matter for both sides, but also that we will both laugh very heartily at ourselves.

Incidentally—moving away from the earlier humanistic plane—that which can be viewed as waiting in the eschatological distance with the "old sorcerer" also pertains, of course (including the fifth and final set of questions), *mutatis mutandis*, to those lesser sorcerer's apprentices of his who are today making villages and cities insecure. I know what I have intended, and continue to intend, in distinction from them as well, but I confess that even concerning them do I find myself in a certain perplexity. In their own way, without possessing Schleiermacher's significance, they certainly mean well, too. If those who follow in his footsteps (at a great human distance from him) are to fall with him, then they might also be able to stand with him. And I certainly would not want to exclude them from my eschatological peace with Schleiermacher, to which I previously alluded. The only thing is that I cannot take my "reunion" with them quite so seriously, nor can I imagine it quite so joyfully, as I can my "reunion" with their forefather, Schleiermacher. When contemplating the great then-and-there of the coming revelation, it is probably not only permitted, but also imperative to think in terms of a certain gradation.

As to a clarification of my relationship to Schleiermacher, what I have occasionally contemplated for here and now—and thus not only with respect to a theological event in the kingdom of glory (which will then form the triumphal ending to my history with Schleiermacher), but, so to speak, with respect also to a millennium preceding that kingdom—and what I have already intimated here and there to good friends, would be the possibility of a theology of the third article, in other words, a theology predominantly and decisively of the Holy Spirit. Everything which needs to be said, considered, and believed about God the Father and God the Son in an understanding of the first and second articles might be shown and illuminated in its foundations through God the Holy Spirit, the *vinculum pacis inter Patrem et Filium*. The entire work of God for his creatures, for, in, and with human beings, might be made visible in terms of its one teleology in which all contingency is excluded. In *Church Dogmatics* IV, 1–3, I at least had the good instinct to place the church, and then faith, love, and hope, under the sign of the Holy Spirit. But might it not even be possible and necessary to place justification, sanctification, and calling under this sign—to say nothing of creation as the *opus proprium* of God the Father? Might not even the christology which dominates everything be illuminated on this basis (*conceptus de Spiritu Sancto!*)? Isn't God—the God confessed by his people through the revelation of his covenant and who is to be proclaimed as such in the world—essentially Spirit (John 4:24, 1 Cor. 3:17), i.e., isn't he the God who in his own freedom, power, and love makes himself present and applies himself? Was it perhaps something of that sort which, without having gotten beyond obscure intimations, was so passionately driving my old friend Fritz Lieb in the past decades of his life, a life which was moved and moving on that basis all along? And is that perhaps also what in our own day the promising young Catholic dogmatician Heribert Mühlen in Paderborn is getting at? Be that as it may, interpreting everything and everyone *in optimam partem*, I would like to reckon with the possibility of a theology of the Holy Spirit, a theology of which Schleiermacher was scarcely conscious, but which might actually have been the legitimate concern dominating even his theological activity. And not his alone! I would also like to apply this supposition in favor of the pietists and (!) rationalists who preceded him, and, of course, in favor of the "Moravians of a lower order" of the eighteenth century, and beyond that, in favor of the "Enthusiasts" who were so one-sidedly and badly treated by the Reformers, and still further back, in favor of all those agitated and contemplative souls, the spiritualists and mystics of the Middle Ages. Could it not be that so many things which for us were said in an unacceptable way about the church and about Mary in Eastern and Western Catholicism might be vindicated to the extent that they actually intended the reality, the coming, and the work of the Holy Spirit, and that on that basis they might emerge in a positive-critical light? And then even (*in etwa* ["more or less"]—as one is wont to say today in bad German) Schleiermacher's miserable successors in the nineteenth century and the existentialist theologians in our twentieth century as well? The whole "history of sects and heretics" could then be discovered, understood, and written not "impartially" but quite critically as a "history" in which everything is thoroughly tested and the best retained, a history of the *ecclesia una, sancta, catholica et apostolica* gathered by the Holy Spirit.

This is merely a suggestion, as is only proper, of what I dream of from time to time concerning the future of theology in general, and in particular concerning the perplexity in which I find myself as I attempt to evaluate

Schleiermacher as well as also those who preceded and succeeded him. I will no longer experience this future, to say nothing of leading the way into it or taking its work in hand.

Not, however, that some gifted young person—in the supposition that he or she is called to it—should now immediately run down the path and into the marketplace for me with a buoyantly written brochure entitled "Toward a Theology of the Holy Spirit" or something of that sort! And how misunderstood my beautiful dream would be if anyone supposed that what is at stake is now to say "the same thing from an anthropological standpoint" once again! As if that were not precisely what is so deeply problematic about Schleiermacher, that he—brilliantly, like no one before or after him—thought and spoke "from an anthropological standpoint"! As if it were precisely the Holy Spirit which encouraged him to do so, or would encourage anyone to do so! As if pneumatology were anthropology! As if I, instead of dreaming of a possibility of better understanding Schleiermacher's concern, had dreamed quite crudely of continuing in his path! I warn! If I am not to have dreamed sheer nonsense, then only persons who are very grounded, spiritually and intellectually, really "well-informed Thebans," will be capable of conceiving and developing a theology of the third article. Those who are not or not yet to that point, instead of boldly wanting to actualize a possibility of the millennium, should prefer to persevere for a little while with me in conscious "perplexity."

INDEXES

I. SCRIPTURE REFERENCES

—280—

II NAMES

III. SUBJECTS